Wild
Northern
California

Help Us Keep This Guide Up to Date

Every effort has been made by the author and editors to make this guide as accurate and useful as possible. However, many things can change after a guide is published—trails are rerouted, regulations change, techniques evolve, facilities come under new management, etc.

We would love to hear from you concerning your experiences with this guide and how you feel it could be improved and kept up to date. While we may not be able to respond to all comments and suggestions, we'll take them to heart and we'll also make certain to share them with the author. Please send your comments and suggestions to the following address:

The Globe Pequot Press
Reader Response/Editorial Department
P.O. Box 480
Guilford, CT 06437

Or you may e-mail us at:

editorial@globe-pequot.com

Thanks for your input, and happy travels!

WILD
Northern
California

A Guide to 41 Roadless Recreation Areas
Including the Entire Sierra Nevada

By
Ron Adkison

FALCON®

Guilford, Connecticut
An imprint of The Globe Pequot Press

AFALCONGUIDE®

Library of Congress Cataloging-in-Publication Data
Adkison, Ron.
      Wild Northern California : a guide to 41 roadless recreation areas,
  including the entire Sierra Nevada / by Ron Adkison.-- 1st ed.
        p. cm.
  Includes index.
  ISBN 1-56044-781-8
     1. Hiking--California--Guidebooks. 2. Trails--California--Guidebooks.
  3. Wilderness areas--California--Guidebooks. 4.California--Guidebooks. I.Title.

GV199.42.C2 A27 2001
917.9404'54--dc21   2001023657

CONTENTS

ACKNOWLEDGMENTS

When I accepted the task of writing this book, I had little idea of the challenge before me. After all, I have been exploring wild country in California since I was a child, so I thought I had a pretty good background to start with. I was wrong. The complexities of wilderness and roadless lands in California are enormous, and without the generous help of the dedicated employees of the USDA Forest Service, Bureau of Land Management, and National Park Service, I would never have been able to get started on this huge project. These professionals answered endless questions, provided me with the voluminous documents I needed, and went out of their way to find obscure maps and information. They all have my utmost respect and admiration, and I am indebted to them for their help and support.

Although there are far too many individuals to name, a few stand out and I want to thank them here:

Jason Van Hook, my trail companion and my nephew, who provided welcome company in the Kiavah, Owens Peak, and Dome Land Wildernesses; my faithful companion Kelly, my Border Collie, who led the way in the Piper Mountain, Sylvania Mountains, Owens Peak, Kiavah, Dome Lane, and South Sierra Wildernesses; Jerry Mosier at the Klamath National Forest; Bob Ramirez at the Shasta-Trinity National Forest; Bob Wetzel at the Stanislaus National Forest; Ralph Moore at Sequoia–Kings Canyon National Parks; John Dell'Osso at Point Reyes National Seashore; Bill Van Bruggen and Rick Connell at the Toiyabe National Forest; David Morton at the Lassen National Forest; Brooks Smith at the Mendocino National Forest; Lisa O'Daly at the Lake Tahoe Basin Management Unit; Jane Goodwin from the Almanor District, Lassen National Forest; the staff at Arcata Resource Area office of the BLM; Ed Patrovsky, a BLM ranger responsible for a vast region of the California desert; Dr. Katie Wash, Outdoor Recreation Planner and Lead Wilderness Specialist at the Ridgecrest BLM office.

Susan Menanno, Lead Wilderness Ranger at the Applegate Ranger District (Red Buttes Wilderness), Rogue River National Forest, was extremely generous in sharing documents and maps, and her vast knowledge of the Red Buttes Wilderness and the Klamath Mountains in California. She provided photos and drafts for the Red Buttes, Siskiyou, Marble Mountain, Russian, and Trinity Alps chapters. Some examples of her work are woven into these chapters, and she is responsible for writing the bulk of the suggested trips for the Trinity Alps and Marble Mountain chapters.

Many thanks to my long-time friend, Randy Judge, who supplied the details for the Virginia Canyon trip in Yosemite, as well as some excellent photos.

Finally, Jay Watson and staff at the Wilderness Society, California and Nevada region, in San Francisco, bent over backwards to answer questions, and provide maps and obscure documents. I am grateful to Jay and the staff for their patience and generous assistance.

LEGEND

Interstate	(00)	Lava Bed	
US Highway	(00)	Crater	
State or Other Principal Road	(00) (000)	Campground	▲
Paved Road		Cabins/Buildings	■
Dirt Road		Peak	9,782 ft.
Trailhead	(T)	Dome	9,782 ft.
Main Trail(s)/Route(s)		Butte	
Cross-country Trail		Elevation	✗ 9,782 ft.
Lakes		Pass/Saddle	)(
River/Stream		Gate	•—•
Falls		Ranger Station	
Spring		Picnic Area	⊼
Marsh		Cave	⊱
Wilderness Area		State Boundary	CALIFORNIA
Roadless Area		City	○
Boundary		Map Orientation	N
Glacier		Scale	0 0.5 1 Miles

WILD NORTHERN CALIFORNIA OVERVIEW MAP

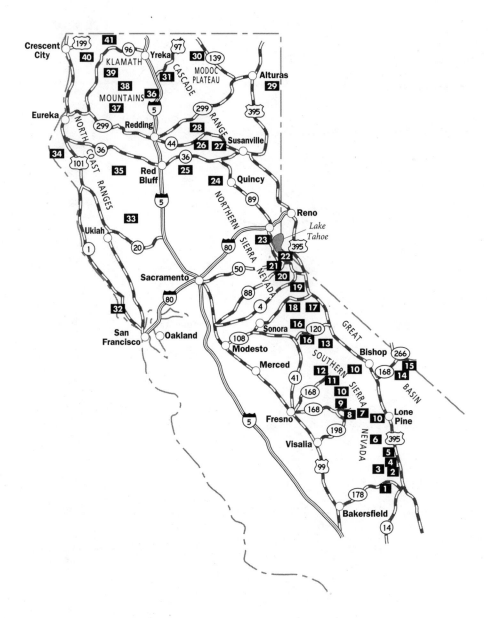

INTRODUCTION

California has a reputation, not only for the landscapes of the cities and of the mind that people have created, but also for its tremendously diverse natural landscapes. Part of California's reputation that is often overlooked regards wilderness. Even in this most populous state, with its huge cities and sprawling suburbs, its traffic jams and infamous smog, there still exists wilderness, and lots of it. In fact, there is more designated wilderness in California than in any other state besides Alaska. Nearly every ecosystem present in California is represented in the state's wilderness areas—desert valleys and mountains, alpine areas, vast forests, foothill oak woodlands, areas of volcanic origin, the seacoast, and even islands off the coast.

This book highlights the best opportunities for self-propelled recreation in northern and central California's roadless lands. The geographic area covered in this book includes the North Coast Ranges north of San Francisco Bay, the Klamath Mountains in northwest California, the southern Cascades, the Modoc Plateau in northeast California, the northern Great Basin, and the entire Sierra Nevada. Although the Sierra Nevada extends farther south than any other area covered in the book, it was included because it is a geographically cohesive unit. Several areas were omitted from this book, either because access is very limited, or because there are few recreational opportunities. These areas include the North Fork and Chanchelulla wildernesses in the North Coast ranges, the Chimney Peak Wilderness in the southern Sierra, and Farallon Islands Wilderness where public access is prohibited.

In the southern Sierra Nevada, a contiguous chain of eight wilderness areas stretches northwest across the range for 140 miles between the Kennedy Meadows Road on the south and the Tioga Road in Yosemite National Park on the north. This chain embraces more than 2.3 million acres of designated wilderness, plus several thousand more acres of roadless potential wilderness, making this region the single largest block of roadless land remaining in the lower 48 states. Save for occasional road corridors, most of the eastern escarpment of the Sierra is protected behind wilderness boundaries from Walker Pass north to Sonora Pass. Much of the northern Sierra is also protected behind the veil of wilderness as far north as Lake Tahoe.

There are only five designated wilderness areas in the vast North Coast Ranges, a region that has been extensively exploited for its productive commercial timberlands. The Yolla Bolly–Middle Eel and the Snow Mountain Wildernesses are the largest, and display the only true subalpine environments in all of California's Coast Ranges.

Northwest California contains nearly one million acres of wilderness in six designated areas of the Klamath Mountains, plus another 350,000 acres of roadless lands adjacent to those wildernesses. The northwest is one of the state's top timber-producing areas, and the effects of many years of large-scale logging has had a tremendous impact on this region. Timber interests, and the Forest Service's assertion that the regional supply of wilderness exceeds the current and projected demand leaves the future of these roadless lands in question. What is left of roadless land in the Klamath Mountains deserves to be protected. The region features incredible biologic and geologic diversity, and in the Klamath National Forest alone there are more than 20 species of cone-bearing trees, more than anywhere else in the world. Many rare plants that occur nowhere else are found in the Klamath Mountains. And wildlife in this region still includes nearly every species that has been present historically.

Northeast and north-central California includes the southern Cascade Range and the Modoc Plateau, a region dominated by volcanic terrain, volcanoes, cinder cones, lava flows, and vast conifer forests.

There are 129 designated wilderness areas in California, spreading across nearly 14 million acres. That may sound like a lot, and it is, but wilderness occupies only about seven percent of the state. And there are many more hundreds of thousands of acres of roadless lands left in California. The California Wilderness Act of 1984 allowed the release of the roadless lands that were not designated wilderness or national forests. Released lands are open to multiple-use management, and some areas have been logged and roads have been constructed. Many other areas remain roadless, and quite a few of them are being managed to retain their roadless character, some for wildlife and watershed management, and other areas for possible future addition to the wilderness preservation system. Many roadless areas on national forest land are called Further Planning Areas, meaning that these areas are being further evaluated for various uses, including possible inclusion in the wilderness preservation system. Wilderness Study Areas (WSAs) are located on both national forest and Bureau of Land Management (BLM) lands. These areas are managed to retain their natural integrity until Congress decides either to release them for multiple-use management or to designate them as wilderness.

There are still many areas in California that should be protected as wilderness, but without a wilderness-designation nomination by land management agencies, no Congressional action can be taken to increase the size of the wilderness preservation system. In some areas the Forest Service has determined that the regional supply of wilderness exceeds the projected demand, and has determined that other areas have no outstanding attributes or characteristics that would warrant their addition to the wilderness system. Yet protectors and defenders of wilderness know that wildlands must be preserved for more than simply recreational value. They must be preserved to maintain their biological integrity. Indeed, wilderness is the only truly biocentric use of land, where the needs of the natural communities and processes take precedence over the needs of humans.

What Is Wilderness?

With the passage of the historic Wilderness Act in 1964, Congress reserved for itself the sole power to legislate wilderness. While most of us know what wilderness is, it is also important to understand the legal meaning of wilderness as expressed in the Act.

The Act empowered three Federal agencies to administer wilderness: the Forest Service, the National Park Service, and the U.S. Fish and Wildlife Service. In 1976, the Bureau of Land Management (BLM) joined their ranks with the passage of the Federal Land Policy and Management Act. In California, all four agencies are responsible for managing wilderness.

The Act states, "In order to assure that an increasing population, accompanied by expanding settlement and growing mechanization, does not occupy and modify all areas of the United States and its possessions, leaving no lands designated for preservation and protection in their natural condition, it is hereby declared to be the policy of the Congress to secure for the American people of present and future generations the benefits of an enduring resource of wilderness. For this purpose there is hereby established a National Wilderness Preservation System to be composed of Federally owned areas designated by Congress as 'wilderness areas,' and these shall be administered for the use and enjoyment of the American people in such manner as will provide for the protection of these areas, the preservation of their wilderness character, and for the gathering and dissemination of information regarding their use and enjoyment as wilderness; and no Federal lands shall be designated as 'wilderness areas' except as provided for in this Act or by a subsequent Act." Wilderness is further defined in the Act as an area that, "in contrast with those areas where man and his own works dominate the landscape, is hereby recognized as an area where the earth and its community of life are untrammeled (or uncontrolled) by man, where man himself is a visitor who does not remain . . ." and is "an area of undeveloped Federal land retaining its primeval character and influence . . . has outstanding opportunities for solitude or a primitive and unconfined type of recreation; has at least 5,000 acres of land . . . and may also contain ecological, geological or other features of scientific, educational, scenic, or historical value."

As California's population continues to expand and occupy once-empty space, so does the pressure of humanity and the need to escape to wild places. Californians should be proud of their wilderness heritage and for the chance to briefly abandon civilization in 14 million acres of wild country, where challenge, self-reliance, quiet, solitude, and the slow pace of wilderness living allows us to detach from the civilized world. There are no manmade attractions in wilderness; the attractions have been created by nature. While there, you will live by nature's terms and on nature's schedule of seasons and sunrises, rather than by your watch, and the rewards are immeasurable.

Make It a Safe Trip

The Boy Scouts of America have been guided for decades by what is perhaps the single best piece of safety advice—Be Prepared! For starters, this means carrying survival and first-aid materials, proper clothing, compass, and topographic maps—and knowing how to use them.

Perhaps the second-best piece of safety advice is to tell somebody where you're going and when you plan to return. Pilots must file flight plans before every trip, and anybody venturing into a blank spot on the map should do the same. File your "flight plan" with a friend or relative before taking off.

Close behind your flight plan and being prepared with proper equipment is physical conditioning. Being fit not only makes wilderness travel more fun, it makes it safer. To whet your appetite for more knowledge of wilderness safety and preparedness, here are a few more tips.

- Check the weather forecast. Be careful not to get caught at high altitude by a bad storm or along a streambed in a flash flood. Watch cloud formations closely, so you don't get stranded on a ridgeline during a lightning storm. Avoid traveling during prolonged periods of cold weather.

- Avoid traveling alone in the wilderness.

- Keep your party together.

- Study basic survival and first aid before leaving home.

- Don't eat wild plants unless you have positively identified them.

- Before you leave for the trailhead, find out as much as you can about the route, especially the potential hazards.

- Don't exhaust yourself or other members of your party by traveling too far or too fast. Let the slowest person set the pace.

- Don't wait until you're confused to look at your maps. Follow them as you go along, from the moment you start moving up the trail, so you have a continual fix on your location.

- If you get lost, don't panic. Sit down and relax for a few minutes while you carefully check your topo map and take a reading with your compass. Confidently plan your next move. It's often smart to retrace your steps until you find familiar ground, even if you think it might lengthen your trip. Lots of people get temporarily lost in the wilderness and survive—usually by calmly and rationally dealing with the situation.

- Stay clear of all wild animals.

- Take a first-aid kit that includes, at a minimum, the following items: sewing needle, snake-bite kit, aspirin, antibacterial ointment, two antiseptic swabs, two butterfly bandages, adhesive tape, four adhesive strips, four gauze pads, two triangular bandages, codeine tablets, two inflatable splints, Moleskin or Second Skin for blisters, one roll 3-inch gauze, CPR shield, rubber gloves, and lightweight first-aid instructions.

- Take a survival kit that includes, at a minimum, the following items: compass, whistle, matches in a waterproof container, cigarette lighter, candle, signal mirror, flashlight, fire starter, aluminum foil, water purification tablets, space blanket, and flare.

- Store your food properly when in bear country. Food storage boxes are located in only a few backcountry locations, most notably in Sequoia–Kings Canyon Wilderness. The best method of protecting your food supply is a bear-resistant food storage canister. These foolproof and bear-proof canisters are widely available at sporting goods stores throughout central and northern California.

Last but not least, don't forget that the best defense against unexpected hazards is knowledge. Read up on the latest wilderness safety information in the recently published *Wild Country Companion.*

YOU MIGHT NEVER KNOW WHAT HIT YOU. Mountains are prone to sudden thunderstorms. If you get caught by a lightning storm, take special precautions. Remember:

- Lightning can travel far ahead of the storm, so be sure to take cover before the storm hits.

- Don't try to make it back to your vehicle. It isn't worth the risk. Even if it's only a short way back to the trailhead, seek shelter instead. Lightning storms usually don't last long, and from a safe vantage point you might enjoy the sights and sounds.

- Be especially careful not to get caught on a mountaintop or exposed ridge; under large, solitary trees, in the open, or near standing water.

- Seek shelter in a low-lying area, ideally in a dense stand of small, uniformly sized trees.

- Stay away from anything that might attract lightning, such as metal tent poles, graphite fishing rods, or pack frames.

- Get into a crouch position and place both feet firmly on the ground.

- If you have a pack (without a metal frame) or a sleeping pad with you, put your feet on it for extra insulation against shock.

- Don't walk or huddle together. Instead, stay 50 feet apart, so if somebody gets hit by lightning, others in your party can give first aid.

- If you're in a tent, stay there, in your sleeping bag with your feet on your sleeping pad.

THE SILENT KILLER. Be aware of the danger of hypothermia—a condition in which the body's internal temperature drops below normal. It can lead to mental and physical collapse and death.

Hypothermia is caused by exposure to cold and is aggravated by wetness, wind, and exhaustion. The moment you begin to lose heat faster than your body produces it, you're suffering from hypothermia. Your body starts involuntary exercise, such as shivering, to stay warm, and it makes involuntary adjustments to preserve normal temperature in vital organs by restricting blood flow in the extremities. Both responses drain your energy reserves. The only way to stop the drain is to reduce the degree of exposure.

With full-blown hypothermia, as energy reserves are exhausted, cold reaches the brain, depriving you of good judgment and reasoning power. You won't be aware that this is happening. You lose control of your hands. Your internal temperature slides downward. Without treatment, this leads to stupor, collapse, and death.

To defend against hypothermia, stay dry. When clothes get wet, they lose about 90 percent of their insulating value. Wool loses relatively less heat; cotton, down, and some synthetics lose more. Choose rain clothes that cover the head, neck, body, and legs and provide good protection against wind-driven rain. Most hypothermia develops in air temperatures between 30 and 50 degrees Fahrenheit, but it can also develop in warmer temperatures.

If your party is exposed to wind, cold, and wet, think hypothermia. Watch yourself and others for these symptoms: uncontrollable fits of shivering; vague, slow, or slurred speech; memory lapses; incoherence; immobile, fumbling hands; frequent stumbling or a lurching gait; drowsiness (*to sleep is to die*); apparent exhaustion; and inability to get up after a rest. When a member of your party has hypothermia, he or she may deny any problem. Believe the symptoms, not the victim. Even mild symptoms demand treatment, as follows:

- Get the victim out of the wind and rain.

- Strip off all wet clothes.

- If the victim is only mildly impaired, give him or her warm drinks. Then get the person into warm clothes and then into a warm sleeping bag. Place well-wrapped water bottles filled with heated water close to the victim.

- If the victim is badly impaired, attempt to keep him or her awake. Put the victim in a sleeping bag with another person—both naked. If you have a double bag, put two warm and naked people in with the victim.

FORDING RIVERS. Although numerous large streams and rivers in wild California are bridged, many are not and must be forded. Especially in late spring and early summer, fording large streams can be dangerous, if not impossible. At other times, when done correctly and carefully, crossing a big river can be safe, but you must know your limits.

The most important advice is "be smart." There are cases where you simply should turn back. Even if only one member of your party (such as a child) might not be able to follow larger, stronger members, you might not want to try a risky ford. Never be embarrassed by being too cautious.

One key is confidence. If you aren't a strong swimmer, you should be. This not only allows you to safely get across a river that is a little deeper and stronger than you thought, but it gives you the confidence to avoid panic. As with getting lost, panic can easily make the situation worse. However, if you lack the swimming skills needed, do not attempt to swim across the river.

When you get to the ford, carefully assess the situation. Don't automatically cross at the point where the trail comes to the stream and head on a straight line for the marker on the other side. Study upstream and downstream and look for a place where the stream widens and the water is not over waist deep on the shortest member of your party. The tail end of an island is usually a good place, and so is a long riffle. The inside of a meander sometimes makes a safe ford, but in other cases a long, shallow section can be followed by a short, deep section next to the outside of the bend where the current picks up speed and carves out a deep channel—so be wary of meanders.

Before starting any serious ford, make sure your matches, camera, billfold, clothes, sleeping bag, and perhaps other items that must stay dry are in watertight bags.

Minimize the amount of time you spend in the water, but don't rush across. Instead, go slowly and deliberately, taking one step at a time, being careful to get each foot securely planted before lifting the other foot. Take a 45-degree angle instead of going straight across, and follow a riffle line if possible.

Don't ford with bare feet. Wear hiking boots without socks or wear sneakers, or tightly strapped sandals.

On small streams, a sturdy walking stick used on the upstream side for balance helps prevent a fall, but in a major river with a fast current, a walking stick offers little help.

Loosen the belt and straps on your pack. If you fall or get washed downstream, a water-logged pack can anchor you to the bottom (where death follows shortly), so you must be able to get out of your pack easily and quickly. Actually, for a short period, your pack might help you become buoyant and float across a deep channel, but in a minute or two, it can become an anchor.

Zero Impact

Going into a wild area is like visiting a famous museum—you do not want to leave your mark on any art treasures. If everybody going through the museum leaves one little mark, the art will be quickly destroyed—and of what value is a big building full of trashed art? The same goes for pristine wildlands. If we all leave just one little mark on the landscape, the backcountry will soon be spoiled.

Wilderness can accommodate human use as long as everybody behaves. But a few thoughtless or uninformed visitors can ruin it for all who follow. All backcountry users have a responsibility to know and follow the rules of no-trace camping.

Nowadays most wilderness users want to walk softly, but some aren't aware that they have poor manners. Often their actions are dictated by the outdated habits of a previous generation of campers who cut green boughs for evening shelters, built campfires with fire rings, and dug trenches around tents. In the 1950s, these "camping rules" may have been acceptable. But they leave long-lasting scars, and today such practices are absolutely unacceptable. Wild places are becoming rare, and the number of users is mushrooming. More and more camping areas show unsightly signs of heavy use.

Consequently, there's a new code of ethics: leave no clues that we were there. Enjoy the wild, but leave no trace of your visit.

Most of us know better than to litter—in or out of the backcountry. Be sure you leave nothing, regardless of how small it is, along the trail or at your campsite. This means you should pack out everything—orange peels, flip tops, cigarette butts, and gum wrappers. Also, pick up any trash that others leave behind.

Follow the main trail. Avoid cutting switchbacks and walking on vegetation beside the trail. Don't pick up "souvenirs," such as rocks, antlers, or wildflowers. The next person wants to see them, too, and collecting such souvenirs violates many regulations.

Avoid making loud noises on the trail (unless you are in bear country) or in camp. Be courteous—remember, sound travels easily in the backcountry, especially across water.

Carry a lightweight trowel to bury human waste 6 to 8 inches deep at least 300 feet from any water source. Pack out used toilet paper.

Go without a campfire. Carry a stove for cooking and a flashlight, candle lantern, or headlamp for light. For emergencies, learn how to build a zero-impact fire from USFS handout pamphlets.

Camp in designated sites when they are available. Otherwise, camp and cook on durable surfaces such as bedrock, sand, gravel bars, or bare ground.

Finally, and perhaps most importantly, strictly follow the pack-in/pack-out rule. If you carry something into the backcountry, consume it or carry it out.

Leave no trace—then put your ear to the ground and listen carefully. Thousands of people coming behind you are thanking you for your courtesy and good sense.

How to Use This Book

This book divides the northern and central parts of the state into 5 regions: Southern Sierra, Northern Great Basin, Northern Sierra, Cascade Range/Modoc Plateau, and North Coast Ranges/Klamath Mountains. Each of the 41 wildlands described in this book are either individual federally designated wilderness areas, or roadless blocks of land under study for wilderness designation, or are managed as roadless nonwilderness to retain their primitive character. Nearly every designated wilderness still has some unprotected roadless lands adjoining its boundaries; these areas are also mentioned in each chapter.

Most of the wildlands in the book are separate areas, but some are parts of vast expanses of contiguous wilderness. For example, the South Sierra, Golden Trout, Sequoia–Kings Canyon, John Muir, Jennie Lakes, Monarch, Ansel Adams, and southern Yosemite Wildernesses are one contiguous wildland in the southern Sierra, forming the largest single block of roadless lands outside of Alaska. Each of these areas has its own distinctive character, so each is covered in a separate chapter.

THE MAPS—The statewide locator map near the beginning of the book shows the 41 wildlands covered here. More detailed maps accompany each wildland chapter. These maps distinguish between designated wilderness and roadless nonwilderness, and they show major access roads, trails, and access points. They are intended to give a general overview of an area and can be useful as one of the first steps in trip planning, but they are not intended as substitutes for applicable USGS quads and wilderness area maps.

INFORMATION BLOCKS—The at-a-glance section introducing each chapter provides these basic facts for each wildland:

1) *Location*—the distance and direction from area boundaries to the nearest and/or largest city or town. This is intended to provide a general idea of an area's location.

2) *Size*—measures the total contiguous roadless area or complex of areas in acres, regardless of land ownership, based upon the best available information.

3) *Administration*—names the state or federal agency responsible for managing the wildlands covered in this book. See Appendix B for a list of these agencies.

4) *Management status*—indicates the area's status as designated wilderness, national park, national monument, wilderness study area, further planning area, roadless nonwilderness managed to retain its primitive character, unprotected roadless nonwilderness, and so on. Forest Plan prescriptions for land management change every 10 to 15 years, so the fate of roadless lands is uncertain and subject to a change in management. Many of the roadless Further Planning Areas are holdovers from the RARE II process that were not designated wilderness in the 1984 California Wilderness Act. Some Further Planning Areas are recommended for wilderness designation, while others are either open to development or could be developed at any time. Readers are encouraged to obtain more information from the managing agency and then work with the agency, conservation groups (see Appendix C), and Congress toward improved management and protection of California's wildlands.

5) *Ecosystems*—based on the U.S. Forest Service, Pacific Southwest Region (Region 5) document *Ecological Subregions of California.* Used by land managers statewide, this text provides standardized descriptions of ecological units in California, describing geology, soils, and landscape features. Vegetation listings for Potential Natural Vegetation (PNV) are based on the Kuchler classification of natural vegetation of California. The Kuchler maps are used by land management agencies for ecosystem management. Natural vegetation is considered as vegetation not appreciably disturbed by man.

6) *Elevation range*—gives the low and high points of an area, in feet above sea level, indicating an area's vertical relief.

7) *System trails*—system trails are those considered maintained by the managing agency. In some places, there are many more miles of unmaintained or abandoned trails, or trails forged by hikers and stock. Where known, the additional miles of these nonsystem trails are indicated in the text.

8) *Maximum core-to-perimeter distance*—the longest distance, in a straight line, that a visitor can be from the nearest road; this figure can be more a function of an area's shape than size. For the eight southern Sierra wildernesses that form a contiguous block, listed above, the core-to-perimeter distance, and the core-to-the-nearest-road distance, is far greater than the individual chapters suggest.

9) *Activities*—those nonmotorized pursuits for which the area is best suited, from both a legal standpoint in the case of wilderness as well as the physical lay of the land. Hiking is the common denominator activity of every area. Where applicable, hunting is mentioned as one of the activities in a broad sense, but please remember that this book is not a hunting guide, which would be a major book in its own right. Legal hunting in season takes place in most of these wildlands, including designated wilderness, except for those in national parks, certain tribal lands, and specially restricted areas.

10) *Maps*—lists all the maps that cover an area, except USGS 1:24,000 maps, which are listed in Appendix D.

11) *Overview*—describes the overall nature of an area's landscapes, its major features, flora and fauna, and occasionally, management status or history. The intent is to provide an overall mental image of the area.

12) *Recreational uses*—this gives a more detailed account of various activities and seasons, access points, trails, and in some cases, use-statistics, and information on wilderness permits. Trip ideas for both winter and summer activities are often included here.

13) *Suggested trip*—each area includes a description of a suggested trip. Most of these trips are in lightly used areas, unless otherwise indicated, with the intention of helping to redistribute local recreational use. Some of the trips are day hikes, others overnighters or extended trips. Some follow trails, while others may be wholly or partly cross-country

trips. Most trips are hikes, though some do double duty as hikes and ski/snowshoe trips.

14) *Distance, Low/high elevations, Difficulty, Best season(s), Topo maps, and Permits*—these listings are self-explanatory. This information will give you a general idea of a trip's difficulty, commitment, and best months for visiting. Topo maps listed are all USGS 1:24,000 quads. Permits are required in some areas, and the ones you need are listed. Many high-use areas have permit quotas and reservation systems in place. Regulations vary between wilderness areas; it is your responsibility to learn them. Most USFS-published wilderness maps contain information about regulations and permits. For more information about how to get permits, phone or visit the national forest offices closest to your trip.

15) *How to get there*—detailed driving directions to trailheads for each suggested trip. Driving distances are rounded to the nearest 0.1 mile; your odometer reading may vary slightly.

16) *Trip narrative*—the suggested trip is described, including major features, trail junctions, potential camping locations, and most of the necessary information needed to get from your starting point to the trip's end. There are also occasional suggestions for side trips.

Appendix A is a checklist of every possible piece of equipment you may need on a wilderness outing. Appendix B lists all of the government agencies responsible for managing wildlands in central and northern California. Appendix C lists the key conservation organizations that focus their efforts on preserving California's wildlands. Appendix D lists every USGS 1:24,000 topographic quadrangle map for all areas covered in the book. Appendix E is a chart, or trip finder, allowing you to quickly browse through the suggested trips detailed in the book. Finally, Appendix F is a timeline showing when California wilderness areas were designated.

Kiavah Wilderness

I

Location: 20 miles west of Ridgecrest and 50 miles northeast of Bakersfield.
Size: 88,992 acres.
Administration: USDAFS–Sequoia National Forest; USDIBLM–Caliente and Ridgecrest resource areas.
Management status: Kiavah Wilderness (88,290 acres); partially roaded nonwilderness (702 acres) allocated for roaded natural management in the Forest Plan.
Ecosystems: Sierran Forest–Alpine Meadows province, Sierra Nevada section, characterized by a moderately high, gently sloping plateau cut by numerous steep and narrow canyons on the west and east sides, alluvial fans, and bahadas (broad slopes where alluvial fans have coalesced into a smooth slope of alluvium); Mesozoic granitic rocks, and Quaternary alluvium; potential natural vegetation Sierran montane forest, northern Jeffrey pine forest, pinyon-juniper woodland, Joshua Tree scrub, and Mojave creosote bush; dendritic drainage pattern with dry stream courses, few perennial springs.
Elevation range: 2,800 feet to 7,120 feet.
System trails: 21.5 miles.
Maximum core-to-perimeter distance: 8 miles.
Activities: Day hiking, backpacking, pinyon nut gathering.
Maps: Sequoia National Forest visitor map; BLM 1:2,500,000 Isabella Lake; see Appendix D for the list of USGS 1:24,000 quads.

OVERVIEW: Rising immediately south of the Kern Plateau and Walker Pass in the southern Sierra is a broad plateau isolated from the bulk of the Sierra Nevada by faulting and erosion. This isolated plateau stretching along the Sierra crest is called the Scodie Mountains, and most of it from the desert floor to the plateau top is protected by the Kiavah Wilderness.

The Scodie Mountains plateau averages about 6,500 feet in elevation and is punctuated by a few prominent summits. Skinner Peak (7,120 feet) in the south, and Pinyon Peak (6,796 feet) in the north are the most significant high points in the Kiavah. Numerous alluvium-filled canyons incise the flanks of the plateau and spread out in broad bahadas in the Mojave Desert to the east and into the Kelso and South Fork valleys to the west and north, respectively. Long, steep ridges separate the canyons east and west of the plateau, but its north and northwest flanks consist of an abrupt 3,000-foot escarpment.

The plateau top supports an extensive woodland of singleleaf pinyon, and the Kiavah and nearby Dome Land are the only wildernesses in California that contain a significant representation of the pinyon-juniper woodland ecosys-

I   KIAVAH WILDERNESS

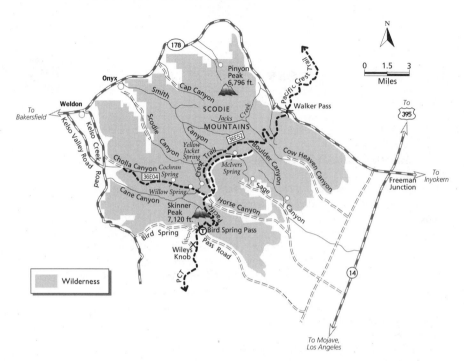

tem. In the northern half of the Scodie Mountains, and in sheltered niches on north-facing aspects, the woodland is studded with tall Jeffrey pines. Sagebrush, Mormon tea, and various coarse shrubs that occupy mid-elevation slopes show the influence of Mojave Desert ecosystems on the Scodies. On alluvial fans and bahadas at the base of the mountains, creosote bush scrub and Joshua tree woodlands dominate on both the east and west sides of the Kiavah.

Several mostly seasonal springs flow from the folds of the canyons, and three others—Yellow Jacket, Willow, and McIvers—flow from the slopes of the plateau. The lack of perennial streams and reliable water restrict quality habitat for wildlife. A small number of mule deer inhabit the Kiavah, and mountain and valley quail are common only where water is available. The USDA Forest Service has developed a number of springs and guzzlers here for wildlife.

RECREATIONAL USES: The Kiavah Wilderness is very little used. Forest Service reports indicate no outstanding features to draw visitors to the area. Yet wilderness enthusiasts will find many attractions, including exceptional opportunities for solitude, a large roadless expanse of pinyon woodland, and far-ranging vistas.

As much as 90 percent of the area's use is concentrated along the Forest Road 27S11 corridor that ascends Horse Canyon from the southeast to the plateau top. Off-highway vehicles frequent this corridor and the four-wheel-drive road that leads 5.5 miles from the microwave tower above Horse Canyon to McIvers Spring, mostly on weekends and during the autumn hunting season.

Because of the lack of reliable water, few backpackers use the Kiavah. Those who do visit are typically northbound Pacific Crest Trail (PCT) through-hikers during May and June. The PCT traverses the Kiavah plateau for about 17 miles between Bird Spring Pass on the south and Walker Pass on the north. There are excellent overnight trips for hikers accustomed to desert travel and willing to pack in one to two gallons of water, and the PCT is the easiest travel route here. The Cholla Canyon Trail leads 4.5 miles from the western wilderness boundary, passing three seasonal springs en route to the FR 27S11 corridor.

Spring wildflower displays are a major attraction in the Kiavah, lasting most years from April well into June. Yet the greatest attractions of the Kiavah are the area's low use and the grand vistas from high points along the plateau top. There are also excellent opportunities for off-trail travel along many of the canyons and across the wooded plateau.

Day Hike

Bird Spring Pass to Skinner Peak

Distance: 8.2 miles, round trip.
Low/high elevations: 5,355 feet/7,120 feet.
Difficulty: Moderately strenuous.
Best seasons: Mid-April through mid-June; mid-September through mid-November.
Topo maps: Cane Canyon-CA, Horse Canyon-CA.
Permits: Not required.

HOW TO GET THERE: From California Highway 178, 59 miles east of Bakers-field, and 29.2 miles west of the junction with CA 14, turn southeast in the hamlet of Weldon onto the signed Kelso Creek Road. Follow this good, paved two-lane road generally south up broad Kelso Valley.

After 10.6 miles, immediately north of an isolated cluster of residences, turn left (east) onto a dirt road where an outdated BLM sign indicates that Bird Spring Pass is 5.4 miles ahead.

The road ahead, recommended for high-clearance vehicles only, is rough, narrow, rocky, subject to washouts, and quite steep in places. It ascends steadily for 6.6 miles to Bird Spring Pass, where the signed Pacific Crest Trail crosses the road. Parking is available in the turnout on the right (south) side of the road.

The Pacific Crest Trail north of Bird Spring Pass is seldom used, save for PCT through-hikers in late spring. This segment is the fastest route to the plateau top, and brings hikers within easy striking distance of the highest point in the Scodie Mountains, 7,120-foot Skinner Peak. The hike is rigorous, gaining nearly 1,800 feet of elevation, though the trail maintains moderate grades.

The sandy tread of the PCT, sometimes trod by grazing cattle, follows a moderate grade northwest from the pass among Joshua trees and a variety of shrubs including big sagebrush, Mormon tea, brittlebush, and hop-sage. In the spring these south-facing slopes are ablaze with wildflowers.

After bending out of a precipitous draw, the trail contours out to the broken granite shoulder of a ridge. The trail ascends into the realm of the pinyon woodland at 6,200 feet, and at 6,520 feet, after 2.5 miles, the trail tops out on the Sierra crest, where you have your first look at Skinner Peak, a granite knob on the northwest skyline lying atop a blocky, pinyon-studded crest. The trail ahead stays just below and west of the crest, carving a swath among pinyons, scrub oak, Mormon tea, beavertail cactus, and yucca. More switchbacks ahead lead you back to the crest, and you proceed briefly northwest to a small notch northwest of Point 6,931.

When the PCT leaves the crest and begins a traverse, leave the trail and ascend the crest northwest, weaving your way among the thick oak and pinyon woodland for 0.4 mile to Skinner Peak, where you find a register can atop the summit boulder. The biggest attraction of Skinner Peak, aside from its remote location, is the sweeping vistas of the southern Sierra and Mojave Desert.

View south along the east slopes of the southern Sierra Nevada from the Pacific Crest Trail below Skinner Peak.

Owens Peak Wilderness 2

Location: 15 miles northwest of Ridgecrest and 60 miles northeast of Bakersfield.
Size: 74,640 acres.
Administration: USDI BLM–Caliente and Ridgecrest resource areas.
Management status: BLM wilderness.
Ecosystems: Sierran Forest–Alpine Meadows province, Sierra Nevada section, characterized by moderately high mountains cut by narrow, steep canyons, with alluvial fans and bahadas; Mesozoic granitic rocks and extensive areas of Quaternary alluvium; potential natural vegetation is pinyon-juniper woodland, Joshua tree scrub, blackbush scrub, and Mojave creosote bush; dendritic drainage pattern with few perennial streams, few springs, and dry meadows.
Elevation range: 3,420 feet to 8,453 feet.
System trails: 23 miles.
Maximum core-to-perimeter distance: 7.5 miles.
Activities: Day hiking, backpacking, mountaineering, rock climbing, pinyon nut gathering.
Maps: BLM 1:2,500,000 Isabella Lake; see Appendix D for the list of USGS 1:24,000 quads.

OVERVIEW: The Owens Peak Wilderness is the southernmost wilderness along the Sierra Nevada crest, extending from Ninemile Canyon in the north to Walker Pass in the south. It encompasses the arid eastern escarpment of the range, numerous rugged peaks along the crest, and the steep slopes and canyons that abut the Kern Plateau on the west. Although the Kiavah Wilderness immediately to the south is geographically located along the Sierra crest as well, the landscape of the Kiavah is more closely related to the Kern Plateau than to the typical Sierra crest landscape of prominent peaks represented here.

Peaks on the Sierra crest dominate the wilderness, marching along in a parade of bold, often imposing summits. Precipitous west-side canyons are short, and few carry reliable water. Spanish Needle Creek, crossed by the Pacific Crest Trail (PCT) in its upper reaches, features a riparian zone dominated by cottonwoods and watered by perennial springs. Smaller west-side drainages, featuring sagebrush-clad valley floors, do not carry year-round flows of water. Broken granite ridges separate the drainages on the west side of the Sierra crest, and many of them are crowned by granite crags and bold peaks with relief of 2,000 feet and more. Lamont Peak, a notable landmark in the Owens Peak Wilderness, is among the summits rising west of the crest.

2 . OWENS PEAK WILDERNESS

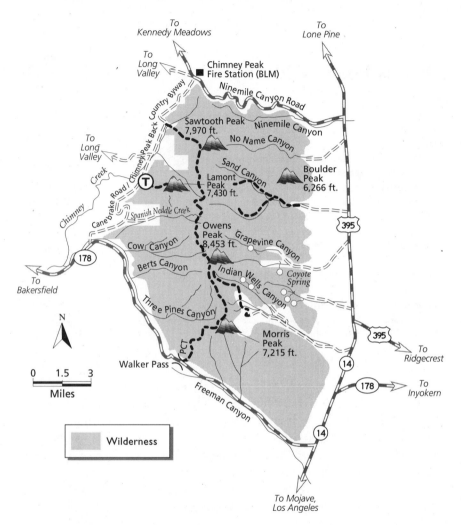

Other major peaks include Spanish Needles, a triad of granite spires, and the lofty pyramid of 8,453-foot Owens Peak. Both peaks are prominent in vistas from U.S. Highway 395 in the Mojave Desert. South of Owens Peak are lower, pinyon-studded summits along the crest, including Morris Peak north of Walker Pass.

Precipitous canyons extend east from the crest, then fan out on broad bahadas above Indian Wells and Rose Valleys. Many of these canyons contain important cultural sites, and desert oases where rich riparian growth crowds numerous perennial springs.

The Owens Peak Wilderness occupies a zone of transition where the Great Basin, Mojave Desert, and Sierra Nevada ecoregions merge. The resulting vegetation patterns represent both foothill and montane ecosystems, and both cold desert and warm desert shrub associations, with each vegetation type finding its own niche on the mountain slopes, peaks, and canyons. Tall Jeffrey pines dot the highest elevations of the wilderness, and on some north-facing aspects, white firs and Jeffrey pines gather into park-like stands.

Much of this landscape of soaring mountains is covered in woodlands of singleleaf pinyon, forming a mantle of gray, gnarled trees. The middle and lower elevations of the west slopes host the taller, long-needled digger pine, recognizable by its large, armored cones. Blackbrush shrublands and Joshua tree woodlands, along with extensive areas of creosote bush scrub, dominate in the lower east-side canyons, alluvial fans, and bahadas, and extend into the lower elevations on the west side of the wilderness as well.

RECREATIONAL USES: Use in the Owens Peak Wilderness is low, not only because the area is often overlooked in favor of friendlier terrain on the Kern Plateau to the west and north, but also because summers are long and hot, there are few reliable water sources, few access points, and only two trails and a few closed four-wheel-drive roads that penetrate the interior.

Primitive four-wheel-drive roads will take you to several east-side canyons, including Indian Wells, Short, Grapevine, Sand, and No Name Canyons. All of these canyons offer good opportunities for off-trail day trips and are particularly attractive from late autumn through spring. Numerous granite outcrops on the ridges separating these canyons attract rock climbers; the most notable is Five Fingers, north of Indian Wells Canyon.

Off-trail travel through most of the Owens Peak area is very difficult and impractical due to steep terrain and dense chaparral. The Pacific Crest Trail (PCT) traverses the wilderness for 21 miles from Walker Pass to Chimney Creek Campground. That trail provides a superb two- to three-day, point-to-point backpack, traversing much of the crest in the wilderness, but water is in short supply, available only at Spanish Needle Creek, about 14 miles northwest of Walker Pass, and at Chimney Creek. Trails lead to superb rock-climbing routes on Spanish Needles and Lamont Peak, which range in difficulty from Class 3 to Class 5+. Other more remote rock-climbing areas in the wilderness are accessible only via tough cross-country scrambles.

Day Hike

Lamont Peak

Distance: 4 miles round trip.
Low/high elevations: 5,500 feet/7,430 feet.
Difficulty: Strenuous.
Best seasons: Mid-May through June; mid-September through October.
Maps: Lamont Peak-CA.
Permits: Not required.

HOW TO GET THERE: From US 395, 54.5 miles south of Lone Pine, or 10 miles north of the U.S. 395/California Highway 14 junction, turn west onto the paved Ninemile Canyon Road, prominently signed for Kennedy Meadows and Chimney Creek Recreation Area. Follow this narrow, winding, steadily ascending road up and over the Sierra crest for 10.6 miles to the BLM's Chimney Peak Work Center and Fire Station. Immediately west of the Fire Station, turn left (south) onto the Canebrake Road, designated the Chimney Peak National Back Country Byway, and signed for Chimney Creek Recreation Area. This graded dirt road is often rough and rocky, with frequent washboards, though it is passable to passenger cars. After 2.9 miles, you pass the pleasant Chimney Creek Campground (no fee, no drinking water), then descend to a Y junction after 4.8 miles. Avoid the westbound road leading to Long Valley Campground and continue straight ahead on the narrow road that winds its way up to a prominent saddle after 7.3 miles. The signed Lamont Peak Trailhead lies along the east side of the road, with ample parking on the west side.

To find the trailhead from CA 178 in the south, follow CA 178 for 71 miles east from Bakersfield, and 3.25 miles east from Weldon, or 17.5 miles west from CA 14, to the northbound Chimney Peak Back Country Byway. The easy-to-miss junction is indicated by a small sign pointing to the Chimney Peak Fire Station, with a much larger destination and mileage sign just up the road north of the junction.

This sandy, washboard road is rocky in places as it steadily ascends 6.5 miles up the south face of the southern Sierra via two switchbacks to the Lamont Peak Trailhead.

The Lamont Peak Trail originated as a climber's route to the Lamont Pinnacles, and it is a no-nonsense pathway ascending 2,000 feet in 2 miles to the summit spire of Lamont Peak. The trail provides superb views of much of the western reaches of the Owens Peak Wilderness, and an exhilarating scramble to the peak's 7,430-foot summit crag.

The signed Lamont Peak Trail begins as a rock-lined path on the east side of the saddle, and winds steadily upward among singleleaf pinyons, digger pines, sagebrush, ceanothus, and scrub oak. A short distance from the trailhead

The Lamont Pinnacles, in the Owens Peak Wilderness, rise northeast of the Lamont Peak Trailhead on Canebrake Road.

the trail inclines steeply, ascending the abruptly rising west slopes of the Lamont Peak massif.

Fine views expand with every step on this tough grind, stretching southward across South Fork Valley to the broad plateau of the Scodie Mountains, and west into the Dome Land country where gentle, forest-covered ridges are punctuated by granodiorite domes and spires.

The trail maintains a steep to very steep grade, allowing you to gain elevation swiftly if not easily. At length the grade moderates as the trail curves around the shoulder of the summit ridge at 7,000 feet. From there inspiring views open up to the east and southeast across oak- and pinyon-clad slopes to the spires of Spanish Needles, then past the pyramid of Owens Peak and Mount Jenkins to the twin summits of Morris Peak, where the distant PCT can be seen traversing its northwest slopes.

The trail then traverses around the ridge, entering a park-like forest of Jeffrey pines, then descends 100 feet into a narrow notch, where white fir joins the forest. Ahead rise the multiple pinnacles of Lamont Peak, and the trail rises steeply from the notch toward the middle, and highest, pinnacle. Just below the top the trail disappears and you must scramble up Class 2 and 3 rock toward the summit. The final few yards provide just enough exposure to plunging cliffs to make things interesting.

Vistas from the summit take in a broad sweep of mostly roadless southern Sierra landscapes, stretching north past Olancha Peak to the lofty peaks of Mount Whitney country. Notches in the Sierra crest to the east frame distant views into the vast valleys and eroded mountain ranges of the Mojave Desert.

Dome Land Wilderness Complex   3

Location: 55 miles northeast of Bakersfield, 12 miles northeast of Kernville, and 25 miles northwest of Inyokern.
Size: 145,935 acres.
Administration: USDAFS—Sequoia National Forest (94,458 acres); USDIBLM–Caliente Resource Area (36,300 acres).
Management status: Dome Land Wilderness (130,758 acres); roadless nonwilderness (Dome Land additions and Woodpecker roadless area, 15,177 acres) allocated for Further Planning status for possible future additions to Dome Land Wilderness.
Ecosystems: Sierran Forest–Alpine Meadows province, Sierra Nevada section, characterized by gentle to moderately steep mountains on a rolling plateau; Mesozoic granitic rocks and older metamorphic rocks, Quaternary alluvium; potential natural vegetation is pinyon-juniper woodland, chaparral, northern Jeffrey pine forest, and Sierran montane forest; numerous seasonal streams, several perennial streams, and large, moderately dry meadows.
Elevation range: 2,800 feet to 9,977 feet.
System trails: 86 miles.
Maximum core-to-perimeter distance: 8.25 miles.
Activities: Backpacking, day hiking, fishing, rock climbing, horseback riding, cross-country skiing, and snowshoeing.
Maps: Sequoia National Forest visitor map; Domeland Wilderness map (topographic, 1 inch/mile); BLM 1:2,500,000 Isabella Lake-CA; see Appendix D for the list of USGS 1:24,000 quads.

OVERVIEW: Of all the wilderness areas in California, perhaps no other is more descriptively named than is the Dome Land. Spreading across the southern end of the Kern Plateau, the Dome Land lies east of the Kern River/South Fork Kern River divide, with the Wild and Scenic South Fork Kern River bisecting the wilderness north to south, roughly through its center.

The heart of the Dome Land on the highland of the Kern Plateau is an area lying above 6,500 feet and dominated by large exposures of granodiorite bedrock. Domes, spires, cliffs, and expanses of bare rock create spectacular landscapes among park-like forests of mixed conifers. Most prominent among the bedrock features are Church, White, Miranda, and Herlihy Domes, though there are literally hundreds of other domes and spires. The western two-thirds of the wilderness contains the highest elevation landscapes, and supports well-developed conifer forests, with white fir and Jeffrey pine dominating. In the highest elevations, red fir and lodgepole pine are common, and are joined in favorable locations by limber and, in the southernmost stands in the state, foxtail pine, a California endemic.

Several meadows add further variety to the landscape, including Manter, Woodpecker, and Smith Meadows in the western half of the wilderness. Rockhouse Basin and Rockhouse Meadow are drier, sagebrush-infested grasslands spreading out along the South Fork Kern River. Several South Fork tributaries originate in the Dome Land or just beyond its boundaries, including Fish, Trout, Tibbets, Manter, Taylor, and Bartolas Creeks.

The high divide along the western boundary is a broken granite ridge capped by 8,000- and 9,000-foot summits, including the wilderness high point at 9,730 feet. The northern wilderness boundary is defined by another prominent divide, including 9,382-foot Bald Mountain and 8,352-foot Pine Mountain. The eastern half of Dome Land, on BLM lands, includes the rugged, pinyon-covered mountains rising east of the South Fork Kern River and south and southeast of Kennedy Meadows, and also parts of Long Valley and the rugged lower gorge of Chimney Creek.

Four separate roadless areas are adjacent to the Dome Land. Since much of the wilderness boundary is drawn along section lines, with little attention to geographic features, these additions would make the Dome Land more of a geographically self-contained unit. Two roadless units—the remaining parts of the original Dome Land roadless area—abut the western wilderness boundary. The Woodpecker roadless area includes a small area of 1,424 acres on the north slopes of Bald and Pine Mountains, including a portion of Fish Creek. The most significant part of the Woodpecker, in terms of size, recreational opportunities, and sensitive ecosystems, is the 10,649 acres surrounding Sirretta Peak. This unit includes part of the divide northwest of the wilderness boundary, and the Trout Creek tributaries of Machine Creek and Little Trout Creek. Sirretta Peak rises to 9,977 feet, making it the highest summit on the southern Kern Plateau, and the highest in the Dome Land Complex.

The Dome Land provides important summer range for part of the Kern River deer herd, and spring and summer range for the Monache deer herd, plus a critical wintering area in Long Valley near the eastern boundary of the wilderness. Other large mammals native to the Dome Land include mountain lion, bobcat, and black bear. An important consideration for recreationists is the large rattlesnake population in the eastern reaches of the wilderness, particularly in the area surrounding the South Fork Kern River.

Cattle graze within the wilderness in two separate grazing allotments, which together carry 275 head of cow-calf pairs from about July 1 to September 15. Much of the wilderness is unsuitable grazing land, however, and visitors will not find widespread cattle.

3   DOME LAND WILDERNESS COMPLEX

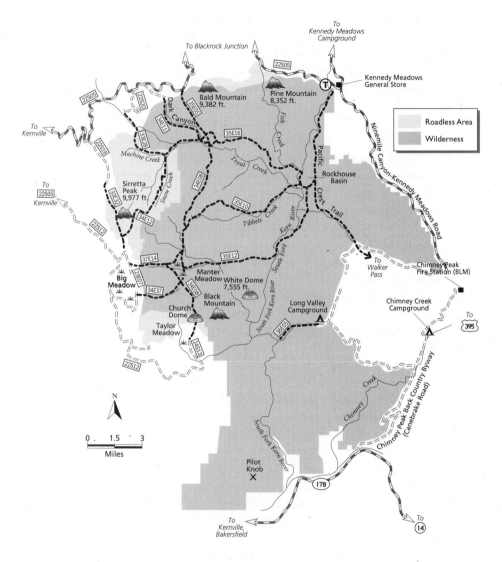

RECREATIONAL USES: The Dome Land is mostly an off-season wilderness, best in late spring/early summer and autumn seasons. Extreme summer heat in all but the highest elevations, combined with water sources that become trickling streams in late season, keeps summer use low. Although day hikers, backpackers, and horseback-riders make up the majority of visitors, hunters in search of mule deer frequent the eastern part of the wilderness in the pinyon woodlands each autumn.

Winter use by cross-country skiers and snowshoers is possible but restricted due to long distances from plowed roads. The Sherman Pass Road (Forest Road 41/22S05) is closed in winter, requiring an approach of 13 miles to reach the Big Meadow trailheads. Access from the east via the South Fork Kern River requires a cold and possibly dangerous ford of the river to reach westbound trails heading for the high country.

The South Fork Kern River provides a natural corridor into the heart of the wilderness, and the Pacific Crest Trail (PCT) follows its course from the north for 7 miles. The Rockhouse Trail (35E12) follows the South Fork for another 4 miles. Access into the higher elevations west of the South Fork is limited by travelers' ability to ford the river. During late spring and early summer, this large stream runs full and is very difficult, if not impossible, to safely ford.

Trout fishing is a big attraction along the South Fork, and this large stream supports populations of rainbow trout. To augment the wild population, the California Department of Fish and Game plants rainbows every two weeks from late May through mid-July. Travel along the South Fork offers open landscapes, gentle terrain, and fine vistas of the domes and spires that characterize most of the wilderness. Fishing is also popular along Trout Creek and in many smaller streams as well, including Manter Creek. Wilderness rock climbing is gaining recognition and popularity in the Dome Land, and there are opportunities to scale seldom-climbed Class 5+ routes. There is also an almost unlimited range of bouldering and scrambling routes.

Trips into the Dome Land originate at ten trailheads, with the four entry points at Big Meadow near the western boundary receiving the heaviest use. Other trails, 34E15 and 34E08, begin near Taylor Meadow several miles southeast of Big Meadow. All of them converge on Manter Meadow, the most beautiful (and most heavily used) montane meadow in the wilderness. The PCT, which enters from the northeast, affords access to three westbound trails—Rockhouse (35E16), Dome Land (35E10), and Manter (35E12)—that lead into the domed landscape of the wilderness. The Manter Trail is extremely steep and rugged, and is the only Dome Land trail not recommended for stock. The Rockhouse Trail from Rockhouse Meadow to Woodpecker Meadow is a closed four-wheel-drive road. Three rarely used trails enter from the north, and all begin along or near FR 22S05. The Machine Creek Trail traverses the Woodpecker roadless area and begins near Boone Meadow, while Wood-pecker Trail (34E08) and Dark Canyon Trail (34E11) descend to Trout Creek from near Bald Mountain on the northern wilderness boundary.

The trail system in the Dome Land traverses the spectrum of wilderness landscapes, and offers numerous opportunities for 15- to 20-mile loops. All but one loop requires fording the South Fork Kern, which is best done during low autumn flows. The Sirretta Trail from Big Meadow to the wilderness boundary at Little Trout Creek traverses the largest unit of the Woodpecker roadless area. The trail ascends to 9,500 feet, passing through the southernmost groves of fox-tail pine. Since it is the only trail open to motorized use in the Dome Land complex, hikers and horseback-riders may encounter motorcycles.

Water-oriented camping areas are not abundant, so backcountry camping is concentrated where water is available. The exception is along the South Fork Kern River, which provides greater opportunities for dispersed camping. The rugged, often chaotic topography, well-developed forest cover, and relative ease of off-trail travel in the northern half of the wilderness offers excellent solitude. Travelers have a better-than-average chance of being alone even on the trail sys-tem beyond Manter Meadow. The most scenic trail in the wilderness, Dome Land Trail (35E10), is a seldom-used route that traverses the rockbound heart of the wilderness. In the summer of 2000, a hot, dry, and historic season of wildland fires, part of the Dome Land was consumed by fire. Contact Sequoia National Forest for information regarding wilderness conditions following the 2000 fires.

Backpack

South Fork Kern River to Rockhouse Basin

Distance: 14 miles, round trip (2 to 3 days).
Low/high elevations: 5,700 feet/6,000 feet.
Difficulty: Moderate.
Best seasons: May through June; mid-September through October.
Topo maps: Crag Peak-CA, Rockhouse Basin-CA.
Permits: Wilderness permits are not required. A California Campfire Permit required for use of open fires or backpack stoves; obtain at any Forest Service or BLM office.

HOW TO GET THERE: From Kernville, drive about 19 miles up the Kern River Road (Sierra Way) then turn right (east) onto the Sherman Pass Road, Forest Road 41/22S05. This road quickly climbs eastward out of Kern River canyon, and after 3.1 miles you pass a gate that is usually closed between late Novem-ber and late May. The road crests Sherman Pass 14.4 miles from the river, and continues east, then north, passing numerous signed spur roads. After driving 17.2 miles from Sherman Pass, you reach the three-way Blackrock Junction.

The South Fork Kern River flows north-south through the heart of the Dome Land Wilderness.

Follow eastbound FR 22S05 toward Kennedy Meadows and US Highway 395. You eventually descend to the bridge spanning the South Fork Kern River, 12 miles from Blackrock Junction. Turn right (south) at the west end of the bridge and drive a few hundred yards to the trailhead parking area.

Or from US 395, about 10 miles north of its junction with California Highway 14, and 54.5 miles south of Lone Pine, turn west where a large sign indicates that Kennedy Meadows is 25 miles ahead. Follow this steadily climbing paved road up to the crest of the Sierra and across the Kern Plateau. After 25 miles you reach a junction. Turn left; the northbound road ends in 3 miles at the Kennedy Meadows Campground. You immediately pass the Kennedy Meadows General Store, then cross the bridge over the South Fork Kern River after another 0.9 mile. Park at the trailhead a few hundred yards south of the road on the west side of the river.

This fine segment of the Pacific Crest Trail along the South Fork Kern River leads to the broad valley of Rockhouse Basin, which features inspiring views into the heart of the Dome Land and productive fishing for brown and rainbow trout. The trip is especially attractive in late spring and early summer when other parts of the Dome Land remain buried in snow.

From the trailhead, a long-closed road follows the west bank of the river for a short distance downriver. In early season when the river is too high to ford, some hikers follow this road and then proceed cross-country to reach Rock-house Basin and the westbound trails into the high country.

If the westbound trails aren't on your itinerary, follow the PCT to Rock-house Basin instead. To find the southbound PCT, walk back to the paved road and pick up the trail just above the east abutment of the bridge. The trail follows a gentle, undulating course all the way to Rockhouse Basin, crossing corrugated slopes above the east bank of the river. Beware of rattlesnakes all along this trail—they are particularly abundant. Big sagebrush dominates the vegetation on the slopes, and there are woodlands of California juniper and singleleaf pinyon with occasional Jeffrey pines.

The river is bordered by meadows, willow thickets, and broad, sagebrush-clad openings. The first few miles closely follow the wilderness boundary, de-lineated by a fence line, with private property and an occasional residence, just beyond. During the initial four miles, the river is close at hand, and there are inspiring views stretching into the domed landscape rising above to the south-west. Vistas also extend into the broad canyon of Trout Creek, bounded by the lofty ridges of Bald and Pine Mountains.

After 5.8 miles, the trail traverses beneath a convoluted granite knob, then quickly tops out on a saddle. From here, it gently descends into what appears to be a dry, sandy wash, but is actually an old four-wheel-drive road. Turn right and follow the wash southwest as it carves a swath through shrublands of sage-brush and rabbitbrush into the broad bowl of Rockhouse Basin.

Once in the basin you are joined on the left by the Rockhouse Trail, another long-closed road. Follow this track northwest down to a signed junction with westbound Dome Land Trail and northwest-bound Woodpecker Trail, both of which require fords of the river.

There are many fine camping areas set above the willow-bordered river and beneath large Jeffrey pines. Peaks of broken granite clothed in a pinyon wood-land bound the eastern margin of the two-square-mile basin, while tall pines stud the steep granite slopes rising to the west. Stegosaurus Fin is the broken knob on the western skyline, one of Dome Land's innumerable granodiorite spires.

Sacatar Trail Wilderness   4

Location: 70 miles northeast of Bakersfield, and 20 miles northwest of Ridgecrest.
Size: 51,900 acres.
Administration: USDIBLM
Management status: BLM wilderness.
Ecosystems: Sierran Forest–Alpine Meadows province, Sierra Nevada section,
characterized by moderately high mountains cut by narrow, steep canyons, and alluvial fans
along the eastern foot of the mountains; Mesozoic granitic rocks; potential natural vegetation
is pinyon-juniper woodland, northern Jeffrey pine forest, blackbrush scrub, and Mojave
creosote bush; many steep canyons with mostly seasonal streams, and few perennial springs.
Elevation range: 3,541 feet to 8,800 feet.
System trails: 9 miles.
Maximum core-to-perimeter distance: 7.75 miles.
Activities: Day hiking, backpacking, pinyon nut gathering.
Maps: BLM 1:2,500,000 Isabella Lake-CA, and Ridgecrest-CA; see Appendix D for the list of
USGS 1:24,000 quads.

OVERVIEW: The Sacatar Trail Wilderness encompasses a nondescript, semi-arid
portion of the southern Sierra Nevada crest between the Ninemile Canyon
Road on the south and the Sequoia National Forest boundary on the north,
about 3.5 miles south of the South Sierra Wilderness. This wildland encompasses a narrow band along the Sierra crest, and includes three prominent west-
trending ridges that reach out toward Kennedy Meadows and the South Fork
Kern River.

The most significant part of the wilderness stretches across the wild, desert-
like eastern face of the Sierra. The wilderness boundary follows the Los Angeles Aqueduct from north to south along the base of the range, where broad
alluvial fans coalesce to form a bahada, a smooth slope of alluvium, rising out
of Rose Valley. The eastern escarpment of the range rises as much as one mile
out of the valley to an undulating crest capped by blocky summits of broken
granite, and fringed by woodlands of singleleaf pinyon.

Five precipitous canyons ranging in length from 3 to 5 miles slice into the
eastern escarpment of the Sierra here. None of them carry perennial flows of
water, though many of them do host springs that nurture dense thickets of riparian growth, including Fremont cottonwood, various willows, and grasses.

4   SACATAR TRAIL WILDERNESS

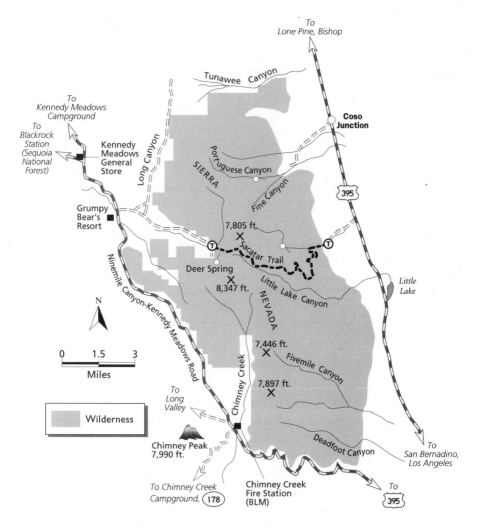

To
Lone Pine, Bishop

Tunawee Canyon

To
Kennedy Meadows
Campground

To
Blackrock
Station
(Sequoia
National
Forest)

Kennedy
Meadows
General
Store

Coso
Junction

Long Canyon

SIERRA

Portuguese Canyon

Fine Canyon

395

Grumpy
Bear's
Resort

7,805 ft.
X

Sacatar Trail

T   T

Deer Spring
X
8,347 ft.

Little Lake Canyon

NEVADA

Little
Lake

Ninemile Canyon-Kennedy Meadows Road

N

7,446 ft.
X

Fivemile Canyon

0   1.5   3

Miles

7,897 ft.
X

Chimney Creek

To
Long
Valley

Wilderness

Deadfoot Canyon

To
San Bernadino,
Los Angeles

Chimney Peak
7,990 ft.

To Chimney Creek
Campground, 178

Chimney Creek
Fire Station
(BLM)

To
395

Only Portuguese Canyon and Lewis Canyon on the eastern slopes have four-wheel-drive roads that afford access to off-trail routes into the wilderness.

Much of the landscape of the Sacatar Trail Wilderness on the Sierra crest and westward is dominated by an array of blocky 7,000- to 8,000-foot ridges and summits, broken granite slopes, and a continuous woodland of pinyon, with occasional junipers mixing among their ranks. Only on the highest northern peaks, approaching 9,000 feet in elevation, do scattered Jeffrey pines stud sheltered niches.

RECREATIONAL USES: This arid to semi-arid wilderness is traversed by only one trail—the Sacatar Trail—which is a historic wagon road across the southern Sierra. Few people visit this wilderness, and most of those who do are autumn hunters and pinyon nut gatherers. The Sacatar Trail Wilderness offers some of the best opportunities for solitude in the southern Sierra, but travel in this trailless place is difficult and time consuming. Ridge-runners and boulder-scramblers will find a wealth of unnamed peaks to bag, but the ability to carry enough water is the single most limiting factor to travel here. It is best suited for off-season travel, during the spring and late autumn. Snowpack is generally light, affording winter access on foot to the backcountry. In fact, winter may be one of the best times to visit, when lingering snow patches can be used to augment your water supply. In some winters, the higher elevations get abundant snow. Travel on skis is difficult due to the nature of the terrain, but snow-shoers can get around much better when the area is snowed in.

The Sacatar Trail is the only easy way to cross the wilderness. This long-closed wagon road samples the spectrum of wilderness ecosystems and landscapes, from the pinyon woodlands of the Sierra crest to the creosote bush shrublands in the desert at the foot of the range. The recommended direction to travel this trail is from west to east, descending the steep eastern escarpment rather than attempting the brutal climb from the desert floor. This is the only trail leading from the foot of the Sierra to the crest that can be traversed on foot during winter; all others, including the nearby Haiwee Pass and Olancha Pass trails to the north, are snowed in during the winter season.

Day Hike or Overnighter

Sacatar Trail

Distance: 9 miles, one way, or any distance as far as time and energy allow.
Low/high elevations: 3,684 feet/7,250 feet.
Difficulty: Moderately strenuous.
Best seasons: April through May; mid-September through November.
Topo maps: Little Lake-CA, Sacatar Canyon-CA.
Permits: Not required. A California Campfire Permit is required for the use of open fires and backpack stoves.

HOW TO GET THERE: Since hiking the Sacatar Trail requires a two-car shuttle, you must first find the obscure trailhead at the end of the hike, along the eastern foot of the Sierra west of U.S. Highway 395. The BLM map or the Little Lake USGS quad are essential aids to finding this trailhead.

Because US 395 is a divided highway, the trailhead access road can only be approached from the southbound lanes. If you are northbound on US 395,

Sacatar Canyon and the Mojave Desert spread out below the Sacatar Trail.

look for the signed Cinder Road turnoff, 19.9 miles north of the US 395/California Highway 14 junction. Note your odometer reading at the junction and continue north on US 395 for another 4.9 miles to the rest area at Coso Junction, where you can make a U-turn and head south. Southbound drivers should note their odometer reading beginning at Coso Junction.

Follow US 395 south for 4 miles from Coso Junction. Then, at a point opposite the northern base of Red Hill, the prominent cinder cone east of the highway, look for an obscure westbound dirt road, and turn right. There is a wire gate you must open and close immediately west of the highway, and an inconspicuous BLM paddle-type sign designates the road as "SE97" and as an "open route."

This dirt road leads southwest across Rose Valley for 0.5 mile to a railroad crossing, then begins a steady ascent of the alluvial fan at the base of the Sierra. There, the road becomes rocky and sandy, and it's recommended for high-clearance vehicles only. After driving 1.25 miles from the highway, cross the concrete-covered First Los Angeles Aqueduct. After another 0.4 mile you reach a north-to-south road atop the Second Los Angeles Aqueduct. Your road, the Sacatar Trail, continues southwest, straight ahead. Since the wilderness boundary is located about 125 feet west of the aqueduct, find a parking spot out of the way, off to the side of the aqueduct road.

The hike begins at the *other* end of the road in Sacatar Canyon. Find that trailhead by following US 395 to the Ninemile Canyon Road, prominently signed for Kennedy Meadows and Chimney Peak Fire Station, 10 miles north of the US 395/CA 14 junction, and 54.5 miles south of Lone Pine. Proceed west on this narrow, winding, and steadily ascending paved road, climbing over the Sierra crest to the Kern Plateau. After 10.6 miles pass the Chimney Creek Fire Station, and continue straight ahead for another 10.4 miles to Grumpy Bear's Lodge and Restaurant, located on the left (southwest) side of the road.

Look for a junction 0.1 mile ahead: the left fork is signed for a Tulare County disposal site, and the right fork is unsigned. Turn right (east) onto the unsigned dirt road and proceed 0.8 mile to a cattle guard and an unsigned junction with a northbound road leading into Long Canyon. Bear right, continuing straight ahead, and after 2 miles, bear right again, staying on the widest, most well-used road. Ignore another northbound road 2.25 miles from the pavement, staying right once again. You reach a three-way junction after 3 miles; follow the middle road, where a homemade sign placed by local landowners points the way to Deer Spring.

Stay left at the following three junctions—the first at 4.2 miles, the second at 4.3 miles, and the third, also signed for Deer Spring, at 4.7 miles. The road narrows beyond that junction, winding southeast through the woodland until it turns south at 5.4 miles, then descends steeply alongside a fence. When you reach the second locked gate along the fenceline on your right (west), your road turns east, and quite soon you reach a fork in the road. Bear left, and after another 150 yards you reach the beginning of the Sacatar Trail, an old doubletrack where a BLM sign declares the wilderness area behind the sign. There is enough space to park two vehicles here, 5.7 miles from the paved road. The road that branches south leads 0.4 mile to its end above perennial Deer Spring at the wilderness boundary, where there are undeveloped campsites used mostly by autumn hunters.

Following the Sacatar Trail from Sacatar Canyon and down the eastern escarpment of the Sierra is one of the more memorable backcountry trips in the southern Sierra. Don't let the long car shuttle deter you from following the trail; you can take a shorter round-trip day hike beginning at either trailhead. A three- to four-mile round-trip hike from the Sacatar Canyon trailhead leads to a high spur ridge, where there are tremendous vistas across the abrupt eastern escarpment of the Sierra to Rose Valley, and to the eroded volcanic desert ranges that stretch eastward toward Death Valley National Park.

Hikers who decide to take the entire trip are advised to hike it from top to bottom, descending 3,500 feet rather than attempting the difficult ascent. You won't find a drop of water along this trail, so be sure to pack an ample supply—*at least* one gallon per person for an overnight trip.

From the BLM "wilderness" sign mentioned above, follow the closed doubletrack of the Sacatar Trail eastward up the broad trough of Sacatar Canyon. Soon the trail crosses a dry, sandy wash, and just beyond, an interesting north-trending draw opens up on the left, rimmed by tall, blocky 8,000-foot peaks.

As the trail ahead begins to ascend toward the crest, you wind among woodlands of pinyon and occasional juniper. Big sagebrush, rabbitbrush, Mormon tea, and bitterbrush scatter out across the dry slopes, with an array of wildflowers to color the landscape during spring.

After rising moderately among wooded hills, the Sacatar Trail tops out on the Sierra Crest after 1.2 miles. The old road then winds downward through the woodland into the upper reaches of Little Lake Canyon, passing many fine potential camping areas. About 1 mile from the crest you reach a hump in the road that barred further travel to motorized vehicles before the area became wilderness in 1994. Beyond that point, the old road becomes more of a trail, its wide bed being reclaimed by time and gravity.

Soon thereafter Little Lake Canyon begins to drop steeply away and the landscape steadily grows more arid. The trail ahead, carved out of the mountainside high above the precipitous canyon, soon leads out of the woodland and onto open slopes, where memorable vistas framed by the canyon walls unfold. The raw landscape of lava flows near Little Lake, the Coso Range, the dry bed of China Lake, and innumerable Mojave Desert mountain ranges march off into the eastern and southeastern distance. Vistas like these are with you for much of the remaining distance.

The trail follows a descending traverse high above Little Lake Canyon where oak groves are massed at the trailside, and willow thickets in the canyon far below attest to the presence of reliable water, too far away and too difficult to reach to be of use for hikers. The trail traverses past a pair of saddles where one could camp and enjoy tremendous and distant landscapes. Beyond the second saddle at 6,500 feet and 4.3 miles, the trail breaks into the open and traverses slopes clad only in coarse desert shrubs.

One long switchback leads to a third and final saddle, 5.1 miles from the trailhead. That saddle, at 5,400 feet, offers the last possible place to camp. The trail ahead descends steadily for 3 more miles into the mouth of an unnamed canyon. The final mile traverses an alluvial fan among a scattering of Joshua trees at the canyon mouth to the wilderness boundary at the Second Los Angeles Aqueduct.

South Sierra Wilderness

Location: 65 miles northeast of Bakersfield, and 4 miles west of Olancha, immediately south of the Golden Trout Wilderness.
Size: 68,263 acres.
Administration: USDAFS–Inyo and Sequoia National Forests.
Management status: South Sierra Wilderness (62,774 acres); the remainder roadless nonwilderness (5,489 acres) allocated to semi-primitive, nonmotorized recreation management.
Ecosystems: Sierran Forest–Alpine Meadows province, Sierra Nevada section, characterized by steep slopes and narrow canyons on the eastern escarpment, and large meadows separated by low ridges in western sections; Mesozoic granitic rocks; potential natural vegetation is northern Jeffrey pine forest, Sierran montane forest, pinyon-juniper woodland, and blackbrush scrub; several perennial and many seasonal streams with a dendritic drainage pattern, many wet meadows.
Elevation range: 6,000 feet to 12,123 feet.
System trails: 78 miles.
Maximum core-to-perimeter distance: 8 miles.
Activities: Backpacking, day hiking, horseback riding, fishing, cross-country skiing, and snowshoeing.
Maps: Inyo and Sequoia National Forests visitor maps; South Sierra Wilderness and Golden Trout Wilderness map (topographic; 1 inch/mile); see Appendix D for the list of USGS 1:24,000 quads.

OVERVIEW: The South Sierra Wilderness is the southernmost link in a contiguous chain of wilderness areas stretching northwest across the Sierra Nevada for 140 miles north to Tioga Road in Yosemite National Park. When you step into the backcountry of the South Sierra Wilderness, you stand at the doorstep of a vast, empty land.

The southern half of the South Sierra is quintessential Kern Plateau landscape. Low, forested ridges crowned by granite knobs separate numerous long and narrow rich meadows. Forests of lodgepole and Jeffrey pine, with red fir in high, sheltered recesses, form park-like forests throughout the landscape. Much of the wilderness south of Round Mountain and east of the South Fork Kern River lies in the rain shadow of the Kern Plateau and Western Divide, and vast woodlands of singleleaf pinyon dominate the forest cover. The Wild and Scenic South Fork Kern River bisects the wilderness north-to-south in its eastern reaches west of the Sierra crest.

5   SOUTH SIERRA WILDERNESS

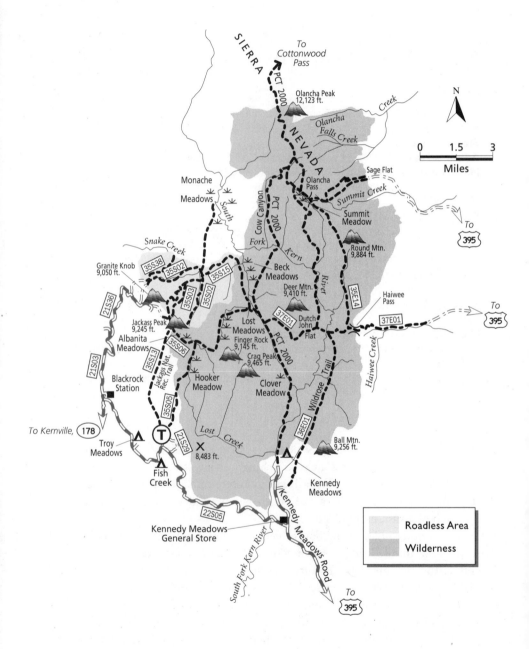

The eastern boundary of the wilderness rises from Kennedy Meadows Campground northeast to the Sierra crest. A 3.5-mile stretch of the crest between the South Sierra and Sacatar Trail Wildernesses was somehow overlooked when wilderness boundaries were drawn, and it is the only part of the Sierra crest, except for highway and forest road corridors, not protected as wilderness between Walker Pass and Lake Tahoe. North of Haiwee Pass, the wilderness boundary dips down to the eastern foot of the Sierra and follows the 6,000-foot contour northward to Olancha Creek and the Golden Trout Wilderness boundary.

The northern portion of the South Sierra Wilderness west of the Sierra crest is bounded on the west by the Sierra Nevada's largest grassland—Monache Meadows. That part of the wilderness embraces the steep slopes between 9,884-foot Round Mountain, and 12,123-foot Olancha Peak—a High Sierra mountain seemingly out of place on the subdued landscape of the Kern Plateau.

Adjoining the northwest corner of the wilderness is the remainder of the South Sierra roadless area not designated wilderness under the California Wilderness Act of 1984. This area lies north of the Granite Knob/Jackass Peak divide, and extends north to Snake Creek, immediately south of Monache Meadows.

Cattle grazing in the meadows of the South Sierra Wilderness and other Kern Plateau grasslands has been going on since the late nineteenth century and continues today, between about July 1 and September 30. Cattle grazing has important historical significance, as ranchers operate here much as their ancestors did more than one hundred years ago. Historic stock driveways are still used to move cattle to and from their summer range.

The fishery of the South Fork Kern River, once the habitat of native South Fork golden trout and Sacramento sucker, was forever altered by the introduction of brown trout in the 1940s. Brown trout are capable of eliminating goldens through predation and they have spread throughout the river and its tributaries. Today, the South Fork's fishery includes rainbow, brown, golden, and rainbow/golden hybrids, along with Sacramento sucker.

Wildlife in the area includes black bear, the sensitive Sierra Nevada red fox, pine marten, and fisher. The huge Monache deer herd, numbering some 8,000 to 9,000 head, is here in summer and autumn, and there are critical springtime fawning areas.

RECREATIONAL USES: Backcountry use of the South Sierra Wilderness is generally light, though the area is becoming more popular in early summer when more northerly wilderness areas are still buried in snow. Day use accounts for the majority of visits by hikers, anglers, and horseback-riders, and they enter from the most easily accessible trailheads, such as Kennedy Meadows Campground on the South Fork Kern River and the Hooker Trailhead near Troy Meadows. The eastside Olancha Pass Trail, part of which is used as a stock driveway, is moderately used in early summer as the preferred route for climbing Olancha Peak, and for access into the Golden Trout Wilderness.

Northbound Pacific Crest Trail (PCT) through-hikers pass through the area, primarily in late spring. Few backpackers regard this as a destination area—the network of maintained and minimally maintained trails, combined with the ease of cross-country travel, makes it ideally suited for loop trips instead. Other parties may be encountered along the PCT, and day hikers often flock to Hooker Meadows, but in most other places, solitude is the rule. The exception is during the autumn deer-hunting season, when usually lonely places in the pinyon woodlands east of the South Fork, particularly in the Haiwee Pass/Dutch John Flat area north to Summit Meadow, attract many hunters. In fact, most trails in the wilderness are used primarily by hunters and range permittees.

The Pacific Crest Trail traverses the wilderness for 17 miles, crossing the South Fork twice via bridges. However, much of the wilderness portion of the river is accessible only by off-trail travel. Numerous closed OHV trails cross portions of the west-central part, east of Monache Meadows.

Six trailheads lead into the South Sierra backcountry. On the west, the Hooker Meadow trailhead on Forest Road 21S29 and the Jackass Trailhead on FR 35E06 will take you to the high western meadows. Kennedy Meadows Campground offers access to the PCT and to the rarely used Wildrose Trail (36E01), which runs for 9 miles along the pinyon-covered mountains east of the river to the Haiwee Trail (37E01). On the east side of the mountains, the Haiwee Trail, used primarily by hunters, begins outside the wilderness boundary and climbs 3,200 feet to Haiwee Pass on the Sierra crest. Farther north, the Olancha Pass Trail (36E02) begins at Sage Flat Trailhead. This 6-mile trail ascends 3,000 feet to Olancha Pass and is moderately graded and well maintained. This is the most popular eastside entry into the wilderness, even though part of the trail is used as a stock driveway.

Winter use of the South Sierra is possible, though moderately long approaches to snow are required. The high meadows in the western part of the wilderness—Albanita, Hooker, and Lost Meadows—consistently have the deepest snowpack. These can be reached via a roundabout route using the northbound PCT from Kennedy Meadows. There is a seasonal locked gate on FR 22S05 a short distance west of the South Fork Kern River bridge west of Kennedy Meadows. You can walk up FR 22S05 until you reach deeper snow, usually around Rodeo Flat on Fish Creek, about 6 miles from the gate. From there you can ski or snowshoe up the Hooker Trail to reach the high meadows.

Albanita Meadows typifies the meadow and forest landscape that dominates much of the South Sierra Wilderness.

Winter access is also possible from the Sage Flat Trailhead. A good snowpack usually blankets the Sierra crest from Summit Meadow northward.

Backpack

Lost Meadows

Distance: 15 miles, round trip.
Low/high elevations: 7,600 feet/8,650 feet.
Difficulty: Moderate.
Best season: Late June through September.
Topo maps: Crag Peak-CA, Monache Mountain-CA.
Permits: Not required. A California Campfire Permit is required for open fires and backpack stoves.

HOW TO GET THERE: From Kernville, drive about 19 miles up the Kern River Road (Sierra Way) then turn right (east) onto the Sherman Pass Road, FR 41/22S05. This road quickly climbs eastward out of Kern River Canyon, surmounts Sherman Pass 14.4 miles from the river, and continues east, then north, passing numerous signed spur roads. After driving 17.2 miles beyond Sherman Pass, you reach the three-way Blackrock Junction.

Follow the eastbound paved road, FR 22S05, toward Kennedy Meadows and U.S. Highway 395. After 5.0 miles, turn left (northeast) onto FR 21S29, signed for "Hooker Trail 1.5." This is a fair dirt road, although rutted and rocky in places. Pass a corral and loading chute after 0.6 mile and reach the Hooker Trailhead at a gate, 1.9 miles from FR 22S05.

Or from US 395, about 10 miles north of its junction with California Highway 14 and 54.5 miles south of Lone Pine, turn west where a large sign indicates that Kennedy Meadows is 25 miles ahead. Follow this steadily climbing paved road to the crest of the Sierra and across the Kern Plateau. After 25 miles you reach a junction. Turn left here (the northbound road ends in 3 miles at the Kennedy Meadows Campground). You immediately pass the Kennedy Meadows General Store, then cross the bridge over the South Fork Kern River after another 0.9 mile. From the river, the road ascends into pine forest, and after another 7 miles you reach right-branching FR 21S29; follow it 1.9 miles to Hooker Trailhead.

Hooker Meadow is one of the best ways to enter the South Sierra Wilderness. Not only is the hike into Hooker an easy one, used by hundreds of mostly weekend day hikers each year, but you are virtually guaranteed to leave those crowds behind once you climb over the ridge to Albanita Meadows. From there, the rich meadows and open lodgepole pine forests are yours to enjoy— along with numerous black bear and mule deer.

The well-worn Hooker Trail leads gradually uphill along an unnamed, seasonal tributary of Fish Creek. Park-like stands of Jeffrey pine, mixed with white fir and Sierra juniper, dominate the forest, and clumps of manzanita inhabit sunny openings. The first mile follows the path of a retired logging road and passes the stumps of selectively cut trees.

The trail requires three easy jump-across fords of the small stream in the first 1.5 miles. The third crossing lies at the southern end of a small, corn lily–fringed meadow, where the trail is obscure. Several yards beyond a very large lodgepole blowdown, look for the well-worn trail ascending a moderate grade away from the drainage, first northeast, then east. The trail rises through Jeffrey pine forest to a broad ridge where you enter the South Sierra Wilderness.

From here you descend an almost imperceptible grade a short distance to a soggy arm of Hooker Meadow, curve northeast around a low forested ridge, and reach the western margin of Hooker Meadow near its southern end. The trail then leads generally north along the western edge of the meadow, where the tread is well-defined in the pine forest but faint in the open grasslands. As you approach what appears to be the upper (northern) end of the meadow, where the grasslands are pinched into a pine-fringed, sagebrush-clad draw, cross over to the east side and enter the upper reaches of Hooker Meadow.

Aspen groves, some of the most extensive on the Kern Plateau, fringe the meadow here. There are many fine campsites all around Hooker Meadow, as well as around Albanita and Lost Meadows up ahead. In some years the small streams draining these meadows may be dry by autumn.

The trail ascends north from Hooker Meadow, crosses an 8,650-foot ridge, then drops to a junction in Albanita Meadows at 4.2 miles. In early summer, particularly following a wet winter, Albanita, Hooker, and Lost Meadows are likely to be very wet, with sizable streams flowing through the grasslands. The trail sign at the junction points east to Lost Meadows and west to Smith Meadow. Albanita offers many fine campsites in the lodgepole pine forest around its margins. About 0.3 mile west of the junction is Aqua Bonita Spring. Although the fence that protected the spring from cattle is now dilapidated, it is still a fine, cold spring bubbling out of the sand into a small pool. In dry seasons, this may be your only source of water.

Lost Meadows, as its name suggests, is well off the beaten path, and you are almost assured solitude in this long, narrow spread. The trail from the junction crosses the stream that drains Albanita Meadows, ascends over a low ridge, then fades out upon reaching Lost Meadows, 1 mile from the junction in Albanita Meadows. The meadows stretch north for 1.5 miles, and there is a reliable spring near the northern end of the meadow.

Fine views reach north from the meadow to the lofty pyramid of Olancha Peak. A base camp can be made in the lodgepole forest next to the meadow. Black bears frequent these meadows, so proper food storage is a must.

Golden Trout Wilderness Complex   6

Location: 40 miles east of Visalia and 15 miles southwest of Lone Pine; adjacent to John Muir, Sequoia–Kings Canyon, and South Sierra wildernesses.
Size: 328,240 acres.
Administration: USDAFS—Sequoia and Inyo National Forests.
Management status: Golden Trout Wilderness (306,000 acres); roadless nonwilderness (Moses roadless area, Sequoia National Forest, 22,240 acres), managed as roadless and recommended for addition to Golden Trout Wilderness.
Ecosystems: Sierran Forest–Alpine Meadows province, Sierra Nevada section, characterized by high, steep mountains at the northern and eastern edge of a rolling plateau, deep stream valleys, extensive meadows, and cirques; Mesozoic granitics, metamorphosed Jurassic marine sedimentary and volcanic rocks, Tertiary andesite, and Pleistocene basalt flows; potential natural vegetation is chaparral, northern Jeffrey pine forest, Sierran montane forest, upper montane-subalpine forests, pinyon-juniper woodland, blackbrush scrub, alpine communities, and Giant sequoia; numerous perennial streams with a complex drainage pattern, and many high elevation lakes.
Elevation range: 3,680 to 12,900 feet.
System trails: 379.1 miles.
Maximum core-to-perimeter distance: 18 miles.
Activities: Backpacking, horseback riding, day hiking, fishing, cross-country skiing, snowshoeing, mountaineering.
Maps: Sequoia and Inyo National Forest visitor maps; Golden Trout Wilderness and South Sierra Wilderness map (topographic, 1 inch/mile); see Appendix D for a list of USGS 1:24,000 quads.

OVERVIEW: The Golden Trout Wilderness spreads out across the most unique landscape in the Sierra Nevada; a vast, rolling tableland known as the Kern Plateau. Large, sprawling meadows, narrow grasslands along stream courses known as "stringers," and rolling, forested ridges and flats dominate the Golden Trout landscape, which contrasts with the southernmost peaks of the High Sierra that bound the wilderness to the northeast and northwest. The northeast corner of the wilderness extends beyond the Kern Plateau to the lower elevations in the desert, encompassing the rugged eastern escarpment of the Sierra Nevada between Cottonwood Creek on the north and Olancha Creek on the south. The Golden Trout is one of the Sierra's largest wildlands, but its landscapes are far different from any other place in the range. The attractions here are not lofty crags and alpine lake basins, but peaceful meadows and vast, open, subalpine forests. Still, the Golden Trout is not simply a featureless land of gentle contours. There are high divides here, and several prominent high points.

Since the Golden Trout abuts the High Sierra on the north and northeast, several peaks, including 12,900-foot Cirque Peak, rise within its boundaries. On the northwest edge of the wilderness is the southern extension of the Great Western Divide, where several peaks exceed 11,000 feet, and one, Florence Peak, reaches 12,432 feet. Slicing across the south-central portion of the wilderness is a high, isolated ridge called the Toowa Range. Crowning this ridge is one of the landmarks and best viewpoints on the Kern Plateau, 11,510-foot Kern Peak.

The main stem of the Kern River flows from north to south through a deep, U-shaped canyon in the center of the wilderness. The Little Kern River, in the western third of the wilderness, drains the slopes of the Western Divide, and the South Fork Kern River drains the Kern Plateau to the east. Both tributaries support their own distinct subspecies of California's state fish, the golden trout.

The South Fork Kern golden trout are native only to the South Fork and Golden Trout Creek, while the Little Kern golden trout are native to only five streams in the Little Kern River drainage. The South Fork subspecies has been transplanted into many streams and high lakes in California, but pure-strain Little Kern goldens are restricted to isolated populations above natural fish barriers in the Little Kern drainage. The Little Kern goldens are listed by the U.S. Fish and Wildlife Service as a threatened species.

The large meadows on the Kern Plateau are among the greatest attractions in the Golden Trout, providing openness and expansive vistas. These grasslands have offered summer forage for livestock since the late nineteenth century and still do, between about July 1 and September 30. However, erosion caused by the effects of grazing has had a significant impact on many meadows in the Golden Trout. As stream bank vegetation is destroyed, gullies form and streams cut deeper channels in meadows. The result is a lowering of the water table and elimination of grasses and sedges, which are then replaced by sagebrush. Many Golden Trout meadows are now a combination of sagebrush and sparse grasses.

Wildlife in the Golden Trout is typical of the Kern Plateau (see South Sierra Wilderness). Due to the well-developed forest cover in the Golden Trout, black bears are common. Most are still wild and avoid humans, and though you may not see one, you'll likely see their tracks on some trails and muddy stream banks. It is always a good idea to protect your food supply, preferably in a bear-resistant canister, when staying overnight in the wilderness. Three major deer herds utilize the Golden Trout: the Tule River, Kern River, and Monache herds. Key winter range is located on the eastern escarpment of the Sierra south of Cottonwood Creek, between 5,000 and 7,000 feet.

6A   GOLDEN TROUT WILDERNESS COMPLEX (WEST)

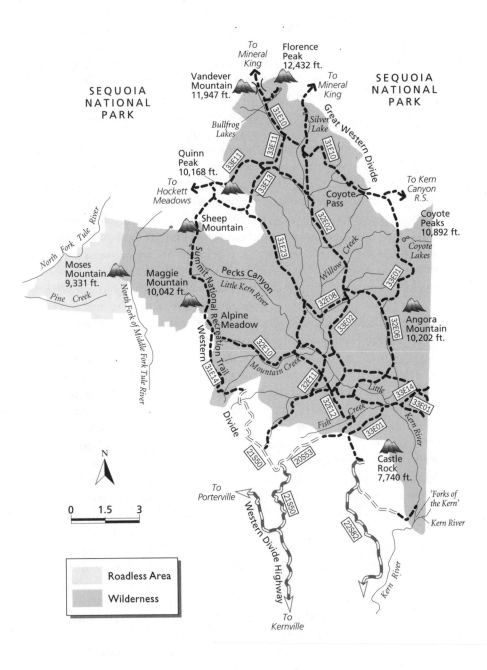

6B GOLDEN TROUT WILDERNESS COMPLEX (NORTH)

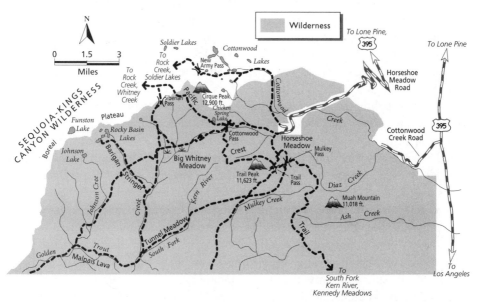

6C GOLDEN TROUT WILDERNESS COMPLEX (SOUTH)

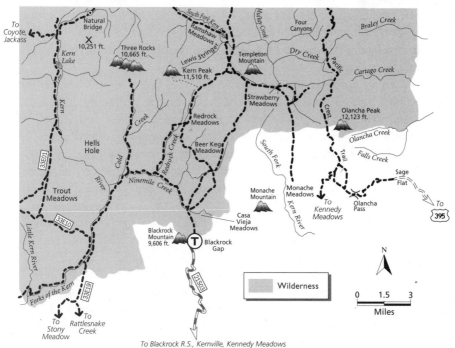

RECREATIONAL USES: With its vast landscape, extensive trail network, hidden meadows, and forests, it's easy to lose yourself in the Golden Trout and enjoy complete solitude. The Pacific Crest Trail (PCT) runs along and near the Sierra crest between Olancha Peak and the Sequoia–Kings Canyon Wilderness boundary. This 25-mile stretch of the PCT is the longest sustained high-elevation trail in the wilderness, staying above 10,000 feet for much of the way while passing high meadows, grand vista points, and the headwaters of numerous streams. Although several PCT through-hikers use the trail each summer, most of the way is lightly traveled, except for the stretch above Horseshoe Meadow, which backpackers frequently use for loop trips from that trailhead. Stock parties frequent the PCT, since there is available forage and a series of corrals located a day's ride apart along the trail between Summit Meadow near Olancha Pass and Poison Meadow near Cottonwood Pass. Several commercial pack stations operate in the Golden Trout, and the wilderness is well suited for the use of pack and saddle stock. Abundant forage, water, comfortable camps, and good stream fishing keep the pack stations running steadily throughout summer.

One of the attractions of the Golden Trout is its vast, open landscapes, and hikers can easily enjoy solitude, even along many of the trails. The landscape here is ideally suited for cross-country exploration, and hikers willing to travel off-trail can find hidden meadows or scale nearby peaks for boundless vistas of wild country. Some places in the Golden Trout have traditionally been heavily used, and these areas include the Horseshoe Meadow/Cottonwood Pass/Chicken Spring Lake area on the northeast, and Rocky Basin Lakes. In the Kern River and Little Kern drainages, Maggie Lakes, Rifle Camp, Grey Meadow, Trout Meadow, Grasshopper Flat, and Kern Flat areas receive concentrated use throughout the season. That leaves the majority of the wilderness lightly to moderately used.

Autumn brings deer hunters to the Golden Trout, most traveling the wilderness with pack and saddle stock, either in private parties or with the use of commercial pack stations. Most of these parties will concentrate where camps and corrals are located. Fenced "tourist pastures" are located at Big Whitney, Little Whitney, Casa Vieja, Redrock, and Trout Meadows, in a meadow on Tamarack Creek, and at Rifle Camp. Other corrals are located along the PCT at Poison, Dutch, and Ash Meadows, Ash Stringer, Death Canyon, and Long Stringer.

Fires are not permitted at Rocky Basin Lakes, or along the PCT between Cottonwood Pass and Sequoia–Kings Canyon Wilderness. Wilderness permits are required for all overnight use. Quotas are in effect for only two of the 30 Golden Trout trailheads. The two quota trailheads, located at Horseshoe Meadow, are the Cottonwood Pass and Cottonwood Lakes trailheads on the Inyo National Forest. Permits for these starting points must be obtained from the Mount Whitney Ranger Station in Lone Pine. Reservations for permits are strongly advised for this high-use area (see Appendix B for addresses and phone numbers).

Backpack

Kern Peak

Distance: 26.6 miles, round trip (3 to 5 days).
Low/high elevations: 8,300 feet/11,510 feet.
Difficulty: Moderate.
Best season: Late June through October.
Topo maps: Casa Vieja Meadows-CA, Kern Peak-CA.
Permits: Wilderness permits are required for overnight use. Obtain at Cannell Meadow Ranger District office in Kernville, or at Blackrock Station near the trailhead. A California Campfire Permit is required for open fires and backpack stoves.

HOW TO GET THERE: From Kernville, drive about 19 miles up the Kern River Road, then turn right (east) onto the Sherman Pass Road, Forest Road 22S05. This road quickly climbs eastward out of Kern River Canyon, surmounts Sherman Pass 14.4 miles from the river, and continues east, then north, passing numerous signed spur roads. After driving 17.2 miles beyond Sherman Pass, you reach three-way Blackrock Junction.

The east-branching road, FR 22S05, leads to Kennedy Meadows and U.S. Highway 395. You continue straight ahead (north), the paved road now bearing the number 21S03. You quickly pass the seasonal Blackrock Station and continue north for 8.1 miles, avoiding several signed spur roads, to the Blackrock Trailhead at the end of the road, 59.2 miles from Kernville.

Or from US 395, about 10 miles north of its junction with California Highway 14 and 54.5 miles south of Lone Pine, turn west where a large sign indicates that Kennedy Meadows is 25 miles ahead. Follow this steadily climbing paved road to the crest of the Sierra and across the plateau. After 25 miles you reach a junction. Turn left; the northbound road ends in 3 miles at the Kennedy Meadows Campground. You immediately pass the Kennedy Meadows General Store, then cross the bridge over the South Fork Kern River. The road leads west for another 12 miles to Blackrock Junction, where you turn right (north), and drive 8.1 miles to the trailhead.

This pleasant backpack through red fir and lodgepole pine forest and verdant, wildflower-filled meadows leads hikers to the best viewpoint on the Kern Plateau, the remote alpine summit of Kern Peak. In addition to being one of the most isolated and seldom-visited mountains on the plateau, Kern Peak offers superb vistas of hundreds of square miles of lonely, relatively unknown wilderness.

From the road's end, walk north past a corral for 0.2 mile to Blackrock Gap, where you enter the Golden Trout Wilderness. The route then descends along a tributary of Ninemile Creek for 1.7 miles under the shade of towering red firs to a junction with an eastbound trail. Continue northwest, skirting the western margin of sloping Casa Vieja Meadows. You will soon pass a southwest-branching trail immediately before bypassing a Snow Survey cabin on your left.

A short distance beyond the cabin, you emerge from lodgepole pine forest to ford Ninemile Creek at the lower end of the meadows. Immediately beyond the ford you meet a westbound trail leading to Jordan Hot Springs.

Resuming your northerly course, you quickly pass a closed eastbound doubletrack that leads past the seasonal ranger station visible 0.1 mile east. Soon leaving the grasslands of the meadows behind, your trail passes over a low gap, descends to a ford of Lost Trout Creek, then traverses lodgepole-shaded slopes to the grassy banks of Long Canyon Creek, about 2.4 miles from Casa Vieja Meadows.

After fording this noisy stream, a short uphill stretch brings you to another junction. The eastbound trail continues ascending Long Canyon, but you turn left (west), climb over a low hill, and enter Beer Keg Meadow where the trail becomes faint. You soon cross two branches of Long Stringer. About 0.5 mile beyond the last ford of Long Stringer, you pass unusual River Spring. Here a large stream emerges from between two small boulders just below the trail. This is the best source of water on this hike, and one of the finest springs anywhere.

Beyond the spring, you soon enter the first of Redrock Meadow's grassy clearings, then bear right where a westbound trail turns left. This sometimes-faint trail ascends the easternmost fork of Redrock Creek, curves in a northwesterly direction through dense lodgepole forest, crosses another small creek, and begins the steep ascent to the crest of the Toowa Range.

You leave the trail at the crest of the Toowa Range, at 10,250 feet and 11.2 miles from the trailhead. Your route, now cross-country, leads westward along the crest of this ridge through a thick forest of lodgepole and foxtail pine. After walking 1 mile along the gentle crest, you reach the steep east slopes of Kern Peak, rising abruptly out of a small cirque. Staying just north of the crest, you head southwestward, and a short but steep scramble up to the low point on the cirque's headwall brings you to the summit ridge. You ascend this ridge through a sparse forest of foxtail pine, the expanding vistas luring you onward to the barren summit of Kern Peak, where a breathtaking view of the Kern River country is revealed. Little remains of the long-abandoned fire lookout tower that once capped this peak. A topographic map may be helpful in identifying distant landmarks.

Sequoia–Kings Canyon Wilderness Complex

7

Location: 55 miles east of Fresno, and 10 miles west of Independence.
Size: 828,730 acres.
Administration: USDI–National Park Service.
Management status: National Park wilderness (736,980 acres); proposed wilderness (91,750 acres) in two separate units, recommended by the NPS for wilderness designation.
Ecosystems: Sierran Forest–Alpine Meadows province, Sierra Nevada section, characterized by complex and very high, steep, and strongly glacier-modified mountains with sharp alpine ridges, aretes, horns, and cols, cirques, and moraines, with broad glacier-modified canyons, moderately deep to deep stream valleys and canyons; Mesozoic granitic rocks, with smaller areas of metamorphosed Jurassic rocks and older metavolcanic and metasedimentary rocks; potential natural vegetation is Sierran yellow pine forest, northern Jeffrey pine forest, Sierran montane forest, upper montane-subalpine forests, Giant sequoia, and extensive areas of alpine communities; abundant perennial streams and rivers with a dendritic drainage pattern, many high-elevation lakes and wet meadows throughout.
Elevation range: 1,900 feet to 14,495 feet.
System trails: 643.6 miles.
Maximum core-to-perimeter distance: 31 miles.
Activities: Backpacking, day hiking, horseback riding, mountaineering, fishing, cross-country skiing, and snowshoeing.
Maps: Sequoia–Kings Canyon National Park visitor map; Sequoia–Kings Canyon Wilderness map (includes John Muir Wilderness; two sheets, topographic, 1 inch/mile); see Appendix D for the list of 38 USGS 1:24,000 quads.

OVERVIEW: Sequoia–Kings Canyon Wilderness is the most diverse wildland in the Sierra Nevada, a land of superlatives with few rivals. The highest peak in the lower 48 states, 14,495-foot Mount Whitney, is found here, as is one of the deepest canyons in North America, Kings Canyon, and the largest trees in the world. The wilderness also supports another rare tree, the foxtail pine, which dominates timberline forests in the upper Kern River drainage. The only other occurrence of this tree in the world is in scattered locations in the Klamath Mountains of northwestern California. Virtually all of the land in these parks without a road is either designated wilderness or is managed as wilderness. Much like the adjacent John Muir Wilderness, Sequoia–Kings Canyon contains some of the most extensive and dramatic high-mountain scenery in the country.

7   SEQUOIA–KINGS CANYON WILDERNESS COMPLEX

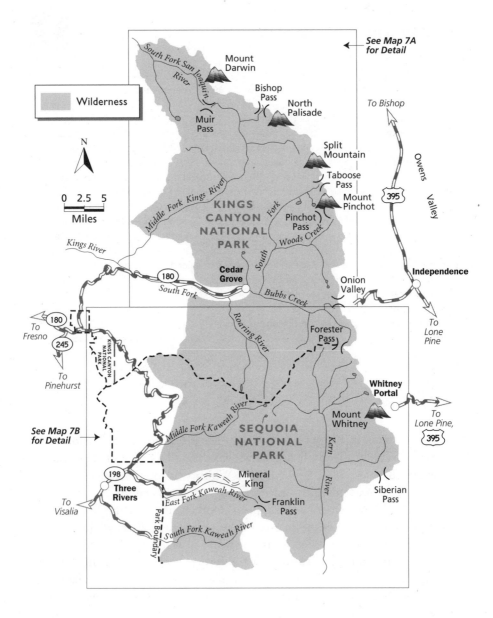

Kings Canyon opens up from Lookout Peak on the western edge of Sequoia–Kings Canyon Wilderness.

The roadless lands recommended for wilderness, and managed as wilderness, include the headwaters of the South Fork Kaweah River in the southwest corner of Sequoia National Park. This is part of a gentle highland called the Hockett Plateau, where there are six Giant sequoia groves, several mid-elevation lakes, rich meadows, and precipitous slopes and canyons. The other unit of roadless land lies along the western park boundary, west of the Generals Highway, and includes parts of both Sequoia and Kings Canyon National Parks. This area includes the North Fork Kaweah River, a narrow and precipitous canyon that plunges from cool forests into the Sierra foothills, and Redwood Mountain, which harbors the world's most extensive grove of giant sequoias.

The wilderness itself, stretching more than 60 miles from north to south and more than 20 miles from east to west, is a land of high divides, deep canyons, large rivers and streams, and hundreds of high-mountain lakes. The Sierra crest defines the eastern boundary of the wilderness, where twelve peaks exceed 14,000 feet in elevation; the lowest point on the crest is 11,300-foot Sawmill Pass. Numerous high divides separate the many canyons in this vast wilderness. The Great Western Divide is the longest, stretching more than 30 miles between Bubbs Creek and the Coyote Peaks near Kern Canyon. Crowned by an array of 12,000-foot and 13,000-foot peaks, the Great Western Divide separates the forested west slopes of the Sierra and the forks of the Kaweah River from

7A SEQUOIA–KINGS CANYON WILDERNESS COMPLEX (NORTH)

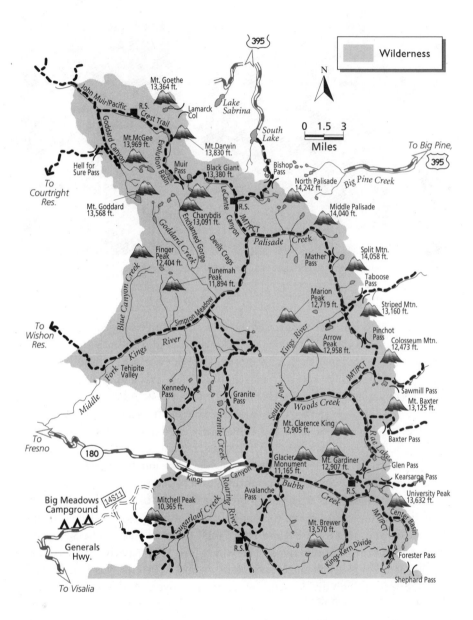

the remarkably straight north-south trough of Kern Canyon. Mineral King, an enchanting valley near the head of the East Fork Kaweah River at the end of a long and rough dirt road on the west slopes of the Great Western Divide, provides the highest elevation trailhead in the parks at 8,200 feet.

At the head of Kern Canyon, and in tributaries below the Sierra Crest and the Great Western Divide, are dozens of broad, lake-filled alpine basins, some of the most remote in the Sierra. The Kern drainage also holds the highest lakes in California, many exceeding 12,000 feet in elevation. Linking the Sierra crest and the Great Western Divide is the Kings-Kern Divide. This concentration of high, rugged granite mountains, best seen from near Kearsarge Pass, is arguably the most spectacular collection of alpine mountains in the United States.

The Kings-Kern Divide not only separates the rivers it was named for, but also separates Sequoia and Kings Canyon National Parks. Kings Canyon National Park is largely roadless, a vast region of deep canyons and high divides. The Monarch Divide/Cirque Crest bounds the gorge of Kings Canyon from the western park boundary to the Sierra crest, stretching some 24 miles and separating the South Fork Kings River from the Middle Fork. In places, these canyons within the wilderness reach 4,000 to 6,000 feet in depth. Dozens of beautiful, high lake basins spread out at the head of the South Fork and its tributaries, Bubbs and Woods Creeks.

Kings Canyon National Park also contains the largest single expanse of treeless alpine country in California. The Middle Fork Kings River is the longest waterway in the wilderness; it begins near Muir Pass on the Goddard Divide, draining the lonely alpine lakes in the northern reaches of Kings Canyon National Park. As the river flows down through incomparable Le Conte Canyon, it is joined by numerous tributaries, including Dusy Branch and Palisade Creek, and quickly gathers strength as it rumbles through Devils Washbowl on its way to Simpson Meadow. At the upper end of Simpson Meadow, Goddard Creek joins from the north. Goddard Creek and its principal tributary, Disappearing Creek, which flows through legendary Enchanted Gorge, have carved out two of the loneliest and most rugged canyons in the Sierra. Below Simpson Meadow the river enters a narrow and profoundly deep canyon bounded by Slide Bluffs to the south and the lofty White Divide to the north. Finally, the canyon opens up near the park boundary in Tehipite Valley, one of the most remote places reached by trail in the wilderness.

The South Fork San Joaquin River begins north of the Goddard Divide in the extreme northern reaches of the wilderness. This river drains lake basins that lie below four major mountain crests: the Goddard Divide to the south, the Sierra crest to the east, the Glacier Divide to the north, and the Le Conte Divide to the west. This is a region of rugged granite peaks, dark metamorphic crags, sprawling alpine lakes, and enchanting valleys. Known as the Evolution

7B   SEQUOIA–KINGS CANYON WILDERNESS COMPLEX (SOUTH)

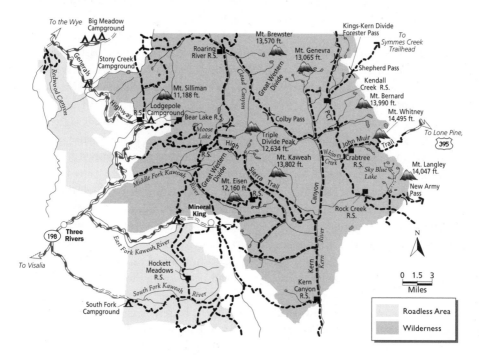

region, the area contains beautiful Evolution Valley, the rockbound lakes of Evolution Basin, and peaks named Darwin, Lamarck, Spencer, Huxley, Haeckel, and Fiske. This is one of the most beautiful places in the Sierra, but its fame, scenery, and two-day access from trails to the east and west make it a popular destination in the wilderness.

Sequoia–Kings Canyon Wilderness features 12,600 feet of relief between its lowest and highest points, the greatest elevation difference in any wilderness in the lower 48 states. Every ecosystem in the Sierra is represented here, from rock and ice in the alpine heights, to oak woodlands and chaparral in the foothills. Consequently, nearly every animal present in the Sierra dwells here. Black bears, and hikers, are abundant enough that proper food storage is *required,* both in the backcountry and the frontcountry of the parks. Hikers have two options for food storage: 1) use the food storage lockers that are in place in 64 locations in the wilderness; 2) use bear-resistant food canisters (available for sale or rent at numerous locations in the parks). Hanging food from the trees using the counterbalance method is rarely effective to thwart the conditioned bears in the wilderness

RECREATIONAL USES: Much of Sequoia–Kings Canyon Wilderness is the realm of the backpacker and horsepacker, though there are a number of lakes and peaks that are accessible to day hikers, particularly in the Sequoia portion of the wilderness. The trail network, combined with dozens of possible starting points, make long-distance backcountry trips here among the finest in the United States. One can go out for as little as a few days, or for two weeks or more, never crossing a road or retracing the same trail.

There are 25 trailheads in the parks spread out along park roads between the South Fork Kaweah River in the south, and Cedar Grove in the north. Most are located along paved park roads, except for those at South Fork Campground and Mineral King. Additionally, trails beginning on national forests to the west and east provide more than two dozen other ways to enter Sequoia–Kings Canyon Wilderness. You can devise loop trips, round trips, and point-to-point trips of widely variable lengths. The John Muir/Pacific Crest Trail traverses the wilderness for 88 miles, crosses 5 high passes (of which Forester Pass at 13,200 feet is the highest along the entire PCT), and traverses seven major drainages. The John Muir and Pacific Crest Trails diverge at Crabtree Meadows west of Mount Whitney. There the Muir Trail heads east, bound for Mount Whitney in 8 miles, while the PCT traverses south and east through forests for another 7.5 miles to the park boundary and on into the Golden Trout Wilderness.

Some of the best lake fishing in the Sierra can be found in this wilderness, and many of the highest lakes contain large golden trout. Most lakes and streams support populations of rainbow, brown, and brook trout as well. A trip into this wilderness not only provides unmatched scenery and good fishing, but there are innumerable opportunities for cross-country travel to lonely lake basins and over high divides. There are many challenging rock climbing and mountaineering areas, including the Evolution region, the Palisades, the forks of the Kings River, the Kings–Kern Divide, and the peaks of the southern High Sierra crest, to name a few. Yet you need not be a seasoned mountaineer to enjoy boundless vistas from High Sierra peaks, for there are dozens of summits that provide walk-up routes.

Most long approaches from westside trails lead gradually into the high country, with a few exceptions; the general rule that the steeper the trail is, the fewer the hikers are, usually applies. A pair of trails beginning near Cedar Grove in Kings Canyon—the lightly traveled Lewis Creek and moderately used Copper Creek Trail to Granite Pass—ascend 6,000 feet and 5,000 feet, respectively, to passes on the Monarch Divide. These trails can be combined into a superb loop trip over the Monarch Divide via the hanging valley of very lightly used Kennedy Canyon. Off-trail routes to Volcanic Lakes and Glacier Valley, to name but two options, make this a fine trip in the otherwise very busy Cedar Grove area.

Approaches from the Jennie Lakes Wilderness in the west to the Roaring River country, including Deadman and Cloud Canyons, will also get you off the beaten track. Other western approaches via the John Muir Wilderness and trailheads at Courtright and Wishon Reservoirs lead to three trails that enter the park wilderness.

Hikers approaching from Owens Valley have eight trailheads from which to begin trips into Sequoia–Kings Canyon Wilderness. Bishop Pass, Kearsarge Pass, Trail Crest on the Mount Whitney/John Muir Trail, and New Army Pass are used by a steady, but quota-regulated, stream of hikers all summer. These trails lead into the most frequently used parts of the park wilderness. Other eastside approaches—including, from north to south, Taboose (6.3 miles), Sawmill (10 miles), Baxter (8 miles), and Shepherd (9.1 miles) passes—lead into less frequently visited country between the most popular Sierra crest passes. If you want to avoid the crowds, choose one of these trails, but bear in mind that their routes are extremely strenuous, rising from the desert to alpine passes and gaining between 5,500 and 6,300 feet of elevation.

Trailhead quotas are in effect at all park trailheads, and also at many trailheads beginning in the adjacent national forests. Wilderness permits are required for all overnight trips. Reservations can be made in advance for two-thirds of the available permits, for a fee, through the Wilderness Office at Sequoia–Kings Canyon National Parks (see Appendix B). Reservations for permits are also available if you intend to enter via the John Muir Wilderness from the Inyo National Forest (eastside). Before you finalize plans for a trip in Sequoia–Kings Canyon Wilderness, request a copy of the backcountry trip planner from park headquarters. The trip planner includes ample information about campfire restrictions, areas either closed to camping or open but with designated sites, food-storage locker locations, and information about reserving permits.

Multi-day Backpack

Rock Creek, Sky Blue Lake

Distance: 25.6 miles, round trip (5 to 7 days).
Low/high elevations: 10,000 feet/12,350 feet.
Difficulty: Moderately strenuous.
Best season: Mid-July through September.
Topo maps: Cirque Peak-CA, Mount Langley-CA, Johnson Peak-CA, Mount Whitney-CA.
Permits: Required for overnight use; obtain at Mount Whitney Ranger Station in Lone Pine (see Appendix B for information on reserving wilderness permits in advance).

HOW TO GET THERE: From U.S. Highway 395 in Lone Pine, turn west onto the signed Whitney Portal Road. Follow this road westward along Lone Pine Creek and through the boulder-covered Alabama Hills for 3.5 miles to the signed Horseshoe Meadow Road, and turn left (south). Ahead you can see the switchbacks of your road ascending the great eastern escarpment of the Sierra Nevada. Follow this good paved road for about 19 miles to a junction. Bear right here and ascend 0.5 mile to the Cottonwood Lakes Trailhead at the road's end.

This exceptionally scenic backpack leads into a remote, trail-less lake basin deep inside Sequoia–Kings Canyon Wilderness; it features broad vistas and productive fishing for golden trout. From the Cottonwood Lakes Trailhead, follow the Cottonwood Lakes Trail north through open lodgepole and foxtail pine forest. The nearly level trail eventually drops down to a crossing of South Fork Cottonwood Creek, and meets the old Cottonwood Creek Trail after 1.6 miles. The following 1.7 miles ascend Cottonwood Creek, passing numerous wet meadows, to the junction with the South Fork Trail. The northwestbound trail leads to Muir Lake and Cottonwood Lakes basin. Bear left onto South Fork Trail and ascend gradually for 0.9 mile to another junction. The South Fork Trail continues ahead to the southwest to South Fork and Cirque Lakes, lying beneath the tall, rubbly pyramid of 12,900-foot Cirque Peak. Bear right at the junction and ascend switchbacks to Cottonwood Lakes basin, 4.5 miles from the trailhead. Here at 11,050 feet, only timberline groves of foxtail pine grow among meadows and talus slopes. The broad sloping platform of Mount Langley, the southernmost 14,000-footer in the Sierra, rises on the northwest skyline.

Cottonwood Lakes 1, 2, 3, and 4 are strictly closed to fishing, since they are a natural fish hatchery and the state's only source of pure-strain golden trout eggs. Good golden trout fishing is available in all other lakes in the Cottonwood drainage. The upper Cottonwood Lakes, Cirque and South Fork Lakes, are the best choices for an overnight stay before tackling New Army Pass on the Sierra crest.

From the junction at Cottonwood Lake 1, proceed west past Lake 2, then begin ascending toward timberline, first past Long Lake, then to round High Lake where, at about 11,450 feet, you find only ground-hugging mats of krummholz. Above High Lake the trail tackles the cirque headwall and you ascend via switchbacks to the broad, gentle Sierra crest of New Army Pass at 12,350 feet, 7.5 miles from the trailhead. Here you enter Sequoia–Kings Canyon Wilderness, and enjoy panoramic vistas across the alpine headwaters of Rock Creek to Siberian Outpost and the Great Western Divide in the distance. Mount Langley lies only 2 miles north on the crest, and provides an easy off-trail walk-up route to its 14,042-foot summit.

The trail descends alpine slopes from the pass, leading to the meadow-carpeted valley of a Rock Creek tributary. After reentering foxtail pine forest, you reach an overused campsite and the junction with the Siberian Pass Trail, 2.3 miles from the pass. Turn north at the junction and descend 0.4 mile to the Rock Creek Trail, where you turn right (northeast) and walk 0.3 mile to Lower Soldier Lake. This area is frequented by backpackers and horsepackers alike, and the Park Service has installed a food-storage locker here because black bears often visit as well. If you find the lake to be too crowded, there are good campsites just above at Upper Soldier Lake, beneath the shattered south face of The Major General.

From Lower Soldier Lake, ascend cross-country to the timberline saddle between Point 11,192 and The Major General, then drop northwest into the beautiful alpine valley of upper Rock Creek. From there simply make your way up the valley along the meandering stream and among flower-filled alpine meadows to the shores of deep, aptlynamed Sky Blue Lake, 2.3 miles from lower Soldier Lake and 12.8 miles from the trailhead. Surrounded by the towering peaks of Newcomb, Pickering, Le Conte, Mallory, and McAdie, this remote basin ranks among the most spectacular in the Sierra. Numerous other lakes can be visited on layover days, and four of them lie above 12,000 feet. Most contain populations of golden trout. Among the peaks that encircle the basin, several can be climbed via Class 3 to 4 routes, including Mallory and Le Conte. Climb gentle slopes to Arc Pass, notching the Sierra crest at 12,880 feet, for a grand vista into Lone Pine Creek and an interesting profile view of Mount Whitney.

Jennie Lakes Wilderness Complex   **8**

Location: 55 miles west of Fresno, and immediately west of Sequoia–Kings Canyon Wilderness.
Size: 12,761 acres.
Administration: USDAFS–Sequoia National Forest.
Management status: Jennie Lakes Wilderness (10,556 acres); the remainder roadless nonwilderness (2,205 acres) allocated to possible future development.
Ecosystems: Sierran Forest–Alpine Meadows province, Sierra Nevada section, characterized by broad ridges, cirque basins, moderately deep stream drainages, and gentle to moderately steep slopes modified by glacial erosion; Mesozoic granitic rocks; potential natural vegetation is Sierran montane, and upper montane-subalpine forests, with small areas of alpine communities; dendritic drainage pattern with numerous perennial streams and montane meadows; few lakes.
Elevation range: 6,640 feet to 10,365 feet.
System trails: 26 miles.
Maximum core-to-perimeter distance: 3 miles.
Activities: Backpacking, day hiking, horseback riding, fishing, cross-country skiing, and snowshoeing.
Maps: Sequoia National Forest visitor map; Jennie Lakes and Monarch Wilderness map (2 inches/mile); see Appendix D for the list of USGS 1:24,000 quads.

OVERVIEW: The small Jennie Lakes Wilderness encompasses the north slopes of a moderately high elevation divide immediately north of Sequoia National Park, and west of Kings Canyon National Park. The wilderness lies almost entirely within the Boulder Creek drainage, a major tributary to the South Fork Kings River. Boulder Creek issues from 9,000-foot Jennie Lake, the highest and largest of the six lakes in the wilderness, and drains north through a 1,000-foot deep canyon that divides the wilderness in half.

Forests of red fir and lodgepole pine dominate the landscape, with expanses of exfoliated granite slabs and rounded granite slopes interrupting the forest cover. Shell Mountain (9,594 feet) dominates the western half of the wilderness, with beautiful Weaver Lake lying below the mountain's slab-covered northwest slopes. West and south of Shell Mountain, Stony Creek gathers its waters and flows south into the North Fork Kaweah River.

8   JENNIE LAKES WILDERNESS COMPLEX AND MONARCH WILDERNESS COMPLEX

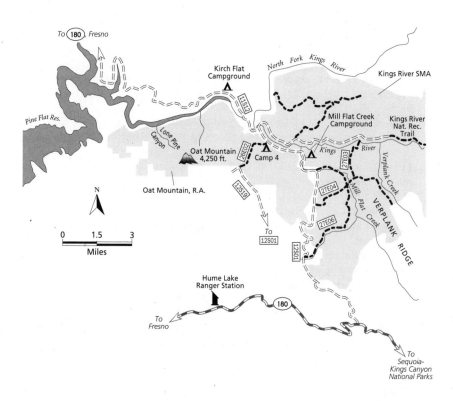

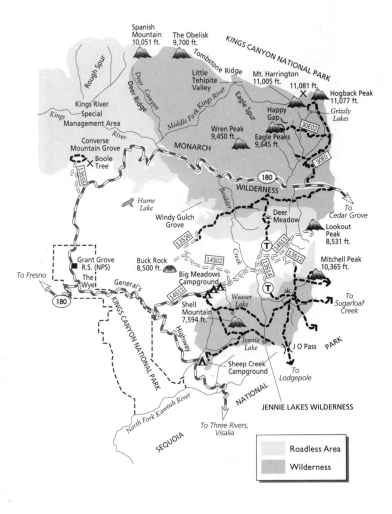

The landscapes of the Jennie Lakes Wilderness are dominated by conifer forests beneath splintered granite peaks.

The eastern half of the wilderness is dominated by a high plateau east of Boulder Creek canyon. Large meadows spread out among the subalpine forests on this plateau, and a high ridge capped by rounded summits bounds this landscape on the east. The ridge divides the Jennie Lakes from Sequoia–Kings Canyon Wilderness and is crowned in the north by 10,365-foot Mitchell Peak, a former lookout tower site and the highest point in the wilderness. The wilderness boundary follows a west-trending ridge that curves around Rowell Meadow from its northeast corner at Mitchell Peak. This lofty ridge is notched by Marvin Pass and crowned by 9,700-foot Mount Maddox, not to mention a classic glacier-scoured dome rising to 9,262 feet.

Three units of roadless land border the wilderness on the southwest and north boundaries. One unit lies east of Stony Creek Campground on the Generals Highway and includes the steep, forested slopes immediately west of a ridge that defines the boundary of Sequoia National Park, southeast of Stony Creek. The two other units lie along the northern boundary, with one area extending southwest from Boulder Creek to Fox Meadow, and the other lying north of the Mount Maddox/Mitchell Peak divide and stretching northeast nearly to Summit Meadow and Lookout Peak. These roadless areas are logical extensions of the Jennie Lakes Wilderness, yet the forest plan has allocated much of this remaining roadless land to timber production and developed recreation.

RECREATIONAL USES: The Jennie Lakes Wilderness is a portal into the Sequoia–Kings Canyon Wilderness more than a destination in its own right. Four trails pass through the Jennie Lakes and reach the high lake basins carved out of the Silliman Crest southeast of the wilderness, then continue into the remote backcountry of the Roaring River and ultimately lead into the upper Kern River basin in the park backcountry. So chances are that all those cars you see in trailhead parking lots belong to hikers who are not even in the Jennie Lakes Wilderness.

Still, the backcountry here does attract its share of visitors. The trail network provides a variety of backcountry trip possibilities, ranging from round-trip day hikes and backpacks, to loop options that take advantage of the 13.5-mile trail looping across a broad stretch of the wilderness and visiting the two major wilderness lakes—Weaver Lake, and Jennie Lake. Of the four trailheads that provide access to the wilderness, the Stony Creek Trailhead (just off the Generals Highway on the southwest) and the Big Meadows Trailhead (on FR 14S11 in the northwest) are the most popular. For a grand tour of the wilderness, begin at either trailhead and follow the loop trail. Starting at Stony Creek, Trail 29E06 ascends 2,500 feet en route to aptly named Poop Out Pass and the junction with the loop. This loop takes you 21.5 miles and offers the spectrum of Jennie Lakes landscapes. Beginning the loop at Big Meadows involves much less climbing and is 2.4 miles shorter, making it a good weekend trip.

The Rowell and Marvin Pass Trailheads lead into the eastern half of the wilderness, which features peaceful forests and bucolic meadows. The loop trail can also be reached via these trailheads. Jennie and Weaver Lakes are major attractions here, and both offer good trout fishing in picturesque settings. Weaver Lake is fringed by lodgepole pine and red fir, with the 800-foot slopes of Shell Mountain rising above it, littered with granite slabs. Jennie Lake lies at 9,000 feet in the basin at the head of Boulder Creek, and is backed up by a 600-foot granite headwall. Both lakes feature outstanding campsites. The eastern plateau surrounding Rowell Meadow offers camping among spreading meadows in open forests of lodgepole pine. Numerous creeks drain the plateau and two small lakes, and off-trail travel is easy and ensures solitude.

The Jennie Lakes Wilderness is well suited for weekend trips and it's a popular area for family day hikes and backpack trips. One outfitter/guide operates out of the Horse Corral Pack Station north of the wilderness, providing services both in the Jennie Lakes backcountry and in Sequoia–Kings Canyon Wilderness.

Black bears are a potential problem not only at backcountry campsites but at trailheads as well. Particularly at the Stony Creek Trailhead, bears can and do break into vehicles in search of food. If you leave any food, food scraps, ice chests, or anything that smells like food in your vehicle, bears will be attracted to it. Typically, they grasp the top of car doors with their claws and bend down the top of the door to gain entry, and once inside, they can do a lot of damage. You will want to protect your food supply at the trailhead and in the backcountry. Bear-resistant canisters work best.

In winter, the Big Meadows Road (FR 14S11) is closed just off the Generals Highway, and numerous cross-country ski trails and snowmobile routes are groomed along forest roads west of the Jennie Lakes Wilderness. Forest Road 14S11 is groomed for snowmobiles 3.8 miles from the highway to the Big Meadows Trailhead, and it can also be used by skiers heading for the Jennie Lakes backcountry. The parking area for these trails is a California Sno-Park, and a Sno-Park permit is required to park your vehicle there. Sno-Park permits for day use or for the season are widely available at sporting goods stores and from the Northern California State Automobile Association office.

Day Hike or Overnighter

Mitchell Peak

Distance: 10.6 miles, round trip.
Low/high elevations: 7,830 feet/10,365 feet.
Difficulty: Moderate.
Best season: July through September.
Topo maps: Mount Silliman-CA, Muir Grove-CA.
Permits: Not required for Jennie Lakes Wilderness. Permits are required for overnight use of Sequoia–Kings Canyon Wilderness. California Campfire Permit required for open fires and backpack stoves.

HOW TO GET THERE: Drive to the signed Big Meadows turnoff on the Generals Highway—the main road leading through Sequoia National Park, connecting California Highway 180 and 198. This turnoff is about 63 miles east of Fresno via CA 180 and the Generals Highway, and 72.5 miles east of Visalia via CA 198 and the Generals Highway.

At this turnoff, turn east and follow the paved road (FR 14S11) toward Big Meadows, indicated by signs at numerous junctions. After driving 9.1 miles from the Generals Highway turn right immediately before the paved road crosses Horse Corral Creek. A sign there points to Rowell Trailhead and Horse Corral Pack Station. Follow this fairly rough dirt road, FR 13S14, generally south for 2 miles to its end at the trailhead parking area, high above Boulder Creek canyon.

This memorable hike to Mitchell Peak features peaceful meadows and forests, with the reward of far-flung panoramas from the 10,365-foot summit. Since the trail gains more than 2,500 feet of elevation, this trip is best taken as an overnighter, spending the night near Rowell Meadow or the meadow immediately south of Marvin Pass. Mitchell Peak is notorious for attracting lightning strikes, so avoid the summit trail during thunderstorms.

The trail (30E08) begins on the east side of the road, just north of the parking area. It heads east through a forest of red and white fir, then soon jogs south and begins traversing rocky and forested slopes far above Boulder Creek canyon. After 1.4 miles the trail bends northeast, traversing sunny, rockbound slopes above Gannon Creek, a noisy Boulder Creek tributary.

The trail eventually approaches a small creek and begins ascending along its course beneath a canopy of lodgepole pines. Leaving that small creek behind, your trail levels off on a meadow-floored, wildflower-brightened, lodgepole-shaded plateau, soon passing just north of the Rowell Meadow Snow Survey shelter. A wilderness ranger uses this cabin as a base camp during the summer season.

The trail continues east from the cabin and soon passes a southbound trail (30E09) leading to JO Pass, Gannon Creek, and Jennie Lake. You continue eastward through the lodgepole pine forest, passing several excellent campsites, to an easy crossing of a small creek. At the trail junction on the east bank of the creek, turn left (north) onto Trail 30E43 toward Marvin Pass.

Your trail leads north through meadow-carpeted lodgepole forest, crosses a small creek, and soon enters a drier forest of red fir and lodgepole pine while ascending to Marvin Pass. After hiking 1 mile from the previous junction, you reach the pass and a trail junction, at an elevation of 9,050 feet. Turning right (east) onto the Kanawyer Gap Trail (30E07), you climb moderately for 0.6 mile to the unmaintained Mitchell Peak Trail, branching left (north) from your trail. This unsigned junction is difficult to locate, obscured as it is by an overgrown clump of chinquapin. From this junction at 9,400 feet, Trail 30E07A gains nearly 1,000 feet in 1.1 miles to the summit of Mitchell Peak.

The trail heads northeast over a 9,600-foot ridge, leaving the Jennie Lakes Wilderness and entering part of the Jennie Lakes roadless area as it ascends steadily to the north ridge of the peak. There it turns southeast and ascends steeply through a stunted timberline forest of lodgepole and whitebark pine to the open, rocky summit. The summit commands a tremendous panorama of the High Sierra and overlooks much of the Jennie Lakes Wilderness.

Monarch Wilderness Complex   9

(See map on pages 48–49)

Location: 70 miles east of Fresno, adjacent to Sequoia–Kings Canyon Wilderness.
Size: 114,347 acres.
Administration: USDAFS–Sequoia and Sierra National Forests.
Management status: Monarch Wilderness (45,000 acres); Kings River Special Management Area (roadless nonwilderness, 48,635 acres), Agnew roadless area (roadless nonwilderness, 8,434 acres), and Oat Mountain roadless area (12,278 acres), all allocated for roadless recreation management in the Forest Plan.
Ecosystems: Sierran Forest–Alpine Meadows province, Sierra Nevada section, characterized by moderately steep to steep mountains and hills in the lower, western foothills, and steep to very steep mountains and slopes in eastern sections, with very deep canyons; Mesozoic granitics, and pre-Cretaceous limestone and metamorphic rocks; potential natural vegetation is blue oak-digger pine forest, chaparral, Sierran montane forest, Giant sequoia, Sierran yellow pine forest, upper montane-subalpine forests, and alpine communities; abundant perennial streams, and rivers (North and South Forks and main stem of Kings River), few wet meadows and high-elevation lakes.
Elevation range: 950 feet to 11,081 feet.
System trails: 25.8 miles in Monarch Wilderness, 3.0 miles in Agnew roadless area, 10.7 miles in Kings River SMA, and 11.0 miles in Oat Mountain roadless area.
Maximum core-to-perimeter distance: 12 miles.
Activities: Backpacking, day hiking.
Maps: Sierra and Sequoia National Forests visitor maps; Monarch Wilderness and Jennie Lakes Wilderness map (topographic, 2 inches/mile); see Appendix D for the list of USGS 1:24,000 quads.

OVERVIEW: Straddling Kings Canyon at its deepest point, the Monarch complex is the most rugged and inaccessible wildland in the Sierra Nevada. The description "complex" is appropriate, for this area includes the Monarch Wilderness (created from the High Sierra Primitive Area in 1984), which is separated by Kings Canyon into two very different units: the Agnew roadless area, which includes part of the high west-slope plateau that was not included in the Monarch Wilderness; the Kings River Special Management Area (SMA), most of which is de facto wilderness in the lower reaches of Kings Canyon; and the Oat Mountain roadless area, which is separated from the Kings Canyon SMA on the southwest by a primitive road corridor.

When combined, these areas feature a very wide range of ecosystems over its more than 10,000 feet of elevation difference; indeed, it displays virtually every ecosystem that exists on the west slope of the Sierra Nevada. It is one of the Sierra's most important wildlands, and certainly one of the most diverse. Vegetation ranges from annual grasslands, blue oak woodlands, and foothill chaparral in lower Kings Canyon, to whitebark pine groves and frost-shattered granite in alpine areas high atop the Monarch Divide in the High Sierra, in an east-to-west distance of 25 miles.

The Oat Mountain roadless area includes the south rim of extreme lower Kings Canyon and north-facing slopes that extend down to the corridor of Forest Road 11S12 along the Kings River, direcly east of Pine Flat Reservoir. Immediately east of the Oat Mountain roadless area is the Kings River SMA. This RARE II area was allocated for Further Planning status from 1979 until 1987, at which time the enactment of Wild and Scenic River legislation established the entire area as a special management area. It includes the roaded corridor along the river and the roadless lands north and south of the river. Although almost all the Kings River corridor is roadless, the area is de facto wilderness and is managed to maintain its undeveloped character.

The Kings River SMA extends upriver from the confluence of the main stem and North Fork Kings River. The north boundary roughly follows Rodgers Ridge, and on the east, the boundary is Deer Ridge and the Monarch Wilderness. South of the river the SMA extends up to the south canyon rim and includes portions of three major tributary canyons: Converse Creek, Verplank Creek, and Mill Flat Creek. A wide range of vegetation types and ecosystems here is important to a variety of wildlife. Below the south canyon rim are two Giant sequoia groves—the Cabin Creek and Converse Mountain Groves.

The Hume and Kings River deer herds migrate from high elevations to winter range in the SMA on Rodgers Ridge, and in the Verplank and Mill Flat Creek drainages. Conifer forests in the upper elevations provide habitat not only for deer, but also for coyote, black bear, marten, porcupine, gray squirrel, and a variety of birds and rodents. Coyotes and deer also make use of low-elevation oak woodlands and chaparral areas, as do ringtail and gray fox.

Kings Canyon reaches its deepest point in the SMA, with an elevation difference of 8,250 feet between the summit of Spanish Mountain and the Kings River at the confluence with Rough Creek, giving it the distinction of being North America's deepest gorge. Much of the canyon in the SMA ranges from 5,000 to 7,000 feet deep. Lying below the extent of ancient valley glaciers, Kings Canyon assumes the classic V-shaped profile of a stream-cut canyon in the SMA. Granitic rocks dominate the landscape of precipitous slopes and deeply incised stream drainages, but in the South Fork canyon at the extreme eastern extension of the SMA, and on Spanish Mountain, there are areas of metamorphic rocks and prominent limestone dikes laced with cave systems. Large populations of various species of bats live in these caves.

The wildest part of the Monarch Complex is the Monarch Wilderness itself, and it is unusual in that the South Fork Kings River and the California Highway 180 corridor separates it into two distinctly different units to the north and south. The larger north unit on the Sierra National Forest is bounded by Deer Ridge on the west, the John Muir Wilderness on the northwest, and the Sequoia–Kings Canyon Wilderness on the east. The wilderness begins on the west at the confluence of the South and Middle Forks of the Kings River. The Middle Fork is an extremely rugged, trail-less gorge nearly 6,000 feet deep at the Monarch/Sequoia–Kings Canyon wilderness boundary in Little Tehipite Valley. West of the Middle Fork, boulder-stacked Tombstone Ridge soars from 3,800 feet on the river to the prominent granite dome of the Obelisk, a major Monarch landmark at 9,700 feet. The high crest stretches westward from the Obelisk to 10,051-foot Spanish Mountain, where the granite crest of precipitous Deer Ridge forms the western boundary and sweeps downward through conifer forests to scrub oak woodlands, chaparral, and grasslands in the Kings Canyon gorge. The principal tributaries to the Middle Fork flowing through precipitous canyons include Tombstone Creek, Brush Canyon, Deer Canyon, and Silver Creek.

From the confluence of the Middle and South Forks at 2,240 feet, the Monarch Divide rises 7,200 feet eastward in 5 miles from chaparral, yucca, and oak woodlands, past limestone dikes and metamorphic outcrops, to the timberline summit of Wren Peak and stunted groves of whitebark pine. From Wren Peak the Monarch Divide stays high, rising in gradual increments toward the highest summits in the wilderness. Mount Harrington, at 11,005 feet, is a prominent landmark with an imposing tower of granite defining its summit. Northeast of Mount Harrington the Monarch Divide rises higher still, reaching its apex atop a rounded, unnamed summit at 11,081 feet. Immediately east of this peak are the twin summits of 11,077-foot Hogback Peak, anchoring the northeast corner of the wilderness. The principal drainages in this area are the forks of Grizzly Creek. Several meadows spread out along the forks of Grizzly Creek, and the only two lakes in the wilderness—the small tarns of Grizzly Lakes—lie below Mount Harrington. As much as 8,700 feet of relief in 5 lateral miles separate the lowest and highest elevations of the Monarch's north unit, so a wide variety of ecosystems exist in a very short distance.

The smaller south unit, located on the Sequoia National Forest, embraces the north-facing slopes above Kings Canyon; it is no less rugged than the north unit, though it lacks alpine heights. This area is incised by numerous precipitous drainages with rushing streams tumbling off a discontinuous divide and off the higher terrain of the nearby Jennie Lakes Wilderness. This area was created from the Agnew RARE II roadless area, and what remains of the Agnew area bounds the wilderness on the south and west. Four named groves of Giant

View from the Kings River Special Management Area of Kings Canyon, to the Obelisk, and Spanish Mountain.

sequoias lie within the Agnew roadless area, and one grove—the Agnew Grove—lies inside the wilderness, one of the few wilderness sequoia groves in the Sierra outside of Sequoia–Kings Canyon Wilderness. The Agnew Grove is located alongside tumbling Rattlesnake Creek, a tributary to Boulder Creek, the principal drainage in the south unit of the wilderness.

RECREATIONAL USES: Since the Monarch Complex spans more than 10,000 feet of elevation with environments ranging from oak woodlands in the foothills to the alpine peaks of the Monarch Divide in the High Sierra, it offers recreational opportunities all year around. Much of this wildland complex is very seldom used. Hunters are the majority of users, yet they come in small numbers. The Oat Mountain area and Kings River SMA provide excellent opportunities for recreation during the late autumn through early spring months, when the higher elevations are blanketed in snow. Numerous tributary drainages in the SMA are incised into granite bedrock, containing many attractive waterfalls, cascades, slides, and pools; unfortunately, most of them aren't accessible by trail. One exception is Mill Flat Creek, where a popular trail leads to the stream's pools, slides, and cascades. The Kings River National Recreation Trail reaches 3 miles up-canyon along the Kings River from the end of the Garnet Dike Road.

The Monarch Wilderness is one of the most lightly used wilderness areas in the Sierra Nevada. Off-trail travel in the lower elevations is impractical if not impossible due to the thick mantle of chaparral and steep terrain.

At the highest elevations, by contrast, the Monarch Divide between Hogback Peak and Mount Harrington is comparably easy to traverse. It offers many fine vistas into the Kings Canyon backcountry of deep canyons, broad cirques, and an array of bold alpine crags, which in number and ruggedness are unrivaled anywhere in the lower 48 states. The best way to reach this high crest is via the Deer Cove Trail (30E01), a brutal 9.4-mile trail that ascends from 4,400 feet in Kings Canyon to 9,685 feet at Grizzly Lakes. Visitors to the north unit of the Monarch on the Sierra National Forest are required to obtain a wilderness permit for overnight use, and the Hume Lake Ranger District office on CA 180 near Dunlap is the most convenient place to get one.

Cross-country routes from the Grizzly Lakes lead to the Monarch Divide, and just over the north side of the divide is the very rarely visited Swamp Lakes basin in Sequoia–Kings Canyon Wilderness. Only two spurs extend off the Deer Cove Trail (30E01) in the north unit of the wilderness. Trail 30E03 branches west from Trail 30E01 north of Deer Cove, heading 0.8 mile toward Choke Creek and eventually disappearing. The other spur, dead-end Trail 30E02, traverses past the clearings of Wildman Meadow for 4 miles to lovely Happy Gap, a broad saddle fringed with gnarled timberline conifers beneath the crags of Eagle Peaks.

Three trailheads provide access to the limited trail system in the south unit of the wilderness in the Sequoia National Forest, where wilderness permits are not required. Trail 30E04, the Kanawyer Trail, stretches 12 miles across the wilderness from FR 13S05 at Evans Grove on the west, to CA 180 in Kings Canyon National Park on the east. The Deer Meadow Trail (30E05) connects with the Kanawyer Trail from the south, traversing 3.5 miles through part of the Agnew roadless area and into the Monarch Wilderness. Due to low use and minimal maintenance, the tread of these trails is often faint and likely to be blocked by blowdowns. Wildness prevails on Monarch trails, with few signs of humanity in the foreground or in the distance. Hikers on Monarch trails are more likely to see the tracks of bear and deer than of other hikers.

Day Hike or Overnighter

Deer Meadow Trail to Agnew Grove

Distance: 8.4 miles, round trip.
Low/high elevations: 6,300 feet/8,600 feet.
Difficulty: Strenuous.

Best season: Mid-June through September.
Topo maps: Cedar Grove-CA, Wren Peak-CA.
Permits: Not required. California Campfire Permit required for open fires and backpack stoves.

HOW TO GET THERE: Drive to the signed Big Meadows turnoff from the Generals Highway (the main road leading through Sequoia National Park, connecting CA 180 and 198). This turnoff is about 63 miles east of Fresno via CA 180 and the Generals Highway, and 72.5 miles east of Visalia via CA 198 and the Generals Highway.

At this turnoff, turn east and follow the paved road toward Big Meadows, indicated by signs at numerous junctions. After driving 4.75 miles from the highway, bear right at the upper (east) end of Big Meadows Campground, where the sign indicates Kings Canyon Pack Station and the Horse Corral Meadow. After driving 9.1 miles from the Generals Highway, continue straight ahead (east), staying on the paved road and bridging Horse Corral Creek, where the signed road to Rowell Trailhead turns right (southeast).

After driving another mile on FR 14S11, turn north onto dirt FR 13S11, which is 10.1 miles from the highway. This is a fair dirt road, narrow and brushy, yet negotiable by passenger cars. The road ends in a loop at the trailhead, 1.1 miles from the pavement of FR 14S11. Parking is available here for up to ten vehicles, and the turnaround can accommodate stock trailers.

This remote, seldom-used trail leads to one of few remaining wilderness groves of Giant sequoias. More than likely, hikers taking this trail will have the area entirely to themselves. This is a rigorous hike, losing 2,200 feet of elevation en route and regaining it on the way back.

Indicated by a semi-permanent sign that reads TRAIL, the Deer Meadow Trail leads north from the road's end, beginning as an old skid trail passing through selectively cut white fir forest. Follow this often-overgrown track for several hundred yards to its end, where another sign that also reads TRAIL marks the beginning of the trail proper. Ahead the trail rises quite steeply at times beneath a moderate canopy of mixed conifers.

The trail briefly levels out on a boulder-stacked ridge, then turns northeast and continues ascending toward Point 8,644. The white fir and Jeffrey pine forest is open enough here to afford tree-framed views of the Monarch Divide, views that improve just ahead as you traverse immediately west of the summit of the point. The trail then descends from this ridge, very steeply at first, through a shady, old-growth red fir forest, typical of north-facing slopes at this elevation in the Sierra, to a small meadow where the tread becomes faint along its southeast margin.

Ahead the tread becomes faint again as you skirt another meadow, this one quite wet with a rich turf of grasses, sedges, and wildflowers. Jump across the trickling stream at the lower end of the spread, then follow the winding trail down to lush Deer Meadow, passing the remains of an old log cabin at the meadow's edge.

The trail then follows around the margin of that crescent-shaped spread, ascends slightly to a minor ridge, then turns northwest where it begins another steep descent. While en route down this narrow ridge, if you step a few paces off the trail, you will enjoy tremendous views into Kings Canyon far below, with the Obelisk rising on the northern skyline. The trail leads you down through red fir forest nearly to a saddle in the ridge before it turns northeast to a broad saddle at 7,700 feet on the Monarch Wilderness boundary. Immediately before entering the wilderness, you have a brief glimpse eastward to several dramatic 12,000- and 13,000-foot peaks rising above the Bubbs Creek area in Sequoia–Kings Canyon Wilderness.

From there the descent continues, moderately at first, then more steeply as you begin following a northwest-trending ridge. As you lose elevation, white fir and Jeffrey and sugar pine begin to dominate the forest. One mile from the wilderness boundary and 900 feet below, you join Trail 30E04 and turn left, continuing the descent through mixed conifer forest. Soon the trail crosses the headwaters draw of an early-season stream, then traverses down to a saddle at 6,320 feet, lying beneath the brushy, pine-topped cone of Peak 6,531.

Agnew Grove covers at least 30 acres on the south slopes of the saddle, above the precipitous drainage of Rattlesnake Creek. Though a small grove, it does contain several large, ancient trees. Another, smaller grove is located on the north slopes of the minor ridge that separates Agnew Grove from Deer Meadow Grove to the south, at about 7,400 feet.

Camping is possible on the saddle above the grove, and Rattlesnake Creek usually provides water until late summer or early autumn. Hikers who do choose to camp here must be extremely cautious with fire.

John Muir Wilderness   10

Location: Southern Sierra Nevada, 50 miles northeast of Fresno, 4 miles south of Mammoth Lakes, 15 miles west of Bishop, and 10 miles west of Lone Pine.
Size: 580,323 acres.
Administration: USDAFS–Inyo and Sierra National Forests.
Management status: National forest wilderness.
Ecosystems: Sierran Forest–Alpine Meadows province, Sierra Nevada section, characterized by complex and very high mountains and ridges, with cirques and glacier-modified valleys, moraines, aretes, cols, horns, and smooth, striated bedrock; Mesozoic granitic rocks, with smaller areas of metamorphosed Jurassic and earlier marine sedimentary and volcanic rocks, and glacial and alluvial deposits; potential natural vegetation is sagebrush steppe, pinyon-juniper woodland, northern Jeffrey pine forest, Sierran montane forest, upper montane-subalpine forests with extensive areas of alpine communities; abundant perennial streams, wet meadows, and lakes throughout (the west slopes are a high, westward-sloping plateau with a dense network of perennial streams and lakes; the east slopes are an abrupt escarpment with steep, narrow stream valleys draining many lakes).
Elevation range: 5,000 feet to 14,495 feet.
System trails: 589.5 miles.
Maximum core-to-perimeter distance: 11.5 miles.
Activities: Backpacking, horseback riding, day hiking, cross-country skiing, snowshoeing, rock climbing, mountaineering, fishing.
Maps: Sierra and Inyo National Forests visitor maps; John Muir Wilderness map (including Sequoia–Kings Canyon Wilderness; two sheets, topographic, 1 inch/mile); see Appendix D for a list of the 32 USGS 1:24,000 quads.

OVERVIEW: The John Muir Wilderness, the second most heavily visited wilderness area in the national wilderness preservation system, sets the standard by which all other high-country wilderness areas are judged. Stretching along the eastern escarpment of the Sierra for some 90 miles between Cottonwood Creek on the south and the Mammoth Lakes area on the north, the John Muir contains 18 named peaks over 12,000 feet, 57 peaks at 13,000 feet or more, and 10 peaks exceeding 14,000 feet. In addition there are scores of unnamed peaks above 12,000 feet. Named in honor of famed naturalist John Muir, this wilderness embraces some of the finest high-mountain landscapes in the Sierra Nevada, a range John Muir called " . . . the most beautiful of all mountain chains."

The wilderness stretches along the eastern escarpment of the Sierra Nevada for 60 miles in a narrow band ranging from one to ten miles wide, be-

10   JOHN MUIR WILDERNESS

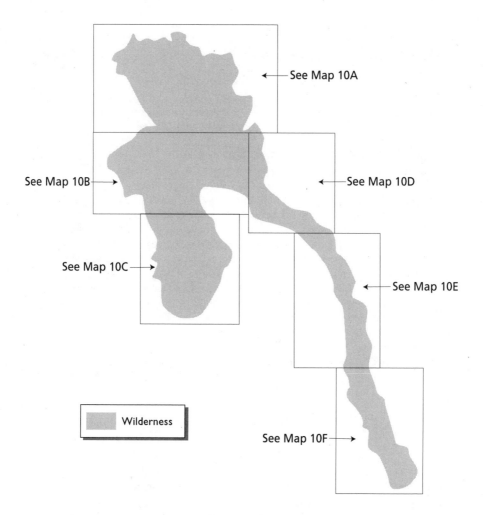

See Map 10A

See Map 10B

See Map 10D

See Map 10C

See Map 10E

Wilderness

See Map 10F

tween Cottonwood Creek on the south and Bishop Creek on the north. At Piute Pass—the head of Piute Creek and the North Fork Bishop Creek drainages—the John Muir Wilderness continues another 30 miles along the eastern slopes to Mammoth Lakes. It also reaches onto the west slopes of the Sierra along the Glacier Divide and the boundary with Kings Canyon National Park, arcing west around that park and extending 20 miles into mid-elevation forests and deep canyons, and across lofty divides. It then reaches south to the northern boundary of the Monarch Wilderness, bounded by the Le Conte Divide and Kettle Ridge along the park boundary on the east, and by roaded country surrounding Wishon and Courtright reservoirs on the west. This portion of the wilderness includes parts of the South Fork San Joaquin River, the headwaters of the North Fork Kings River, and tributaries to the Middle Fork Kings River.

North of the Glacier Divide and South Fork San Joaquin River, the John Muir follows the dips and swells of the west slopes past the Mono Divide to Mono Creek canyon and over the Silver Divide to Fish Creek. Finally, it rises to the Mammoth Crest, where to the north and west it merges with the Ansel Adams Wilderness.

The eastern escarpment of the range within the John Muir rises abruptly from broad alluvial fans on the fringes of the desert expanse of Owens Valley, and it is the most profound face of high mountains in the United States. It rises in elevation from 6,000 to 8,000 feet from the foot of the range to the crest, in a lateral distance averaging a mere 5 to 6 miles. Its total elevation difference is as much as 10,000 feet from the Owens Valley floor. Once tributaries to the Owens River that now feeds the Los Angeles Aqueduct system, scores of tumbling streams cascade down through some of the most rugged canyons in the nation. Each canyon is surrounded at its head by great cirques and cliffs, permanent snowfields, and small glaciers and peaks ranging from 12,000 to 14,000 feet. Among the snowfields are the Palisade Glaciers, at the head of Big Pine Creek; these are some of the southernmost glaciers in the U.S. Chains of high lakes rest at the head of nearly all the eastside canyons in hanging cirques. Below the lake basins, the plunging U-shaped canyons, excavated by glaciers in their upper reaches, drain turbulent streams bound for the desert. Farther north, beyond Bishop Creek, canyons, including Rock, McGee, and Convict Creeks, are less precipitous, displaying glacier-carved, U-shaped profiles and prominent moraines that reach almost to the foot of the range. Of all the eastside drainages, none is larger than expansive Bishop Creek. The three forks of this drainage boast about 100 lakes, a number unsurpassed in any drainage in the eastern Sierra Nevada.

Nearly all of the lands in the John Muir were modified by glaciation, save for the lowest parts of the eastern slopes south of Big Pine Creek. Vast expanses of ice-carved bedrock dominate the John Muir near and above timberline, and there are few wildlands in the wilderness preservation system that can rival the John Muir's 957 high lakes. The John Muir contains vast areas above timberline, and, combined with Sequoia–Kings Canyon Wilderness, this region of the High Sierra forms one of the largest contiguous areas above 10,000 feet in the United States. Alpine fell-fields and alpine meadows dominate the landscape above 10,800 feet, below which are extensive timberline stands of whitebark and lodgepole pine. Foxtail pines replace whitebarks in the southern reaches of the wilderness at timberline, often growing straight and tall up to

10A JOHN MUIR WILDERNESS

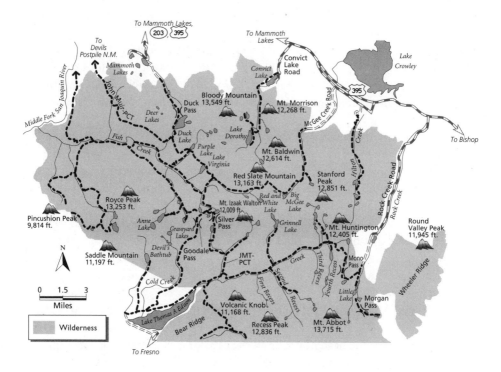

their elevational limit at about 11,200 feet. Lodgepole pine is the dominant conifer in the John Muir. In the lower elevations, Jeffrey pine dominates, joined in places by white fir, red fir, and occasional groves of aspen.

Because of the high elevations of the John Muir, wildlife is scarce. Black bears, common to the forests of the west slope, were once rare east of the Sierra crest. Eastside drainages are now seeing a marked increase in black bears conditioned to scavenging for human food. In Independence Creek, for example, hikers following the trail from Onion Valley to Kearsarge Pass are *required to* store food in bear-resistant canisters, and bears have developed the habit of destroying vehicles at the Onion Valley Trailhead in search of food. Other areas where human/bear encounters are likely include eastside canyons on the White Mountain Ranger District and in northern areas of the Mammoth Ranger District. While traveling in the John Muir backcountry, travelers will occasionally observe mule deer, yet the most readily observed wildlife include yellow-bellied marmot, pika, and golden-mantled ground squirrel. Clark's nutcrackers are common avian denizens of pine forests, while above timberline gather small flocks of the delicate rosy finch.

10B JOHN MUIR WILDERNESS

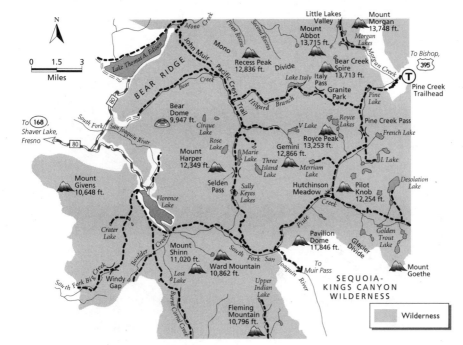

The two remaining remnant populations of California bighorn sheep are located on the eastern slope of the Sierra in the southern John Muir Wilderness, in two separate California Bighorn Sheep Zoological Areas. One surrounds Mount Williamson, the other, Mount Baxter. Sheep from these populations have been reintroduced in the Wheeler Ridge area between Pine Creek and Rock Creek, and in the Mount Langley area above the Cottonwood Lakes. Regulations to limit human disturbance are in effect, prohibiting dogs and closing the two zoological areas to entry generally between July and mid-December.

Fishing is a popular attraction in the John Muir, and aerial stocking generally relies on hatchery-raised trout. The exception is the golden trout, unsuccessfully raised in fish hatcheries. The State of California relies on Cottonwood Lakes 1, 2, 3, and 4, and their tributaries as the sole source of pure-strain golden trout eggs. Thus fishing in these lakes is strictly prohibited.

RECREATIONAL USES: Few wilderness areas of the U.S. can compare to the John Muir in the variety and quality of its high-mountain backcountry recreation. The area's trail network, combined with cross-country hiking opportunities

10C JOHN MUIR WILDERNESS

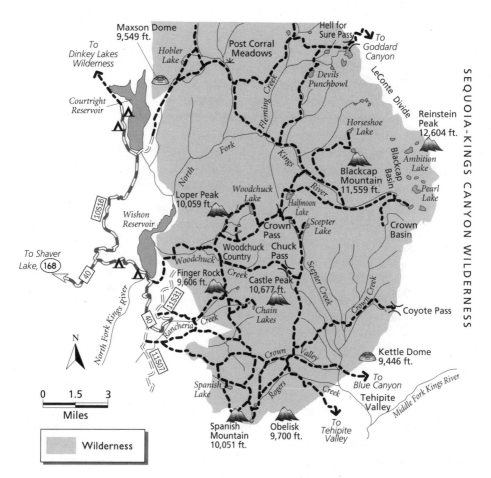

ranging from easy to challenging, make the John Muir suitable for incompara-ble high-country hiking that can last as little as one day to as much as several weeks. Yet hiking is not the only popular self-propelled activity here. The John Muir provides some of the most abundant and challenging mountaineering in the United States. Famous peaks such as Mount Whitney, Mount Tyndall, Mount Williamson, and North Palisade all feature climbing routes beginning at Class 4 and reaching well into the Class 5 range. Many other peaks, both named and obscure, attract peak-baggers of all abilities. The rewards of scaling peaks in the John Muir are tremendous, and their vistas are unrivaled.

The John Muir is very heavily used, and throughout the summer season on its nearly 600 miles of trails you are very likely to meet other parties coming and going. Some trails, of course, are more popular than others, and solitude can still be found in much of the vast backcountry. Off-trail travel to remote lake basins can provide complete solitude. On 31 of the 76 access points to the John Muir, trail quotas (in effect from the last Friday in June through mid-September) decrease overcrowding and enhance opportunities for solitude. Wilderness permits are required for overnight use but not for day use, except in the Mount Whitney Zone, where permits are also required for day hiking along the Mount Whitney Trail. On the Sierra National Forest (westside entry), two-thirds of each trailhead quota is available by advance reservation, with the remainder being available on a first-come, first-served basis on the day of entry. Reservations require a fee and they can be made by mail through district ranger stations. For eastside entry via the Inyo National Forest, reservations for quota and nonquota trailheads can be made up to six months in advance. (See Appendix B for a list of managing agencies to contact for information.)

Among the users of the John Muir are clients of commercial outfitter/ guides, which amount to roughly one-fourth of the total annual use of the backcountry. Sixteen commercial pack stations, serving many popular trailheads, all offer backcountry trips into the John Muir. In addition to horse packing, there are numerous commercial guides who offer trips for backpacking, mountaineering, climbing, fly fishing, and ski touring.

Many eastside trails south of Bishop Creek are extremely strenuous, beginning at low elevations near the foot of the mountains and ascending thousands of feet to lofty passes on the Sierra crest. The Mount Whitney, Symmes Creek, Baxter Pass, Sawmill Pass, and Taboose Pass Trails all gain more than 6,000 feet of elevation on their short, abrupt courses to the Sierra crest. Not only are these trails arduous, they provide few places to camp. They do provide considerable solitude, and most hikers use them en route to mountaineering routes and to the backcountry of Sequoia–Kings Canyon Wilderness. Eastside drainages from Big Pine Creek north, and particularly the forks of Bishop Creek, are less difficult to access, and not only provide ways to reach deep into the backcountry, but provide destinations as well. Stocking of rainbow, brook, brown, and golden trout takes place in 280 of the John Muir's 957 lakes.

Paved roads provide access to most trailheads on both the east and west sides of the wilderness. Stock use by private parties and outfitters is moderate to high on both sides of the John Muir, with stock parties concentrating use in Mono Creek, Humphreys Basin, Graveyard Meadows, French Canyon, Piute Creek, and along the John Muir/Pacific Crest Trail.

Winter access is almost entirely restricted to the eastside trailheads, where plowed roads in Big Pine Creek, Bishop Creek, Rock Creek, and the Mammoth Lakes area provide high-elevation starting points for winter recreation. Snowshoeing, skiing, and ski mountaineering to places like the Palisades, the forks of Bishop Creek, Humphreys Basin, Little Lakes Valley, Pioneer Basin,

10D   JOHN MUIR WILDERNESS

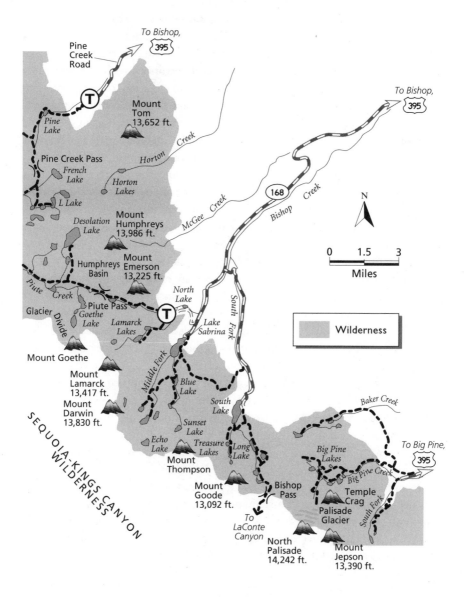

To Bishop, 395

Pine
Creek
Road

T

Pine
Lake

Mount
Tom
13,652 ft.

Horton   Creek

To Bishop, 395

Pine Creek Pass

French
Lake

Horton
Lakes

L Lake

Horton

McGee   Creek

Bishop   Creek

168

Desolation
Lake

Mount
Humphreys
13,986 ft.

N

Mount
Emerson
13,225 ft.

Humphreys
Basin

North
Lake

0   1.5   3
Miles

Piute   Creek

Piute Pass

Glacier

Goethe
Lake

South
Fork

Lake
Sabrina

Lamarck
Lakes

T

Divide

Wilderness

Mount Goethe

Mount
Lamarck
13,417 ft.

Middle Fork

Blue
Lake

Mount
Darwin
13,830 ft.

South
Lake

Baker   Creek

Sunset
Lake

SEQUOIA-KINGS CANYON

Echo
Lake

Treasure
Lakes

Long
Lake

Big Pine
Lakes

To Big Pine, 395

WILDERNESS

Mount
Thompson

Mount
Goode
13,092 ft.

Bishop
Pass

Big Pine Creek

Temple
Crag

Palisade
Glacier

South Fork

To
LaConte
Canyon

North
Palisade
14,242 ft.

Mount
Jepson
13,390 ft.

and the Duck Lake/Mammoth Crest area make much of the John Muir a premier year-round backcountry destination.

The heaviest use areas are listed by ranger district below:

West Side:

Kings River Ranger District: Red Mountain Basin, Woodchuck Basin, Crown Valley.

Pineridge Ranger District: Florence Lake, Bear Creek, Mono Creek, Devils Bathtub, Graveyard Meadows.

East Side:

Mount Whitney Ranger District: Cottonwood Lakes basin, Mount Whitney Trail, North Fork Trail, Kearsarge Pass Trail.

White Mountain Ranger District: Little Lakes Valley, Hilton Lakes, Long Lake (Bishop Creek), Blue Lake (Sabrina Basin), First through Third lakes (Big Pine Creek).

Mammoth Ranger District: Cascade Valley, Duck and Purple Lakes.

Multi-day Backpack

North Lake to Pine Creek

Distance: 22 miles shuttle trip (3 to 5 days).
Low/high elevations: 7,400 feet/11,440 feet.
Difficulty: Moderate.
Best season: Mid-July through September.
Topo maps: Mount Darwin-CA, Mount Tom-CA, Mount Hilgard-CA.
Permits: A wilderness permit is required for overnight use, and entry quotas are in effect. Obtain at the White Mountain Ranger District office in Bishop. Reservations for permits can be made up to six months in advance (see Appendix B for information).

HOW TO GET THERE: From U.S. Highway 395 in Bishop, turn west onto California 168 where a sign lists mileage to South Lake, Lake Sabrina, and North Lake. Follow this paved road up Bishop Creek canyon, and after 14 miles, avoid the left-branching road leading to South Lake and continue straight ahead for 3 more miles to the signed, right-branching North Lake Road. Follow this dirt road for 1.75 miles to the signed hiker's parking area just above North Lake.

To find the Pine Creek Trailhead, drive 10 miles north of Bishop on US 395, then turn west and proceed 10 more miles up the paved Pine Creek Road to the hiker's parking area just east of the pack station.

This memorable backcountry trip leads for miles through timberline and alpine terrain, past dozens of lakes both large and small, and features good fishing, abundant side-trip options, superb alpine vistas, and vegetation ranging from Jeffrey pine forest to alpine tundra.

10E JOHN MUIR WILDERNESS

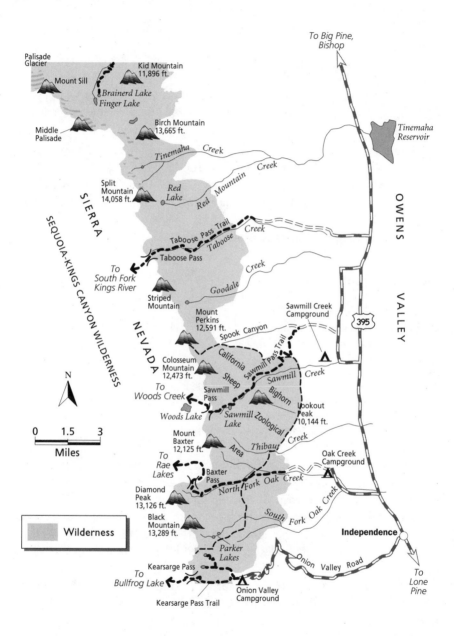

Palisade
Glacier

Kid Mountain
11,896 ft.

Mount Sill

Brainerd Lake
Finger Lake

Birch Mountain
13,665 ft.

*Tinemaha
Reservoir*

Middle
Palisade

Tinemaha   Creek

Creek

Split
Mountain
14,058 ft.

*Red
Lake*

Red   Mountain

SIERRA

SEQUOIA-KINGS CANYON WILDERNESS

Taboose Pass Trail

Creek

Taboose

Taboose Pass

To
South Fork
Kings River

Creek

Goodale

Striped
Mountain

Mount
Perkins
12,591 ft.

Sawmill Creek
Campground

NEVADA

Spook   Canyon

California

Sawmill Pass Trail

395

OWENS   VALLEY

N

Colosseum
Mountain
12,473 ft.

Sheep

Sawmill   Creek

To
Woods Creek

Sawmill
Pass

Bighorn

Woods Lake

*Sawmill
Lake*

Zoological

Lookout
Peak
10,144 ft.

0   1.5   3

Miles

Mount
Baxter
12,125 ft.

Area

Thibaut   Creek

Oak Creek
Campground

To
Rae
Lakes

Baxter
Pass

North Fork Oak Creek

Diamond
Peak
13,126 ft.

Black
Mountain
13,289 ft.

South Fork Oak Creek

Independence

Wilderness

*Parker
Lakes*

Onion   Valley   Road

Kearsarge Pass

To
Bullfrog Lake

Onion Valley
Campground

To
Lone
Pine

Kearsarge Pass Trail

To Big Pine,
Bishop

10F JOHN MUIR WILDERNESS

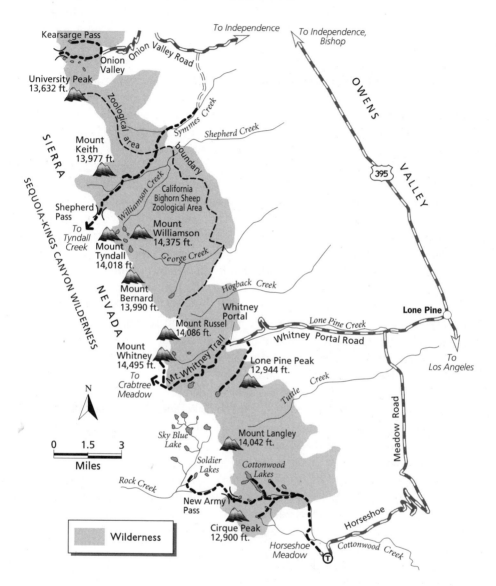

Kearsarge Pass

To Independence

To Independence, Bishop

Onion Valley Road

Onion Valley

University Peak 13,632 ft.

Zoological area

Symmes Creek

Shepherd Creek

OWENS

395

VALLEY

SIERRA

Mount Keith 13,977 ft.

boundary

Williamson Creek

California Bighorn Sheep Zoological Area

SEQUOIA-KINGS CANYON WILDERNESS

Shepherd Pass

To Tyndall Creek

Mount Williamson 14,375 ft.

Mount Tyndall 14,018 ft.

George Creek

NEVADA

Mount Bernard 13,990 ft.

Hogback Creek

Whitney Portal

Lone Pine

Mount Russel 14,086 ft.

Lone Pine Creek

Whitney Portal Road

Mount Whitney 14,495 ft.

Mt. Whitney Trail

Lone Pine Peak 12,944 ft.

To Los Angeles

To Crabtree Meadow

Tuttle Creek

N

Mount Langley 14,042 ft.

Meadow Road

Sky Blue Lake

0   1.5   3

Miles

Soldier Lakes

Cottonwood Lakes

Rock Creek

New Army Pass

Horseshoe

| | Wilderness |

Cirque Peak 12,900 ft.

Horseshoe Meadow

T

Cottonwood Creek

Campfires are prohibited from the trailhead to Piute Pass, but are permitted west of the pass in the Sierra National Forest and in the Pine Creek drainage.

From the hiker's parking area, walk back to the North Lake Road, turn right, and hike 0.5 mile to the trailhead at the upper end of the campground. A short distance beyond, the southbound Lamarck Lakes Trail forks to your left at a large information sign. You turn right and ascend westward through the shade of aspen, lodgepole, and limber pine. After fording the North Fork Bishop Creek twice, you begin following switchbacks up talus slopes below the broken red cliffs of the Piute Crags. Above that ascent, you reach Loch Leven, the first lake in this small but highly scenic basin.

The trail ascends more gradually to Piute Lake, beyond which you soon leave the last gnarled whitebark pines behind and ascend the final alpine slopes to Piute Pass. Your view eastward from the pass takes in the U-shaped valley containing Piute and Loch Leven lakes. Westward, your view is strictly alpine. Immediately to your west lies the broad expanse of alpine Humphreys Basin, one of the largest and most gentle lake basins in the Sierra Nevada. There are more than 20 alpine lakes here, most of which offer challenging fishing. North of the pass, convoluted red and brown cliffs soar to the pinnacle-topped summit of 13,986-foot Mount Humphreys, the highest peak this far north in the Sierra.

From the pass, descend westward to round Summit Lake and continue your trail walk through the tundra-dominated landscape of Humphreys Basin. All the lakes in this basin are accessible by easy cross-country jaunts, and they're so numerous that it is easy to have one entirely to yourself.

Your route soon passes to the north of Golden Trout Lake, where camping is restricted to no less than 500 feet from the lakeshore. Lodgepole pine forest increases as you descend along Piute Creek, offering more sheltered camping than in exposed Humphreys Basin.

After a few short switchbacks, the trail levels off in a thick, shady lodgepole pine forest, and you pass occasional small, wildflower-decorated meadows. With the pyramidal hulk of Pilot Knob looming directly above to the north, you hop across multi-branched French Canyon Creek and soon meet the French Canyon Trail on your right, just north of the small green spread of Hutchinson Meadow.

Turn northeast onto this trail and begin a long, gentle ascent of French Canyon. You soon break into the open, following the edge of a narrow two-mile-long meadow. Merriam Peak and the broken, craggy summits of the Sierra crest stand majestically above the canyon in the north. Midway up the meadow you pass a faint westbound trail that climbs to seldom-visited Merriam Lake. At the head of the meadow, you hop across the Royce Lakes outlet creek, which features a memorable waterfall a short distance above the trail.

From the crossing, you quickly pass the last remnants of gnarled conifers and continue your jaunt through open, alpine meadows. About 0.8 mile below Pine Creek Pass, you meet a southbound trail that provides access to several large lakes, including Moon Lake, and "L" Lake. Short cross-country jaunts in that basin lead to many more infrequently visited alpine lakes.

After a short, stiff climb beyond that trail, you level off on a large grassy bench. From here a cross-country route of moderate difficulty will lead to the Royce Lakes chain, well off the beaten path. Continuing northward on the trail, you skirt two small tarns and a few persistent whitebark pines, then cross the Sierra crest at 11,120-foot Pine Creek Pass. Views are good southward to the western peaks of the Glacier Divide. You'll see a host of high peaks surrounding the Pine Creek drainage to the north, dominated by the jagged crag of 13,713-foot Bear Creek Spire.

You then begin a short descent through alpine meadows along the headwaters of Pine Creek before reentering timberline forest, eventually passing the signed trail leading west to Granite Park and Italy Pass.

As your descent proceeds, you cross a multi-branched creek, skirt the western shore of Upper Pine Lake, then Pine Lake, both of which offer excellent views across their deep blue waters. You soon ford the outlet creek of Pine Lake and pass the last few campsites along Pine Creek, shaded by lodgepole pines. A traverse of north-facing slopes, under the precipitous north wall of Peak 12,280, brings you to a series of short switchbacks where you lose 400 feet of elevation.

Suddenly, your trail emerges onto an access road to the old Brownstone Mine. You follow this narrow dirt road as it descends via switchbacks into lower Pine Creek canyon. After hiking 1.1 miles along this road, leave it and proceed eastward on another trail. Your final descent begins immediately across the canyon from the Union Carbide tungsten mill. The trail crosses several small creeks in a Jeffrey pine and red fir forest, and eventually you reach the pack station, pass a few scattered buildings, and finally reach the hiker's parking area at 7,400 feet.

Dinkey Lakes Wilderness   ▮▮

Location: 45 miles northeast of Fresno.
Size: 30,000 acres.
Administration: USDAFS–Sierra National Forest.
Management status: National Forest wilderness.
Ecosystems: Sierran Forest–Alpine Meadows province, Sierra Nevada section, characterized by high, steep mountains with glacial cirques, domes, and moderately high ridges and wide valleys; Mesozoic granitic rocks and small areas of volcanics; potential natural vegetation is Sierran montane forest, and upper montane-subalpine forests forest types, and small areas of alpine communities; numerous perennial streams, moderate- to high-elevation lakes, and large, wet meadows.
Elevation range: 8,200 feet to 10,619 feet.
System trails: 50 miles.
Maximum core-to-perimeter distance: 3.5 miles.
Activities: Backpacking, day hiking, horseback riding, cross-country skiing and snowshoeing, fishing.
Maps: Sierra National Forest visitor map; Dinkey Lakes Wilderness map (topographic, 2 inches/mile); see Appendix D for a list of USGS 1:24,000 quads.

OVERVIEW: Although separated from the true High Sierra by a mid-elevation, forested plateau, the Dinkey Lakes Wilderness stands high enough to have hosted mountain-carving glaciers in the distant past. The results can be seen today in the form of numerous subalpine lakes, cirques, smoothed and polished granitic bedrock, and quarried peaks that rise well above timberline. The Dinkey Lakes is joined by four other southern Sierra wildlands—Kaiser, Dome Land, Sacatar Trail, and Owens Peak—that are separated by narrow road corridors from the 2.3 million acres of contiguous wilderness south of central Yosemite.

The bulk of the Dinkey Lakes landscape is dominated by subalpine forests, moderately high, rolling ridges with areas of frost-shattered and ice-polished granite bedrock and domes, seven very large, wet meadows, and numerous smaller grasslands, many of which occupy former lakebeds. A high divide along the southwestern boundary is crowned by half a dozen peaks exceeding 10,000 feet in elevation, including the 10,619-foot summit of the south peak of Three Sisters, 10,349-foot Brown Peak, and 10,318-foot Eagle Peak. A short, northeast-trending spur ridge extends into the wilderness from Three

11 DINKEY LAKES WILDERNESS

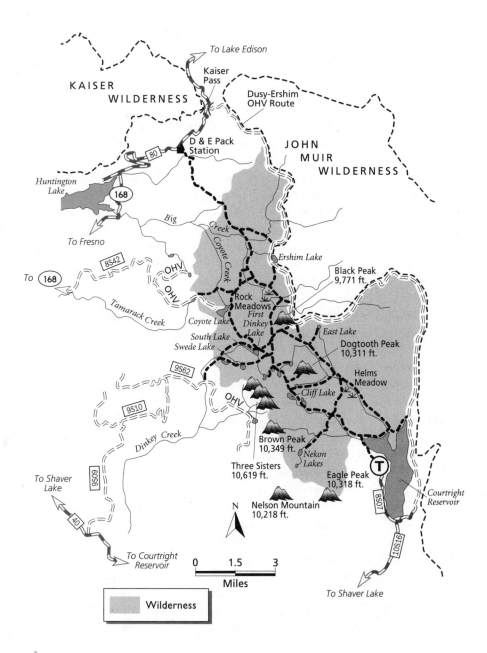

To Lake Edison

Kaiser Pass

KAISER WILDERNESS

Dusy-Ershim OHV Route

D & E Pack Station

JOHN MUIR WILDERNESS

Huntington Lake

168

To Fresno

To 168

8S42

OHV

OHV

Tamarack Creek

Big Creek

Coyote Creek

Ershim Lake

Black Peak 9,771 ft.

Rock Meadows

Coyote Lake

First Dinkey Lake

South Lake

Swede Lake

East Lake

Dogtooth Peak 10,311 ft.

Helms Meadow

9S62

OHV

Cliff Lake

9S10

Dinkey Creek

Brown Peak 10,349 ft.

Three Sisters 10,619 ft.

Nekon Lakes

Eagle Peak 10,318 ft.

T

9S09

To Shaver Lake

40

N

Nelson Mountain 10,218 ft.

Courtright Reservoir

8S07

To Courtright Reservoir

0   1.5   3

Miles

10S16

To Shaver Lake

Wilderness

Sisters, dividing the waters of Dinkey Creek to the north from tributaries to Courtright Reservoir to the south. Dogtooth Peak, rising to 10,311 feet, crowns the northeastern extension of this ridge. The entire landscape was scraped bare by glacial ice; the most obvious examples are along the flanks of the high divide, where 14 high lakes rest in a series of timberline cirques scooped out of the granite slopes.

The center of the wilderness and its northeast boundary are crossed by an ill-defined divide that directs north-flowing tributaries to the San Joaquin River and southbound streams to the Kings River. The high divide along the southwestern boundary drains streams westward into Dinkey Creek, another Kings River tributary.

Mule deer from the Huntington and North Kings herds occasionally appear in the Dinkey Lakes area, but due to the lack of preferred browse shrubs, they are few in number. Black bear, on the other hand, are quite common, as they are throughout most of the Sierra's west slope, but encounters between bears and humans have not yet become a problem. Other wildlife in the Dinkey Lakes area is not readily observed, as in most middle- and high-elevation areas of the Sierra. Golden-mantled ground squirrels are one of the most frequently seen rodents, and marmots and pikas inhabit rocky areas at timberline and above. The extensive forests of the Dinkey Lakes also support marten and fisher, while Sierra Nevada red fox and coyote range throughout the area.

RECREATIONAL USES: Not only do fishing opportunities exist in the Dinkey Lakes area, but the two prominent peaks rising above the lakes—10,619-foot Three Sisters and 10,311-foot Dogtooth Peak—can be scaled via Class 2 and Class 3 routes, respectively, providing expansive and complementary perspectives that encompass a large slice of the Sierra Nevada.

This region of the upper west slope of the central Sierra Nevada is a popular OHV destination, and there are several four-wheel-drive OHV routes available for motorized recreation. The Dinkey Lakes Wilderness would be contiguous with the vast John Muir Wilderness immediately to the east but for the narrow corridor of the Dusy-Ershim OHV route (7S32), linking Kaiser Pass in the north with Courtright Reservoir in the south. Three other OHV routes approach the wilderness boundary along its western margin. They are popular during the summer season and receive heavy use on holiday weekends. Some day hikers and anglers use these routes as well, but the majority of them approach the Dinkey Lakes from paved and well-maintained forest roads.

This wilderness has three primary trailheads: Cliff Lake Trailhead at Courtright Reservoir on the southeast; Dinkey Creek Trailhead on the west; and the California Riding and Hiking Trailhead at D and F Pack Station on the Kaiser Pass Road (FR 80), two miles from the northwest wilderness boundary. The

Dogtooth Peak serves as foreground to far-ranging vistas of the central Sierra Nevada.

Dinkey Creek Trailhead is most heavily used, owing to its easy access from California Highway 168 on the west and short trail (less than 3 miles) into the heart of the Dinkey Lakes basin.

Many trails provide opportunities for loop trips and round trips of several days' duration, though the majority of visitors, most of them day hikers, congregate in the Dinkey Lakes basin. Dinkey Lakes receives generally light backcountry use, except for the basin area. Most hikers opt to visit better-known areas in the adjacent John Muir Wilderness instead; that leaves thousands of acres of unspoiled subalpine forests, vast meadows, lofty summits, and trail-less lake basins to explore in the Dinkey Lakes country in relative solitude.

Forty to fifty percent of backcountry visitors fish in lake-filled High Sierra wilderness areas such as the Dinkey Lakes. Fourteen of the Dinkey's seventeen major lakes are stocked by air with golden, brook, and rainbow trout. The two commercial pack stations operating in this area depend for much of their business on fishing enthusiasts. The California Riding and Hiking Trail is a long-distance approach from the D and F Pack Station on Kaiser Pass Road in the northwest, but it receives the majority of pack and saddle stock use from private parties and the pack station. The large meadows in the northern reaches of the wilderness provide abundant feed for stock and are often used as base camps for stock parties.

Wilderness permits are required for overnight use of the Dinkey Lakes Wilderness, but there are no quotas. You can get permits from the Eastwood visitor center at Huntington Lake on CA 168, from the Dinkey Creek Ranger Station, from the Pineridge Ranger Station in Prather northeast of Clovis, and from the Courtright Village Homeowners Association building, near Cliff Lake Trailhead at Courtright Reservoir.

Winter access is limited by the long distances from plowed roads. The best access is from CA 168 in the northwest, which is plowed to Sierra Summit Ski Area. From there you can ski or snowshoe up Forest Road 80 (Kaiser Pass Road) to the D and F Pack Station and follow the route of the California Riding and Hiking Trail for 2.5 miles into the northern reaches of the wilderness.

Day Hike or Overnighter

Courtright Reservoir to Dogtooth Peak

Distance: 11.6 miles, round trip.
  Low/high elevations: 8,475 feet/10,311 feet.
Difficulty: Moderate.
Best season: July through September.
Topo maps: Courtright Reservoir-CA, Dogtooth Peak-CA, Nelson Mountain-CA, Ward Mountain-CA.
Permits: Wilderness permit required for overnight use. Obtain at Pineridge Ranger District Office in Prather just off CA 168, 22.5 miles northeast of Clovis.

HOW TO GET THERE: From Clovis, proceed northeast on CA 168 for about 40 miles to the community of Shaver Lake. Turn right (east) near the southern end of Shaver Lake where a sign indicates Dinkey Creek and Wishon Dam. Follow this paved road generally eastward for 11.6 miles to a junction just south of Dinkey Creek.

Turn right (south) just beyond the pack station, where the sign indicates McKinley Grove, Wishon Reservoir, and Courtright Reservoir. Follow this paved road southeast, pass through the McKinley Grove of Giant Sequoias and, after 13.6 miles, reach a junction with the right-branching road to Wishon Reservoir. Turn left here and follow the good paved road toward Courtright Village (no services) and to the Cliff Lake Trailhead, about 10 miles from the previous junction.

This trip is an excellent introduction to the attractions of the Dinkey Lakes country. Rising from the dome-encircled shores of Courtright Reservoir through shady, subalpine forests and rich meadows, the trail passes beautiful and aptly named Cliff Lake, then tops out on a timberline divide. A short spur trail leads from there to the foot of a bold granite crag, Dogtooth Peak, where a moderate Class 3 scramble leads to the summit and tremendous vistas.

From the 8,475-foot parking area, your trail heads northwest through a red fir and lodgepole pine forest on a slightly descending grade. You will soon pass a doubletrack joining your trail on the right. As you approach the northwest end of Courtright Reservoir, the forest becomes dominated by lodgepole pine. Hop across the creek draining Cliff Lake and enter the Dinkey Lakes Wilderness.

Your trail then meanders northwestward through heavy lodgepole pine forest, reaching a four-way junction 3.0 miles from the trailhead. The northeast-bound trail leading to Helms Meadow and beyond is seldom used, while the southwest-bound trail, equally seldom trod, leads to the Nelson Lakes basin.

You continue northwest on the Cliff Lake Trail and eventually begin an ascent up switchbacks along a south-facing slope clothed in western white pine and manzanita—enjoying fine views along the way. The trail levels off above the switchbacks, and you soon find yourself walking above the northeast shore of beautiful Cliff Lake at 9,500 feet, 5 miles from the trailhead. There are numerous possibilities for camping above this shore of the lake. With a backdrop of 400-foot-high cliffs and an open, boulder-dotted forest, it is an excellent and justifiably popular campsite.

The trail becomes faint as it passes above the lake, so watch for blazed trees. It becomes easy to follow once again as you reach a signed junction. The left-branching, descending trail leads to campsites above the upper end of Cliff Lake. Bullfrog Lake lies just over the ridge to the northeast, but continue your northwest-bound ascent; after 0.75 mile you reach 9,920-foot pass.

Instead of descending northwest into the Dinkey Lakes basin, as most hikers do, turn right (east-northeast) at the pass and walk 0.75 mile along the ridge among stunted mountain hemlocks and whitebark pines to the ridge immediately west of Dogtooth Peak. The peak itself is accessible only by a Class 3 climb, but the ridgetop provides superb vistas for those not inclined to scale the crag. From the peak or the ridge just below it, a vast sweep of Sierra Nevada terrain unfolds. The gentle terrain on the sandy ridge just below the peak has excellent camping, but hikers planning to stay overnight must pack adequate water and employ zero-impact practices to the fullest.

Kaiser Wilderness

Location: 50 miles northeast of Fresno, and immediately north of Huntington Lake.
Size: 22,700 acres.
Administration: USDAFS–Sierra National Forest.
Management status: National forest wilderness.
Ecosystems: Sierran Forest–Alpine Meadows province, Sierra Nevada section, characterized by complex, moderately high mountains modified by glacial erosion, shallow to moderately deep stream valleys, many cirques; Mesozoic granitic rocks; potential natural vegetation is upper montane-subalpine forests, and small areas of alpine vegetation communities; complex drainage pattern with many perennial streams, numerous lakes, and wet meadows.
Elevation range: 7,200 feet to 10,320 feet.
System trails: 29 miles.
Maximum core-to-perimeter distance: 4.8 miles.
Activities: Backpacking, day hiking, horseback riding, fishing, cross-country skiing, and snowshoeing.
Maps: Sierra National Forest visitor map; Kaiser Wilderness map (topographic, 2 inches/mile); see Appendix D for a list of USGS 1:24,000 quads.

OVERVIEW: The small wildland of the Kaiser Wilderness stretches along a moderately high east-west ridge, separated from the High Sierra by the canyon of the South Fork San Joaquin River. Kaiser Ridge's average elevation, exceeding 9,000 feet, forms the divide through the wilderness. Kaiser is separated from the John Muir Wilderness by the mile-wide corridor of Forest Road 80 (Kaiser Pass Road), and only 2 miles separate the Kaiser from the Ansel Adams Wilderness to the northeast.

Because of the east-west orientation of the granite ridge, glaciers carved the north slope into a scalloped outline of deep cirques that contain all but two of the 24 lakes in the wilderness. The cirques, lakes, granite cliffs and several timberline peaks, and the alpine crest surrounding 10,320-foot Kaiser Peak, combine to make the Kaiser a miniature version of the High Sierra.

The south slopes of Kaiser Ridge rise abruptly from just above the forested shores of Huntington Lake, a well-developed resort with paved roads, campgrounds, and marinas. Forests of white fir and Jeffrey pine mantle the rounded, granite-slab-covered southern slopes, interrupted by occasional fields of montane chaparral. Midway up these slopes there are small, wet meadows

12   KAISER WILDERNESS

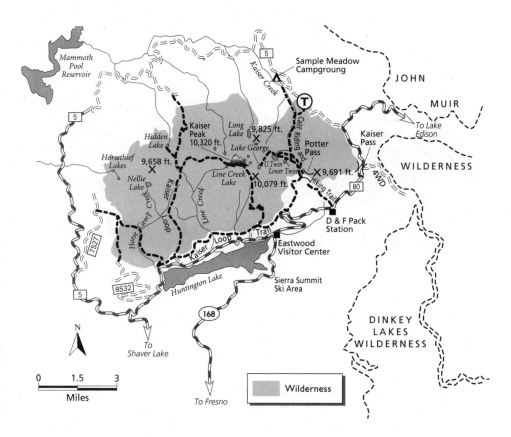

along the many perennial streams, fringed with corn lilies and willows; forests of red fir and western white pine dominate. Still higher, near the crest of Kaiser Ridge, lodgepole pine forests often share space with red fir and western white pine. The pine and fir forests are open along the crest, making cross-country travel easier—except for the many blocky granite peaks that stand in the way.

On the highest reaches of Kaiser Ridge, particularly around Kaiser Peak, there are stands of whitebark pine, often stunted and growing in ground-hugging mats of krummholz. On the north slopes and in the high cirques is mountain hemlock, a cold- and snow-tolerant tree, graceful with its drooping branches and blue-green foliage. The most windswept slopes and ridges feature shallow soils, granite slabs, and picturesque, wind-flagged Jeffrey pines and tenacious Sierra junipers.

Much of the Kaiser is hidden from view by visitors at Huntington Lake and travelers along California Highway 168. Only from FR 80 northeast of Kaiser

Lower Twin Lake lies on the north slopes of the frost-shattered granite crest of Kaiser Ridge.

Pass can travelers see into this wilderness high country. And the views are grand, reaching into the broken granite cliffs surrounding the Twin Lakes cirque, home to ten of the Kaiser's 24 lakes.

RECREATIONAL USES: The Kaiser is a natural high-mountain getaway because it is the Sierra Nevada high country closest to hundreds of thousands of central San Joaquin Valley residents. Use is moderate to high, with the greatest amount on summer weekends and holidays. A hike of one to two hours is all that's required to get to some of the Kaiser's most scenic destinations. There's an excellent trail network for day hikes, overnight trips, and extended backpacks. Since most of the high lakes have no trail access, you can devise your own challenging cross-country routes to seldom-visited timberline and subalpine lakes.

The 15.5-mile Kaiser Loop Trail offers a strenuous day hike, or a more leisurely backpack, with side-trip options of visiting two lakes by trail and many others cross-country. Part of the loop follows the southern wilderness boundary above Huntington Lake. The trail then ascends to the 9,000-foot crest of Kaiser Ridge and on up to Kaiser Peak before dropping back toward the lake. This fine trip surveys the spectrum of wilderness landscapes—the far-ranging vistas that take in the vast San Joaquin River drainage almost in its entirety, from the Ritter Range above the North Fork to the peaks of the Le Conte Divide above the South Fork.

Bow and rifle hunters visit the Kaiser from late summer through mid-autumn, though few of them venture very far into the wilderness, preferring instead to hunt the forest roads. Private horse parties are occasional visitors to the Kaiser, but the D and F Pack Station on the Kaiser Pass Road south of Potter Pass accounts for the majority of stock use here. Many wilderness lakes are stocked with rainbow, brown, brook, and golden trout. Some lakes, such as Nellie Lake on the south slope and Upper Twin Lake on the north slope get fished heavily, but they're still very productive.

In winter, CA 168 is plowed to the Sierra Summit Ski Area, just two miles south of the junction with Kaiser Pass Road. From here skiers, snowshoers, and snowmobilers can follow Kaiser Pass Road east to Kaiser Pass, but beyond that point only self-propelled winter recreationists can enter the wilderness. Follow Kaiser Ridge from the pass or use a southern approach to the backcountry via Potter Pass, beginning at the D and F Pack Station/Trailhead, 6.8 miles from the ski area.

Day Hike or Backpack

George Lake, Kaiser Peak

Distance: 6 to 9 miles, round trip (2 to 3 days).
Low/high elevations: 8,100 feet/10,320 feet.
Difficulty: Moderate to strenuous.
Best season: July through September.
Topo map: Kaiser Peak-CA.
Permits: Required for overnight use; obtain at the Pineridge Ranger District office in Prather, or at the Eastwood visitor center/ranger station at the east end of Huntington Lake, between Memorial Day and Labor Day.

HOW TO GET THERE: From Fresno, follow CA 168 for 71 miles northeast into the Sierra, en route passing through the town of Shaver Lake to the east end of Huntington Lake and a signed junction. Turn right (northeast) there onto the paved, two-lane Kaiser Pass Road (FR 80), signed for Mono Hot Springs, Lake Edison, and Florence Lake.

This steadily ascending road becomes a narrow, winding, and steep single lane of pavement after 6.7 miles (drive with extreme caution). Top out on 9,160-foot Kaiser Pass after 7.4 miles, then descend for 2.1 miles to the junction with FR 5, signed for Sample Meadow Campground, and turn left (west). Follow this good gravel road for 2.2 miles to the spacious trailhead parking area on the east side of the road. There is space here for 15 to 20 vehicles, and at an information signboard on the west side of the road is where the trail begins.

The subalpine lake basin northeast of Kaiser Peak is one of the most scenic spots in the entire wilderness, set beneath the splintered granite crest of Kaiser

Ridge. Unless you like lots of company, avoid this hike on holiday weekends. With three trails leading to Upper Twin Lake, the basin is at times downright overcrowded. Off-trail exploration will lead to some of the highest lakes in the Kaiser, as well as to Kaiser Peak, the apex of the wilderness.

The trail winds a level course along the edge of selectively logged forest, staying inside an unlogged forest of lodgepole pine and red and white fir. After a few hundred yards you enter the Kaiser Wilderness, then begin gradually descending along the sometimes rocky trail. Lodgepole pine dominates the forest here among boulder-dotted grassy openings that host sagebrush, aspen, currant, and numerous wildflowers.

The descent ends when you reach the alder-lined banks of Kaiser Creek, where you turn left and follow the east bank briefly upstream. Quite soon the trail appears to end, and you should then make a hard right turn and cross the large logs spanning the creek. The stock ford lies a few yards downstream. Just a few yards beyond, you probably won't notice the seldom-used Kaiser Creek Trail joining your trail on the right (north).

Soon you will cross back to the east bank of Kaiser Creek at another log/stock ford crossing, then resume the pleasant, gradual uphill walk through the pine and fir forest. After 1.9 miles you rock-hop the Round Meadow branch of Kaiser Creek. Beyond that crossing the trail ascends a steady, moderate to sometimes steep grade, rising through an increasingly rockbound landscape with extensive areas of bare granite and glacier-deposited boulders (erratics). Red fir and western white pine become the dominant forest trees during this ascent.

After 2.3 miles, at 8,480 feet, you reach a junction on a sagebrush-clad slope. The left fork is signed for Badger Flat, which you can use to loop back to this junction from Upper Twin Lake. But for now, you turn right onto the fork signed for Twin Lakes (the George Lake Trail). Your trail quickly tops a rise and turns west, traversing open slopes above the verdant spread of Round Meadow. This traverse soon curves northwest and crests a minor saddle set beneath a broken slope of metamorphic rocks.

Beyond that saddle you soon come to another small creek and once again you will cross its course via logs. On the west bank of that stream, turn left (south), and after a brief ascent, you then stroll down to the northeast shore of the lovely, trout-filled waters of Upper Twin Lake. Broken, ice-chiseled granite rises behind the lake to tree-studded Kaiser Ridge.

Although this is a large lake, there are only a handful of suitable campsites above its west and northwest shores. The heavily impacted sites adjacent to the lakeshore are posted "closed to camping" and must be avoided. Fishing is often excellent for the abundant pan-sized trout.

At the trail junction above Upper Twin Lake, the right-branching trail leads west, ascending 500 feet in 1 mile to George Lake. One of the more unusual sights along the trail is the Upper Twin Lake outlet stream, which quickly enters a cave below the lake and flows underground for several hundred yards before resurfacing. The trail ascends to a ridge above the lake, where fine views stretch northeast to the Silver Divide. The trail then drops back to the lakeshore and continues west. Beyond Upper Twin, it ascends steadily through pine and fir forest, eventually turning south to ascend the outlet stream to rectangular, island-dotted George Lake at 9,100 feet, backed up by a smooth, 800-foot headwall.

From George Lake you can scramble cross-country up to College, Campfire, and Jewel Lakes, Jewel being one of the highest wilderness lakes at 9,800 feet. To reach the Kaiser Loop Trail and Kaiser Peak, there is a rigorous off-trail route for jaded scramblers that ascends a broken granite slope for 700 feet in 0.5 mile, rising southwest from the lake to a 9,800-foot saddle fringed with stunted whitebark pine. There you meet the Kaiser Loop Trail and follow it for 0.8 mile to the alpine summit, a worthy destination featuring long-range vistas of 40 miles of High Sierra peaks.

Ansel Adams Wilderness Complex   13

Location: 70 miles east/northeast of Merced and 70 miles northeast of Fresno.
Size: 250,807 acres.
Administration: USDAFS–Sierra and Inyo National Forests; USDI NPS–Devils Postpile National Monument.
Management status: National forest and national monument wilderness (229,593 acres); with the remainder roadless nonwilderness (San Joaquin roadless area, 21,214 acres), some of which may be allocated for potential development of mountain bike trails and downhill ski area expansion.
Ecosystems: Sierran Forest–Alpine Meadows province, Sierra Nevada section, characterized by glacier-modified mountains, sharp alpine ridges and peaks, with long, deep, U-shaped valleys, glacial cirques, moraines; Mesozoic granitic rocks, metamorphosed Jurassic and earlier marine sedimentary and volcanic rocks; potential natural vegetation is Sierran montane forest, northern Jeffrey pine forest, Sierran yellow pine forest, upper montane-subalpine forests, and alpine communities; many perennial streams and high-elevation lakes.
Elevation range: 3,500 feet to 13,157 feet.
System trails: 348.8 miles.
Maximum core-to-perimeter distance: 8 miles.
Activities: Day hiking, backpacking, horseback riding, fishing, cross-country skiing, snowshoeing, and mountaineering.
Maps: Sierra and Inyo National Forests visitor maps; Ansel Adams Wilderness map (topographic; 1 inch/mile); see Appendix D for a list of USGS 1:24,000 quads.

OVERVIEW: Originally established in 1964 as the Minarets Wilderness, the Ansel Adams was expanded in 1984 and renamed for the renowned landscape photographer. The Ansel Adams Wilderness extends along the west slopes of the Sierra Nevada from Lake Thomas A. Edison north to Rodger Peak and the boundary with Yosemite Wilderness. North of Rodger Peak, the Ansel Adams stretches along the eastern slopes of the range to California Highway 120 near Tioga Pass. The Ansel Adams, together with nearby Yosemite Wilderness, form the northern end of true High Sierra wilderness. The vast highlands that begin far to the south in Sequoia–Kings Canyon Wilderness finally begin to give way to more extensive lower elevation country in the Ansel Adams and in Yosemite. Timberline in the Ansel Adams begins to show the effects of its more northerly latitude and so is generally lower than it is farther south, ranging between 9,600 and 10,400 feet.

13A   ANSEL ADAMS WILDERNESS COMPLEX (NORTH)

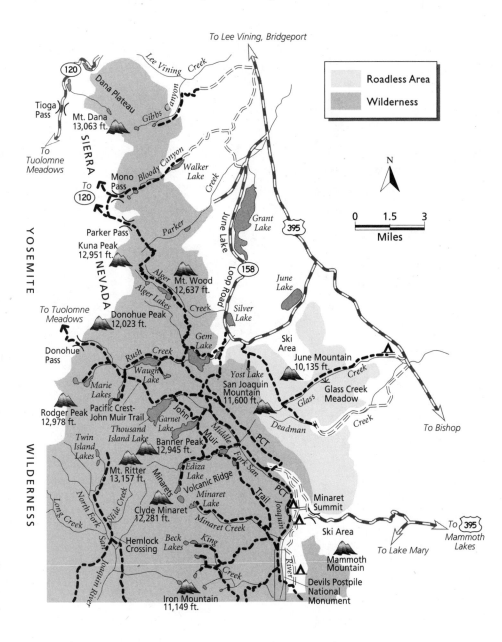

13B ANSEL ADAMS WILDERNESS COMPLEX (SOUTHWEST)

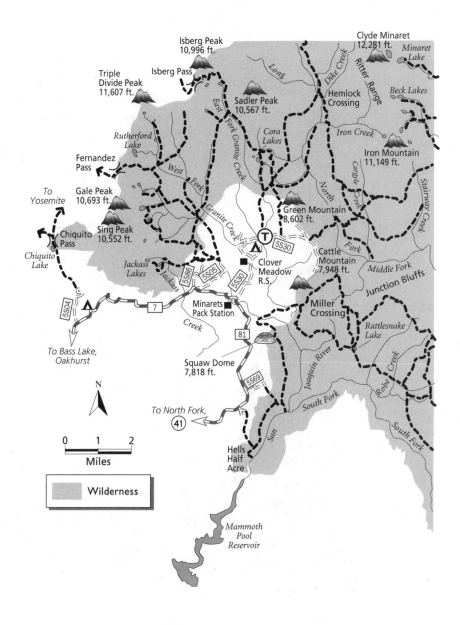

The southern reaches of the Ansel Adams spread out west of the John Muir Wilderness and Lake Edison, reaching into the lower canyons of the South and Middle Forks of the San Joaquin River, and including the 3,000-foot-deep gorge of the river's main stem. This region of glacier-carved canyons and chaparral- and forest-covered slopes contains few trails and is seldom visited.

Much of the Ansel Adams is dominated by high country, and it is some of the best known and most heavily used high country in the Sierra. The northern reaches of the wilderness stretch across the eastern face of the Sierra, in a narrow band dominated by 12,000-foot peaks and plateaus of granite and metamorphic rock, and of precipitous, glacier-carved canyons, including Gibbs, Bloody, Parker, Alger, and Rush Creeks. Each one of these canyons is served by good trails that ascend quickly from Jeffrey pine and aspen stands to timberline lakes beneath lofty peaks and permanent snowfields. Trails in Bloody Canyon, Alger Creek, and Rush Creek lead to high, Sierra crest passes that lead into Parker Pass Creek and the Lyell Fork Tuolumne River in the southern Yosemite Wilderness. Rush Creek is the most expansive of the eastside drainages, with more than two dozen lakes and tarns ranging in elevation from 9,000 to nearly 12,000 feet. Easy access from the June Lake Loop Road makes the Rush Creek drainage one of the most popular destinations in the wilderness.

Bounding Rush Creek to the south is the Sierra crest, which makes an uncharacteristic turn at Rodger Peak from west to east, instead of its typical northwest-to-southeast orientation. There the crest reaches past a series of modest, 10,000-foot summits, rises to the broad dome of 11,600-foot San Joaquin Mountain, then turn southeast and dips to 9,100 feet at Minaret Summit. The summit is significant in that it affords the only road access over the Sierra crest in a 140-mile span north of the Kennedy Meadows Road. Minaret Summit is also the lowest point on the Sierra crest in a 170-mile stretch between the Golden Trout Wilderness and the Carson-Iceberg Wilderness north of Sonora Pass.

This 9-mile-long low point in the Sierra crest in the Ansel Adams is even more significant as a migration corridor for both plant and animal species between the east and west slopes of the range. North and east of San Joaquin Mountain and the Sierra crest is a large block of roadless land, including the headwaters of Glass and Deadman Creeks and extending eastward to the volcanic domes along the western edge of the Inyo Craters volcanic field. This area supports well-developed stands of Jeffrey pine in lower elevations near 8,000 feet, and pure stands of red fir, rare east of the crest, in middle elevations. Glass Creek Meadow spreads out in the heart of the roadless area, immediately south of 10,135-foot June Mountain, and this spread supports populations of the rare Yosemite toad, a federally listed "species of concern." The crest area, including San Joaquin Mountain,

13C   ANSEL ADAMS WILDERNESS COMPLEX (SOUTHEAST)

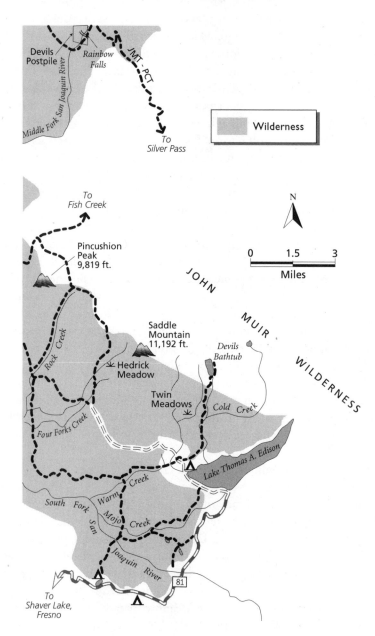

has extensive areas of alpine fell-fields and stands of whitebark pine, growing in krummholz form. White Wing Mountain, rising to 11,014 feet, is a prominent crag that soars 3,500 feet above Reversed Creek and the June Lake Loop Road in the northwest corner of the roadless area. Access to this area is limited to an unmaintained trail linking a trailhead near Obsidian Dome on the east to Yost Lake in the northwest, and the short but rigorous Yost Lake and Fern Lake Trails beginning on the June Lake Loop Road. Cross-country hiking and skiing are possible, and skiing is a popular activity along the crest northwest of Minaret Summit.

In the heart of the Ansel Adams is the high divide of the famous Ritter Range, which includes the landmark spires of the Minarets. Separating the North and Middle forks of the San Joaquin River, the Ritter Range features tremendous relief—up to 5,000 feet—between the two canyons. Anchored in the north to the Sierra crest by 12,978-foot Rodger Peak and extending northwest into Yosemite as the Cathedral Range, the Ritter Range marches southeast into the Ansel Adams for 15 miles in a parade of bold peaks. These include 12,311-foot Mount Davis, 12,945-foot Banner Peak, 13,157-foot Mount Ritter, and 12,281-foot Clyde Minaret. Permanent snowfields and small glaciers cling to the flanks of this lofty divide. On its eastern slopes, traversed by the John Muir Trail, are many very popular, and highly scenic, alpine and timberline lakes, including incomparable Thousand Island Lake, one of the largest backcountry lakes in the Sierra. In contrast, the west slopes of the Ritter Range fall away into a seldom-visited canyon of profound depth and beauty—the North Fork San Joaquin River canyon.

The southwest corner of the Ansel Adams encompasses a high divide of 10,000- to 12,000-foot peaks that form the boundary of Yosemite Wilderness, and divides the headwaters of the Merced River to the west and north, from Granite Creek, a major tributary to the North Fork San Joaquin River. Carved out of the east, or Ansel Adams, side of the divide are dozens of timberline and alpine lake basins in the headwaters of the forks of Granite Creek, Norris Creek, and Chiquito Creek; these are among the more popular destinations in the wilderness.

RECREATIONAL USES: The Ansel Adams Wilderness is heavily used throughout the summer season, yet it gets only about one-fifth the number the John Muir does. Backpacking, horseback riding, fishing, mountaineering, and climbing are the principal activities. Use is heavy in several long-time favorite areas, while other places receive very little use. The comprehensive trail network in the Ansel Adams leaves few areas trailless, and those areas are attractive to experienced cross-country backpackers, where they will find challenge, superb scenery, and exceptional solitude.

Wilderness permits are required year-round for overnight use. Only 13 of the most popular trailheads (out of 42) have seasonal quotas in effect between the last Friday in June and September 15. The most likely days for quotas to fill are Thursdays, Fridays, and Saturdays. Reservations for permits on the Sierra National Forest (westside entry) may be made for a fee by mail, beginning March 1. Two-thirds of each trailhead's quota of permits may be reserved, and these permits can be picked up in person at Clover Meadow Station in the Granite Creek area. The remainder are available on a first-come, first-served basis.

The eastern side of the Ritter Range, a long-time favorite destination, can be reached via three eastside trailheads: Silver Lake (Rush Creek), Agnew Meadows, and Reds Meadow. Excellent stream and lake fishing, good trail access, camping in timberline and alpine settings, and first-class alpine landscapes attract backpackers, horse packers, and mountaineers every summer. Quotas on trails in this area have markedly reduced the overcrowding prevalent in the 1970s, and reasonable solitude can be enjoyed there on weekdays, particularly in early autumn. The high divide along the Yosemite boundary in the southwest portion of the wilderness is also a very popular destination. Much of this backcountry is served by an excellent network of trails, and the four major trailheads in the Clover Meadow area—Norris, Fernandez, Mammoth, and Isberg—receive a steady stream of summer use. Most hikers to this corner of the Ansel Adams Wilderness hike in to the high lakes along the divide, and some take loop trips over the divide and into Yosemite and back.

Mountaineering in the Ansel Adams, particularly in the Ritter Range, began in earnest back in the 1930s, and the range continues to be a popular location for climbing. Relatively short access, compared to many other High Sierra alpine areas, and an abundance of prominent peaks, featuring routes ranging from scrambles to Class 5.8, attract accomplished climbers and weekend peak-baggers alike. Eighteen named spires comprise the Minarets, and throughout the wilderness there are another 11 named peaks exceeding 12,000 feet, numerous alpine peaks rising above 11,000 feet, the Ansel Adams' two 13,000-footers—Mount Ritter and Mount Dana—all accessible from trailheads in a day or less.

Fishing is an important attraction in the area's backcountry lakes and streams. Seventy-four out of more than 130 lakes are stocked by air. Not only do backpackers enjoy angling for brook, brown, rainbow, and golden trout, but five commercial pack stations depend on backcountry fishing for their clients during the summer season. Other commercial guides in the Ansel Adams offer trips for backpacking, mountaineering, and ski touring. In the Minarets Ranger District, which includes all of the wilderness west of the Ritter Range, outfitter/guide clients account for nearly 50 percent of wilderness users.

The Ritter Range towers above the North Fork San Joaquin River canyon in the Ansel Adams Wilderness.

In winter, westside trailheads are difficult and arduous to reach. Clover Meadow, for example, lies more than 30 miles from the nearest plowed road. Eastside approaches are best. Plowed roads to the Mammoth and June Mountain ski areas provide relatively quick access for skiers and snowshoers. Each winter a handful of dedicated ski mountaineers tackle the Mammoth-to-Yosemite high route, yet the Ansel Adams is accessible to less dedicated winter travelers as well. Snowshoe and ski trips are possible into the Yost, Fern, and Rush Creek drainages from the June Mountain ski area. White Wing Mountain, which divides Fern and Yost Creeks, offers exceptionally challenging skiing for accomplished telemark skiers. Skiing the road over Minaret Summit takes you into the Middle Fork San Joaquin River Canyon and the eastern slopes of the Ritter Range. Perhaps one of the best short day or weekend trips follows the Sierra crest from Minaret Summit toward San Joaquin Mountain. Although this divide is buffeted by strong winds, with prominent cornices developing on the leeward side, it offers gentle to moderate touring terrain and matchless vistas.

Backpack

North Fork San Joaquin River

Distance: 28 miles round trip (4 to 6 days).
Low/high elevations: 7,000 feet/8,900 feet.
Difficulty: Strenuous.
Best season: July through September.
Topo maps: Timber Knob-CA, Cattle Mountain-CA, Mount Lyell-CA, Mount Ritter-CA.
Permits: Required for overnight use; obtain at Clover Meadow station en route to the trailhead.

HOW TO GET THERE: There are two possible ways to reach the trailhead: from the town of North Fork or from Bass Lake.

To reach North Fork, drive north from Fresno for 28.5 miles via California Highway 41, then turn right (east) where a sign reads ROAD 200, O'NEALS, NORTH FORK, NATIONAL FOREST SCENIC BYWAY. Follow this road for about 17 miles to North Fork, then turn right where a sign points to South Fork and Mammoth Pool. Stay right just past the sawmill in South Fork, where a sign points to Rock Creek and Mammoth Pool. Drive this two-lane paved road, Forest Road 81 (the Sierra Vista Scenic Byway), into the western Sierra, following signs indicating Mammoth Pool and Clover Meadow.

After driving 35.8 miles from South Fork, stay left where a right-branching road descends to Mammoth Pool Reservoir. A sign here points left to Minarets Station; continue driving this good paved road and eventually pass the Minarets Work Center on your left, and then reach a three-way junction after driving 13.8 miles from the Mammoth Pool turnoff. A sign here points left to FR 7, Minarets Pack Station, and Beasore Meadows. Turn right at that junction and drive 1.8 miles to the Clover Meadow Ranger Station, where you can obtain your wilderness permit.

Alternatively, from the north shore of Bass Lake, turn north onto Beasore Road, FR 7, and follow signs pointing to Beasore Meadows and Clover Meadow. FR 7 is a narrow, winding, steadily ascending paved road, with signs at junctions along the way pointing to Clover Meadow. Just before reaching the turnoff to Upper Chiquito Campground, the road narrows to one lane, and its surface becomes very rough, with broken pavement and potholes. At the junction with southbound FR 81, 30 miles from Bass Lake, continue straight ahead (east) on FR 5S30 for 1.8 miles to Clover Meadow Ranger Station.

Continue straight ahead past the ranger station for 0.5 mile to a junction with a northwest-bound road signed for Isberg Trail and Mammoth Trail. Turn left and follow this road for 1.2 miles to a junction alongside West Fork Granite Creek, then turn right (east) toward the Isberg Trail. Follow this graded dirt road for another 1.3 miles to the signed Isberg Trailhead, then continue ahead for another 200 yards to the parking area on the south side of the road.

The trail to Hemlock Crossing and the North Fork San Joaquin River canyon is a dead-end trail that offers tremendous solitude in a canyon that ranks among the most dramatic in the Sierra. The lakes at the head of the North Fork are not served by trails and are rarely visited. And since much of the trail *descends* into the canyon, many hikers choose another trail to avoid the long haul back out.

The crossing of the North Fork at Hemlock requires a deep ford of the vigorous river, and it remains a difficult ford until August, usually. Even then the crossing is knee-deep to thigh-deep, but once you reach the east bank of the river, you have reached a wonderland of high country on the North Fork Trail. At the head of the North Fork lying beneath the towering peaks of the Ritter Range, you'll find several lonely lake basins, accessible cross-country.

From the parking area, stroll west back down the road to the signed Isberg Trail and turn right (north) onto the wide and dusty singletrack. The trail rises gently at first through a forest of Jeffrey pine and red fir; it briefly traverses above the East Fork Granite Creek and then angles uphill, rising at a moderate grade and passing through dense forest. At length the trail breaks out of the forest onto steep, open granite slopes studded with Jeffrey pine and Sierra juniper.

The views from this rocky, northeast-bound traverse are far ranging. Look out to the southeast across the densely forested west slopes of the Sierra to the high peaks of the Silver Divide, to Kaiser Ridge to the south, and to an array of ice-chiseled alpine crags stretching away to the southeast horizon.

The traverse soon leads you into The Niche, a narrow gap in a high granite ridge carved by the East Fork Granite Creek. Here, after 2 miles, you enter the Ansel Adams Wilderness. Beyond The Niche, a pleasant stroll along the East Fork through open lodgepole and western white pine forest leads 0.3 mile northeast to the junction with the trail that leads northwest to Cora Lakes, Isberg Pass, and Yosemite. Turn right (northeast) at the junction and you quickly reach the banks of the East Fork. Hikers can rock-hop the creek just downstream from the stock ford. The trail ahead rises gently among clumps of azalea, through the forest and past wet meadows rich with the color of shooting star, groundsel, aster, American bistort, and yampah.

Soon you arrive at another junction; continue straight ahead toward Hemlock Crossing. After 0.3 mile, at an unsigned junction, bear right. The trail ahead is uneventful as you proceed across gentle, pine and fir-forested terrain. After 1.1 miles from the previous junction, rock-hop small Chetwood Creek and then begin ascending the slopes of the ridge to the north. It's a steady ascent up this ridge through pine and fir forest to the 8,900-foot-high point. Along this stretch you will begin to enjoy tremendous views of the towering Ritter Range and the deep trough of the North Fork San Joaquin River canyon.

About 2.3 miles north of Chetwood Creek and 6.3 miles from the trail-head, you descend east along a small creek, then rise to the shoulder of a granite ridge plunging into the North Fork canyon. You then descend along the northwest side of the ridge, dropping 1,200 feet in 2 miles en route to Hemlock Crossing, on a series of tight, rocky switchbacks.

Unforgettable views accompany you much of the way. The canyon below is nearly devoid of forest, hosting only pockets of pine and fir among an array of ice-polished domes composed of the same dark metamorphic rocks as that of the Ritter Range. The Ritter Range soars more than 4,000 feet above the canyon. It is crowned by 13,157-foot Mount Ritter in the northeast, the high towers of the Minarets in the east, the dark pyramid of Iron Mountain in the southeast, and an array of 10,000- to 12,000-foot peaks in between.

At length the plunging trail levels out among domes, then winds down to Hemlock Crossing at 7,600 feet, 8.6 miles from the trailhead. There, beneath Dome 8,286 and the great peaks of the Ritter Range, you will find several fine campsites among a scattering of pine and fir. The crossing itself is a ford immediately below a low waterfall, and often remains knee deep, with a moderate current, throughout summer.

On the east bank of the vigorous river, trails lead northwest and southeast. The southeast-bound trail ultimately leads to Devils Postpile on the Middle Fork San Joaquin River. The northwest-bound trail follows the spectacular North Fork up-canyon among an array of domes for 5 miles, where it fades out in rocky terrain in a 9,300-foot valley between the Twin Island and Catherine Lakes basins. For experienced hikers this area is excellent for cross-country exploration of the lakes in Bench Canyon, at the head of the North Fork beneath Mount Davis and Rodger Peak, and in the Lake Catherine basin beneath Banner Peak and Mount Ritter.

Piper Mountain Wilderness   14

Location: 20 miles northeast of Big Pine.
Size: 72,575 acres in three units separated by vehicle corridors.
Administration: USDIBLM—California Desert District, Ridgecrest Resource Area.
Management Status: BLM wilderness.
Ecosystems: Intermountain Semi-Desert and Desert province, Southeastern Great Basin section, characterized by steep mountains, narrow canyons, gently to moderately sloping alluvial fans and nearly level floodplain and basin floor; Mesozoic granitic, Precambrian sedimentary and metamorphic, Paleozoic marine sedimentary, Triassic marine sedimentary, Triassic-Jurassic metamorphosed volcanic, and Tertiary volcanic rocks, with extensive areas of alluvial and lakebed deposits; potential natural vegetation is Mojave creosote bush and desert saltbush, and pinyon-juniper woodland; medium- to high-density drainage pattern with dry stream drainages.
Elevation range: 3,430 feet to 8,805 feet.
System trails: Approximately 19 miles of closed four-wheel-drive roads.
Maximum core-to-perimeter distance: 6.5 miles.
Activities: Day hiking, backpacking.
Maps: BLM 1:2,500,000 Last Chance Range; USGS 1:100,000 Bishop-CA, Last Chance Range-CA; see Appendix D for a list of USGS 1:24,000 quads.

OVERVIEW: The Piper Mountain Wilderness is one of the gems of California's Great Basin wildlands, and its desert mountains and canyons are as seldom visited as any other remote corner of the state's vast deserts. The wilderness includes a northeastern subrange of the Inyo Mountains known (but not labeled on most maps) as the Chocolate Mountains; the northwestern reaches of the Last Chance Range; and the upper end of Eureka Valley immediately north of the northwestern corner of Death Valley National Park. The Piper Mountain Wilderness is bounded on the northeast by Fish Lake Valley and the North Eureka Valley Road, on the west by Deep Springs Valley and California Highway 168, and on the south by Death Valley Road. All of these roadways, including the highway through Deep Springs Valley, are very lightly traveled.

One of the concessions made when this area was designated wilderness under the California Desert Protection Act of 1994, was to allow two vehicle corridors through the wilderness to remain open to motorized vehicles. Separated by these vehicle corridors, the Piper Mountain Wilderness lies in three units.

14A PIPER MOUNTAIN WILDERNESS (WEST)

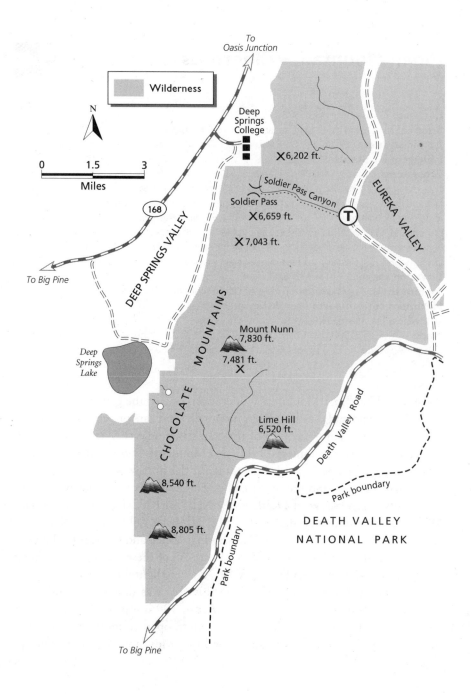

To
Oasis Junction

Wilderness

N

0   1.5   3
Miles

Deep
Springs
College

X 6,202 ft.

Soldier Pass Canyon
Soldier Pass
X 6,659 ft.

168

X 7,043 ft.

EUREKA VALLEY

T

DEEP SPRINGS VALLEY

To Big Pine

CHOCOLATE   MOUNTAINS

Mount Nunn
7,830 ft.

7,481 ft.
X

Deep
Springs
Lake

Lime Hill
6,520 ft.

Death Valley Road

8,540 ft.

Park boundary

8,805 ft.

DEATH VALLEY
NATIONAL PARK

Park boundary

To Big Pine

The largest, western unit of the wilderness embraces the crest of the Chocolate Mountains, its eastern slopes down to Eureka Valley, and the range's steep western face immediately above Deep Springs Valley. A seldom-used double-track links Gilbert Pass on CA 168 in the north with the Death Valley Road in the south, and also separates the central and western units of the wilderness. The central part of the wilderness includes the northern end of Eureka Valley and the extensive bahada that rises to a very colorful and deeply dissected northwestern subrange of the Last Chance Range. Horse Thief Canyon and the Loretto Mine Road separate the southeastern unit of the wilderness, which is a continuation of the Last Chance subrange that extends southeast to the Eureka Valley Road and the boundary of Death Valley National Park.

The wilderness features classic desert valley and mountain landscapes. Coarse desert shrubs dominate the vegetation, with creosote bush in the valleys and on the bahadas, and shadscale, littleleaf horsebrush, and Mormon tea in higher elevations. The highest peaks in the wilderness are located in the south end of the Chocolate Mountains, near its divergence from the Inyos. There, a number of 8,000-foot summits dominate the landscape, but as the range extends northeast, the peaks become lower in elevation and the range narrows considerably—to only 3.5 miles wide at its narrowest point. The northern reaches of the Chocolate Mountains reflect the arid climate that prevails, with only widely scattered singleleaf pinyon and Utah juniper growing on the most sheltered, north-facing slopes. The broad dome of Piper Mountain (labeled "Chocolate Mountain" on the topo map), the namesake of the wilderness, anchors the northeast end of the range, and though its summit approaches 8,000 feet, only a few gnarled pinyons and junipers dot its highest slopes.

RECREATIONAL USES: The quintessential desert landscape of the Piper Mountain Wilderness, shimmering in heat waves and forbidding for much of the year, offers a premier refuge from civilization during the cooler months. Few people visit this wilderness, and most who come to this region are en route to Death Valley via the lightly traveled Death Valley Road. Four-wheel-drive enthusiasts utilize the vehicle corridors that slice through the wilderness, and some occasionally trespass into the wilderness, despite warning signs and stiff fines.

Few hikers venture into the Piper Mountain Wilderness. Students from Deep Springs College in Deep Springs Valley are the most frequent visitors, occasionally hiking over Soldier Pass from the west, and they outnumber all other visitors to the summit of Piper Mountain, though they come here in very small numbers.

The landscapes of the wilderness offer a variety of desert excursions, from day hikes to overnighters and extended trips, and are limited only by the traveler's imagination, ability, and preparation. As in any other waterless desert area, the ability to carry, or cache, water is the single most limiting factor to

14B   PIPER MOUNTAIN WILDERNESS (EAST)

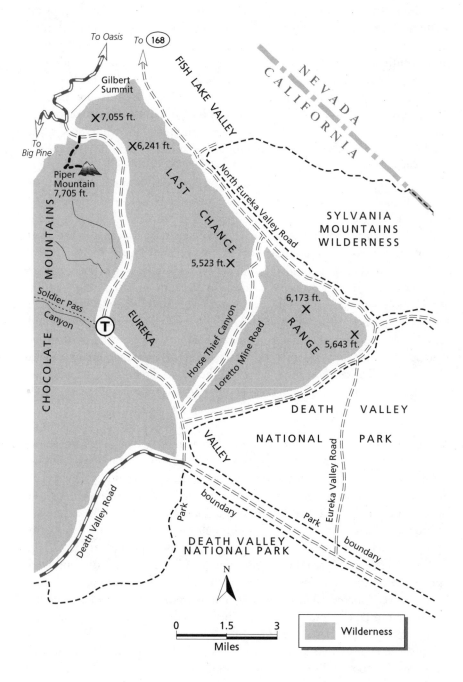

To Oasis

To (168)

Gilbert Summit

FISH LAKE VALLEY

NEVADA

CALIFORNIA

X 7,055 ft.

To Big Pine

X 6,241 ft.

LAST

Piper Mountain 7,705 ft.

CHANCE

North Eureka Valley Road

SYLVANIA MOUNTAINS WILDERNESS

CHOCOLATE

MOUNTAINS

5,523 ft. X

Soldier Pass

Canyon

(T)

EUREKA

Horse Thief Canyon

Loretto Mine Road

6,173 ft. X

RANGE

5,643 ft. X

DEATH   VALLEY

NATIONAL   PARK

VALLEY

Eureka Valley Road

Death Valley Road

Park

boundary

Park

boundary

DEATH VALLEY NATIONAL PARK

N

0   1.5   3

Miles

Wilderness

travel here. The roads that surround the wilderness, and the two four-wheel-drive routes that cut through it, offer access to potential water cache locations for hikers planning extended trips. The country here is wide open, and one can walk for miles across desert flats, ascend lonely canyons, or follow the crest of the Chocolate Mountains and enjoy panoramic vistas and utter solitude.

Access can be gained from the south at almost any point along Death Valley Road between Little Cowhorn Valley and the floor of Eureka Valley. The Loretto Mine Road and the four-wheel-drive road between Gilbert Summit and Eureka Valley afford access to the eastern side of the Chocolate Mountains and to the two eastern units of the wilderness.

Day Hike

Soldier Pass Canyon

Distance: 6.4 miles, round trip.
Low/high elevations: 4,160 feet/5,500 feet.
Difficulty: Moderate.
Best seasons: Mid-March through May; late September through November.
Topo maps: Soldier Pass-CA (the addition of the Horse Thief Canyon quad is useful for finding the trailhead access road).
Permits: Not required.

HOW TO GET THERE: From U.S. Highway 395 at the north end of Big Pine, turn east onto CA 168, signed for Ancient Bristlecone Pine Forest, Westgard Pass, Deep Springs, and Highway 95 junction. Be sure to top off your gas tank in Big Pine, and carry ample water and other supplies; the desert ahead is remote and assistance is far away.

After 1.5 miles the highway bridges the Owens River, and a short distance ahead, 2.4 miles from US 395, you find the right-branching, eastbound Death Valley Road, signed for Saline Valley, Eureka Valley, and Scotty's Castle. Turn right onto this two-lane, paved road, which ascends steadily, winding up the western slopes of the Inyo Mountains via Waucoba Canyon. After 10 miles, the centerline stripe ends and the pavement narrows and becomes rougher.

Pass the junction with the Saline Valley Road near the crest of the Inyos after 13.2 miles, then follow the long descent into Eureka Valley. After you follow a right-angle bend on the valley floor, you proceed southeast straight across the valley to a second right-angle bend. On the left (north) side of the pavement at that bend, a poor doubletrack branches north, 31.9 miles from US 395. BLM signs at the junction declare this road to be an "open route," and a "designated corridor through wilderness area." A high-clearance vehicle is recommended to traverse this sandy and gravelly doubletrack, though carefully driven cars can usually negotiate the route.

View east down Soldier Pass Canyon to the Last Chance Range.

After driving north for 1.1 miles, avoid a right-branching doubletrack, and continue straight ahead for 0.1 mile to a junction in a broad wash (labeled "3500T" on the Horse Thief Canyon quad), where another designated vehicle corridor branches right (northeast). Stay left here, and skirt the southwest base of Point 3900, the only feature of relief in the broad valley, after 3.5 miles. Soldier Pass Canyon is now visible ahead to the northwest, the only prominent canyon slicing back into the eastern flanks of the Chocolate Mountains.

After driving 5.25 miles from Death Valley Road, a closed doubletrack branches left (northwest). A BLM sign immediately north of the junction designates the main road as a corridor through wilderness, and a barricade blocks the northwest-bound road leading into Soldier Pass Canyon. There is room enough for two vehicles to park here at the trailhead on the left (west) side of the road.

Soldier Pass is a deep notch on the crest of the Chocolate Mountains, and can be approached from either side of the range. The eastside approach via Soldier Pass Canyon is the longest, but it provides one of the finest canyon hikes in the Piper Mountain Wilderness. The reason for the name of the pass and the canyon is uncertain, but it probably was used by soldiers in the late nineteenth century. Maps as old as 1879 feature the label "Soldier Pass."

Follow the closed four-wheel-drive doubletrack over coarse sand west from the trailhead, ascending the gently sloping bahada toward the mouth of Soldier Pass Canyon. Although ample signs identify the area as wilderness, and specify penalties for vehicle trespass, some people still occasionally drive up the road into the canyon. Report any violations you witness to the BLM office in Ridgecrest.

The bold eastern face of the Chocolate Mountains rises 2,000 feet above the mouth of the canyon, and the steep slopes are studded with desert-varnished granite boulders and stiff desert shrubs. The broad basin of Eureka Valley spreads out behind you, rimmed by barren, colorful mountains, with the sparkling-white Eureka Dunes rising at the southeastern end of the valley. Vegetation on the bahada below the mouth of the canyon is dominated by shadscale, indigo bush, burro bush, and creosote bush.

After 1.2 miles, the doubletrack dips into the broad wash at the canyon's mouth, and you proceed into the canyon via the sandy wash. A short but prominent side canyon joins on the right at 1.8 miles, slicing northward into the broken granite mountains that rise more than 1,000 feet above the canyon. Upon closer inspection you will see that these mountains are not nearly as barren as they appear from a distance. A wide variety of desert shrubs mantle the slopes in a perpetually gray-green veneer, and in spring, particularly following a wet winter, colorful wildflowers decorate the canyon.

Beyond the north-trending side canyon, Soldier Pass Canyon grows increasingly narrow, and at 2.3 miles a boulder jam blocks the wash, barring further progress to trespassing motor vehicles. After a brief scramble through the boulder jam, note that the wash continues to grow smaller, and as you rise above 5,000 feet, cliffrose and desert-olive appear. There are traces of a foot path in this part of the canyon, as well as occasional cairns showing the route ahead. As you approach the head of the canyon, minor scrambling over and around boulders is necessary.

When the canyon forks north and south, just below the broad saddle of Soldier Pass, you will find traces of a constructed trail that ascends the final 300 feet up to the pass. The pass, at 5,500 feet, lies at the east end of an extensive, shrub-dotted flat. Views extend westward across the flat, past the invisible trough of Deep Springs Valley to the southern crest of the White Mountains, and southeast back down Soldier Pass Canyon to the colorful Last Chance Range.

Soldier Pass can be the end of a day hike, or the beginning of a longer foray into the wild Chocolate Mountains. One could establish a base camp at the pass and take day-hike excursions to nearby peaks, though some imagination would be required to find a tent site among the boulders and shrubs at the pass. The pinyon- and juniper-studded north slopes of Peak 6659 beckon to peak-baggers immediately south of the pass. Lesser summits to the north are all accessible via scrambling routes, and all offer broad vistas of lonely desert mountains and valleys.

Sylvania Mountains Wilderness   **15**

Location: 30 miles east of Bishop and 30 miles northeast of Big Pine.
Size: 17,820 acres.
Administration: USDIBLM—California Desert District, Ridgecrest Resource Area.
Management Status: BLM wilderness.
Ecosystems: Intermountain Semi-Desert and Desert province, Southeastern Great Basin section, characterized by steep mountains, moderately steep hills, gently to moderately sloping alluvial fans, and nearly level floodplain and basin floor; Jurassic and Cretaceous granitic, Tertiary and Quaternary volcanic, Precambrian sedimentary, and early Paleozoic, mostly Ordovician, sedimentary rocks, and Quaternary alluvial deposits; potential natural vegetation is desert saltbush, Mojave creosote bush, Joshua tree scrub, sagebrush steppe, and pinyon-juniper woodland; concentric drainage pattern of dry stream courses, few springs.
Elevation range: 4,640 feet to 7,970 feet.
System trails: 13.7 miles (closed four-wheel-drive roads).
Maximum core-to-perimeter distance: 3 miles.
Activities: Hiking, backpacking, pinyon nut gathering.
Maps: BLM 1:2,500,000 Last Chance Range; USGS 1:100,000 metric Last Chance Range-CA/NV; see Appendix D for a list of USGS 1:24,000 quads.

OVERVIEW: The Sylvania Mountains are a nondescript northern subrange of the Last Chance Range, straddling the California-Nevada border above the southeastern margin of the Fish Lake Valley. The Sylvania Mountains Wilderness and the nearby Piper Mountain Wilderness are the northernmost BLM wilderness areas in the California desert. Unlike many other high desert ranges in eastern California, the Sylvanias have no distinct crest, but rather are an aggregate of rounded summits and long ridges dissected by innumerable draws and canyons. These drainages, dry except in times of flood, radiate in all directions, like the spokes of a wheel, from a central highland of 6,000- to 7,000-foot summits and ridges.

Bahadas dominate the landscape in the lower elevations of the wilderness on its western, northwestern, and southwestern sides. The gentle slopes of the bahadas rise gradually from Fish Lake Valley to the high northern portion of the Sylvanias, where long ridges and an array of rounded summits dominate the landscape. Farther south, above Cucomungo Canyon, the wilderness assumes a far more rugged character, with broken slopes of barren bedrock incised by prominent canyons, most notable of which is White Cliff Canyon.

15 SYLVANIA MOUNTAINS WILDERNESS

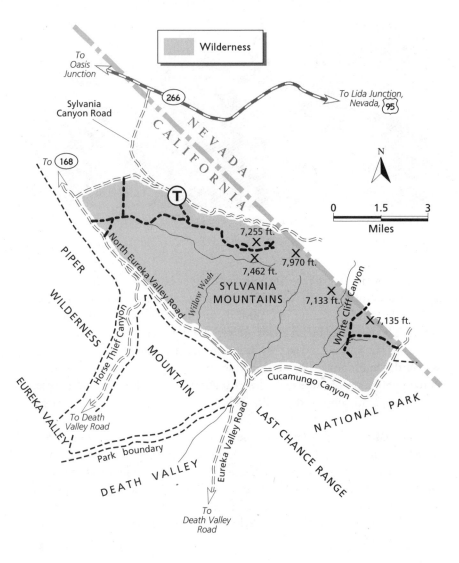

The wilderness includes the broad bahada (a gently sloping depositional surface, formed at the base of mountain ranges in arid regions by coalescing alluvial fans) that rises east from the upper Fish Lake Valley, and the western part of the Sylvania Mountains to the California-Nevada border. The more extensive part of the range reaches into Nevada, beyond the wilderness boundary, where there are many old prospects and mines, and a network of low standard

The snow-capped White Mountains rise west of the wooded heights of the Sylvania Mountains.

roads that provide access into the pinyon-juniper woodlands. The Sylvania Canyon Road, North Eureka Valley Road, and Cucomungo Canyon Road follow the wilderness boundaries in California on the north, west, and south, respectively. These remote desert roads are very lightly used.

There are few springs in the Sylvanias, and most of those lie on the Nevada side of the mountains. They do provide enough water, however, to sustain a limited population of mule deer, desert bighorn sheep, chuckar, and coyote. The most frequently observed wildlife include a variety of lizards, and antelope ground squirrels.

The alluvial fans and bahadas in the Sylvanias support one of the northernmost populations of Joshua trees in California. Joshua trees do extend north of the wilderness along the eastern flanks of Fish Lake Valley, and continue northward into Nevada nearly to the town of Tonopah. Most desert travelers wouldn't expect to see Joshua trees this far north, and they are an attractive addition to the landscape of the lower Sylvanias, often framing distant views of the Sierra Nevada.

RECREATIONAL USES: The Sylvania Mountains encompass some of the most remote high desert wilderness in California, a place where there are tremendous opportunities for solitude and off-trail exploration, and far-ranging, contrasting vistas. Hikers have yet to discover the Sylvanias, so backcountry use is almost nonexistent in this isolated desert range. Two factors limiting travel here are the lack of trails and the lack of water. The wilderness is best suited to exploratory day trips or overnighters. To enjoy memorable wildflower displays, visit the Sylvanias from March through May. Gathering pinyon nuts is an added bonus to an autumn outing. Avoid visiting the Sylvanias during the oppressive heat of summer between June and September.

A variety of backcountry trips can be taken in the Sylvanias, either by following closed four-wheel-drive roads or by striking out on your own across the open landscape. One can wander for miles among Joshua tree woodlands across the bahadas, or traverse high ridges among woodlands of singleleaf pinyon.

Three closed four-wheel-drive roads offer access into the northern portion of the wilderness, and all of them gradually rise along the bahada and converge in an unnamed canyon which can be followed to its head in the pinyon-covered highlands. In the extreme southeastern reaches of the wilderness, two other closed four-wheel-drive roads, spanning 4 miles, wind among pinyon-covered hills and open canyons between old mining prospects. White Cliff Canyon, in the eastern part of the wilderness, extends north from the Cucomungo Canyon Road for 3 miles into Nevada. The lower reaches of this aptly named canyon feature one of the most rugged landscapes in the wilderness, where the canyon's wash is flanked by 800-foot cliffs.

Day Hike

Sylvania Mountains

Distance: Variable, up to 9 miles or more, round trip.
Low/high elevations: 5,656 feet/7,280 feet or higher.
Difficulty: Moderate.
Best seasons: March through May; late September through November.
Topo maps: Sylvania Canyon-CA/NV, Sylvania Mountains-NV/CA.
Permits: Not required.

HOW TO GET THERE: From U.S. Highway 395 at the north end of Big Pine, turn east onto California Highway 168. Follow this narrow, steep, and winding paved road over Westgard Pass, then Gilbert Summit, then follow the downgrade into Fish Lake Valley. After driving 38 miles from US 395 you reach Oasis Junction; turn right, and follow CA 168/266 first east, then southeast, for 4.3 miles to the Nevada state line, beyond which the road becomes NV 266.

Drive 0.8 mile beyond the state line to a junction with an unsigned, southbound dirt road, and turn right (south). Follow this good, graded dirt road, the Sylvania Canyon Road, for 4.1 miles to a junction with a closed southbound doubletrack, indicated by a BLM wilderness signpost and blocked by a line of rocks. Park at the junction with the closed road and begin hiking there.

Joshua trees stud the lower slopes and bahadas of the Sylvania Mountains.

This interesting hike explores the northernmost canyon in the Sylvania Mountains, surveying the spectrum of wilderness landscapes and ecosystems. The Sylvanias are bone dry, so don't take the hike without carrying plenty of water, and then do so only during the cooler months of the year.

The closed doubletrack heads south from the Sylvania Canyon Road, gradually rising across the bahada at the western foot of the range. Hop-sage, Mormon tea, cheesebush, deerhorn cholla, and Joshua trees dominate the vegetation here. It's an interesting admixture of California desert plant communities where species of the Mojave and Great Basin deserts converge.

Vistas are far ranging from the open landscape, stretching past the rugged, colorful ranges of the Piper Mountain Wilderness to the alpine crest of the White Mountains and the high peaks of the Sierra Nevada. After almost one mile, the doubletrack dips into a wash and bends left (southeast). There you meet the closed four-wheel-drive road shown on the map. Its track down the wash to the west has been erased by runoff, but it is traceable farther west where it leaves the wash and crosses the bahada, leading toward the North Eureka Valley Road.

A lone pinyon stands at the junction, offering the only shade for miles in this open desert. Heading southeast up the wash, you follow the course of a gradually developing canyon, rising steadily uphill. Rabbitbrush, a typical denizen of desert washes, is common, and gnarled cliffrose shrubs stud the slopes above in the lower reaches of the canyon. Joshua trees persist in the canyon to the 7,000-foot level, and by the time you have ascended to 6,300 feet, pinyons appear on north-facing slopes.

At this point, you have finally begun to enter the Sylvania Mountains. Here you also begin to rise above the deep alluvial deposits, and the granitic core of the range begins to crop out on the slopes of the canyon. Soon the canyon ceases to grow deeper and ahead it maintains itself as a modest 200-foot deep-crease cleaving the slopes of the range. Outcrops of limestone and other mineral-rich metamorphics appear at about the 3-mile point, as do various prospect pits, along with a scattering of cans and other relics of various vintages.

Above 7,000 feet, singleleaf pinyon and Utah juniper gather to form a scattered woodland, while big sagebrush, cliffrose, Mormon tea, and rabbitbrush dominate the shrub cover on the gentle slopes of the Sylvanias. The old doubletrack winds its way up the drainage, and at 4 miles you reach a badly eroded spur road, leading 0.25 mile to a hilltop prospect. Soon thereafter the grade moderates as you enter the headwaters basin of the wash, a broad bowl mantled in a thick pinyon woodland. At 4.3 miles the doubletrack forks. Follow the left fork, and after several yards, turn left again onto a faint doubletrack. This road ascends 0.3 mile to a point on a ridge at 7,280 feet, offering one of the best vistas in the northern Sylvanias.

Or you might choose to walk south across the pinyon-covered landscape to either Point 7,462 or Point 7,458. Those points lie atop the rim of the "high" Sylvanias, and from there you gain tremendous views over rugged, unnamed canyons and the broken, rocky slopes and ridges of the southern Sylvanias.

Yosemite Wilderness   16

Location: 70 miles east of Modesto and 12 miles southwest of Bridgeport.
Size: 705,551 acres.
Administration: USDI–National Park Service.
Management status: National Park wilderness (704,624 acres); roadless nonwilderness (927 acres) recommended by the NPS for wilderness designation.
Ecosystems: Sierran Forest–Alpine Meadows province, Sierra Nevada section, characterized by an extensive plateau interrupted by steep, high mountains with cirques, aretes, horns, cols, and smooth, striated bedrock, broad, U-shaped valleys, and deep, narrow canyons; Mesozoic granitics, with smaller areas of metamorphosed Jurassic and earlier marine sedimentary and volcanic rocks, metamorphosed Paleozoic marine sedimentary rocks, and glacial and alluvial deposits; potential natural vegetation is Sierran yellow pine forest, Sierran montane forest, blue oak-digger pine forest, upper montane-subalpine forests, and alpine communities; abundant perennial streams and rivers, cirque lakes, and wet meadows throughout.
Elevation range: 2,900 feet to 13,114 feet.
System trails: 800 miles.
Maximum core-to-perimeter distance: 15 miles.
Activities: Backpacking, day hiking, horseback riding, cross-country skiing, snowshoeing, rock climbing, mountaineering, fishing.
Maps: Yosemite National Park visitor map; USGS 1:125,000 Yosemite National Park and Vicinity-CA; see Appendix D for a list of USGS 1:24,000 quads.

OVERVIEW: Although Yellowstone was our nation's first national park, created in 1872, the idea of creating a public park for the use and recreational enjoyment of visitors was born in Yosemite. Indeed, Yosemite played a key role in the concept of conservation of wildlands, not only in California, but throughout the country. In 1864, Yosemite Valley and the Mariposa Grove of giant sequoias was deeded as a park to the state of California by the Federal government. And in 1890, the Yosemite Act set aside Yosemite National Park as a forest preserve, which required that all resources in the park be retained in their natural condition. Finally in 1984, the California Wilderness Act set aside virtually all roadless land in Yosemite as wilderness, encompassing nearly 95 percent of the park. The exceptions are the five High Sierra Camps in the Yosemite backcountry, which, with their improvements such as cabins, are islands of civilization within Yosemite Wilderness.

There are few people who have never heard of or seen photographs of Yosemite. When the word Yosemite is mentioned, what likely comes to mind are the big granite walls of Yosemite Valley. The 2,000- to 3,000-foot sheer granite cliffs that flank Yosemite Valley feature some of the most difficult big-wall climbs in the world, and also make the valley one of the world's most beautiful and dramatic glacial valleys. Only the valley's walls and the canyon rims above lie within Yosemite Wilderness (the valley floor is outside of wilderness boundaries), and there is much more to this national park wilderness than great cliffs of stone. Other places like Tuolumne Meadows and Hetch Hetchy Reservoir are examples of Yosemite's diversity, and the roads leading to those places, along with the road into the Yosemite Valley, are only gateways to the vast Yosemite Wilderness.

The wilderness is separated into two distinctly different halves by the Tioga Road (California Highway 120). On the north, Yosemite is bounded by the Emigrant Wilderness, and on the south by the Ansel Adams. From west to east, Yosemite Wilderness stretches from chaparral- and digger pine-covered foothills to towering alpine peaks along the Sierra Nevada crest.

Some of the most resistant, unjointed granite in the Sierra dominates in Yosemite, and in combination with the erosive power of ancient glaciers, we have one of the most dramatic glaciated landscapes in the Sierra. Although individual glaciers scoured the great canyons of the Merced and Tuolumne rivers, the ice fields coalesced in the higher elevations and created a virtual ice cap, with only the highest peaks and ridges (nunataks) exposed above the ice. The results are seen today in the form of knife-edged ridges (aretes), splintered crests, sharp peaks (horns) and, where glaciers flowed over highly resistant granite and smoothed the rocks below, a profusion of domes. Yosemite may well contain the greatest concentration of domes in the Sierra. Also common are hanging valleys, created as glaciers deepened and widened principal drainages, leaving tributaries lying far above. Yosemite's great waterfalls plunge from some of these hanging valleys. Glaciers also carved basins that contain 526 lakes of more than one acre in size, along with innumerable ponds and tarns.

The northern half of Yosemite Wilderness is the least known and least traveled. North of the Tioga Road are broad, forested ridges and the high crest between Mount Hoffman and Tuolumne Peak. Farther north lies the cavernous gorge of the Grand Canyon of the Tuolumne River, which in places exceeds 3,000 feet in depth. Beyond that canyon is a series of moderately high, mostly bare granite ridges separating numerous long, parallel, U-shaped valleys covered in conifer forests and rich meadows. Each canyon begins below the Sierra crest in high alpine valleys draining countless timberline lakes.

The southern half of the wilderness is more complex, and much of it is more heavily used than the northern half. Many consider this part of Yosemite to be

16A   YOSEMITE WILDERNESS (NORTHWEST)

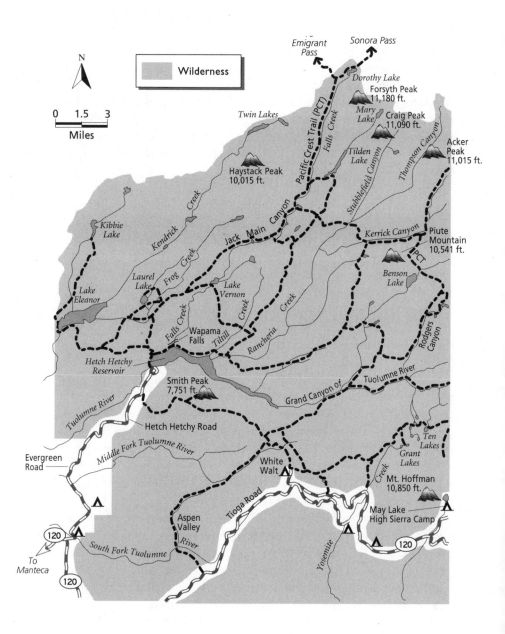

N

Wilderness

0   1.5   3
Miles

Emigrant Pass

Sonora Pass

Dorothy Lake

Forsyth Peak
11,180 ft.

Twin Lakes

Mary Lake

Craig Peak
11,090 ft.

Pacific Crest Trail (PCT)

Falls Creek

Tilden Lake

Acker Peak
11,015 ft.

Stubblefield Canyon

Thompson Canyon

Haystack Peak
10,015 ft.

Kendrick Creek

Jack Main Canyon

Kerrick Canyon

Piute Mountain
10,541 ft.

Kibbie Lake

Frog Creek

PCT

Benson Lake

Laurel Lake

Lake Vernon

Creek

Rancheria

Creek

Lake Eleanor

Falls Creek

Wapama Falls

Tiltill

Rodgers Canyon

Hetch Hetchy Reservoir

Smith Peak
7,751 ft.

Grand Canyon of

Tuolumne River

Tuolumne River

Hetch Hetchy Road

Ten Lakes

Middle Fork Tuolumne River

Grant Lakes

Evergreen Road

White Wolf

Creek

Mt. Hoffman
10,850 ft.

Aspen Valley

Tioga Road

May Lake
High Sierra Camp

120

South Fork Tuolumne

River

Yosemite

120

To Manteca

120

16B YOSEMITE WILDERNESS (NORTHEAST)

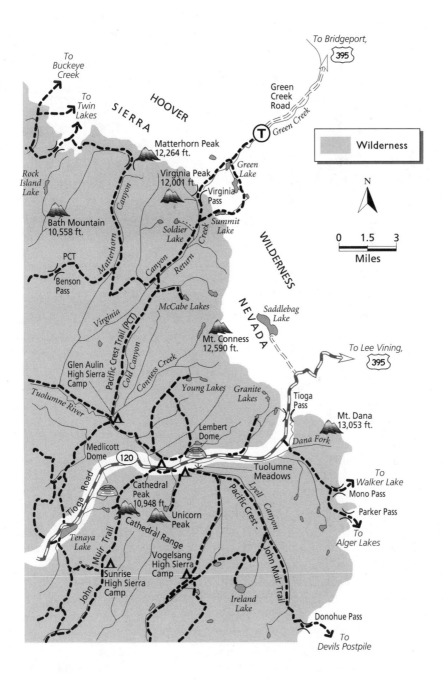

16C YOSEMITE WILDERNESS (SOUTH)

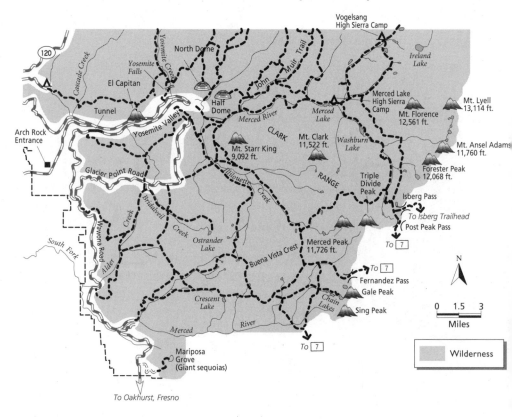

the northern end of the true High Sierra, and indeed, this area contains the northernmost 13,000-foot peak in the range and the last great expanse of alpine high country. The Sierra crest immediately south of Tioga Pass contains a small outcrop of reddish metamorphic rocks, of which Mount Dana and Mount Gibbs are composed. The crest trends generally south for 11 miles from Mount Dana to 13,114-foot Mount Lyell, Yosemite's highest peak. A spur ridge known as the Cathedral Range stretches northwest from Lyell toward Tuolumne Meadows. Lyell Canyon is in this horseshoe-shaped drainage basin between the high crests, and it is one of the most beautiful, and most heavily used, high valleys in Yosemite. Although Lyell Canyon is in a fork of the Tuolumne River, all the wilderness south of the Cathedral Range drains the forks of the Merced River.

The Cathedral Range is one of Yosemite's landmarks, and contains spectacular splintered crags such as Cathedral Peak, Unicorn Peak, and the Cockscomb.

Southwest of Mount Lyell, Yosemite shares a common boundary with the Ansel Adams Wilderness. The boundary lies along a lofty, unnamed crest of 10,000- to 12,000-foot peaks. Another subrange—the Clark Range—juts northwest into Yosemite from this crest. Between the high divides of the Clark and Cathedral Ranges, the Merced River branches into several forks which gather their waters from dozens of alpine lakes. These forks come together at Merced Lake, where the river begins its tumultuous journey through Little Yosemite Valley, past Half Dome, and finally plunges over Nevada and Vernal Falls into Yosemite Valley. The southwestern reaches of Yosemite Wilderness beyond the Clark Range are an expansive, forest-covered plateau, with only the high prominences of Buena Vista Crest reaching above forests of pine and fir. This plateau drains Illilouette, Bridalveil, and Chilnualna Creeks, and the South Fork Merced River which bounds the southern edge of the wilderness.

Except for the low-elevation canyons of the Tuolumne and Merced Rivers, much of Yosemite lies at high elevations, and 55 percent of the wilderness contains subalpine and alpine ecosystems. Soils in the wilderness are thin, with granitic bedrock dominating, yet the wilderness still supports well-developed conifer forests. As you rise from the west, you'll notice that ponderosa pine, Douglas-fir, incense-cedar, and black oak form the lowest forest belt up to about 5,000 feet. Between 5,000 and 7,000 feet, a mixed conifer forest dominates, including white fir, sugar pine, and red fir. Lodgepole pine and red fir make up the forest above 8,000 feet where bedrock begins to dominate the landscape. Jeffrey pine and the tenacious Sierra juniper inhabit the most exposed, rocky sites above 8,000 feet, and from about the 8,500-foot level, lodgepole pine forms continuous stands. You'll find mountain hemlock on sheltered, generally north-facing slopes. Lodgepole pine begins to give way to the Sierra's most dominant timberline tree, the whitebark pine, at 9,500 to 10,000 feet, which itself fades out between 10,500 and 11,000 feet.

With over 10,000 feet of vertical relief and varied topography, Yosemite supports an astounding 1,460 species of plants occupying 40 recognized plant communities. Almost 80 of these plant species are recognized as being either rare or sensitive in the wilderness. Yosemite's diversity of habitats supports 78 species of mammals, of which the mule deer and black bear are the largest and most readily observed, along with 247 species of resident and seasonal birds, 39 species of reptiles and amphibians, and 11 species of fish.

RECREATIONAL USES: The Yosemite Wilderness is an extremely popular destination for both day-hikers and backpackers, and with its extensive network of 800 miles of trails, there are innumerable opportunities to explore the spectrum of Yosemite landscapes. The famous John Muir Trail (JMT) begins in Yosemite Valley and winds past Tuolumne Meadows en route to Donohue Pass and points south. The Pacific Crest Trail shares its route with the JMT south of Tuolumne Meadows, then follows an up-and-down course through canyons and over ridges through the lonely northern half of the wilderness. Many trails are heavily used, including the Merced Lake Trail into Little Yosemite Valley, and the High Sierra Loop, which connects the five High Sierra Camps both north and south of Tuolumne Meadows.

About 40 to 50 percent of backpackers begin their trips at trailheads in Tuolumne Meadows, as the overflowing parking lots on any summer day attest. Yet only about 10 percent of an estimated more than 500,000 Yosemite hikers stay overnight in the backcountry. Backcountry use is often concentrated in the upper Merced River and Cathedral Range areas, leaving the forested southwest part of the wilderness and the canyons and cirque basins in the northern part generally uncrowded. Required wilderness permits further reduce the impacts visitors have on the land and each other. Each trailhead has a daily quota that limits the number of backpackers entering the wilderness. Wilderness permit stations are located at Yosemite Valley, Wawona, Big Oak Flat, Hetch Hetchy, and Tuolumne Meadows, where 50 percent of each trailhead's quota for permits are available on a first-come, first-served basis the day of, or one day prior to, your trip. The remainder are available by reservation, for a fee, from two days to 24 weeks in advance of your trip. From May through September, reservations are strongly advised. (See Appendix B for addresses and telephone numbers of Yosemite National Park and permit reservation system.)

The Yosemite trail network allows for a wide variety of extended loop trips, ranging from two or three days to a week or more. There are more than 30 trailheads in the park, most along primary paved roads, and all are well signed. Trails follow nearly every canyon bottom in the wilderness, and many lead to high lakes and cross lofty divides. Many backpackers enter remote sections of Yosemite Wilderness on the south and east from the adjacent Ansel Adams and Hoover Wildernesses. Taking these "back door" routes into the park usually provides the greatest opportunities for solitude. In fact, entering the northern reaches of Yosemite's high northern canyons from the east, or Hoover, side, provides short, one-day access to some of the most lightly used parts of the wilderness. Although long distance through-hikers pass through Yosemite on the John Muir and Pacific Crest Trails, most hikers use only segments of those trails while looping through the wilderness. A popular one-way trip of about a week follows a 78-mile section of the Pacific Crest Trail from Tuolumne Meadows north to Sonora Pass.

Yosemite is famous for its big walls and smooth, unjointed granite, and rock climbers from around the world flock to the park to challenge the big walls on one-day and multi-day climbs. Most of the popular routes, however, are locat-

RANDY JUDGE PHOTO

Shepherd crest rises above Virginia Canyon in northern Yosemite Wilderness.

ed along the fringes of the wilderness.

Day-hikers make up the majority of wilderness users, and the variety of potential day hikes is enormous. Ice-scoured lake basins, alpine peaks such as Mount Dana, high passes, meadows and river valleys, and the top of such prominences as El Capitan and North Dome, are all accessible via day hikes.

Winter use of Yosemite Wilderness is concentrated in the Badger Pass area and the Glacier Point Road, which provides access to valley overlooks and the excellent ski-touring terrain in the forested southwest part of the wilderness. Day-skiers also use the Mariposa Grove and Crane Flat areas on the west, while fewer still take multi-day trips up the Tioga Road (closed in winter) into the Tuolumne Meadows area. California Highway 120 is plowed on the east side of Tioga Pass as far as the Saddlebag Lake Road, at about 9,600 feet, 2 miles below Tioga Pass. Starting a ski or snowshoe trip there allows you to quickly reach the high country of the Yosemite Wilderness.

Yosemite is well known for its bear population, and at trailheads *hundreds* of vehicles are damaged every year by bears in search of human food. Do not leave anything in your vehicle overnight that looks or smells like food, including ice chests, grocery bags, or food wrappers. Anywhere you travel in the Yosemite Wilderness, you are urged to carry and store your food in a bear-resistant food canister, since these are the only sure way to protect your food supply. If you

Return Creek in Virginia Canyon.

RANDY JUDGE PHOTO

don't already own one, they are available for rent in the park at Yosemite Valley Sports Shop, Mountain Shop in Curry Village, Crane Flat Grocery Store, Wawona Store, Tuolumne Meadows Store, and Hetch Hetchy Entrance Station.

Backpack

Green Creek to Virginia Canyon, Soldier Lake

Distance: 19 miles, loop trip (3 to 5 days).
Low/high elevations: 8,100 feet/10,600 feet.
Difficulty: Moderately strenuous.
Best season: Mid-July through September.
Topo map: Dunderberg Peak-CA.
Permits: Required for overnight use; obtain at the Bridgeport Ranger Station.

HOW TO GET THERE: From U.S. Highway 395, 3.8 miles south of the Bridgeport Ranger Station and 85.75 miles north of Bishop, turn southwest onto the signed Green Creek Road. Bear left after 1 mile where a sign points to Green

Creek. After another 2.5 miles, turn right; the Virginia Lakes Road continues straight ahead. Proceed another 5.8 miles to the trailhead at the end of the road.

This memorable trip begins in the Hoover Wilderness and crosses the Sierra crest via two high passes, one with a trail, the other with only a boot-worn path. The trip leads into Virginia Canyon, a deep, U-shaped valley typical of Yosemite's "north boundary" country. Virginia Canyon sees few visitors, and the steep trailless scramble up to 10,624-foot Soldier Lake virtually guarantees solitude. The loop can, of course, be taken in either direction, but it is probably easier to cross Virginia Pass and its snowfield first, and return via Summit Pass and the Green Creek lakes basin. Remember that campfires are not allowed above 9,000 feet in the Green Creek drainage, nor are they permitted above 9,600 feet in Yosemite Wilderness.

The trail begins at the northwest end of the parking area and heads southwest through a forest of lodgepole and Jeffrey pine, aspen, and juniper. Ahead lie the conical alpine peaks encircling the upper West Fork Green Creek and Glines Canyon. During the first 2.3 miles to Green Lake you will notice the East Fork Green Creek opening up to the south, exposing the massive red flanks of Dunderberg Peak which, at 12,374 feet, is the highest summit in the Green Creek area.

After 2.3 miles of steady ascent from the trailhead, you reach a junction with the right-branching trail to West Lake. Turn right there; you will be returning in a few days via the left fork. The trail follows the north shore of 9,000-foot Green Lake past the northbound West Lake Trail and passes numerous campsites between the outlet and the lake's west end. If you started late in the day, camp here, since there are no more sites between the lake and Virginia Canyon. The poor trail ahead leads steadily up the trough of Glines Canyon, passing willow thickets and a diminishing forest of lodgepole and whitebark pines. It is a steady ascent of 1,600 feet in 2.5 miles from Green Lake to the 10,600-foot notch of Virginia Pass, and you can expect to cross a small permanent snowfield just below the pass. Once you reach the pass, you are treated to inspiring vistas into the north boundary country of the park. Views reach down past the meadows and timberline trees into upper Virginia Canyon and stretch past Excelsior Mountain to the bold granite peaks of the Shepherd Crest. To the west across the canyon rise 11,695-foot Stanton Peak, 12,001-foot Virginia Peak, and 12,240-foot Twin Peaks.

A faint trail steadily descends south from Virginia Pass down into thickening lodgepole forest in Virginia Canyon. When you reach the canyon floor, an off-trail detour is possible that leads west to the unnamed lake east of Virginia Peak, or up-canyon to a higher lake resting beneath the north side of the peak. Those basins hold snow well into the summer, so don't expect to find a dry campsite at least until mid-August.

The trail stays on the east side of Return Creek for 1.5 miles from the pass to the junction with the Summit Pass Trail, branching left (northeast). Follow the Virginia Canyon Trail west from the junction to a ford of Return Creek, which will be difficult until the snow melts. There is a good campsite at the crossing, and fishing for rainbows in Return Creek can be productive.

Follow the west side of the creek downstream for 0.5 mile, where you will find a tumultuous stream plunging down the west canyon wall. There you leave the trail and pick your way up the steep, rocky slope alongside this stream, rising above timberline during the mile-long, 1,300-foot ascent. The climb ends at beautiful Soldier Lake, nestled in a hanging valley far above Virginia Canyon. You will find good but exposed camping areas at this alpine lake, and several short but rewarding side-trip options. Ascend Gray Butte to the northeast of the lake for fine views up and down the canyon, or climb nearby Stanton or Virginia Peaks. Spiller Lake lies over the divide about 1 mile to the west, and is seldom visited.

To return via Summit Lake, backtrack to the Summit Pass Trail and turn right, and in 1 mile ascend 800 feet to the pass, nearly at timberline. Summit Lake spreads out immediately east of the 10,200-foot pass, as do the colorful metamorphic peaks surrounding the Green Creek drainage.

The trail descends into increasingly heavy forest via the East Fork Green Creek, which must be forded several times, past Hoover, Gilman, Nutter, and East Lakes; in 5.3 miles, you're back at Green Lake. From there it's only 2.3 miles back to the Green Creek Trailhead.

Hoover Wilderness Complex

Location: 9 miles west of Bridgeport and 60 miles east of Sonora.
Size: 121,001 acres.
Administration: USDAFS–Toiyabe National Forest.
Management status: National Forest Wilderness (48,601 acres); roadless nonwilderness (72,400 acres) recommended for wilderness designation in the forest plan.
Ecosystems: Sierran Forest–Alpine Meadows province, Sierra Nevada section, characterized by high, steep, strongly glacier-modified mountains with sharp peaks and ridges, aretes, cols, horns, cirques, moraines, deep, narrow canyons and broad glacial valleys; Mesozoic granitics, large areas of pre-Mesozoic sedimentary and metamorphic rocks, Pliocene volcanic and mudflow deposits, glacial deposits; potential natural vegetation is sagebrush steppe, northern Jeffrey pine forest, upper montane-subalpine forests, and extensive aeas of alpine communities; medium density of perennial streams, many high-elevation lakes and wet meadows.
Elevation range: 7,200 feet to 12,590 feet.
System trails: 115.7 miles.
Maximum core-to-perimeter distance: 7 miles.
Activities: Backpacking, day hiking, horseback riding, fishing, mountaineering, cross-country skiing, and snowshoeing.
Maps: Toiyabe National Forest visitor map; Hoover Wilderness map (topographic, 1 inch/mile); see Appendix D for a list of USGS 1:24,000 quads.

OVERVIEW: Along the eastern slopes of the central Sierra Nevada, the Hoover Complex is one of a long chain of wildlands that protects the eastern escarpment of the Sierra from south of Walker Pass at the southern end of the range, to the Carson-Iceberg Wilderness in the headwaters of the East Fork Carson River. The Hoover embraces one of the northernmost and last expressions of true High Sierra landscapes—deep U-shaped valleys, high-elevation lakes, nine 12,000-foot peaks, and several small glaciers. The Hoover Complex bounds both Yosemite and Emigrant wildernesses on the west, but unlike other east-slope wildlands in the Sierra, the Hoover is more a destination wilderness than a travel corridor.

The Hoover is located far enough north in the eastern Sierra, and lies at high enough elevations that, when combined with three distinctly different rock/soil types, its landscapes more closely resemble parts of the Rocky Mountains than the Sierra Nevada. Forest cover is limited to middle elevations along a narrow band in the Hoover, with Jeffrey pine, red fir, and lodgepole pine

17A HOOVER WILDERNESS COMPLEX (NORTH)

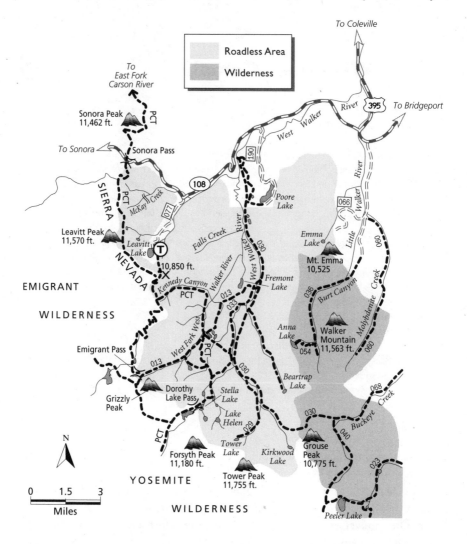

below and whitebark pine and mountain hemlock near timberline. Above the forest zone are alpine cushion plants, rock, and ice, and below are slopes of sagebrush, bitterbrush, and some of the most extensive groves of aspen in the Sierra. Ridges are broad, and the landscape is open and expansive.

Three distinct units make up the Hoover Complex: the narrow, 23-mile-long strip of the Hoover Wilderness, the Hoover East roadless area to the northeast, and the Hoover West roadless area to the northwest. The two roadless areas are managed by the Toiyabe National Forest as wilderness.

The Hoover Wilderness stretches along the Sierra crest from about one mile north of Tioga Pass to Hawksbeak Peak at the head of the West Walker River. Here the peaks are composed of the nearly white granite of the Sierra Nevada batholith and many of them shelter small glaciers and permanent snowfields. On the crest is Mount Conness, highest in the wilderness at 12,590 feet, with the Conness Glacier spreading out on the peak's northeast face. Farther north, 12,446-foot Excelsior Mountain harbors another small icefield.

Yet where the Sierra crest bends from north-south to northwest-southeast, between Twin Peaks and Kettle Peak, it shelters the greatest concentration of permanent ice in the Hoover. This part of the crest—Sawtooth Ridge—is the most famous area in the Hoover. Along this ridge is 12,264-foot Matterhorn Peak, the 12,240-foot summits of Twin Peaks, and an array of jagged horns and narrow cols. About a dozen small glaciers lie beneath this crest, at the head of five precipitous U-shaped gorges that plunge thousands of feet to Robinson Creek and Twin Lakes.

East of the Sierra crest in the Hoover Wilderness, a series of high ridges separate the deep, U-shaped glacier-carved canyons of Lundy Canyon and Virginia, Green, Robinson, and Buckeye Creeks. These ridges, which are crowned by some of the highest peaks in the Hoover, are great rubbly masses of gray and reddish metamorphic rocks, one of the most extensive exposures of metamorphics in the Sierra.

The Hoover East roadless area embraces Crater Crest and upper Tamarack Creek north of Sawtooth Ridge, then reaches north past lower Robinson Creek to Buckeye Ridge, lower Buckeye Creek, Flatiron Ridge, and lower Molybdenite Creek. The Hoover West roadless area stretches north and west, embraces the entire upper basin of the West Walker River, and stretches along the Sierra crest to Sonora Pass. Here volcanic peaks dominate the West Walker valley. On the valley floor, granite domes rise above rich meadows and a discontinuous forest of mixed conifers and lodgepole pine. Rising at the head of the valley are granite crags of the Sierra crest, including the 11,000-foot summits of Forsyth, Tower, and Ehrnbeck Peaks, and the landmark Hawksbeak Peak. Ancient glaciers carved this landscape, but scraped away the veneer of volcanic rock only on the Sierra crest southeast of Grizzly Peak and in the West Walker valley. The result is a stark contrast between light gray granite, smoothed and polished by glacial ice, and dark volcanic slopes and ridges. Lakes are abundant in granitic terrain, but are rare where volcanics dominate. The volcanic soils have a greater water-holding capacity than granitic soils, so the dark slopes are mantled in a rich verdure of summer greenery, including vast fields of mule's ears, a showy sunflower that grows almost exclusively on volcanic soils.

Mule deer habitat in the Hoover is extensive, with spring, summer, and autumn range located throughout the grassy, shrub-dotted foothills and lower

17B   HOOVER WILDERNESS COMPLEX (SOUTH)

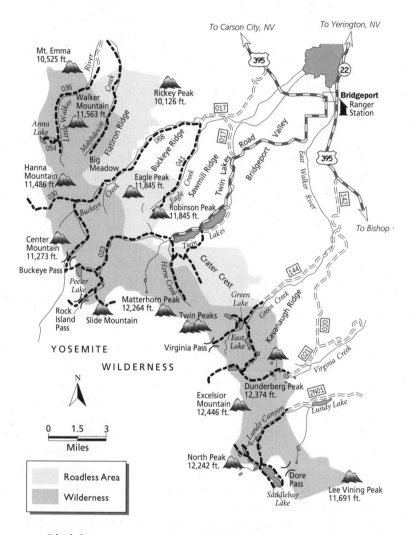

canyons. Black bears are numerous, and all backcountry travelers are advised to store their food supply properly, preferably in a bear-resistant canister. Cattle and sheep still graze in parts of the Hoover complex. In the high sagebrush grasslands at the north end of the complex, particularly near Emma Lake, Molybdenite Creek, and Burt Canyon, bands of sheep will be found throughout summer.

RECREATIONAL USES: The Hoover has an extensive trail network for day hiking, weekend backpacking, and extended round-trip and loop-trip backpacking. The southern half of the Hoover receives the highest use, and for good reasons.

Green Lake and Virginia Pass on the east side of the Sierra in the Hoover Wilderness.

Trailheads at Green Creek and Virginia Lakes are high and dramatic, with alpine high country and more than a dozen timberline lakes only a short walk away. Saddlebag Lake, the highest trailhead in the Sierra at 10,100 feet, is located at timberline, affording an alpine starting point for short day hikes or weekend backpacks beneath the highest peaks of the Hoover. A water-taxi service is provided at Saddlebag Lake Resort, where boats will take you to the upper end of the mile-long lake for a modest fee. A boot-worn path ascends to the Sierra crest above Steelhead Lake, about 2.5 miles from Saddlebag Lake, and leads into the McCabe Lakes and Virginia Canyon in Yosemite Wilderness.

Trails beginning at Saddlebag Lake connect with the Mill Creek Trail in Lundy Canyon. Since Lundy Canyon is one of the Hoover's lowest-elevation trailheads, and the trails involve significant ascents to high country, both the Mill Creek and Lake Canyon Trails are among the least used in the southern Hoover.

Trails beginning at Twin Lakes on Robinson Creek in the middle reaches of the wilderness have traditionally been the most consistently popular in the Hoover, and justifiably so. From Mono Village at the end of the road at Twin Lakes, Sawtooth Ridge and Matterhorn Peak thrust 5,000 feet skyward in a lateral distance of 3 miles, making the scene one of the most spectacular in the Sierra. It is also a very popular rock-climbing and mountaineering area, with several no-nonsense approach routes using the four canyons draining Sawtooth Ridge, including a trail that ascends Horse Creek. For the backpacker, and occasional cross-country skiers and snowshoers in winter, a good trail (023) leads up the valley of Robinson Creek for about 4 miles to Barney Lake. There the canyon grows steeper and trails begin to peel off in different directions. First an unmaintained trail leads west and over the ridge into the South Fork Buckeye Creek and the junction with Trail 040, which in turn leads on up to Buckeye Pass on the Sierra crest. Farther on, another fork (Trail 048) leads to unusual Peeler Lake, straddling the Sierra crest and draining both east and west across the divide. Finally, at the head of Robinson Creek, trails branch southwest to Snow Lake and Rock Island Pass (023), and southeast to cross the crest into Slide Canyon in Yosemite. These trails from Robinson Creek cross the Sierra crest at four passes barely 2.5 miles apart, and create numerous loop possibilities in the remote north boundary country of Yosemite, some by trail, others by relatively easy cross-country travel.

The next drainage north of Robinson Creek is Buckeye Creek, an immense U-shaped trough 3,000 to 4,000 feet deep. Long meadows, peaceful aspen groves, a meandering fish-filled stream, and broad, towering ridges follow the Buckeye Creek Trail (068) for over 9 miles up the canyon to The Roughs and Buckeye Forks, and beyond to Kirkwood and Buckeye passes. Also beginning at Buckeye Trailhead is one of three dead-end trails in the northern Hoover complex. Trail 041 leads 5 miles up the narrow Eagle Creek valley to its end at 9,800 feet. There are no lakes to attract visitors to Eagle Creek, and the trail is lightly used. It does afford access to Victoria, Eagle, and Robinson Peaks, all easy walk-ups (Class 2 routes) featuring outstanding vistas.

At the north end of the Hoover complex, three high ridges, Flatiron, Hanging Valley, and the West Walker divide, separate two lonely canyons also traversed by dead-end trails. Obsidian Campground, set along the rushing waters of Molybdenite Creek among scattered lodgepole pine and aspen, separates the trailheads for the Molybdenite Creek Trail (060) and the Burt Canyon/Little Walker River Trail (036). The Little Walker River drains the broad, open volcanic ridges at the north end of the Hoover complex, and with rough access roads, only two backcountry lakes, and dead-end trails, this area sees few backcountry visitors. Emma Lake is a fine short day hike from the Stockade Flat Trailhead at the end of Forest Road 066 west of the campground. Both lower Molybdenite Creek and the Little Walker River are excellent fly-fishing streams, while Anna Lake at 10,500 feet, perched on a high, hanging shelf above the Little Walker, offers challenging deep-water lake fishing. For those who enjoy wandering beyond the reach of trails, there's a cross-country route over Hanging Valley Ridge between the Little Walker River and Molybdenite Creek.

The West Walker River flows through a large expanse of roadless country in the Hoover West roadless area. Here is also the greatest selection of trails and off-trail routes in the Hoover complex, making the West Walker one of the premier destinations for backcountry recreation in the northern High Sierra. The primary trail through the dome-rich valley of the West Walker begins at

An old mining road scars the volcanic landscape of the Sierra Crest in the Hoover Complex.

Leavitt Meadows on California Highway 108, adjacent to the campground there. This trail leads 7 miles up the valley, beyond which more than a half-dozen other trails fork off in various directions. The PCT traverses the spine of the Sierra in the Hoover complex from Sonora Pass to the Kennedy Canyon saddle. From there the trail leads down the broad trough of Kennedy Canyon into the West Walker valley, and finally ascends an idyllic, lake-filled basin to Dorothy Lake Pass on the Yosemite Wilderness boundary. Any number of the trails here can be combined to form loop trips, and can be extended by following trails into Yosemite Wilderness to the south and Emigrant Wilderness to the west.

Leavitt Meadows provides a good but low-elevation (7,100 feet) start to trips that can range from one day to a week or more. Four-wheel-drive vehicles can follow the very rough Leavitt Lake Road for 3.2 miles from CA 108 and begin their backcountry explorations of the Hoover complex at timberline. Sonora Pass also provides a high-elevation starting point (9,628 feet) for the southbound PCT, and the first 7.6 miles of that mountaintop trail stay above timberline on alpine slopes.

Wilderness permits are required for overnight use of the Hoover complex. For trailheads at Saddlebag Lake or Lundy Canyon on the Inyo National Forest, obtain permits from the Mono Basin visitor center located east of U.S. Highway 395 at the north end of Lee Vining. For trailheads at Virginia Lakes, Green Creek, Tamarack Creek, Twin Lakes, Buckeye Creek, Molybdenite Creek, Burt Canyon, and Emma Lake, obtain permits at the Bridgeport

Ranger Station at the south end of Bridgeport on US 395. Overnight users entering via Leavitt Meadows, Leavitt Lake, and Sonora Pass may self-register for permits at the hiker's parking area adjacent to Leavitt Meadows Campground on CA 108. Or you may obtain permits from the Summit Ranger District office of the Stanislaus National Forest, on CA 108 about 30 miles northeast of Sonora. Trailhead quotas are in effect between July 1 and September 15 at all trailheads on the Toiyabe National Forest except Tamarack Creek, Molybdenite Creek, Burt Canyon, Emma Lake, Leavitt Meadows, Leavitt Lake, and Sonora Pass. One-half of each quota may be reserved between March 1 and May 30 each year (contact Bridgeport Ranger Station for information; see Appendix B). The remaining permits are available on a first-come, first-served basis only on the day of your trip. To backpack in the Sawtooth Ridge Zone above Twin Lakes, including the drainages of Horse, Little Slide, Blacksmith, and Cattle Creeks, you must obtain a special Explorer Wilderness Permit, build no fires, camp more than 100 yards from travel routes, and not have more than 8 people in your backpacking group.

Multi-day Backpack or Horsepacking Trip

Leavitt Lake Loop

Distance: 20.8 miles, semi-loop trip (3 to 5 days).
Low/high elevations: 8,550 feet/10,824 feet.
Difficulty: Moderately strenuous.
Best season: Mid-July through September.
Topo maps: Sonora Pass-CA, Pickel Meadow-CA, Tower Peak-CA, Emigrant Lake-CA.
Permits: Required for overnight use. See driving directions for locations to obtain permits.

HOW TO GET THERE: The unsigned Leavitt Lake Road branches southwest from CA 108, 11.1 miles southwest of the CA 108/US 395 junction and 68.7 miles northeast of Sonora.

Westbound drivers coming from US 395 should first self-register for a wilderness permit from the dispenser at the signed Backpacker Trailhead Parking, 100 yards south of the Leavitt Meadow Campground and 7 miles from US 395. After that formality, continue ascending CA 108 for another 4.1 miles, where you will find the unsigned Leavitt Lake Road branching left (southwest) at a sharp curve in the highway alongside Leavitt Creek.

Eastbound drivers should follow CA 108 for 28.5 miles from Sonora to the Summit Ranger District office, located alongside the highway at the Pinecrest turnoff, and obtain permits there. When the office is closed, you may self-issue permits from a dispenser outside the office. Continue following the highway

Grizzly Peak on the Sierra crest rises at the head of the West Fork West Walker River, near Emigrant Pass.

up to Sonora Pass, 65 miles from Sonora, then descend to cross the signed Soda Creek bridge 3 miles southeast of the pass, and continue ahead for another 0.75 mile to the Leavitt Lake Road and turn right (southwest).

The unmaintained Leavitt Lake Road is extremely rough and rocky and very steep in places, with deep potholes and ruts, and there are three stream fords. A high-clearance four-wheel-drive vehicle is essential for navigating this road. Drivers of low-clearance two-wheel-drive vehicles should not attempt it; just park off the highway and walk the road for 3.2 miles to the trailhead, adding 1,350 feet of elevation gain to the trip.

Follow this rough road to the first stream ford at 1 mile, then ascend steeply to the second ford at 2.1 miles, where you will find a spacious car camping area. After 2.9 miles you reach the shallow ford of Leavitt Lake's outlet stream, then continue an undulating course above the lake's northeast shore, passing spur roads leading left and right to camping areas in timberline groves of whitebark pines. Continue straight ahead, first east, then southeast, ascending away from the lake. After 3.2 miles, you reach the spacious parking area where the road is gated ahead. There you will find an information signboard with a map of the area, and room enough to park at least 12 vehicles.

This view-packed, high-elevation backpack surveys the glaciated landscapes of the West Walker River canyon in Hoover West. The return leg of the loop

Volcanic mountains, including Leavitt Peak, at left, rise above Leavitt Lake in the northwestern reaches of the Hoover Complex.

tours the high eastern reaches of the Emigrant Wilderness. The trip features long traverses along the Sierra crest, abundant fishing opportunities, and many options for off-trail exploration to lonely canyons and lake basins.

The trip begins above Leavitt Lake in the kind of timberline landscape one usually has to hike into for several days to enjoy. Much of this trip follows an old road that provides access to several mining claims in the Snow and Huckleberry Lakes area of the Emigrant Wilderness. Even though this road has seen little use since 1967, it remains as an abominable scar on the alpine landscape of the Sierra crest. One advantage of the road is that it provides easy access to the backcountry, and its grades are milder than most trails in the area.

The trip begins at the locked gate above the trailhead at 9,700 feet, and you follow the old mining road up a steep grade among stunted whitebark pines. You ascend steadily through the Ski Lake basin for 1.1 miles and rise above timberline to a 10,650-foot pass on a high volcanic ridge. Snow often remains on the north side of the pass throughout summer. Only alpine cushion plants carpet the ground on this high ridge, including alpine sunflower, dwarf lupine, dwarf sulphur buckwheat, blue flax, and wallflower. Behind you are expansive views of the distant Sweetwater Mountains, Leavitt Lake, Leavitt Peak, and Sonora Peak, and ahead are far-ranging vistas extending deep into the Sierra backcountry. The broad valley of the West Walker River, punctuated by granite domes, spreads out to the southeast, with the bold peaks of Forsyth and Tower rising at the valley's head. Lovely Kennedy Canyon lies far below to the south, its broad trough embraced by alpine ridges of volcanic rocks.

The road descends south from the pass, then curves west to meet the PCT at 1.3 miles. Vistas from here reach into the deep valley of Kennedy Creek and far down the west slopes of the range to The Dardanelles and beyond. About 50 yards beyond the junction, hikers are directed by signs onto a steep foot trail that shortcuts the long switchbacks of the old road. By following either the road or the trail, you descend steadily for another 1.3 miles to the Kennedy Canyon saddle, where the PCT branches left (northeast) away from the road. En route down to the saddle you will see the road ahead as it ascends 1,200 feet from the saddle to Point 10,824. Since it is far easier to descend those 1,200 feet on the return trip, most people will turn left onto the PCT at the saddle. There are good campsites in groves of whitebark pines at the broad saddle, and perennial Kennedy Creek begins in a draw immediately southwest of the crest.

Descending Kennedy Canyon via the PCT is a delightful walk through timberline groves of whitebark into the lodgepole pine forest below. Eventually the trail turns southeast away from Kennedy Canyon and soon enters the granite-dominated terrain of the West Walker valley. As you work your way up the western fringes of the valley, you cross two usually dry drainages before skirting the rich grasslands of Walker Meadows. After 6.9 miles the trail crosses a bridge spanning the West Fork West Walker River, and on the other side you find a signed junction. Trails branch east to Long Lakes, southeast to Piute Meadow, and southwest to Dorothy Lake Pass, Cinko Lake, and Emigrant Pass. Turn southwest and follow the banks of the large, turbulent West Fork for 0.25 mile, where the PCT ascends southwest away from the creek. Your trail (013) continues a moderate ascent over rocks, tree roots, and slabs for about 1 mile to a ford of the West Fork beneath the ice-polished flanks of Dome 10,100. The trail continues up the lovely granite-bound canyon beneath the shade of mountain hemlocks and lodgepole pines. The West Fork is always close at hand, its waters ranging from quiet riffles to boisterous cascades and inviting pools.

Ascending the rocky trail up the canyon is struggle enough on foot, and it's easy to imagine the difficulty of emigrants using this route to cross the Sierra in 1852 and 1853. This is part of the West Walker–Sonora Road, a short-lived emigrant trail across the Sierra. After 1.4 miles from the PCT, and 8.5 miles from the trailhead, an eastbound spur trail branches left, bound for Cinko Lake and the PCT. Set at 9,200 feet in a granite bowl at timberline, Cinko Lake is a worthwhile, mile-long round-trip detour, offering good, though popular, campsites.

Your trail, signed at the junction for Grizzly Meadows and Emigrant Pass, continues up-canyon on the south side of the creek, rising steeply. Soon you regain granitic terrain, and the trail grows obscure as you rise over much bedrock to timberline. Eventually you reach an expansive meadow, from where broad Emigrant Pass can be seen just ahead, with castle-like Grizzly Peak standing guard over the pass to the southwest. The trail promptly disappears upon reaching this meadow, so you make your way southwest along the main drainage toward the broad pass. When you top the ridge you'll realize it isn't really the pass at all, and soon you reach a junction in a higher meadow with the old mining road, which heads south toward Grizzly Meadow, Snow Lake, and Bond Pass. Bear right and follow the doubletrack northwest through alpine meadows, where fine views reach past Grizzly Peak, the southernmost volcanic peak on the Sierra crest, to the ice-polished granite ridges and high peaks of northern Yosemite.

Emigrant Pass is actually a very broad gap on the crest, and it is uncertain where you cross until you notice water flowing westward. The doubletrack leads you on a high traverse, and soon sprawling Emigrant Meadow Lake comes into view, surrounded by granite domes, alpine meadows, and clumps of whitebark pine. The traverse leads north to the alpine gem of High Emigrant Lake at 9,700 feet, 1.2 miles from the junction below Emigrant Pass, and 11.9 miles from the trailhead. Cross the outlet just below the lake's small rock dam. Your last chance for camping below timberline south of Kennedy Canyon saddle is in this basin, either near High Emigrant Lake, or in the Red Bug Lake basin a short distance northwest.

The doubletrack leads beyond High Emigrant Lake and passes verdant volcanic slopes, as you rise toward the head of the lake's basin. The 1,100-foot ascent that lies ahead follows moderate switchbacks up the slopes of Peak 10,824. What makes the ascent tolerable, even enjoyable, are the incomparable vistas that expand with every step. They reach a crescendo as you approach Peak 10,824 at 14.8 miles, beyond which begins a protracted descent on switchbacks. Whitebark pines reappear at 10,200 feet, and ahead the road leads past a plunging gorge that drops into Kennedy Creek canyon far below. Just beyond, the road begins a long traverse toward Kennedy Canyon saddle, but there is often a long, very steep snowfield blocking the road just ahead, and it is very dangerous to traverse.

In response, hikers have forged a bypass trail (unsuitable for stock) that descends the steep scree slopes for 500 feet into upper Kennedy Creek and ultimately up to Kennedy Canyon saddle. Once you reach the PCT junction at the saddle after 18.2 miles, retrace your route for another 2.6 miles to Leavitt Lake.

Emigrant Wilderness ■ 18

Location: 30 miles northeast of Sonora, and 22 miles west of Bridgeport.
Size: 112,376 acres.
Administration: USDAFS–Stanislaus National Forest.
Management status: National Forest Wilderness.
Ecosystems: Sierran Forest–Alpine Meadows province, Sierra Nevada section, characterized by a high, glaciated plateau, sharp alpine ridges, and cirques; Mesozoic granitic and Jurassic volcanic rocks, small areas (roof pendants) of Jurassic metamorphic rocks, and glacial and alluvial deposits; potential natural vegetation is Sierran yellow pine forest, Sierran montane forest, upper montane-subalpine forests and alpine communities; numerous perennial streams with a parallel drainage pattern, abundant wet meadows, and many moderate- to high-elevation lakes.
Elevation range: 4,800 feet to 11,570 feet.
System trails: 180 miles.
Maximum core-to-perimeter distance: 7.5 miles.
Activities: Backpacking, horseback riding, day hiking, fishing, cross-country skiing, and snowshoeing.
Maps: Stanislaus National Forest visitor map; Emigrant Wilderness map (topographic; 1 inch/mile); See Appendix D for the list of USGS 1:24,000 quads.

OVERVIEW: Long before the ancestral Sierra Nevada was uplifted to its present height, volcanic eruptions from the east flowed over much of the landscape north of Yosemite National Park. These flows buried most of the exposed granitic bedrock in the region. When the glaciers formed, they began to carry away much of the volcanic debris that buried the landscape, re-exposing the granitic bedrock.

Beyond the northern end of the High Sierra, this glacially re-exposed granite gives way to deep volcanic deposits not completely removed by glaciation, thus forming a landscape much different than areas farther south in the Sierra. The contrast between the two rock types is often striking, and typifies the landscapes in the Emigrant Wilderness.

Immediately north of Yosemite Wilderness, on the west slopes of the Sierra Nevada, is the Emigrant Wilderness, a high, glacier-carved landscape that is, in essence, the northern extension of the Yosemite backcountry. Yet compared to the moderately dissected landscape of northern Yosemite, much of the Emigrant is dominated by a high, gently sloping plateau with shallow drainages separated by low, glacier-scoured ridges.

18   EMIGRANT WILDERNESS

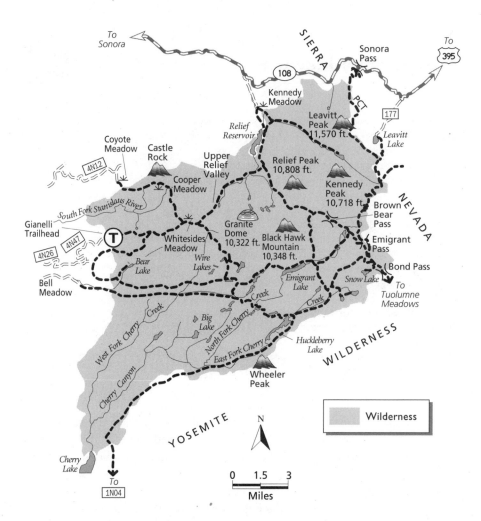

The Emigrant is dominated by granitic rocks, although along the northern boundary and in the northeast corner of the wilderness, volcanic rock caps the bedrock of the Sierra Nevada batholith. The majority of the Emigrant's 100 lakes are located in the granitic landscape that dominates the south half of the wilderness. Lakes range in size from less than one acre to 213-acre Emigrant Lake, and some lakes are estimated to be more than 200 feet deep. This part of the wilderness contains a profusion of domes, much bare granite, open sub-alpine forests, and the many forks of the Cherry Creek drainage, a large tributary to the Tuolumne River.

The northwest corner of the Emigrant lies at the head of the South Fork Stanislaus River and the Clavey River, a little-known tributary to the Tuolumne. This is an area of high tablelands, timberline forests, rich meadows, few lakes, and unusual volcanic outcrops. Peaks such as Castle Rock, The Three Chimneys, and East Flange Rock describe some of the erosional forms expressed in the area's volcanic rocks.

The northeast corner of the Emigrant is the most rugged, features the highest peaks, and has the deepest canyons. The principal drainages are Summit Creek and Kennedy Creek, both tributaries to the Middle Fork Stanislaus River. There are fewer lakes here, since volcanic rocks dominate the landscape, but despite the lack of lakes, the landscapes are dramatic. Kennedy Creek is a cavernous trough bounded by lofty ridges, and contains the largest wetland ecosystem on the Stanislaus National Forest. From the 7,800-foot floor of this U-shaped canyon, slopes rise abruptly to such prominences as 11,570-foot Leavitt Peak, 10,718-foot Kennedy Peak, and 10,808-foot Relief Peak. Large Kennedy Lake spreads out on the valley floor, with a handful of small lakes and tarns resting in hanging valleys above. The forks of Summit Creek are born from lakes that dot the flanks of rugged Granite Dome, and Relief Creek, a western tributary, drains through the lovely grasslands of Upper and Lower Relief Valleys, important rest and resupply points along the short-lived West Walker–Sonora emigrant road that traversed the wilderness in the early 1850s.

The average elevation along trails in the Emigrant is about 8,500 feet, but since the area was so thoroughly scoured by ice-age glaciers, soils are thin to nonexistent. More than half of the wilderness is either barren bedrock or mantled with grasslands and alpine vegetation. Less than one-third is covered with conifers. Many areas of granitic terrain in the Emigrant represent timberline environments at relatively low elevations. Emigrant Meadow Lake, for example, rests in a broad granite basin at about 9,400 feet, and only stunted groves of whitebark pine stud the basin among grasslands and alpine vegetation. Timberline in this part of the Sierra generally averages between 9,800 and 10,000 feet.

Throughout the Emigrant there is a series of dams on lakes and in meadows constructed in the 1930s to provide reliable habitat for trout both within and outside the wilderness. Eleven of the eighteen wilderness dams were used to augment downstream flow during late summer and early fall. These dams altered the lakes they impound by raising and lowering lake levels by 6 to 10 feet. Four other dams were built simply to raise the levels of Huckleberry, Cow Meadow, Red Can, and Yellowhammer Lakes by 3 to 4 feet. Three meadow maintenance dams were constructed at Whitesides, Cooper, and Horse Meadows to sub-irrigate the spreads for grazing purposes. Although the decision was controversial, the Forest Service will maintain eight of the original eighteen dams, while the remainder will be allowed to deteriorate.

Granitic and volcanic terrain form contrasting landscapes in the Emigrant Wilderness.

Wildlife in the Emigrant is diverse, with many species reflecting the biological diversity of the ecosystems here. Two federally listed endangered species, the bald eagle and peregrine falcon, and seven sensitive species, including fisher, marten, Sierra Nevada red fox, willow flycatcher, goshawk, great gray owl, and California spotted owl, find habitat in the Emigrant. Other rare wildlife includes wolverine, Sierra Nevada snowshoe hare, Mount Lyell salamander, and Yosemite toad. Yet most visitors probably will not observe any of these animals. The most common sightings include mule deer, marmot, pika, golden-mantled ground squirrel, and, occasionally, black bear. In the Emigrant, and throughout most of the Sierra, black bears are abundant, and proper food storage by backcountry visitors is strongly advised.

Although a modest number of deer hunters use the Emigrant in autumn, the abundance of fish-filled lakes and streams is one of the Emigrant's major attractions in summer. Of more than 100 wilderness lakes, 73 are stocked with rainbow, golden, brook, and brown trout, many of them every one to three years (stocking schedules vary). Many lakes contain self-sustaining trout populations.

While most of the Emigrant has been protected from development since 1931, the presence of a small area of mineralization known as the Bigelow Peak roof pendant resulted in the development of 44 mining claims between Snow and Huckleberry Lakes, beginning in the 1940s. This area contains deposits of scheelite, a source of tungsten. Due to the remote location of the claims and the short operating season, the claims were only marginally economical. Today only fifteen of the claims are valid and there has been no significant mining activity since 1967. Some debris and mining scars are still evident in the area, but the greatest impact was the construction of a road from Leavitt Lake near Sonora Pass, to Snow Lake near the boundary with Yosemite. This abominable scar across the alpine landscape of the Sierra crest will last for generations to come, though nature is slowly reclaiming the road. As long as the claims are valid, mining may occur again in the future, and the road may carry vehicles and heavy equipment deep into the wilderness. For the time being, hikers and horse packers take advantage of the road to reach the heart of the Emigrant high country.

RECREATIONAL USES: The interconnecting trail network and ease of off-trail travel make the Emigrant one of the premier destinations in the Sierra. Unlike much larger wilderness areas to the south, the highlights of the Emigrant can be enjoyed on a weekend backpack or even on a day hike. Backpacking is the most popular activity in the Emigrant, accounting for more than 80 percent of total overnight use in the wilderness. Stock use, including both private groups and three commercial pack stations, make up the remainder of overnight users. Despite many exceptional day-hiking opportunities, only about 20 percent of wilderness users, or an estimated average of about 2,500 people, day hike in the Emigrant. That may sound like a lot of people, yet the Emigrant receives much less use than most Sierra wilderness areas.

Backpackers don't always want to share space with stock parties in the backcountry. If you are one of them, avoid the following sites that are frequented by stock parties: Kennedy, Emigrant, Huckleberry, Emigrant Meadow, Buck, Wood, Deer, and Cow Meadow Lakes; and Cooper and Whitesides Meadows.

Fifteen trailheads provide access to the Emigrant trail network, some of them alongside paved highways, but most lying along fair to good unpaved forest roads. Nearly 75 percent of wilderness visitors enter at three trailheads: Kennedy Meadows, Crabtree Camp, and Gianelli. All other trailheads are lightly used, yet given the open nature of the Emigrant and its innumerable lake basins and glacier-carved topography, the backcountry has the capacity to absorb many visitors. The wilderness rarely seems crowded.

The Emigrant provides many excellent opportunities for ski mountaineering, ski touring, and snowshoeing, although winter use is limited by snow levels and unplowed roads. Most winter trips begin from the Gianelli and Coyote Meadow trailheads, but since both lie at about 8,500 feet, winter users often simply drive until they reach the snow line, then proceed on skis. When California Highway 108 is opened in spring over Sonora Pass, a wide range of challenging high-elevation terrain is accessible. Blue Canyon, west of Sonora Pass, and the Leavitt Lake area, east of the pass, offer outstanding spring skiing.

Wilderness permits are required for overnight stays in the Emigrant between May 1 and October 31. There are no trailhead quotas in effect, and permits may be obtained at Stanislaus National Forest district offices. In Pinecrest, about 30 miles northeast of Sonora on CA 108, you can self-register for permits after business hours from a dispenser outside of the office. Visitors approaching from U.S. Highway 395 via CA 108 can self-register for eastside entry points (Leavitt Meadows, Leavitt Lake, Sonora Pass) at the signed Backpacker Trailhead Parking area adjacent to Leavitt Meadows Campground, 7 miles east of US 395.

Backpack or Horsepacking Trip

Gianelli Trailhead to Upper Relief Valley

Distance: 16.4 miles, round trip (2 to 4 days).
Low/high elevations: 8,560 feet/9,200 feet.
Difficulty: Moderate.
Best season: July through early October.
Topo maps: Cooper Peak-CA, Pinecrest-CA.
Permit: A wilderness permit is required for overnight camping, and can be obtained at the Summit Ranger Station, located at the junction of CA 108 and the Pinecrest/Dodge Ridge Road. On weekends, hikers self-issue permits from the dispenser outside the ranger station.

HOW TO GET THERE: Proceed east from Sonora on CA 108 for about 30 miles, then turn right (east) onto the paved two-lane road where a sign indicates PINECREST-1. The Summit District ranger station is located on the east side of the highway at this turnoff. After driving 0.4 mile, turn right again and follow signs to Dodge Ridge Ski Area. Turn right once again after another 3.0 miles; a sign here points to Aspen Meadow, Bell Meadow, and Crabtree Camp. This turn is located just before a large sign at the entrance to Dodge Ridge Ski Area.

After turning right here onto Forest Road 4N26, your road leads southwest for 0.4 mile to a stop sign. Turn left (southeast) there and ascend steadily to the junction with the southbound road to Bell Meadow, 1.7 miles from the stop sign and 5.5 miles from the highway. Stay left (east) at that junction, drive through the Aspen Meadow Pack Station complex on the dirt road, beyond which you follow one-lane pavement on a steady ascent.

The pavement ends 1.3 miles beyond the pack station. The wide dirt road ahead is rough, with washboards and rocky stretches for the remaining distance to Gianelli Trailhead. After driving 1.4 miles from the end of the pavement, stay left (east) where a signed spur road branches right to Crabtree Trailhead. Continue ascending, now on FR 4N47, for another 4.1 miles to the trailhead parking area, 12.3 miles from the highway.

High Emigrant Lake is one of the highest elevation lakes in the Emigrant Wilderness.

This scenic subalpine trip features broad vistas and spreading meadows, and it surveys contrasting landscapes of granitic and volcanic terrain. It can be taken as an introduction to the Emigrant Wilderness, or combined with any number of other wilderness trails to form loops ranging in length from 3 to 7 days or more.

The rock-lined trail begins at the north end of the parking area and ascends gradually northeast through a shady forest of red fir, mountain hemlock, and western white pine to a granitic ridge, the Stanislaus River/Clavey River divide. Here, trailside trees filter the northward view across the South Fork Stanislaus River canyon. The trail follows an eastbound course just below the ridge, then turns south at a ridgeline saddle. The trail ahead ascends gently to moderately through a shady pine, fir, and hemlock forest and among granite slabs to the west shoulder of Burst Rock. There you pass a sign that details the brief history of the emigrant trail known as the West Walker–Sonora Road, a very difficult route that gave the Emigrant Wilderness its name.

The trail ahead gently ascends sandy slopes south of Burst Rock, then gradually descends to an open saddle. A descent of 250 feet through subalpine forest follows east of Burst Rock. At the bottom of this descent, in a saddle fringed with stunted trees and red heather, you pass an unmarked trail on your left leading a short distance north to 8,800-foot Powell Lake. You next climb 250 feet over a north-south ridge, topping out at 9,200 feet in a mixed conifer for-

High Emigrant, Emigrant Meadow, and Middle Emigrant lakes spread out in the alpine landscape of the eastern Emigrant Wilderness.

est, then descend 350 feet to reach a junction in Lake Valley, 3.0 miles from the trailhead. The signed southbound trail leads to Chewing Gum Lake in 0.7 mile, then continues beyond to the trailheads at Crabtree Camp and Bell Meadow.

Bearing left at this junction, you soon leave tarn-dotted Lake Valley behind and begin climbing moderately beneath a canopy of pines and past wildflower-filled openings. Nearing the top of this ascent, you traverse an open, grassy ridgetop offering great views north and east. This ridge is capped by volcanic deposits, unlike the initial segment of the hike that passed over granitic rock exclusively. Soon passing back into the realm of granite, you begin another descent of 350 feet, and reach a junction with a southbound trail leading to Y-Meadow Dam, 4.5 miles from the trailhead. Bearing left here you proceed northeast through a gradually thinning forest. Soon you break into the open and head east across aptly named Whitesides Meadow, meeting the northwest-bound trail to Cooper Meadow near the east end of this large grassland. Staying right at this junction, your trail soon leaves that spread, skirts the edge of a small meadow filled with lupine and groundsel, and meanders up to a junction with the popular right-branching trail leading to Salt Lick Meadow and the lake-filled terrain in the heart of the Emigrant Wilderness.

Bearing left here, your trail begins a northeasterly course, first on the north side, then on the south side of the ridge, alternating between volcanic and granitic terrain. About 1.25 miles from Whitesides Meadow you pass the small meadow and trickling stream forming the headwaters of Relief Creek, and begin descending.

You soon are skirting the western edge of Upper Relief Valley's subalpine grassland, gloriously brightened by colorful blooms. You pass a southbound trail leading to Salt Lick Meadow after a short jaunt into the valley. Good campsites can be found around the valley and near the two small, shallow lakes at its northern end.

Experienced cross-country hikers might consider a 2.5- to 3-mile jaunt east from Upper Relief Valley to several remote alpine lakes lying in cirques just north of 10,322-foot Granite Dome, the large, rounded alpine mountain rising east of the valley.

Carson-Iceberg Wilderness Complex   **19**

Location: 80 miles northeast of Stockton and 5 miles west of Walker.
Size: 204,200 acres.
Administration: Stanislaus National Forest (west of Sierra crest), Toiyabe National Forest (east of Sierra crest).
Management status: National Forest wilderness (160,000 acres), with the remainder roadless nonwilderness managed as Further Planning Areas and recommended for wilderness additions.
Ecosystems: Sierran Forest–Alpine Meadows province, Sierra Nevada section, characterized by complex, high, and strongly glaciated mountains with sharp alpine ridges, cirques, and deep stream valleys; Mesozoic granitic rocks, with Pliocene volcanics, Jurassic metamorphic rocks, and early Mesozoic volcanic rocks; potential natural vegetation is northern Jeffrey pine forest, Sierran montane forest, upper montane-subalpine forests, and alpine communities; numerous perennial streams, wet meadows, and high-elevation lakes.
Elevation range: 4,800 feet to 11,462 feet.
System trails: 212.4 miles.
Maximum core-to-perimeter distance: 12.5 miles.
Activities: Backpacking, day hiking, horseback riding, fishing, cross-country skiing, snowshoeing, and mountaineering.
Maps: Stanislaus National Forest visitor map; Toiyabe National Forest visitor map; Carson-Iceberg Wilderness map (topographic; 1 inch/mile); see Appendix D for the list of USGS 1:24,000 quads.

OVERVIEW: The Carson-Iceberg Wilderness is one of the northernmost wildlands in the range with High Sierra-like landscapes, stretching along the Sierra crest between Ebbetts Pass in the north and Sonora Pass in the south. The wilderness is almost equally divided between the west and east slopes of the Sierra Nevada, including the headwaters drainages of the North and Middle Forks of the Stanislaus River on the west slope, and the headwaters of the East Fork Carson River on the east slope.

In its highest elevations, the Carson-Iceberg is dominated by volcanic rocks, much like the Mokelumne Wilderness to the north. Lower elevations on both the west and east slopes are dominated by granitic rocks. Areas on the west slope have had much of the volcanic veneer stripped away by glaciation, while those areas on the east were not buried as deeply in volcanics, and were only moderately glaciated.

The Sierra crest rises abruptly from Sonora Pass in the southeast to 11,459-foot Sonora Peak. It continues northwest past 11,233-foot Stanislaus Peak, then dips much lower to 9,000-foot summits as it winds its way toward Ebbetts Pass in the northwest. Only Disaster Peak and Arnot Peak exceed 10,000 feet on the crest northwest of Stanislaus Peak. A more prominent divide extending northeast from Sonora Peak is capped by numerous 10,000-foot peaks and topped by 11,398-foot White Mountain. This divide, featuring both granitic and volcanic terrain, embraces the headwaters of the East Fork Carson River and Silver King Creek, one of the river's principal tributaries. Separating the East Fork from its tributary drainages—Silver King Creek and Wolf Creek—are three high, northeast-trending divides, each capped by 8,000- to 10,000-foot peaks. The highest and most spectacular of these divides rises immediately east of Ebbetts Pass. It is crowned by 10,935-foot Highland Peak and 10,772-foot Silver Peak, both of which dramatically rise more than 3,500 feet above Wolf Creek on the east and Silver Creek on the west.

West of the crest, a prominent divide extending southwest from the vicinity of Wolf Creek Pass features several prominent 9,000-foot peaks—Hiram, Airola, and Iceberg—and the unusual high volcanic formations of The Dardanelles. This divide not only separates the North and Middle forks of the Stanislaus River, it divides two very different west-slope landscapes. South and east of this divide is the deep canyon of the Clark Fork Stanislaus River (a candidate for Wild and Scenic River status) and its principal tributaries, Disaster and Arnot Creeks. The Iceberg, a prominent granite peak, rises above the Clark Fork canyon. Northwest of the divide is a gently sloping landscape dominated by ice-scoured granite bedrock, featuring numerous parallel, joint-controlled drainages that flow southwest into Union and Spicer Meadow Reservoirs. Defining the northern boundary of the Carson-Iceberg west of the Sierra crest are portions of another high divide capped by 9,000-foot peaks that include Folger, Peep Sight, Henry, and Bull Run.

There are numerous tarns in the Carson-Iceberg, but only 14 named backcountry lakes. This wilderness is still a popular destination despite the lack of lakes, yet it is much more lightly used than the lake-filled Emigrant Wilderness south of Sonora Pass. The attractions of the Carson-Iceberg include its openness, large meadows, many streams, long-distance vistas, and overall size, which affords considerable solitude.

Four roadless areas adjacent to the Carson-Iceberg were given Further Planning status in the California Wilderness Act of 1984, three on the Stanislaus National Forest on the west slope, and one area on the Toiyabe National Forest on the east slopes below Ebbetts Pass. While three of these roadless areas will likely someday be added to the Carson-Iceberg Wilderness, the Pacific Valley roadless area on the Stanislaus National Forest could be developed into an alpine ski area.

19A CARSON-ICEBERG WILDERNESS COMPLEX (WEST)

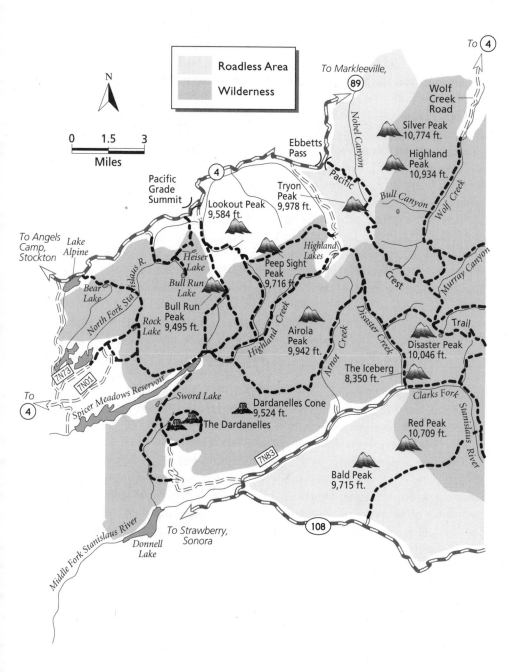

19B CARSON-ICEBERG WILDERNESS COMPLEX (EAST)

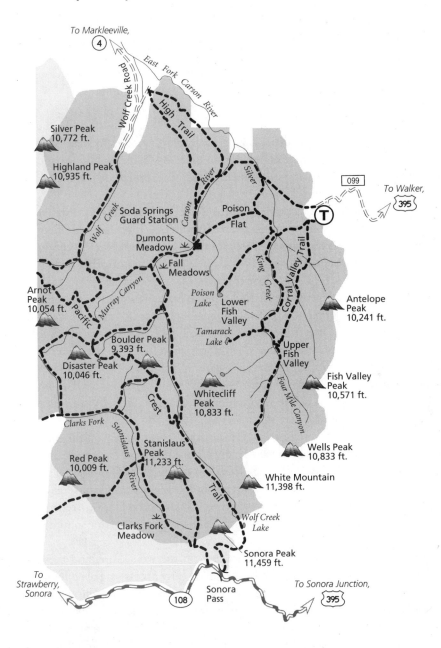

Mule deer habitat is excellent in the Carson-Iceberg, particularly on the east slope, and the herds attract many hunters into the backcountry in autumn. Black bear habitat is also abundant, and backcountry travelers are advised to protect food supplies. There are problem bears here, and they have no fear of humans and an insatiable appetite for backpackers' food. East-slope drainages support the only native populations of Piute cutthroat trout in existence, including Silver King Creek upstream from Llewellyn Falls, and all of the Corral Valley and Coyote Valley drainages, which are closed to fishing.

RECREATIONAL USES: With its vast landscape and over 200 miles of trails, the Carson-Iceberg offers excellent trips ranging from easy day hikes to week-long backpack trips. Its open terrain allows for ample cross-country hiking, and considerable solitude can be found on many trails, since much of the wilderness remains relatively "undiscovered" by California hikers.

The eastern slopes of the wilderness, in the Toiyabe National Forest, are far more lightly used than the more-accessible western slopes. The Carson-Iceberg is the closest high-country wilderness to western Nevada population centers in the Carson City and Reno areas, and Nevada hikers represent nearly one-half of the visitors to the eastern slope. For solitude, open landscapes, panoramic vistas, and excellent fishing, you can't find a much better destination than the eastern half of the Carson-Iceberg. Five trailheads provide access on the east side. From the Sierra crest at Sonora Pass, the PCT heads northwest over the crest, into the East Fork Carson River, then north along the crest for 31 miles to Ebbetts Pass on California Highway 4. Many hikers follow only segments of the PCT, making one- to two-week backpack trips. The Sonora Pass to Ebbetts Pass segment has much to recommend it, including grand vistas, considerable solitude, and a relatively short and simple car shuttle.

Other trailheads that access eastside trails include Corral Valley on the eastern wilderness boundary, Wolf Creek Meadow and High Trail trailheads, and Nobel Creek Trailhead. The Wolf Creek Meadow and High Trail trailheads receive considerable use from parties with pack and saddle stock. Corral Valley affords access to a network of trails in the eastern half of the Carson-Iceberg, though the majority of hikers flock to Poison Lake—a good place for solitude-seekers to avoid.

Fifteen trailheads service the Carson-Iceberg on the west slope, and these are popular with day-hikers and backpackers alike. Easy access via paved highways and high-standard forest roads, combined with proximity to Central Valley population centers, make many westside trailheads very popular, particularly on summer weekends. The most popular are along CA 4 at Stanislaus Meadow, and the Heiser Lake Trailhead at Mosquito Lake immediately west of Pacific Grade Summit. These trailheads are extremely busy with day hikers en route to Heiser Lake (2.1 miles) and Bull Run Lake (3.6 miles).

Wilderness permits are required for overnight stays. For westside entry, permits are available from any Stanislaus National Forest office. For eastside entry, visitors can self-register at trailhead dispensers. There are no trailhead quotas.

Winter access to the Carson-Iceberg high country is gained only by long approaches, since both CA 4 and CA 108 are gated and closed in winter. CA 4 is plowed to the Silver Tip Campground at the junction with the road to Mount Reba Ski Area. One could drive to that point, then ski or snowshoe up CA 4 and enter the wilderness at almost any point along the northern boundary. On the east slope, you can access the wilderness via Forest Road 099, the Golden Gate Road, leading to the Corral Meadow Trailhead. Snow depth will determine how far you can drive on this road (see *How to get there* below). Since this road has several extremely steep grades, considerable caution is advised, along with a set of chains for your vehicle. When snow conditions are good, you'll find many miles of superb ski-touring terrain from Corral Valley Trailhead.

Backpack

Fish Valley Loop

Distance: 14 miles or more, semi-loop trip (3 to 5 days).
Low/high elevations: 7,700 feet/8,900 feet.
Difficulty: Moderate.
Best season: July through September.
Topo maps: Coleville-CA, Lost Cannon Peak-CA.
Permits: Required for overnight use; self-register for permits at the dispenser adjacent to the trailhead.

HOW TO GET THERE: From U.S. Highway 395, 1.3 miles north of the town of Walker or 50 miles south of Carson City, Nevada, turn west onto the signed Mill Canyon Road and drive 0.3 mile to a junction. Bear right there onto Golden Gate Road, FR 099, signed for Little Antelope Pack Station. The wide and graded dirt road crosses Little Antelope Valley, then begins a very steep ascent of the eastern escarpment of the Sierra. High-clearance vehicles are recommended for the rocky road ahead, although passenger cars still frequently make it.

Ford a small, shallow stream 3.3 miles from the highway, and another after 3.8 miles; beyond this, the grade moderates. You reach a signed junction 6.3 miles from the highway, with the road straight ahead leading to the pack station and the southbound road leading to Corral Valley Trailhead. Turn left and follow the narrow and very rocky road for 0.4 mile to the information signboard and the wilderness permit dispenser, adjacent to the stock trailer parking area. From there continue ahead for 0.1 mile to the trailhead at the road's end, where there is space enough for 8 to 10 vehicles.

This seldom-used trail visits a series of lovely eastern Sierra meadows and features inspiring alpine vistas, productive fishing in lower Silver King Creek, and ample opportunities for off-trail exploration. In fact, the Silver King Creek environs offer some of the best off-trail side-trip options in the wilderness. In autumn there are memorable foliage displays as the abundant aspens turn golden, but be sure to wear blaze orange if you visit from late September through October, when deer are in season.

A map on the information signboard at the stock trailer parking area lists the streams that are strictly closed to fishing to protect native Piute cutthroat trout populations. There is good fishing below Llewellyn Falls and in nearby Tamarack Lake, which includes golden trout. Since most visitors to this area are en route to either Poison or Tamarack Lakes, the peaceful meadows along the route provide considerable solitude.

The trail begins from the west side of the trailhead parking area as the wide track of a long-closed road, but soon narrows to a singletrack leading gently uphill beneath a canopy of white fir and aspen. Quite soon the trail from the Little Antelope Pack Station joins on the right, and immediately thereafter you enter the Carson-Iceberg Wilderness and begin a moderate to steep ascent. After 0.75 mile you exit the forest and open up on a broad flat covered in sagebrush, snowberry, and mule's ears.

As the trail ahead proceeds gently across the brushy flat, fine vistas extend down to the sprawling meadows of Silver King Valley to the northwest, all the way to the distant Freel Peaks in the Carson Range. They even extend to the more distant Crystal Range summits in the Desolation Wilderness, west of Lake Tahoe. Perhaps the most outstanding views are of numerous alpine summits reaching westward into the Carson-Iceberg interior.

After 1 mile, you reach a signed junction where the westbound trail leads to Long Valley and Poison Lake, and the rocky southbound trail heads for Corral Valley. For now, head toward Corral Valley, since taking the loop in this direction involves less ascending, and you will also leave most of the other hikers behind who are bound for Poison Lake. A few hundred yards west of the junction is a very large cairn built long ago by lonely Basque sheepherders.

The trail into Corral Valley descends nearly 500 feet in 1.3 miles, skirting an extensive aspen grove en route to the verdant meadows on the valley floor. There, with a backdrop of 10,241-foot Antelope Peak, you jump across two forks of the small creek, then enter lodgepole pine forest on the meadow's southern margin. The trail ascends gradually southwest from Corral Valley, along the needle-carpeted forest floor. After red fir and western white pine join the forest ranks, the trail inclines more steeply, finally switchbacking to a grassy

The seldom-used trail into Upper Fish Valley.

saddle at 8,900 feet on a blocky granite ridge. There the forest yields to large, fragrant specimens of curl-leaf mountain mahogany, lying in the foreground of your view to the lofty divide that defines the western skyline.

The trail then descends 650 feet on the hot and dry south slopes of the ridge and passes through an open woodland of Jeffrey pine, Sierra juniper, and mountain mahogany. The trail is quite steep, eroded, and rocky, yet it is still much easier to go down than up. It eventually levels off at the sagebrush-studded clearing of Coyote Valley, and across the small valley to its southern edge it will be faint and soggy in early summer. As in Corral Valley, there are many potential camping places.

The trail ahead leads gradually uphill away from the meadows and enters an open forest of lodgepole pine, Sierra juniper, and aspen. Soon you approach the next ridgeline saddle at 8,500 feet, where fine views extend into the alpine heights of upper Silver King Creek and Fourmile Canyon.

The trail descends gradually from the saddle and crosses a broad, sloping meadow en route to a reconstructed segment of trail not shown on maps. The trail now switchbacks gently through aspens and junipers into Upper Fish Valley. On the valley floor at the eastern margin of the mile-long meadow is a signed junction. From here you will follow the trail to the northwest, down Silver King Creek, but by now most travelers will be in search of campsites. There are few near the junction. Good sites can be found in the lodgepole pine forest near the north end of Upper Fish Valley; on the west bank of the creek near the Connels Cow Camp cabin, now owned by the Forest Service; or up the valley toward the mouth of Fourmile Canyon. Although signs of cattle grazing are evident, cows no longer graze in this area. Upper Fish is a beautiful valley, fringed by lodgepole pine and aspen and bounded by alpine volcanic peaks approaching 11,000 feet.

Possible side-trips include a 1,600-foot ascent in 2.8 miles of unmaintained trail that begins at Connels Cow Camp and leads to Whitecliff Lake. The lake contains no fish and is seldom visited, but it rests in a scenic bowl beneath the east face of Whitecliff Peak at 9,709 feet. Another trip, recommended for experienced cross-country backpackers only, ascends Fourmile Canyon to a broad Sierra crest saddle. It then follows the crest from the saddle, goes up and over 10,833-foot Wells Peak and down to a narrow, 10,000-foot saddle where it picks up the Silver King Trail. After heading north for 3.8 miles, the trail puts you back at the mouth of Fourmile Canyon.

To finish the loop trail from Upper Fish Valley, proceed northwest, then north for 4.2 miles down Silver King Creek to a signed junction. There, you reach the westbound trail signed for Poison Lake, and the eastbound trail, your return route, signed for Rodriguez Flat. Turn right, ford the grassy-banked stream one last time immediately below the confluence with Corral Valley

Creek, and begin the 2.3-mile, 1,100-foot ascent back to the Corral Valley Trail junction. The trail winds upward at a moderate grade, over slopes littered with both volcanic and granitic boulders, with occasional junipers, Jeffrey pines, aspens, and clumps of mountain mahogany offering small pockets of shade along the way. Fine vistas back into the interior of the Carson-Iceberg expand as you gain elevation, and eventually familiar sights come into view, including Antelope Peak and Corral Valley. After 2.3 miles, turn left at the junction and retrace your route for 1 mile to the trailhead, enjoying views into Walker Valley, Smith Valley, and distant barren Nevada mountain ranges along the way.

Mokelumne Wilderness 20

Location: 70 miles east of Sacramento and 18 miles south of South Lake Tahoe.
Size: 104,500 acres.
Administration: USDAFS–Stanislaus, Eldorado, and Toiyabe National Forests.
Management status: National Forest wilderness.
Ecosystems: Sierran Forest–Alpine Meadows province, Sierra Nevada section, characterized by moderately high to high, steep mountains, deep stream valleys, cirques, and hanging valleys; Mesozoic granitics, Pliocene and Miocene lava flow deposits, and glacial deposits and alluvium; potential natural vegetation is Sierran montane forest, northern Jeffrey pine forest, upper montane-subalpine forests, Sierran yellow pine forest, and alpine communities; dendritic drainage patterns with many perennial streams, numerous moderately high to high lakes.
Elevation range: 4,000 feet to 10,381 feet.
System trails: 118 miles.
Maximum core-to-perimeter distance: 7.25 miles.
Activities: Day hiking, backpacking, horseback riding, fishing, cross-country skiing, and snowshoeing.
Maps: Eldorado, Stanislaus, and Toiyabe National Forests visitor maps; Mokelumne Wilderness map (topographic; 1 inch/mile); see Appendix D for the list of USGS 1:24,000 quads.

OVERVIEW: Between Ebbetts Pass and Carson Pass on the Sierra crest, the Mokelumne Wilderness occupies a transition area in the Sierra Nevada. Elevations are lower north of Ebbetts Pass, and there are few areas rising above timberline, yet the Mokelumne still displays the profound effects of glacial modification upon its landscape, typical of the High Sierra. The Mokelumne Wilderness includes the Sierra crest from Forestdale Divide to Carson Pass; the bulk of the wilderness encompasses the headwaters of the North Fork Mokelumne River on the west slope. A detached unit of the wilderness, lying to the east and separated by the Blue Lakes Road (Forest Road 015) and an OHV road corridor, includes part of the Sierra crest immediately north of Ebbetts Pass, and a high, north-trending divide crowned by Jeff Davis and Markleeville Peaks, east of the Sierra crest in the East Fork Carson River drainage. Streams draining north from the high divide extending west from Round Top to Covered Wagon Peak flow into the Silver Fork of the American River. The southern wilderness boundary immediately north of California

Highway 4 generally follows the crest of a high, 8,000-foot volcanic divide separating the North Fork Mokelumne River in the north from the North Fork Stanislaus River in the south.

Round Top, the highest peak in the wilderness at 10,381 feet, is the remnant of a volcanic vent from which most of the volcanic deposits in the wilderness were erupted between 4 and 20 million years ago. Much of the Sierra crest and the landscape east of the crest is dominated by volcanic material, while on the west slope, stream erosion and glaciation stripped away much of the overlying volcanics, re-exposing the granitic bedrock lying below. The variation between the volcanic and granitic landscapes has created many dramatic landforms.

Numerous glacial features are evident, mostly in areas dominated by granitics, including tarns, lateral and terminal moraines, stepped valleys, and cirque lakes. There are 220 glacial lakes and tarns in the Mokelumne; 18 of the largest lakes are stocked every one to three years with fingerling trout, including brook, rainbow, Lahontan cutthroat, and golden trout.

Broad, U-shaped valleys characterize the principal drainages on the west slope, including Summit City Canyon and the upper North Fork Mokelumne River canyon. The North Fork extends from its headwaters on the 9,000- and 10,000-foot peaks on the Sierra crest in the Carson-Iceberg Wilderness, then flows through the Mokelumne Wilderness to an elevation of 3,949 feet at Salt Springs Reservoir on the southwestern boundary. On its 18.5-mile course, the North Fork flows through a dramatic, granite-bound gorge, ranging from 3,000 to 4,000 feet deep.

Over 6,000 feet of elevation separate the highest and lowest elevations in the Mokelumne. The soils are volcanic and granitic, and the west slopes of the Sierra Nevada are moist while the east slopes are drier. Consequently, there is a wide variation in vegetation types, ranging from foothill woodlands of ponderosa pine and canyon live oak, to alpine vegetation. The highest peaks along the Sierra crest and east of the crest are composed of volcanic material, and support rich timberline and alpine vegetation. Round Top has been designated a special interest area, not only because of its unique geological features, but also due to its botanical diversity. More than 580 different species of plants have been identified here. Riparian vegetation, most well developed in the North Fork canyon, includes white alder, mountain alder, cottonwood, willows, creek dogwood, western azalea, and bitter cherry.

Typical of much of the Sierra Nevada, the Mokelumne contains quality habitat for common animals such as black bear, gray squirrel, and mule deer. The Mokelumne includes critical fawning habitat and summer range for mule deer. Sensitive wildlife species known to occur in the Mokelumne include marten, California spotted owl, flammulated owl, great gray owl, northern

20   MOKELUMNE WILDERNESS

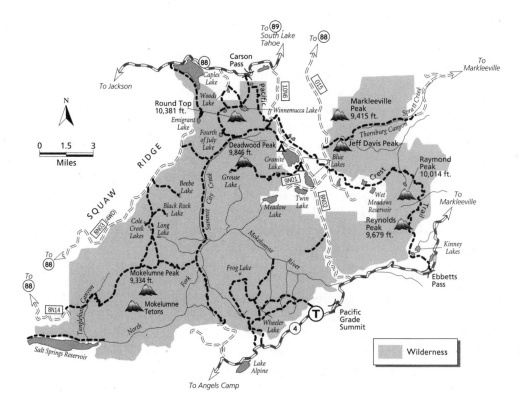

goshawk, and mountain quail. Wintering bald eagles, a federally listed threatened species, have been sighted around the shores of Salt Springs Reservoir.

As with many high-elevation wilderness areas in the Sierra north of Yosemite, the Mokelumne supports cattle and sheep grazing. The grazing allotments in the Mokelumne are more extensive than in most other regional wildernesses and the impacts of grazing are found at many wilderness destinations which, unfortunately for visitors, provide some of the best forage. Long, Black Rock, Cole Creek, Beebe, and Wheeler Lakes are all frequented by grazing cattle during the summer.

RECREATIONAL USES: The Mokelumne Wilderness provides the setting for superb backcountry adventures, its dramatic landscapes ranging from deep canyons to alpine heights and from ice-scoured granite to the verdant slopes of the volcanic peaks. Yet far fewer people come to the Mokelumne than to nearby wilderness areas, such as the Desolation and Carson-Iceberg. High lakes are the biggest attraction in the Sierra Nevada backcountry. The lakes of the Mokelumne are no exception, particularly those around the wilderness perimeter, but since they attract a disproportionately large number of visitors, much of the rest of the wilderness is free of backpackers. Much of the North Fork Mokelumne River canyon is trailless, and trails reach the river at only three points: Blue Hole, at the upper end of Salt Springs Reservoir; between Camp Irene crossing and the confluence with Summit City Creek; and Jackson Canyon, north of Wheeler Lake. With relatively few destination lakes and large areas where there are no trails, the Mokelumne Wilderness provides exceptional opportunities for solitude.

Since the Mokelumne is surrounded by roads, access is easy via 24 trailheads with 11 receiving the bulk of use. These include, in descending order of popularity: Carson Pass, Caples Dam, Woods Lake, Horsethief Springs, Salt Springs Reservoir, Lost Cabin, Tanglefoot, Woodchuck Basin, Middle Creek Campground, Horse Canyon, and Wet Meadows. In a typical year, more than half of overnight visitors enter the wilderness from trailheads in the Carson Pass area, and these trailheads are also very popular with day-users en route to Frog, Winnemucca, and Round Top Lakes. Other popular day-use destinations in the Mokelumne include Emigrant Lake, Granite Lake, and the Raymond Creek Meadows area north of Ebbetts Pass. These areas are not only popular because of their easy access, but also because they are some of the most spectacular places in the wilderness. The majority of overnight and day use is on summer weekends.

Most hikers take round trips to lake basins in the higher elevations. The trail along Salt Springs Reservoir to Blue Hole on the North Fork Mokelumne is popular in the early season, usually beginning in April, three months before the high country opens up. In fact, that is the only early-season snow-free trail in the wilderness; all other trails leading to the North Fork begin at high elevations. The Pacific Crest Trail passes through eastern portions of the wilderness between Ebbetts Pass and Carson Pass. Except for stretches between Ebbetts Pass and Raymond Lake, and from Frog Lake to Carson Pass, major users of the trail are summer through-hikers northbound on the PCT. The Tahoe-Yosemite Trail also traverses the wilderness north to south, from Carson Pass to Mount Reba via Summit City Creek and the North Fork Mokelumne River. The Emigrant Summit Trail, a National Recreation and Historic Trail that was used by thousands of emigrants between 1849 and the mid-1850s, follows the western wilderness boundary along Squaw Ridge and passes through the wilderness from Emigrant Valley to Caples Lake. Use of pack and saddle stock in the wilderness, by private parties and one commercial outfitter, is low in the Mokelumne, except during the autumn deer-hunting season.

Winter use of the wilderness is made possible by the plowed route of California Highway 88 over Carson Pass and by the proximity of the Mount Reba and Kirkwood ski areas to the wilderness boundary. Cross-country skiing is very popular along the marked Winnemucca Lake Loop, beginning at Carson Pass. Carson Pass is a California Sno-Park site, requiring a fee and a permit, and it is the most heavily used Sno-Park site in the state. Skiers and snowshoers seeking more solitude can enter the wilderness from the vicinity of the Mount Reba Ski Area along the south boundary. Mount Reba sits at the west end of a high volcanic divide south of the North Fork Mokelumne River canyon. High elevations, deep snows, and a series of north-facing bowls below this ridge provide some outstanding ski opportunities.

Wilderness permits are required for overnight use of the Mokelumne from April 1 through November 30, and there are no daily entry quotas. Permits are available by self-registration at the Markleeville Chamber of Commerce/USFS ranger station, and from the following ranger stations: Eldorado National Forest Information Center in Camino; Amador Ranger District office in Pioneer; Calaveras Ranger District office in Hathaway Pines; Carson Ranger District office in Carson City, Nevada; Carson Pass Information Station; and the Alpine Ranger Station. Self-issue parking fees are collected at the Carson Pass Pacific Crest trailheads, both at the pass, and 0.25 mile west of the pass.

Backpack

Wheeler Lake, Underwood Valley

Distance: 15 miles, loop trip (3 days).
Low/high elevations: 7,500 feet/8,846 feet.
Difficulty: Moderate.
Best season: July through September.
Topo map: Pacific Valley-CA.
Permits: Required for overnight use between April 1 and November 30.

HOW TO GET THERE: Hikers approaching from the east will follow CA 4 southwest from its junction with CA 89 (5 miles southeast of Markleeville). After 6.2 miles, the centerline on CA 4 disappears, and the road becomes a steep, narrow, and winding route stretching southwest as far as Lake Alpine. The road crests the Sierra at Ebbetts Pass after 13.2 miles, descends to the North Fork Mokelumne River, then rises to Pacific Grade Summit, 21.2 miles from CA 89. The spacious Sandy Meadow Trailhead lies on the south side of the highway, adjacent to stock corrals, 1.1 miles west of Pacific Grade Summit.

Hikers approaching from the west will follow CA 4 for 56 miles northeast from Angels Camp to the trailhead. If you reach Pacific Grade Summit, you've gone 1.1 miles too far.

High volcanic ridges bound the southern reaches of the Mokelumne.

This fine hike leads through subalpine forests in the southern reaches of the Mokelumne Wilderness, offering occasional long-range vistas deep into its rugged interior. Wheeler Lake can be busy on summer weekends, but it features good fishing, good campsites, and a spectacular setting beneath a crest of high volcanic peaks. Underwood Valley offers an off-trail destination to one of the most seldom-visited glacial valleys in the Mokelumne.

The trail begins on the north side of the highway, several yards west of the trailhead parking area, and is indicated by a sign reading TRAIL. You rise moderately at first through red fir and lodgepole pine forest, then level out just before topping a low saddle. Enter the Mokelumne Wilderness on the north side of the saddle, then begin a steady descent that leads to a long traverse of corrugated slopes, where small meadows and early season rivulets interrupt the forest of lodgepole and western white pine, red fir, and mountain hemlock—the typical timberline forest of the Northern Sierra.

After 1.5 miles, you reach the sloping spread of Sandy Meadow, backed up by volcanic summits. Here a trailside post points left (west) to Avalanche Meadow, and right (northwest) to Wheeler Lake. Either trail can be taken to reach the lake, though the right-hand trail is more direct and involves less climbing. Save the Avalanche Meadow Trail for the return trip.

After turning right, begin descending steadily through viewless forest for about 0.5 mile to a rock-hop crossing of Meadow Creek. Beyond the crossing the trail heads west, and soon you reach another stream; this one usually requires a shallow ford.

Ahead you begin a steady ascent through increasingly rocky terrain studded with erratic boulders, to a pair of small and shallow, but picturesque, tarns. Soon thereafter you will reach Wheeler Lake's large outlet stream, which you will have to cross twice.

A steady ascent through a mixed conifer forest leads you on a winding course past ice-polished granite to the east shore of Wheeler Lake. The lake is popular enough to host a few hiking or horsepacking parties on most summer weekends, but on weekdays you may have the lake to yourself.

The verdant volcanic slopes of an 8,800-foot ridge rises behind the lake; the lake basin, however, is scooped out of granitic bedrock. Fishing is best in deep water from the north shore near the lake's outlet. The better campsites are located among granite knolls north of the lake in the open, mixed conifer forest that surrounds it. Rangers recommend these sites but discourage the use of campsites along the fringe of the meadows beyond the south and west shores. These sites have been overused and many are closed to camping.

Few hikers continue on past Wheeler Lake—the trail around its south and west shores is faint, and remains wet and soggy usually until midsummer. From the west shore, head north into the forest, where the tread is better defined, leads over a low saddle, then gradually drops to a junction 0.6 mile from the lake. The northbound trail descends 1,500 feet in 2.5 miles through Jackson Canyon to the North Fork Mokelumne River. Turn left at the junction; the signpost points to Frog Lake. This trail stays north of a small, cascading stream and ascends very steeply. Just as it approaches the banks of the stream, it bends northwest and the grade moderates as you make your way up, then down, to another small creek.

From here the trail rises 250 feet in a third of a mile to a saddle at 8,555 feet. Vistas from just off the trail are panoramic, encompassing much of the rugged interior of the Mokelumne. The trail descends north from the saddle, sometimes steeply, toward a lower bench dominated by conifer-studded granite domes. After descending 400 feet in 0.4 mile, the trail turns west to reach a small meadow alongside a stream, where you meet the northbound spur trail leading to Frog Lake, 6.4 miles from the trailhead. Turn left at this junction, and you should leave most other hikers behind as you first ascend to an 8,300-foot ridge, then descend to a long southeast traverse about 350 feet above Underwood Valley. The valley's meadows, gently-sloping floor, and year-round stream, all surrounded on three sides by dark volcanic ridges, make it a scenic place to pass your first or second night on the trail, and there is an excellent chance of enjoying the valley in complete solitude.

After 9 miles, cross the headwaters of the Underwood Valley creek in the timberline forest, avoid an unmaintained westbound trail, and prepare for a strenuous 800-foot ascent of the valley's headwall, topping out at 8,650 feet after 1 mile. This slope holds snow well into summer, making the ascent difficult at least until August most years. Continue northeast up the ridge, ignoring the southbound, descending trail leading to a pair of trailheads along CA 4. The ascent leads to Point 8,846, where far-ranging panoramas stretch north across the Mokelumne and south across the high country of the Carson-Iceberg Wilderness.

Staying in form with the roller-coaster nature of this trip, you now follow the trail steeply downhill to Avalanche Meadow, reentering pine, fir, and hemlock forest, and again cross slopes that are likely to be snow-covered well into summer. After 11.0 miles, you reach Avalanche Meadow, at 8,100 feet. This is a lovely subalpine spread lying beneath fluted volcanic cliffs, at the head of the Wheeler Lake cirque. Take the eastbound trail at the junction in Avalanche Meadow. This trail follows a high traverse for 2.5 miles past the Cliff Meadow cirque, back to the junction at Sandy Meadow. From here, retrace your inbound trail for 1.5 miles to the Sandy Meadow Trailhead.

Dardanelles Roadless Area   21

Location: 7 miles south of South Lake Tahoe.
Size: 14,500 acres.
Administration: USDAFS–Lake Tahoe Basin Management Unit.
Management status: Roadless nonwilderness, managed for nonmotorized recreation.
Ecosystems: Sierran Forest–Alpine Meadows province, Sierra Nevada section, characterized by a broad, high basin, high-elevation alpine crests, and sharp volcanic peaks; Pliocene and Tertiary volcanic rocks, with smaller areas of Mesozoic granitic rocks, and glacial deposits; potential natural vegetation is upper montane-subalpine forests, and alpine communities; many perennial streams, wet meadows, and numerous moderately high lakes.
Elevation range: 6,400 feet to 10,061 feet.
System trails: 26.1 miles.
Maximum core-to-perimeter distance: 3 miles.
Activities: Day hiking, backpacking, fishing, cross-country skiing, and snowshoeing.
Maps: Lake Tahoe Basin Management Unit visitor map; see Appendix D for a list of USGS 1:24,000 quads.

OVERVIEW: Although the Dardanelles roadless area was released for nonwilderness uses by the 1984 California Wilderness Act, the area is managed to preserve its natural condition and to provide an area of nonmotorized recreation. The backcountry of the Lake Tahoe region is the most intensively used by recreationists in all of California. The famous Desolation Wilderness immediately west of Lake Tahoe is very heavily used, and is omitted from this book based on the advice of land managers.

Often called "Meiss Country" after a local ranching family, the Dardanelles roadless area is not to be confused with "The Dardanelles," a high volcanic ridge on the western slope of the Sierra farther south in the Carson-Iceberg Wilderness.

The Dardanelles, with its broad meadows, timberline lakes, and alpine peaks, provides an attractive alternative backcountry destination to the often overcrowded Desolation country. South of Lake Tahoe, the lake's principal tributary is the Upper Truckee River. The Upper Truckee features a V-shaped headwaters bowl where the Sierra Nevada crest and the Carson Range diverge, heading northwest and northeast, respectively. This part of the Sierra was buried in volcanic material millions of years ago. Some of these volcanics were stripped away by glacial advances, re-exposing the granitic bedrock of the Sierra.

21   DARDANELLES AND FREEL
ROADLESS AREAS

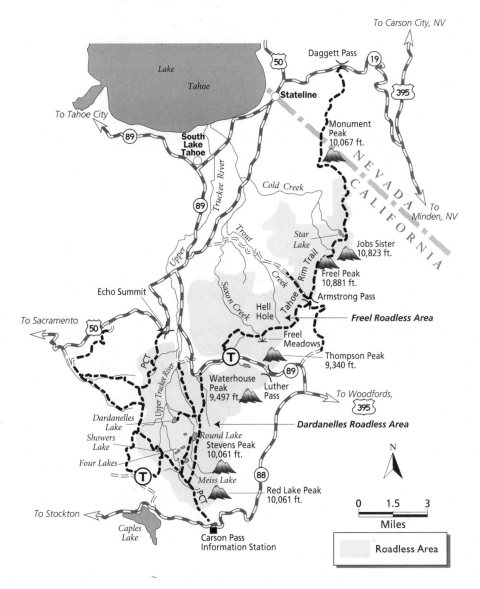

Much of the Upper Truckee basin is bounded by volcanic ridges, and the Carson Range summits of Stevens and Red Lake Peaks bear the distinction of being the highest peaks this far north in California composed of mudflow breccia. The most distinguishing features of the Upper Truckee are its broad subalpine meadows, the willow-fringed river banks, and open stands of lodgepole pine. Vistas from the upper basin and from the Pacific Crest Trail are outstanding as they stretch across much of the roadless area, which features stratified volcanic peaks and ridges, mats of krummholz whitebark pine, and verdant blankets of grasses and forbs. There is little evidence of outside development or highway noise here since the landscape is naturally enclosed.

The northern half of the area, being lower in elevation, supports well-developed forest cover and greater exposures of granitic bedrock. Numerous lakes dot the landscape of the Dardanelles, most of them in granite bowls. Round and Meiss Lakes are located in more open settings among volcanic rock. Each of these lakes provides a different setting, and they are the destinations of most hikers.

Cattle graze the Upper Truckee in summer on the 700 AUM Meiss Meadow Allotment. The historic Meiss Cabin, built in 1878, still stands in the very upper reaches of the basin and is used in summer by the range permittees, and in winter, by a permittee for guided winter recreation classes.

RECREATIONAL USES: The Dardanelles is second only to the Desolation Wilderness in popularity in the Lake Tahoe region, and only the Desolation has a greater number of lakes. Four trailheads provide access to the Dardanelles backcountry. Because three of them are reached by paved highways and because of the network of good, mostly gentle trails (some of them old jeep roads), the area is attractive to families, day-hikers, and weekend backpackers. Many of them are locals.

The Carson Pass Northbound PCT Trailhead, located about 0.25 mile west of Carson Pass, affords quick access through open country over the divide and into the Upper Truckee basin. Big Meadow on the north is the most heavily used trailhead, and it affords two-hour access to Dardanelles and Round Lakes. Echo Summit on California Highway 50 is a southbound PCT starting point to the Dardanelles. Schneider Camp on the southwest side of the area is the least-used entry point, so it provides more solitude than other trails. Hikers willing to travel off-trail can enjoy plenty of solitude, even though the area is popular, and the openness and gentle nature of much of the Dardanelles lends itself to off-trail exploration.

High-elevation winter use of the Dardanelles is made possible by plowed highways to the north and south. Skiers and snowshoers can enter from the south on the Pacific Crest Trail just west of Carson Pass at the Sno-Park, from

The Carson Range bounds the eastern reaches of the Dardanelles Roadless Area.

the north at the Echo Summit Sno-Park on CA 50, or from the unplowed Big Meadows trailhead on CA 89. Because of high winds and dry snow, the high ridges of the Carson Range and Sierra crest are often blown clear of snow, and avalanche danger is high, which means ski-touring and snowshoeing are better on the lower slopes and basin floors.

Day Hike or Backpack

Showers Lake

Distance: 8.2 miles, loop trip.
Low/high elevations: 8,300 feet/9,200 feet.
Difficulty: Moderate.
Best season: July through September.
Topo map: Caples Lake-CA.
Permits: California Campfire Permit required for open fires and backpack stoves.

HOW TO GET THERE: From CA 88 above the north shore of Caples Lake, about 102 miles east of Stockton and 3 miles west of Carson Pass, turn north where a sign indicates the CalTrans Caples Lake Maintenance Station. Drive past the maintenance station, and after 0.4 mile, turn right (north) onto Forest Road 10N13 where a sign points to Schneider. The road turns to dirt at this point.

Follow this occasionally rough and dusty road for 1.7 miles to the upper end of a broad meadow and park. The road continues on beyond a stock gate, but it is a poor doubletrack.

This hike, traversing subalpine terrain for the entire distance, is by far the least-used trail in Dardanelles roadless area, save for the Showers Lake environs. Subalpine Showers Lake is often crowded, especially on summer weekends. Solitude-seeking backpackers might consider locating their campsites in the Upper Truckee River basin, in one of the westside bowls along the latter part of the hike, or setting up a dry camp on the Sierra crest.

From the east end of the large meadow known as Schneider Camp, the trail leads eastward and begins ascending volcanic slopes clothed in sagebrush and a variety of wildflowers. As you near the top of your climb, you pass a few stunted whitebark pines, and after hiking 1.1 miles from the trailhead, you reach your high point of 9,200 feet atop the alpine Sierra Nevada crest. The views are excellent.

Just after reaching this high point, you pass by an eastbound trail descending Dixon Canyon and proceed north along the wildflower-clad east slopes of the Sierra Nevada crest. Quite soon, Round Lake and the Four Lakes come into view in the Upper Truckee River basin; beyond, Lake Tahoe begins to dominate your northward view.

The contouring trail soon begins a descent toward Showers Lake, which is visible in a shallow basin to the north. After entering subalpine forest, your steep, gravelly route joins the Pacific Crest Trail (PCT) just before reaching Showers Lake. You turn left and soon begin skirting the numerous east-shore campsites set amid mountain hemlock, red fir, lodgepole, and western white pine. On any given summer weekend, unoccupied campsites around this lake may be hard to find.

You soon pass a sign pointing to Echo Summit and then descend northward to cross the dam-regulated outlet creek below Showers Lake before doubling back up that creek and curving west into a willow-cloaked meadow. You soon pass another sign pointing to Echo Summit, then begin traversing a timberline bowl flanked by volcanic mudflow boulders on the left and glacially re-exposed granite on the right. Upon leaving this bowl, you pass into a drier forest of mountain hemlock and lodgepole pine and then through one of the many stock gates (which you should be sure to close) encountered along the hike.

You soon meet the homebound segment of your loop on the wildflower-speckled Sierra crest, about 1.75 miles from Showers Lake. Turn left here and head south toward Schneider Camp. You'll pass drift-bent lodgepole pine and shelter-giving stands of mountain hemlock before you encounter a sign bolted high on a lodgepole pine informing northbound motorcyclists (rarely seen on this trail) that the terrain north of the sign is closed to motorized recreation.

Your southbound course leads through two timberline bowls west of the Sierra crest. Occasional views—northward into the Desolation Wilderness country, westward across the conifer-clad western slope of the Sierra, and southward to the volcanic divide separating the American and Mokelumne Rivers—help pass the time during your southbound trek.

You eventually break into the open as you begin an eastward traverse and are treated to superb views of the Carson Pass region, Elephants Back, impressive Round Top, and Caples Lake. Descending amid thickening forest, you soon amble out onto a doubletrack, turn left, and hike 0.5 mile back to the trailhead.

Freel Roadless Area

(See map on page 161)

Location: 3 miles southeast of South Lake Tahoe.
Size: 15,600 acres.
Administration: USDAFS–Lake Tahoe Basin Management Unit.
Management status: Roadless nonwilderness, managed for nonmotorized recreation.
Ecosystems: Sierran Forest–Alpine Meadows province, Sierra Nevada section,
characterized by high to moderately high, steep-sided mountains, narrow canyons, glacial
cirques and moraines; Mesozoic granitic rocks; potential natural vegetation is upper montane-
subalpine forests, Sierran montane forest, nothern Jeffrey pine forest, and alpine communities;
dendritic drainage pattern with perennial streams, and numerous wet meadows.
Elevation range: 6,500 feet to 10,881 feet.
System trails: 28 miles.
Maximum core-to-perimeter distance: 2.25 miles.
Activities: Day hiking, backpacking, mountain biking.
Maps: Lake Tahoe Basin Management Unit visitor map; see Appendix D for a list of USGS
1:24,000 quads.

OVERVIEW: The Lake Tahoe region, California's recreational Mecca, is well en-
dowed with wild country that provides ample opportunities for self-propelled
travel beyond the roads, resorts, and other developments that surround the
lake. One such wildland, the Freel roadless area, lies along the spine of the
rugged Carson Range immediately southeast of the city of South Lake Tahoe.
Freel embraces the northwest slopes of the Carson Range in the Tahoe Basin,
and its boundary stretches along the Carson crest from Luther Pass nearly to
the Nevada state line.

The Freel Peak massif, rising to 10,881 feet, is the centerpiece of this
roadless area and also bears the distinction of being the highest point in the
Lake Tahoe basin and in the Carson Range. The Carson Range lies in some-
what of a rain shadow east of the Sierra Nevada crest, so it supported only
small mountain glaciers that carved out a trio of minor cirques: Hell Hole,
upper Cold Creek basin, and Star Lake basin. Star Lake is one of the major
attractions of the Freel area. Resting at 9,100 feet, this 7-acre lake is the
highest-elevation lake in the Tahoe Basin. Northeast of Freel Peak rises
10,823-foot Jobs Sister, and to the southwest on the Carson crest is the
notch of 8,700-foot Armstrong Pass. Perched on a high bench in the south-

Freel Meadows in the Freel roadless area.

western corner of the wild area are the subalpine grasslands of Freel Meadows, lying at 9,200 feet at the head of Saxon Creek.

The western portion and lower elevations of the Freel area support a mixed conifer forest of Jeffrey pine, red fir, white fir, and western white pine. Higher elevations and the eastern part of the area are dominated by lodgepole pine and mixed subalpine forest, including mountain hemlock on sheltered, generally north-facing slopes. The highest peaks support extensive mats of krummholz whitebark pine. Freel Peak, Jobs Sister, and nearby Jobs Peak, outside the Freel area on the Toiyabe National Forest, are among the few peaks in the Tahoe Basin with a definite timberline. Small groves of aspen are scattered in favorable sites throughout the area. Freel Peak supports one of the few areas of alpine cushion plants this far north in the Sierra Nevada.

Surface water is not abundant, owing to the deep soils of decomposed granite. Where water is present, it flows year-round. Saxon Creek, Trout Creek, and Cold Creek are the principal drainages. Freel Meadows and the boggy meadows of Hell Hole are watered by perennial springs.

Much of the Freel area within the roadless area boundary is undisturbed, and access was very limited until construction began on the Tahoe Rim Trail in 1984. Although this is the least visited backcountry area on the California side of Tahoe Basin, there are numerous attractions. High, rocky alpine peaks, extensive forests, and rich meadows are among its features. Panoramic vistas from the Carson crest are found, particularly from Freel Peak.

The only notable intrusions into the natural integrity of the Freel area are a small electronic site atop Freel Peak, which is slated for removal, an inactive mining claim on Saxon Creek, and a small earth dam at Star Lake. Grazing permittees also run cows in part of the Freel in summer. Visitors that are uncomfortable with cattle in the backcountry should voice their concerns directly to the USFS, and *not* take action on their own against the cattle or their owners—always respect private property. Since the Tahoe Rim Trail concentrates use along its course, opportunities for solitude are classified as moderate. Although less than 800 acres of this wild area lie within 0.25 mile of a road, the average core-to-perimeter distance is short. From the backcountry, travelers do have occasional views of urban areas in the Tahoe Basin, and airline traffic from the Lake Tahoe Airport can be occasionally seen and heard. Yet the vertical relief of the area provides a sense of solitude.

RECREATIONAL USES: The Tahoe Rim Trail is the primary travel route through the Freel roadless area, and it is shared by hikers, horseback-riders, and mountain bikers. In fact, mountain bikers make up the majority of backcountry users, and the Freel area is one of the best places for mountain biking in California. The Tahoe Rim Trail traverses the entire area for 22.5 miles between Luther Pass in the southwest and Kingsbury Grade (Nevada Highway 19) in the northeast. The trail is heavily used throughout by thousands of mountain bikers each summer, many of whom ride the distance between the two highways in one day.

Star Lake is the primary attraction for hikers, and foot access to the lake is from the Tahoe Rim Trail in the northeast, from a trailhead that accesses Armstrong Pass from Willow Road, an unsigned, rough road east of Luther Pass on the southeast side of the Carson Range in the Toiyabe National Forest. Another primary destination is Freel Peak, which is best climbed from Armstrong Pass, via a challenging boot-worn trail. Fountain Place, in Trout Creek canyon, is on private property. FR 12N01 leads to this private property, and near the posted boundary, a trail skirts the private property, leading southwest into the deep cirque of Hell Hole. Travelers must also be aware of another parcel of private land, northwest of Star Lake. The road that heads northwest from the lake leads, in about 0.5 mile, onto the Trimmer Ranch property, the largest private inholding in the Lake Tahoe basin. Respect private property and do not trespass.

There is some winter use of the Freel backcountry, though the landscape is not ideally suited for backcountry skiing. Snowshoeing on the Tahoe Rim Trail from Luther Pass is the best way to tour the backcountry in winter.

Day Hike or Overnighter

Freel Meadows

Distance: 7.6 miles, semi-loop.
Low/high elevations: 7,716 feet/9,280 feet.
Difficulty: Moderate.
Best season: July through September.
Topo maps: Freel Peak-CA.
Permits: California Campfire Permit required for use of open fires and backpack stoves.

HOW TO GET THERE: The trailhead lies on the north side of California Highway 89 near the west end of a very large meadow and Grass Lake, about 1.75 miles northwest of Luther Pass and about 6.6 miles southeast of the junction of CA 89 and westbound CA 50. Park in the turnout on the south side of the highway at the west end of the above-mentioned meadow. Then walk east along the highway for about 100 yards and turn onto the signed, westbound Tahoe Rim Trail on the highway's north side.

Utilizing a segment of the 150-mile-long Tahoe Rim Trail, this Carson Range hike leads to two lovely meadows, once seldom visited and then only by hikers. Returning on the old Tucker Flat Trail offers an alternative to hikers not wishing to retrace the entire route.

The trail begins by following blazed trees west as it parallels the highway before bending north in a forest of Jeffrey pine and red and white fir. You soon cross a small, alder-lined creek; notice the Tucker Flat Trail branching right and ascending along the course of that creek. It forms the homebound segment of this hike.

Continue along the Tahoe Rim Trail and eventually cross a larger stream before following switchbacks up toward Peak 8997 in a pleasant pine and fir forest. When the trail levels off, cross a small creek hidden under large granitic boulders below an aspen-covered meadow. Soon thereafter your route bends into another gully and crosses its small creek amid aspen, lodgepole pine, and red fir.

After hiking 1.8 miles from the trailhead, you top a boulder-strewn ridge amid western white pine and red fir, and briefly glimpse Lake Tahoe in the northwest and snowy Sierra Nevada summits in the southeast.

The trail then leads generally east while climbing up and around Peak 9078, almost touching its rocky summit. Occasional openings in the forest reveal the Crystal Range and other Desolation Wilderness peaks in the northwest.

East of Peak 9078, the trail descends to Tucker Flat saddle at 8,800 feet. The old Tucker Flat Trail crosses the Tahoe Rim Trail at this point, branching right and descending back to CA 89—your return route—then branching left and descending into Tucker Flat.

You, however, work your way east along the wide forested ridge, and after hiking 0.75 mile from Tucker Flat saddle, you begin traversing above west (or lower) Freel Meadow. This small but beautiful spread is dotted with boulders and brightened by a variety of wildflowers. Its margins are forested with lodgepole and whitebark pine and a few mountain hemlocks. The small creek flowing through the southern edge of the meadow, the headwaters of Saxon Creek, carries a reliable flow of water.

Proceeding east, your trail passes over a low divide and skirts the northern margin of east (or upper) Freel Meadow. The trail traverses above the meadow and provides good views as far south as Stanislaus Peak.

Eventually, retrace the route back to Tucker Flat saddle, turn left, and begin a steep southbound descent. Your route follows the main creek downstream; you cross it twice, then angle through a meadow-floored flat where the trail becomes muddy at times. Aspen soon joins the pine and fir forest as you begin descending along the course of a small creek, which quickly leads you back to the Tahoe Rim Trail; turn left and backtrack to the trailhead.

Granite Chief Wilderness   23

Location: 6 miles west of Tahoe City, and 10 miles south-southwest of Truckee.
Size: 26,850 acres.
Administration: USDAFS–Tahoe National Forest and Lake Tahoe Basin Management Unit.
Management status: National Forest Wilderness (25,680 acres); the remainder roadless nonwilderness (1,170 acres), in two separate units, allocated to Further Planning status.
Ecosystems: Sierran Forest–Alpine Meadows province, Sierra Nevada section, characterized by moderately high peaks, steep mountain slopes, cirques, and deep stream valleys; Miocene and Pliocene volcanics, and small areas of Mesozoic granitic rocks; potential natural vegetation is Sierran montane forest, upper montane-subalpine forests, and alpine communities; numerous perennial streams with a complex drainage pattern, and few high-elevation lakes.
Elevation range: 4,800 feet to 9,006 feet.
System trails: 32 miles.
Maximum core-to-perimeter distance: 3 miles.
Activities: Backpacking, day hiking, horseback riding, cross-country skiing, snowshoeing, fishing.
Maps: Tahoe National Forest visitor map; see Appendix D for a list of USGS 1:24,000 quads.

OVERVIEW: The Desolation Wilderness west of Lake Tahoe is the Sierra Nevada's final expression of granitic, glacier-carved alpine grandeur. Farther north, the Sierra crest becomes dominated by volcanic rocks, elevations are lower, and conifer forests cover all but the highest prominences. Just before the Sierra crest dives down to Donner Pass and becomes ill-defined to the north of Interstate 80, there lies one last stretch of wild country, crowned by a series of 8,000-foot peaks, in a landscape that has been isolated from development by its sheer ruggedness and inaccessibility. This wildland is protected as the Granite Chief Wilderness, an area named for its only peak exceeding 9,000 feet.

The Granite Chief Wilderness boundary follows the Sierra crest from near Barker Pass in the south to 9,006-foot Granite Chief in the north, then turns northwest along the Forest Hill Divide, stretching past 8,971-foot Needle Peak and 8,891-foot Lyon Peak. Only the two small roadless areas immediately east of the crest lie within the Lake Tahoe Basin; all other drainages in the Granite Chief flow west. The Middle Fork of the American River and Five Lakes Creek, a tributary to the Rubicon River, are the principal drainages in the

23   GRANITE CHIEF WILDERNESS

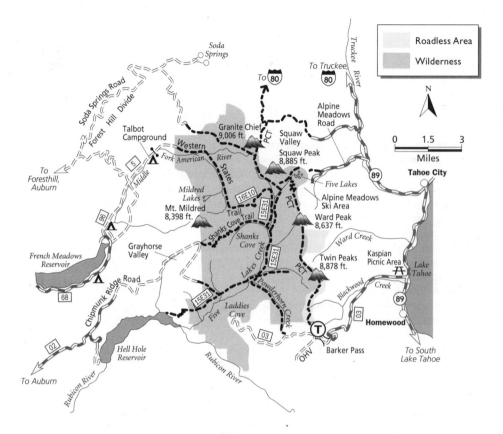

wilderness. The Granite Chief was extensively glaciated and displays typical glacial features such as cirques and U-shaped valleys, but contains few lakes. The granitic core of the Sierra in the Granite Chief is buried beneath deep andesite lava flows and mudflow deposits. Lakes were formed in the few areas where glaciers removed these soft volcanic rocks and exposed resistant granitic bedrock. These include the Five Lakes near the Sierra crest, Little Needle Lake at the head of the Middle Fork American River, and the Mildred Lakes high on the flanks of Mildred Ridge above Picayune Valley.

The Granite Chief is dominated by soils derived from volcanic mudflow material. These soils are generally deep and nutrient rich, with moderate water-holding capacity. Consequently, the slopes of the high, rounded ridges that separate the two principal drainages support a mosaic of rich vegetation, ranging from discontinuous conifer forest to montane chaparral, fields of mule ears, and slopes mantled in rich displays of wildflowers and grasses.

Whitebark pine—the quintessential timberline conifer of the Sierra—grows on the highest peaks and ridges. Several large meadows interrupt the expanse of forest in the Granite Chief, most notably along Five Lakes Creek, at Diamond Crossing, and in Picayune Valley. A well-developed riparian zone hugs the banks of many of the Granite Chief's stream courses, including black cottonwood, thin-leaf alder, and aspen.

The roadless areas adjacent to the Granite Chief include a 600-acre northern unit and a 570-acre southern unit. The north unit lies immediately south of Ward Peak and the Alpine Meadows ski area and may be developed for alpine skiing. The south unit lies immediately east of the Sierra crest between Barker Peak and Twin Peaks and is recommended to remain undeveloped in the current forest plan. The Pacific Crest Trail north of Barker Pass traverses this roadless area at the head of Blackwood Creek.

Typical of much of the Sierra, the Granite Chief provides habitat for black bear, mountain lion, and upland birds such as Sierra blue grouse and mountain quail. Mule deer depend on the Granite Chief for summer range and fawning areas that include the entire northwest corner of the wilderness within the French Meadows State Game Refuge, and the area along Five Lakes Creek from the junction of the Shanks Cove and Five Lakes Trails, which is one mile north past Big Spring. In both fawning areas, wilderness visitors are prohibited from entering with dogs between May 17 and July 15. Viable fisheries in the Granite Chief include Whiskey, Picayune, Bear Pen, and Five Lakes Creeks, which contain rainbow, brook, and brown trout. The three largest of the Five Lakes are stocked with brook trout, but fishing is generally poor. All other wilderness lakes contain no fish.

RECREATIONAL USES: The Granite Chief provides outstanding opportunities for day hiking, backpacking, horsepacking, cross-country skiing, and snowshoeing, and with few exceptions, it also provides good opportunities for solitude, in contrast to the nearby Desolation Wilderness four miles to the southeast. Unlike many other California wilderness areas where group size is limited to 15 people, groups in the Granite Chief are limited to 12.

The Five Lakes basin, located on the eastern boundary of the wilderness between the Squaw Valley and Alpine Meadows ski areas is very heavily used by day-hikers throughout summer. An average of 80 hikers on weekend days and 40 hikers on weekdays follow the 2-mile trail from the Alpine Meadows Road trailhead to this attractive lake basin, making it the highest-use area in the wilderness.

The interior of the wilderness is lightly used by backpackers and horsepackers, and access can be gained from eight trailheads, including the aforementioned Five Lakes Trailhead. The Barker Pass Pacific Crest Trail (PCT)

Trailhead is used by an average of 5 to 6 hikers per day, most of whom are day-hikers following the PCT north for less than four miles to the wilderness boundary. The PCT follows the Sierra crest from Barker Pass north for 14 miles, exiting the wilderness immediately east of Granite Chief. The most frequent users of this trail are PCT through-hikers, who generally pass through the Granite Chief in July or August on their northbound trek. The Talbot Trailhead on the west side of the wilderness about 4 miles northeast of French Meadows Reservoir is the only wilderness trailhead featuring a developed campground. The Western States Trail (16E10) begins there, leading 4 miles to Picayune Valley, and thence another 4 miles over an 8,000-foot ridge to Whisky Creek and the Five Lakes Trail. An average of 4 to 8 hikers use this trailhead each day during summer to enter the Granite Chief. Less-used trailheads that require four-wheel-drive vehicles for access are the Grayhorse and Buckskin Trailheads, located northeast of Hell Hole Reservoir in Grayhorse Valley; in turn, they provide access to the Shanks Cove and Steamboat Trails, respectively.

The Tevis Cup Trailhead on the northwest side of the Granite Chief also affords access for four-wheel-drive vehicles only to the Tevis Cup Trail—a high-elevation trail ascending to the spectacular headwaters of the Middle Fork American River and the PCT immediately south of the granite dome of Granite Chief. On the southwest side the Powderhorn Trailhead, located 2 miles west of Barker Pass, provides access to the steep, 3-mile Powderhorn Creek Trail leading to Diamond Crossing in Five Lakes Creek valley. Finally, the huge Squaw Valley Ski Area parking lot is the Granite Chief Trailhead, which provides access to the PCT, 1 mile north of the wilderness boundary, on a 2.5-mile trail.

The most popular destinations in the wilderness are all in the Five Lakes Creek drainage: Whisky Creek, Big Springs, and Diamond Crossing. There are many other fine destinations in the Granite Chief along the major stream and trail corridors and at remote, trailless places such as Little Needle and Mildred Lakes, where backcountry travelers can enjoy excellent opportunities for solitude and some of the finest landscapes in the Northern Sierra.

Horseback riding amounts to only about 5 percent of total wilderness use, and most horsepackers use the wilderness during the autumn hunting season. Two commercial outfitters provide horsepacking trips into the Granite Chief, mostly to destinations along Five Lakes Creek and at Shanks Cove, and mostly during deer hunting season.

Winter use of the Granite Chief is almost exclusively confined to Five Lakes basin, which attracts many cross-country skiers and snowshoers, mostly because of its short distance from the plowed Alpine Meadows Ski Area Road. The Barker Pass Road on the southern edge of the wilderness is closed

Twin Peaks and the Sierra crest in the southern reaches of the Granite Chief.

by a locked gate just off of California Highway 89 at the Kaspian Picnic Area. But the road makes an excellent, though long and avalanche-prone, approach to the PCT trailhead at Barker Pass. The terrain between Barker Pass and Twin Peaks provides challenging ski mountaineering for advanced backcountry skiers.

Day Hike, Overnighter, or Ski/snowshoe Tour

Barker Pass to Twin Peaks

Distance: 9.2 miles, round trip.
Low/high elevations: 7,600 feet/8,840 feet.
Difficulty: Moderately strenuous.
Best seasons: July through September for hiking; January through March for skiing and snowshoeing.
Topo map: Homewood-CA.
Permits: California Campfire Permit required for open fires and backpack stoves.

HOW TO GET THERE: From CA 89 on the west shore of Lake Tahoe, 4.2 miles south of Tahoe City, and 0.8 mile north of Tahoe Pines, turn west onto Forest Road 03, the Barker Pass Road, signed for KASPIAN PICNIC GROUND and BLACKWOOD CANYON. A gate is locked immediately west of this junction from late autumn through May. Skiers and snowshoers must begin their trip there.

Follow this paved, narrow, winding, and steep road for 6.9 miles to the end of the pavement immediately west of the Sierra crest. The wide, red cinder road then descends for 0.5 mile to the turnoff to the prominently signed Barker Pass PCT Trailhead. Turn right and drive about 75 yards to the turnaround at the road's end. At the trailhead you will find an information signboard with a map of the Granite Chief Wilderness, two picnic tables, a pit toilet, and car camping areas.

This view-packed trip follows a segment of the Pacific Crest Trail along the crest of the northern Sierra and features grand vistas of Lake Tahoe, the Granite Chief Wilderness, and the ice-scoured landscape of the Desolation Wilderness. Winter travelers will begin their trip at the Kaspian Picnic Area just off CA 89 and ski or snowshoe 7.4 miles up the Blackwood Canyon Road to the Barker Pass PCT Trailhead. Avalanches commonly occur in the upper reaches of the Blackwood Creek drainage near Barker Pass, and it is advisable to obtain reports on snow conditions from Forest Service offices in South Lake Tahoe or Truckee before setting out. Early winter generally provides more stable snow conditions, but snowpack may be light. Climbing skins are recommended for skiers, since this trip traverses steep terrain.

With the fluted volcanic cliffs of Peak 8,614 rising to the south and long views down the ice-scoured granite landscape of the Rubicon River to the west, 7,700-foot Barker Pass is a spectacular trailhead. It gets even better as you head northwest along the PCT, if you avoid a northbound doubletrack that also begins at the trailhead. The trail traverses the slopes of 8,166-foot Barker Peak through red and white fir and western white pine forest and openings mantled in summer by mules ears, larkspur, pennyroyal, paintbrush, and many other colorful blooms. Expansive vistas stretch southwest across the domed landscape of the upper Rubicon River valley, and high peaks of the Crystal Range in Desolation Wilderness begin to appear farther southwest. After 0.8 mile the PCT is crossed by an old logging road along the eastern edge of selectively cut forest, and soon thereafter you reach a saddle on the Sierra crest at 8,050 feet. A short detour to the east of the trail reveals a splendid view of Lake Tahoe and the Carson Range to the east. You'll see the rubbly summits of Twin Peaks on the northeast skyline.

Cross-country skiers and snowshoers should consider following the crest from this point to Twin Peaks, thus avoiding the avalanche-prone east-facing cirques that the trail traverses ahead. The crest route undulates over two broad, 8,600-foot summits, then becomes quite challenging as it turns northeast toward Twin Peaks—it becomes very narrow and is punctuated by low, blocky towers. Consider a route on the west side of the towers in winter.

In summer, hikers will continue ahead on the PCT, pass through a shady red fir and mountain hemlock forest, pass a corn lily–studded clearing at the head of a Blackwood Canyon tributary, and after 1.4 miles, crest a narrow saddle on a spur ridge east of Peak 8,620. From here the PCT descends 250 feet via switchbacks on a northbound course into the headwaters bowl of the North Fork Blackwood Creek. This bowl, and those up ahead, with their shady canopy of red fir and mountain hemlock, harbors snowfields that linger into July and, following wet winters, persist into August. From the North Fork bowl, your last reliable water source in summer, the PCT continues descending, losing another 400 feet and avoiding the rocky buttresses and talus slopes that define the southeast face of the crest. Then, after 3 miles, switchbacks lead you on a 600-foot ascent in 1 mile to the Granite Chief Wilderness boundary, beyond which the trail continues ascending, gaining another 200 feet in 0.2 mile to regain the Sierra crest at 8,400 feet, on the south slopes of Twin Peaks. This gentle part of the crest, protected by a dense stand of timberline conifers, offers a good winter campsite.

From here, the PCT begins a traverse along the west slopes of Twin Peaks. Leave the trail on the crest and angle up toward the north, but stay to the left (west) of the talus slope and ascend through the timberline forest of red fir, western hemlock, and western white and whitebark pine. You will soon break out of the forest onto an open slope, verdant with summer greenery, then angle right (northeast) and scramble the remaining short distance via metavolcanic rock slabs to the square-edged summit of west Twin Peak, at an elevation of about 8,840 feet. It's 0.4 mile and 450 feet above the PCT, and its conical neighbor immediately to the east is several feet higher but more difficult to scale. Skiers will enjoy the exhilarating descent from the peak back to the PCT upon returning. Vistas from the summit area are panoramic and far-ranging, encompassing a vast sweep of the northern Sierra.

Bucks Lake Wilderness Complex   24

Location: 9 miles west of Quincy and 35 miles northeast of Chico.
Size: 37,000 acres.
Administration: USDAFS–Plumas National Forest.
Management status: National forest wilderness (21,000 acres); the remainder mostly roadless nonwilderness allocated for potential timber harvest in the Forest Plan.
Ecosystems: Sierran Forest–Alpine Meadows province, Sierra Nevada section, characterized by a north/northwest-aligned mountain crest, steep and glacially scoured on the east and gently sloping on the west; Mesozoic granitic rocks, Paleozoic marine sedimentary and metamorphosed volcanic rocks, Pliocene volcanic mudflow deposits, and glacial deposits; potential natural vegetation is Sierran montane forest, upper montane-subalpine forests; dendritic drainage pattern with many perennial streams, springs, and small, wet meadows, and several moderately high glacial lakes.
Elevation range: 2,160 feet to 7,120 feet.
System trails: 40.4 miles.
Maximum core-to-perimeter distance: 3.5 miles.
Activities: Hiking, backpacking, horseback riding, cross-country skiing, and snowshoeing.
Maps: Plumas National Forest visitor map; Bucks Lake Wilderness visitor map (topographic; 2 inches/mile); see Appendix D for a list of USGS 1:24,000 quads.

OVERVIEW: The Bucks Lake Wilderness is the northernmost wildland in the Sierra Nevada, and despite its moderate elevations and northerly latitude, it represents classic Sierra landscapes. In fact, Bucks Lake country contains the final, northernmost extension of the Sierra crest. At the north end of the wilderness, the crest is severed by the deep canyon of the North Fork Feather River, and from there to Lake Almanor it is no longer distinct.

The northwest-southeast trend of the crest in the Bucks Lake Wilderness separates two distinctly different landscapes. The crest itself is gentle, gradually sloping to the west, representing the ancient erosional surface of the land before it was uplifted. Several hills crown this divide, with Mount Pleasant rising to 7,120 feet, the highest point in the wilderness. Most of the Bucks Lake is dominated by granitic rocks, and the northeastern slopes of the crest were gouged and polished by mountain glaciers, which left behind large expanses of bare rock and several small lakes. The largest cirque, Silver Lake, is a broad, mile-wide, ice-sculpted bowl spread out below Spanish Peak on the Sierra crest. The long arms of two large mile-long moraines extend from the Silver

24   BUCKS LAKE WILDERNESS COMPLEX

Lake and nearby Gold Lake cirques, embracing the drainage of Jacks Meadow Creek below Spanish Peak. Thirteen lakes, only four accessible by trails, lie below the crest on this ice-gouged side of the range. Three Lakes and Grassy Lakes lie immediately south of the crest and west of Mount Pleasant.

White fir, and sugar and Jeffrey pine form discontinuous stands on the northeastern slopes, with lodgepole pine growing in low-lying areas near lakes and wet meadows. The crest supports almost pure stands of red fir, some of the most extensive in the Sierra. A proposed 1,300-acre Research Natural Area in the red fir forest surrounding Mount Pleasant reflects the pristine nature of these forests. The west slope, in marked contrast to northeastern slopes, is a gently sloping surface with broad, rounded ridges separated by numerous shallow drainages that contribute to the large reservoir of Bucks Lake just outside the wilderness boundary. Wet meadows rich with corn lilies, aspen groves, alder-lined streams, and fields of montane chaparral interrupt the mixed conifer forest on these slopes.

In the northern reaches of the wilderness, the crest bends to the west and forms the rim of the North Fork Feather River canyon, and the wilderness includes the 6-mile-wide canyon wall, from the crest nearly to the river. With more than 4,000 feet of relief in two lateral miles, a variety of ecosystems are represented on these slopes, ranging from the red fir and western white pine forests of the crest to stands of Douglas-fir, incense-cedar, ponderosa pine, black oak, California laurel, and live oak on the slopes near the river. Moist streamsides support big-leaf maple and dogwood and an understory of bracken fern and thimbleberry.

Three separate units of roadless land lie adjacent to the wilderness: one block stretches along the north wall of the North Fork Feather River canyon northeast of the wilderness; and the other two units lie north and northwest of Bucks Lake on the west slopes. These two are separated by a four-wheel-drive road corridor leading to Camp Rogers Saddle and Three Lakes. The central unit rises immediately north of Bucks Lake, and includes a high ridge capped by 7,183-foot Bald Eagle Mountain, and 6,819-foot Bucks Mountain.

The westernmost roadless unit includes the high rim and the southeast wall of the North Fork Feather River canyon and lower Bucks Creek, a productive trout fishery. Although these roadless lands have minimal recreational value, they are important to preserving the integrity of the ecosystems in this northernmost extension of the Sierra crest.

In addition to black-tailed and mule deer, black bear, coyote, and mountain lion, there are certain species in the Bucks Lake area that are dependent upon the old-growth forests remaining in both the wilderness and adjacent roadless areas. These include the endangered bald eagle and peregrine falcon, and the sensitive goshawk, great gray owl, spotted owl, fisher, marten, Sierra Nevada red fox, and willow flycatcher.

RECREATIONAL USES: The Bucks Lake Wilderness has an excellent network of trails and, with the exception of the trails in the southeast part of the wilderness, most are very lightly used. Six trailheads provide access to the trail system: three near the boater's Mecca of Bucks Lake; two Pacific Crest Trail trailheads (one on the south at Bucks Summit, the other on the north at Belden on the North Fork Feather River), and one at Silver Lake on the northeast slope.

The Silver Lake area is very popular with anglers, picnickers, and campers, particularly on summer weekends. Proximity to the town of Quincy, and its spectacular scenery and good fishing make the Silver Lake area a justifiably popular destination. Day hikers from Silver Lake flock to Gold Lake and, to a lesser extent, to Rock Lake and Mud Lake, all less than two miles from the Silver Lake Trailhead. In late summer when their waters have warmed, swimming

Gold Lake is one of few lakes in the Bucks Lake Wilderness.

and diving are popular activities at these cirque lakes. More hardy souls hike the rigorous trail to Spanish Peak, the former site of a fire lookout tower with far-ranging vistas. Hikers who enjoy the challenge of off-trail walking and the promise of solitude amid dramatic landscapes will enjoy cross-country routes to three lonely lake basins northwest of Silver Lake in the headwaters of the Mill Creek drainage. (There are two Mill Creeks in the Bucks Lake Wilderness: one drains south into Bucks Lake, and the other drains north into the North Fork Feather River.)

Pacific Crest Trail (PCT) through-hikers bound for Oregon and points north are the most frequent users of the 18.25-mile segment of PCT that traverses the wilderness from south to northwest. Except for the steep ascent from Bucks Summit to Spanish Peak and the abrupt descent from the crest to the North Fork Feather River, the trail maintains gentle grades. Most PCT travelers don't linger very long in the Bucks Lake country, since they are usually anxious to reach the traditional resupply point at Belden in the North Fork canyon.

The PCT can be combined with the Right Hand Branch Mill Creek Trail and the Mill Creek Trail, beginning at one of the three Bucks Lake trailheads, for a rewarding 18.2-mile loop surveying the forested west slope and the red fir forests along the crest. Miles of excellent ski-touring and snowshoeing terrain exist upon the gentle crest. Shady forests, miles of moderately high elevations, and an average snowpack of 10 to 12 feet make the area ideally suited to winter backcountry recreation from December through May. And winter access is provided from two trailheads along the plowed Bucks Lake Road (Forest Road 414). Beginning at either the Bucks Summit Trailhead at 5,500 feet or the Bucks Creek Trailhead on the eastern arm of Bucks Lake at 5,200 feet, round trips and loops are possible. For longer day or overnight ski tours, experience in wilderness skiing is required, since the forest-covered terrain can be disorienting.

Day Hike

Spanish Peak

Distance: 7.5 miles, round trip.
Low/high elevations: 5,800 feet/7,017 feet.
Difficulty: Moderate.
Best season: July through September.
Topo map: Bucks Lake-CA.
Permits: California Campfire Permit required for open fires and backpack stoves.

HOW TO GET THERE: From California Highway 70/89 in Quincy, turn west onto the two-lane pavement of FR 119, prominently signed for Meadow Valley and Bucks Lake. After 8.5 miles, turn right (northwest) onto FR 24N29X, signed for Silver Lake. This is a rough gravel road with frequent washboards; it is narrow and winding, steep in places, and quite rocky over the final 3 miles.

Follow this road for 6 miles, then turn left into Silver Lake Campground. The confined trailhead parking area is located at the road's end, on the northeast shore of Silver Lake next to the dam. If the parking area is full, as it often is on summer weekends, park at the campground entrance and walk 0.4 mile to the trailhead.

This trip to Spanish Peak is one of the more well-used trails in the Bucks Lake Wilderness, but to compensate for lack of complete solitude, the trail traverses the most scenic, and largest, lake basin in the wilderness. The reward for the stiff climb to Spanish Peak is unparalleled vistas of the Northern Sierra and the southern Cascade Range.

From the road's end at Silver Lake, the trail begins by following along the Silver Lake dam, where you enjoy excellent views into the ice-sculpted cirque above. Soon after you leave the dam, the signed Gold Lake Trail branches left away from the shoreline fishing access trail. Quickly thereafter you reach the boundary of the Bucks Lake Wilderness and a trail register.

From here you begin ascending steeply up the rocky moraine, where only a few white firs and Jeffrey pines cast scant shade among the fields of manzanita and huckleberry oak. After two short but steep pitches you crest the huge moraine, where far-flung vistas reach northwest past Silver Lake to distant Lassen Peak, east to sprawling American Valley, and southeast past Spanish Peak to the bold crags of Sierra Buttes.

Then you begin a gentle traverse across the south slopes of the brushy moraine, studded with widely scattered white fir, and Jeffrey and sugar pine. After 1.0 mile, just after leaving the moraine and bending south, you reach a junction indicated by a trailside post. The Gold Lake Trail continues south for 0.5 mile to Gold Lake, but you want to bear right onto the Granite Gap Trail. This trail ascends steeply over ice-gouged granite, then traverses to a minor saddle shaded by lodgepole pines. A faint northbound path leads 150 yards to the rock- and tree-lined tarn of Mud Lake. Your trail ascends steeply beyond the junction and, just before reaching a higher saddle in a brushy moraine, you meet the unsigned trail to Rock Lake branching left (south). The fir-fringed Sierra crest now lies only 500 feet above you and a band of ice-polished granite.

The Granite Gap Trail turns rocky and begins ascending very steeply through a jumble of huge boulders, above which the tread grows more obscure. When the boulders are behind you, the still-steep trail ascends southwest up a shallow draw, where snow is likely to linger well into July. At the head of the draw you meet the PCT after 1.9 miles and turn left. The trail ahead is pleasantly undulating, and breaks in the red fir forest allow views to Gold Lake's deep blue oval, below. Notice the distinct line of staghorn lichen on the reddish gray trunks of red firs alongside the trail; on each and every tree that line represents the average 10- to 12-foot snow depth here at 7,000 feet.

The trail reaches a small, wet meadow at 2.9 miles, where in early summer there is a profusion of buttercups. Here the signed Right Hand Branch Trail to Bucks Lake turns southwest, but its seldom-used tread is nearly invisible. A moderate ascent leads 0.25 mile from the meadow to a broad, open spur ridge projecting east from the crest. The PCT continues south across a long-closed doubletrack. You turn left onto the eastbound branch of the doubletrack, signed for Spanish Peak. The ridge contrasts with the shady red fir forests behind you; it hosts montane chaparral dominated by pinemat manzanita and huckleberry oak and is studded by only a scattering of red fir and western white pine. Follow the old road gently up to a dilapidated outhouse, from which a rocky trail leads to the open summit area of Spanish Peak at 7,017 feet, 3.75 miles from Silver Lake. Only the concrete foundation and a scattering of detritus remain of the old fire lookout tower that once stood here.

The vistas from this peak are tremendous, and few PCT through-hikers pass up the side-trip to enjoy them. Views stretch along the eastern escarpment of the crest past Lake Almanor to distant Lassen Peak, Brokeoff Cone, and Reading Peak in Lassen Volcanic National Park. On the eastern horizon, beyond Meadow Valley and Quincy, are the long rolling ridges rising at the headwaters of the Feather and Yuba Rivers. The peaks of the far Northern Sierra march into the southeastern distance, including Mount Elwell above Lakes Basin, and Sierra Buttes. The vast, gentle west slope of the Northern Sierra, incised by the cavernous defile of the Middle Fork Feather River, stretches away toward the invisible Sacramento Valley.

Ishi Wilderness Complex

25

Location: 20 miles east of Red Bluff.
Size: 61,127 acres.
Administration: USDAFS–Lassen National Forest.
Management status: Ishi Wilderness (41,100 acres); the remainder partially roaded nonwilderness (20,027 acres) in two separate units, allocated to Further Planning in the Forest Plan for possible addition to Ishi Wilderness.
Ecosystems: Sierran Forest–Alpine Meadows province, Sierra Nevada Foothills section, characterized by mountain foothills with a complex of long, nearly flat ridges and moderately deep and wide stream valleys with floodplains and terraces; Late Pliocene and Quaternary volcanic rocks and mudflow deposits; potential natural vegetation is blue oak–digger pine forest, with smaller areas of chaparral, and northern yellow pine forest; several perennial streams and springs.
Elevation range: 870 feet to 4,350 feet.
System trails: 30.2 miles.
Maximum core-to-perimeter distance: 5.75 miles.
Activities: Day hiking, backpacking, catch-and-release fishing.
Maps: Lassen National Forest visitor map; Ishi Wilderness visitor map; see Appendix D for a list of USGS 1:24,000 quads.

OVERVIEW: The Ishi Wilderness and surrounding roadless units represent the most unique wildland in California. The Ishi occupies the western foothills of the extreme southern extension of the Cascade Range and is the only wilderness that preserves a significant area of the Sierra/Cascade foothill ecosystem. The Ishi is essentially a gently westward-sloping plateau incised by several deep and wide stream valleys. Ledges, cliff bands, columns, and towers of volcanic rock interrupt the gentle nature of the landscape. The canyons display a modified stair-step profile of volcanic terraces and low cliff bands.

The Ishi contains numerous unique features, including extensive pineries, or groves, of Pacific ponderosa pine forest type, and unique geologic features, including the recommended Graham Pinery Research Natural Area and the proposed Black Rock Special Interest Area.

The "Ishi B" Further Planning Area is mostly roadless terrain that lies adjacent to the wilderness in two separate units to the north and south. The northern unit is the Antelope Creek Portion and contains landscapes similar to the wilderness, including the deep canyons of the North and South Forks of Antelope Creek. An

25   ISHI WILDERNESS COMPLEX

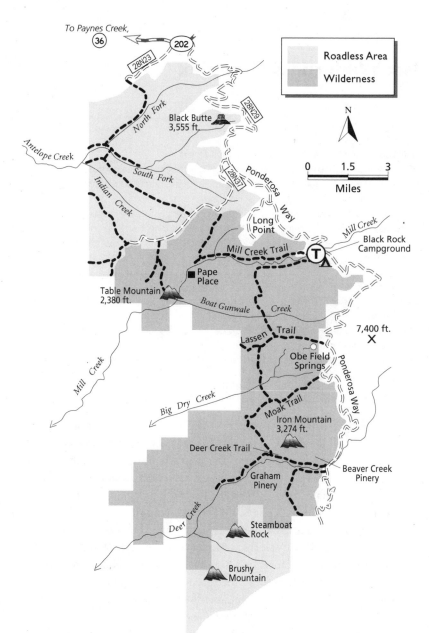

off-highway-vehicle (OHV) trail that follows the northern divide of Mill Creek separates the Antelope Creek Portion from the wilderness, and another OHV trail follows Indian Ridge to the south of Antelope Creek's south fork. The remainder of the unit is roadless, with the exception of two sections of private land. The Indian Creek recommended Research Natural Area is located in this unit, and contains a high-quality representative of the blue oak-digger pine forest type.

The southern unit of "Ishi B," the Brushy Mountain portion, contains a large amount of private land. Its natural integrity has been altered by roads, OHV use, cabins, and other developments, and access to this unit is restricted because of the private lands.

Deer Creek and Mill Creek are the principal drainages in the Ishi Wilderness, and both are large streams listed in the Nationwide Rivers Inventory for addition to the Wild and Scenic Rivers System. Mill Creek originates on the slopes of Lassen Peak in Lassen Volcanic National Park, some 30 miles from the Ishi Wilderness, and Deer Creek gathers its waters from the highlands west of Lake Almanor. These creeks and the forks of Antelope Creek support resident trout and an important anadromous fishery of spring and fall chinook salmon and steelhead migrations.

The highest elevations in the Ishi lie along the eastern boundary, where the low foothills begin to rise steadily to 4,000-foot ridges. Incense-cedar, black oak, ponderosa, sugar pine, and Douglas-fir forests dominate the sheltered aspects in the higher elevations, while greenleaf manzanita chaparral occupies sunny slopes. Mid-elevation slopes host digger pine and open woodlands consisting of blue, interior live, and black oak. A series of long and gentle, east-to-west ridges separates the drainages of Mill, Boat Gunwale, Big Dry, and Deer Creeks. Alder, big-leaf maple, California bay, poison oak, and the vines of California wild grape are found in the most sheltered recesses of the canyons. The dry ridges and lower slopes in the Ishi support grassy, oak-dotted slopes and pockets of chaparral.

Wildlife in the Ishi is as diverse as its landscapes. Black bear, mountain lion, coyote, wild turkey, California quail, wild hog, and bobcat find habitat here, and so do Golden eagles, prairie falcons, and red-tailed hawks. The Tehama black-tailed deer herd, California's largest migratory herd, uses the Ishi complex as a migratory route and winter range. The Brushy Mountain portion of "Ishi B" supports a wild horse herd of approximately 21 animals.

RECREATIONAL USES: Use of the Ishi Wilderness is generally low, and many visitors are attracted by the area's history. The people of the Southern Yana and Yahi Yana, who occupied the area between Paynes Creek and Deer Creek for over 3,000 years, were eventually exterminated by early settlers beginning in the 1840s. Ishi, the famous sole survivor of the Yahi Yana, hid from settlers for many years in this rugged canyon country, and finally left the homeland that now bears his name in 1911. There are numerous cultural sites here, including ambush and massacre sites.

Late autumn through spring is the typical season of use in the Ishi country, making it one of the few wild areas in California accessible for winter hiking. Although the area lies only about 20 miles from Sacramento Valley population centers, access is long, difficult, and restricted in many places by private property. The seven trailheads that provide access to the Ishi are all reached off Ponderosa Way (Forest Road 28N29). All wilderness trails are maintained on a cyclical, rotational basis, and many are subject to slumping and washouts in places. Critical repairs are made on an as-needed basis, if funding allows. On the northern wilderness boundary, on the rim above Mill Creek, the Peligreen Jeep Trail four-wheel-drive road affords access to Rancheria and Table Mountain/Black Oak Grove Trailheads. Part of the Rancheria Trail into Mill Creek is open to vehicular travel by owners of the Pape Place in lower Mill Creek, a private inholding within the wilderness.

The Mill Creek Trail on the north and Deer Creek Trail on the south are the most frequently used trails in the wilderness. Most wilderness visitors either take day hikes or overnight trips. Three other east-to-west trails traverse the Ishi. The Lassen Trail, Moak Trail, and Devils Den Trail are all lightly used ridgetop trails, with Lassen receiving the most use.

A north-to-south trail traversing the Ishi connects Mill Creek to Deer Creek. Beginning at Ponderosa Way on the south bank of Mill Creek just beyond Black Rock, this up-and-down route ascends dry ridges, dips into canyons, and follows portions of the Lassen and Moak trails en route to Deer Creek. Since the trail is very lightly used, it provides the greatest opportunity for solitude of any trail in the Ishi, and it surveys the area's spectrum of landscapes.

Fishing in the drainages of the Ishi complex is catch-and-release only, restricted to artificial lures with barbless hooks. Most backpackers use terraces adjacent to Mill and Deer Creeks for camping, leaving the upland ridges free of campsites and the impacts of overnight visitors. Anyone willing to pack water and camp on these ridgetops will enjoy considerable solitude. The creek-bottom campsites are still so infrequently used that there are few, if any, impacts from overuse. Rather, the impacts present come from misuse.

Since much of the Ishi lies within the boundaries of the Tehama State Wildlife Area, where hunting is not allowed, most of the use of forest roads around the boundaries of the wilderness is by visitors staying in the small, primitive Black Rock Campground, OHV users, and weekend motorized recreationists. Black Rock Campground, set in an oak woodland along the banks of Mill Creek, is an attractive base for day-hiking forays. Probably the only drawback to this no-fee campground is the abundance of poison oak on the slopes above it.

Day Hike or Overnighter

Mill Creek

Distance: 9 miles or more, round trip.
Low/high elevations: 1,700 feet/2,200 feet.
Difficulty: Easy.
Best seasons: March through May; late September through December.
Topo maps: Panther Spring-CA, Barkley Mountain-CA.
Permits: Wilderness permits are not required. A California Campfire Permit is required for open fires and backpack stoves.

HOW TO GET THERE: From California Highway 36, 23 miles east of Red Bluff and 48 miles west of Chester, turn south to the small hamlet of Paynes Creek, where a sign points the way to Tehama Wildlife Area and Ishi Conservation Camp. After 0.3 mile, turn right (south) at the Paynes Creek Store, drive through town, then ascend into the foothills. After 2.9 miles, pass the Tehama Wildlife Area headquarters, then the Ishi Conservation Camp at 3.0 miles. Avoid the southbound High Trestle Road 5.6 miles from CA 36, and also the Hogsback Road at 8.2 miles.

Turn right (southeast) onto Ponderosa Way (FR 28N29) after 8.7 miles. Signs here indicate mileage to Panther Springs and to Black Rock—your destination. Prepare for a long, slow drive to Black Rock because the road is winding, steep, narrow, and rough. Although a high-clearance vehicle isn't usually required, one is recommended. The road ahead ascends to 4,200 feet, and if it is snow-covered or wet, drive with caution.

The ford of North Fork Antelope Creek at 12.5 miles can be hazardous following heavy rains or during snowmelt runoff. Avoid the left (northeast) turn onto Upper Middle Ridge Road at 16.3 miles. Ponderosa Way passes South Antelope Campground at 18.2 miles, the Panther Springs Station at 19.9 miles, then ascends through the forest past the Peligreen Jeep Trail and the Long Point Road before descending toward Mill Creek.

At the bottom of the grade in Mill Creek canyon, 24.8 miles from CA 36, you meet an unsigned westbound road that leads into private property. You can find pullouts in which to park along the first 0.3 mile of this road, or you can continue ahead along Ponderosa Way. The entrance to Black Rock Campground is 0.3 mile ahead (east). Either park near the entrance or drive into the campground.

Mill Creek., the largest stream in the Ishi Wilderness.

The trailhead proper is located at the west end of Black Rock Campground, in the shadow of the haystack-shaped monolith of Black Rock. The trail begins behind the information signboard and ascends briefly up to the westbound spur road that leads to a small block of private property. Once you reach the road, follow it west, downhill, for 0.3 mile to a locked gate. There the trail begins, ascending north of the road to a gate and trail register.

The Mill Creek Trail then follows a fenceline, skirts private property for about 0.5 mile, and enters the Ishi Wilderness along the way. There are several boggy sections along the trail, watered year-round by upslope springs. The trail ahead follows well above large Mill Creek and passes through open oak woodlands.

The trail bends in and out of numerous shallow, south-trending draws, some of which carry water, and traverses open slopes and terraces en route down Mill Creek. Mill Creek averages 30 feet wide, even during periods of low flows in late autumn. Many deep holes lie between rapids and cascades.

The canyon opens up as you travel downstream, with a scattering of oaks to provide occasional shade. This is certainly not a trail to take during the hot summer months, when daytime high temperatures routinely exceed 100 degrees F. There's poison oak along the Mill Creek Trail, though it's not abundant. Watch for it along the banks of the many side streams you'll cross on the way down-canyon.

Don't expect to be following the creek closely. Although you will have occasional glimpses of the powerful stream and are seldom out of earshot, you must leave the trail in most instances to reach the creek or camping areas on terraces just above it. The basalt cliffs that rim Long Point rise far above the north side of the canyon, and numerous vigorous springs issue from their base. The Mill Creek canyon is lovely foothill country, featuring a variety of landscapes and environments, ranging from basalt pillars and cliffs to open, grassy, oak-studded slopes, and from park-like groves of ponderosa pine to a scattering of spreading digger pine stands.

There are many possible terrace-top campsites along the Mill Creek Trail, and there is no particular destination. Remember that the trail ends after 6.2 miles at the private property of the Pape Place. Probably the best place to end your tour of Mill Creek is at the confluence with Avery Creek at 4.3 miles, or Rancheria Creek at 4.9 miles.

Lassen Volcanic Wilderness Complex   26

Location: 45 miles west of Redding, and 10 miles north-northwest of Chester.
Size: 92,302 acres.
Administration: USDI–National Park Service; USDAFS–Lassen National Forest.
Management status: National Park wilderness (78,982 acres in two separate units, with the east unit immediately west of Caribou Wilderness); National Forest roadless Further Planning Areas (8,900-acre Heart Lake FPA, and 4,420-acre Wild Cattle Mountain FPA).
Ecosystems: Sierran Forest–Alpine Meadows province, Southern Cascades section, characterized by moderately steep to steep shield and composite volcanoes, plug domes, and cinder cones, surrounded by volcanic plateau; Pliocene and Pleistocene basalt and andesite lava flows and pyroclastic deposits, with smaller areas of rhyolite and dacite lava flows, andesitic mudflow deposits, and glacial deposits; potential natural vegetation is Sierra montane forest, upper montane-subalpine forests, yellow pine-shrub forest, and alpine communities; numerous moderately high lakes, perennial streams, and thermal areas.
Elevation range: 5,300 feet to 10,457 feet.
System trails: 145.2 miles.
Maximum core-to-perimeter distance: 7 miles.
Activities: Backpacking, day hiking, horseback riding, fishing, cross-country skiing, and snowshoeing.
Maps: Lassen National Forest visitor map; USGS 1:62,500 Lassen Volcanic National Park map; see Appendix D for a list of USGS 1:24,000 quads.

OVERVIEW: Lassen Volcanic Wilderness lies in two distinctly different units bisected by the paved Lassen Park Road. The eastern unit is the largest, with an average elevation of 6,500 feet, and its landscapes are very similar to the adjacent Caribou Wilderness to the east. This unit is a forested volcanic plateau studded with cinder cones, several young lava flows, and numerous lakes. Yet unlike the Caribou, there are several perennial streams which drain more than two dozen lakes. The northern reaches of the east unit drain into Hat Creek, a Pit River tributary. Streams in the southern reaches drain into Kings Creek, Hot Springs Creek, Warner Creek in Warner Valley, and finally into the North Fork Feather River.

The western unit contains the dacite plug domes of Chaos Crags in the north. Lassen, Eagle, and Ski Heil Peaks, along with Mount Diller and Brokeoff Mountain, form a ridge of impressive alpine peaks in the southwest corner. Lassen Peak's south slope and summit area lie outside the wilderness boundary.

Reading Peak, rising to 8,701 feet east of Lassen Peak, is the easternmost alpine summit in the wilderness, harboring more than a half dozen lakes and tarns beneath its glacier-carved north face. Although few lakes exist in the western unit of the wilderness, there are numerous alpine cirques—the forested valley of upper Manzanita Creek, and a beautiful trailless basin at the head of Blue Lake Canyon, west of Eagle Peak and Pilot Pinnacle.

Brokeoff Mountain, the high ridge between it and Lassen Peak, and Mount Conard in the south are all remnants of the former rim of Mount Tehama. Thought to have been 1,000 feet higher than present-day Lassen Peak, Mt. Tehama was a composite volcanic cone that existed hundreds of thousands of years ago but eventually collapsed. Glaciers have since modified this high landscape into the only alpine environment in the park, with timberline groves of mountain hemlock and whitebark pine and alpine cushion plants mantling the open slopes above 9,000 feet.

Although the last eruptions occurred between 1914 and 1917, altering the summit area and northeast slopes of Lassen Peak, geothermal activity continues today in the southern reaches of the park. Places like Boiling Springs Lake, Bumpass Hell, and Devils Kitchen contain fumaroles and hot springs similar to geothermal features in Yellowstone National Park.

With a diversity of vegetation and terrain, wildlife is abundant in the wilderness. More than 150 species of birds have been recorded here, including two endangered species, bald eagle and peregrine falcon. Large numbers of black-tailed deer use the wilderness for summer range. Also present are bobcat, black bear, wolverine, marten, and mountain lion. Fishing is a popular backcountry activity in many lakes, but fish stocking was discontinued in 1974 so that trout populations could return to their natural state.

Two Further Planning Areas, recommended in the Lassen National Forest Plan for wilderness designation, lie adjacent to Lassen Volcanic Wilderness. The largest is the Heart Lake area, immediately west of the southwest corner of the park. This area includes the Heart Lake basin north of the Rocky Peak divide, the South Fork Bailey Creek, and the North Fork in middle Blue Lake Canyon. South of Rocky Peak, this roadless area extends to Glassburner Meadows and Huckleberry Lake. The Heart Lake National Recreation Trail traverses the area through the southwest corner of Lassen Volcanic Wilderness. Wild Cattle Mountain Further Planning Area includes a portion of Mill Creek, which originates on the south side of Lassen Peak in Little Hot Springs Valley. Mill Creek, which flows through the Ishi Wilderness in the western Cascade foothills en route to the Sacramento River, is a candidate for Wild and Scenic River status. This creek is significant in that it is one of very few streams remaining in California to have its biological integrity still intact from its source to the Sacramento River and thence to the Pacific Ocean. The Wild Cattle

26   LASSEN VOLCANIC WILDERNESS COMPLEX

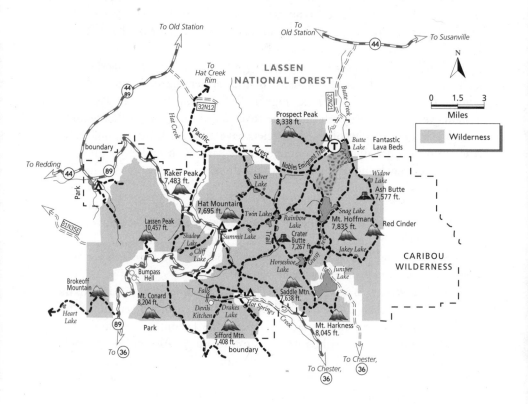

Mountain roadless area, ironically, does not include Wild Cattle Mountain, but it does include a southern extension of the Lassen volcanic plateau, numerous meadows, and several lakes, including Blue, Ridge, Duck, Patricia, and Elizabeth Lakes. Several trails, including Growler, Childs Meadows, and the North Arm Rice Creek Trails traverse the area and connect with other trails in Lassen Volcanic Wilderness.

RECREATIONAL USES: As the east and west units of Lassen Volcanic Wilderness are so different, so too are the recreational opportunities. The west unit offers few trails but features grand alpine landscapes. A good but steep trail ascends 2,600 feet in 3.7 miles from the park road near the southwest entrance to 9,235-foot Brokeoff Mountain, on the rim of the ancient Mount Tehama volcano. Another short but scenic trail rises from the Sulphur Works fumaroles to Ridge Lakes, which lie in a small cirque at 8,000 feet beneath 9,087-foot

Mount Diller. A dead-end trail leads 3.5 miles from the Manzanita Lake Campground in the northwest corner of the wilderness to the upper valley of Manzanita Creek, spreading out below the west slopes of Lassen Peak. Two other trails traverse the eastern slopes of Lassen Peak; one follows the East Fork Hat Creek to Shadow Lake, the largest lake in the west unit of the wilderness, and the other follows the West Fork. Both trails meet at Terrace Lake below Reading Peak. Off-trail hiking is possible from the park road to the crest of high peaks southwest of Lassen Peak. Blue Lake Canyon lies in a remote, trailless basin west of that high crest, and is managed as "trailless wilderness." It can be reached by crossing the high crest between Eagle Peak and Mount Diller or by entering from the west on Forest Road 31N35 in the Lassen National Forest.

The east unit of the wilderness is the largest and most diverse, and has the greatest concentration of trails. Many lakes are scattered across this landscape, as well as rich meadows, geothermal features, cinder cones, lava flows, and several perennial streams. Trails crisscross the area, beginning at four principal trailheads: Butte Lake in the northeast, Summit Lake in the west, and Warner Valley and Juniper Lake in the south. The area is well suited for day hiking, and trails can be combined to form a variety of loop trips for extended backpacking.

Although this part of the wilderness is mantled in forests of pine and fir, there are several high points, including Cinder Cone, Prospect Peak, and lookout-capped Mount Harkness, where trails lead to panoramic vistas. The Pacific Crest Trail (PCT) traverses the wilderness for 17.4 miles from north to south between Soap Lake and Little Willow Lake. Uncharacteristic of this usually high, open route, the PCT in Lassen Volcanic Wilderness follows the forested volcanic plateau and affords few vistas.

There are numerous meadows, peaks, lakes, thermal areas, and other sensitive places in the wilderness that are closed to camping. Many of these closed areas are open to camping in winter. A list of these areas can be obtained from the park at the locations listed below under *Permits*. Wilderness permits are required for all overnight use of the wilderness, year-round, and are also required for day use by stock parties. No overnight camping is allowed with pack and saddle stock. There are no trailhead quotas, and permits can be obtained in person, or by phoning or mailing in a request to park headquarters at least two weeks in advance of the trip. There are numerous regulations specific to Lassen that are listed on the permit, including the prohibition of campfires and the requirement to pack out used toilet paper.

Lassen receives copious amounts of snow during winter, and the park road is plowed from the southwest entrance to the Lassen Chalet parking lot at 6,700 feet. The park road is used for cross-country skiing and snowshoeing in winter between the chalet and Manzanita Lake. There are almost unlimited wintertime opportunities throughout the park for overnight trips and day trips, including ski touring and ski mountaineering. Wintertime campsites must be located at least one mile from any Park Service public use facility or plowed road.

Backpack

Butte Lake–Snag Lake Loop

Distance: 11.9 miles, loop trip (2 to 3 days).
Low/high elevations: 6,043 feet/6,400 feet.
Difficulty: Moderate.
Best season: July through early October.
Topo maps: Prospect Peak-CA, Mount Harkness-CA.
Permits: Wilderness permit required for overnight use. Permits can be obtained through the mail by phoning Park Headquarters (see Appendix B), or at the following locations: Loomis Museum, Park Headquarters, Southwest Information Station, Southwest Entrance Station, and Manzanita Lake Entrance Station (when Loomis Museum is closed), and at the Hat Creek Information Center (Lassen National Forest), located at the junction of California Highway 44/89 in Old Station.

HOW TO GET THERE: Follow CA 44 east from Redding for 73 miles or west from Susanville for 40.5 miles, and turn onto the southbound dirt road signed for Butte Lake, Forest Road 32N21. This road is wide but usually has a rough, washboard surface. As you drive south, avoid various right and left turns, all signed.

After 6.5 miles, you reach the self-pay station at the park boundary and the Butte Lake Campground entrance. Bear left at this junction and after 0.1 mile you will reach the large trailhead parking area above the north shore of Butte Lake.

This fine hike tours the eastern reaches of Lassen Volcanic Wilderness, passes through rich forests, visits two large lakes, and circumnavigates one of the youngest lava flows in the park. The gentle grade of the trail, ample campsites, and delightful scenery make this a fine weekend trip for any hiker. The final leg of the loop trip traces Nobles Emigrant Trail, a route that played an important role in the settlement of northern California.

From the parking area, ignore the northbound trail to Bathtub Lake (route of Nobles Trail) and head east, briefly following a service road, to the trail proper. Soon after passing a destination and mileage sign, you enter a park-like forest of pine and fir on a smooth tread of volcanic sand. Soon a moderate grade leads you up the slopes of Knob 6272 and then switchbacks lead down to an easy log crossing of Butte Creek at the north end of Butte Lake.

Thermal features, such as Boiling Springs Lake, often lie close to snow-clad peaks in Lassen Volcanic Wilderness.

Beyond the crossing, the trail hugs the lake's east shore where you may see rainbows leaping from its cold, clear waters. As you approach the south end of the lake, lodgepole pine and aspen join the forest of pine and fir, which accompanies you to a signed junction 2.0 miles from the trailhead. Bear right here toward Snag Lake and begin climbing gently southward.

You will probably not realize you have gained the ridge until you begin descending the other side. This gentle descent leads 0.5 mile through thick forest, ending near the east shore of immense Snag Lake, rimmed on three sides by low, forested ridges, and on the fourth by the lava beds that created it.

The trail then heads south, across a grassy, aspen-clad slope above the east shore. After 6 miles you should bear right where another trail joins on your left bound for Juniper and Jakey Lakes. Your trail heads southwest, crosses four springs, and reaches the bridged crossing of Grassy Creek after another 0.1 mile.

Beyond the crossing, a level stint through lodgepole forest leads to another southbound trail heading to Horseshoe and Juniper Lakes. Turning right, another pleasant 0.4-mile jaunt leads to yet another junction with a left-branching trail bound for more backcountry lakes. Stay right again and continue north well above the west shore of Snag Lake. Quite soon you will enter a charred forest blackened in the summer of 1987. You reach the head of the lake opposite the lava beds 1.2 miles from the last junction.

After you stroll 1.6 miles from Snag Lake, a trail joins your route on the left, entering on a slightly higher contour. A sign here advises you to stay on the trail to avoid tracking the cinder fields. Bear right at the junction, and your trail begins climbing the cinder fields opposite the colorful Painted Dunes. With a view of prominent Cinder Cone ahead of you and snow-streaked Lassen Peak behind, you reach an unsigned junction after 0.3 mile. You can either turn right to climb the steep southern slopes of Cinder Cone—its summit offers exceptional views over the Fantastic Lava Beds, Painted Dunes, and much of the route you have traveled thus far—or bear left, climbing 0.2 mile to the wide track of Nobles Emigrant Trail.

A fine panorama unfolds upon reaching that trail, stretching across the lava beds to Red Cinder Cone, Mount Hoffman, Mount Harkness, and Fairfield Peak. Turning right onto Nobles Trail, you climb easily toward a low saddle, flanked on the left by a forest of Jeffrey pine and on the right by the smooth, nearly barren slopes of Cinder Cone.

A 0.1-mile stroll along the trail leads to a junction with a trail climbing out of the cinder fields below. Staying to the left, proceed through the long saddle at the forest's edge, where a profusion of round black boulders litters trailside slopes. Known to geologists as volcanic bombs, these rocks were ejected in a molten state, probably from the main crater atop Cinder Cone.

Descending northeast from the saddle, you reach another junction with a trail that climbs 0.5 mile to Cinder Cone's summit, 0.4 mile from the previous junction. Bearing left at that juncture, your trail descends into a forest of large Jeffrey pines, and once again skirts the edge of the lava flow amid pine forest, reaching the left-branching trail to Prospect Peak after another 0.8 mile. Prospect Peak, 2.8 miles distant and 2,000 feet above, offers a commanding view and is a worthwhile side-trip if time and energy allow.

Continuing ahead, you quite soon reach a signed spur trail leading 100 yards to the edge of the lava, from which issues trickling Cold Spring. The remainder of the trip continues along the edge of the lava beds, soon passing below the campground. You should avoid the use trails leading up to it. Reach the road's end near the ranger station, 0.4 mile from the Prospect Peak Trail, and follow it uphill for the final 0.2 mile to the parking area.

Caribou Wilderness   **27**

Location: 10 miles north of Chester, 60 miles east of Redding, and immediately east of Lassen Volcanic Wilderness.
Size: 20,625 acres.
Administration: USDAFS–Lassen National Forest.
Management status: National Forest wilderness.
Ecosystems: Sierran Forest–Alpine Meadows Province, Southern Cascades section, characterized by a gently rolling volcanic plateau and numerous cinder cones; Pliocene and Pleistocene volcanic rocks; potential natural vegetation is Sierran montane forest, and upper montane-subalpine forests; numerous lakes, few surface streams, small areas of wet meadows.
Elevation range: 6,400 feet to 8,374 feet.
System trails: 21 miles.
Maximum core-to-perimeter distance: 2.6 miles.
Activities: Backpacking, day hiking, horseback riding, fishing, cross-country skiing, and snowshoeing.
Maps: Lassen National Forest visitor map; Caribou Wilderness visitor map; see Appendix D for a list of USGS 1:24,000 quads.

OVERVIEW: Extending east from Lassen Volcanic Wilderness is a moderately high, gently rolling plateau with an average elevation of about 7,000 feet. Much of this plateau has been set aside for preservation since 1932. Today the Caribou Wilderness is still one of the most pristine forested landscapes remaining in California's Cascades.

The glaciated volcanic plateau within the boundaries of the Caribou Wilderness is covered by moderately dense conifer forest and punctuated by numerous volcanic buttes and cinder cones. This wildland would be more aptly named "thousand lakes" than its neighbor several miles to the northwest, since it contains 23 named lakes and innumerable tarns and ponds. Seventy-five percent of the wilderness is mantled with conifers or covered in water, while the remainder is barren volcanic rock, mostly on cliff faces and the slopes of the high cinder cones. There are no perennial surface streams in the Caribou, yet the area produces high-quality water for the headwaters of the Susan River and Pine Creek, water that goes underground and resurfaces beyond the wilderness boundaries. Bailey Creek, a seasonal tributary to the Feather River, drains the southern Caribou lakes near Hay Meadow.

27 CARIBOU WILDERNESS

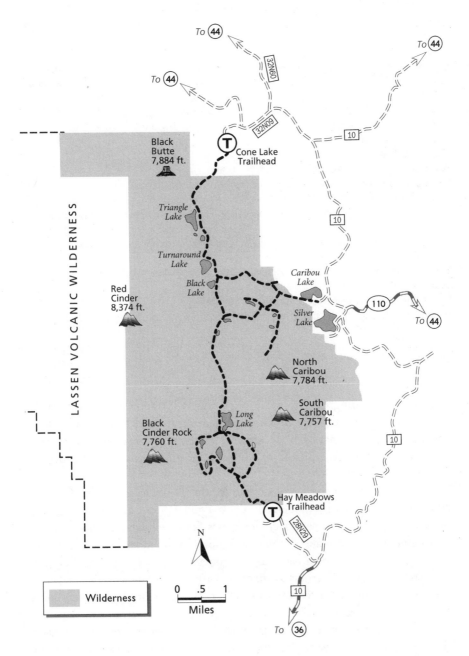

To (44)

32N60

To (44)

To (44)

To (44)

32N09

10

Black
Butte
7,884 ft.

(T) Cone Lake
Trailhead

*Triangle
Lake*

*Turnaround
Lake*

*Black
Lake*

*Caribou
Lake*

10

Red
Cinder
8,374 ft.

*Silver
Lake*

110

To (44)

North
Caribou
7,784 ft.

LASSEN VOLCANIC WILDERNESS

South
Caribou
7,757 ft.

*Long
Lake*

10

Black
Cinder Rock
7,760 ft.

Hay Meadows
Trailhead

(T)

28N29

N

10

0   .5   1

Wilderness

Miles

To (36)

Although most of the major lakes accessed by trails in the Caribou are moderately popular, opportunities for solitude are excellent when traveling off-trail, and the trailless terrain between the main north-south trail and Lassen Volcanic Wilderness to the west is very seldom visited.

RECREATIONAL USES: Three trailheads provide access to the Caribou backcountry, and the trails are gentle, leading to major wilderness lakes less than two miles from any trailhead. The area is well suited for day hiking, though the majority of wilderness users stay overnight in the backcountry. The Caribou is used lightly by horseback riders, most of whom visit on weekends.

All trailheads are moderately to heavily used on weekends, and the Silver Lake Trailhead on the east consistently gets more than half of this wilderness area's visitors. Hay Meadow Trailhead on the south, and Cone Lake Trailhead on the north split the remainder. While many travelers come to the Caribou to simply enjoy camping by the lakes and in the forests, fishing is also a big attraction. Since the lakes are low in fertility and unable to support a self-sustaining fish population, 21 of Caribou's lakes are stocked by air with rainbow trout.

The primary wilderness trail runs north-south between Hay Meadow and Cone Lake Trailheads; the lakes closest to each trailhead are most heavily used, especially on weekends. Lakes along this trail between Long Lake in the south and Turnaround Lake in the north are much less frequently visited. Two connecting trails access the primary trail from the Caribou Lake Trailhead on the east.

Off-trail travel is easy but can be confusing because of the moderate forest cover. Few visitors scale the high points of this wilderness, but those who do enjoy excellent vistas across the Caribou and Lassen Volcanic Wildernesses. Winter use is possible but is very light—the roads aren't plowed. This region averages a 6-foot snowpack through April, so the only way to reach the Caribou's trailheads is by a long ski in, or with a snowmachine. Snowmachine use is frequent in winter along Forest Road 10 around the boundaries of the Caribou.

Backpack or Day Hike

Cone Lake to Hay Meadow

Distance: 10.75 miles, point-to-point, or any length round trip for as long as time and energy allow.
Low/high elevations: 6,400 feet/7,080 feet.
Difficulty: Moderate.
Best season: July through early October.
Topo maps: Bogard Buttes-CA, Red Cinder-CA.
Permits: Wilderness permits not required. A California Campfire Permit is required for open fires and backpack stoves.

Turnaround Lake in the northern reaches of the Caribou Wilderness.

HOW TO GET THERE: To get to the Hay Meadow and Cone Lake Trailheads from the west and south, follow California Highway 36 to its junction with southbound Plumas County Road A-13, 5 miles east of Chester and 29 miles west of Susanville. From this junction, turn onto a northbound road directly opposite CR A-13 and proceed north, turning left onto signed Forest Road 10 after 0.2 mile, avoiding the eastbound road to the Chester Landfill. Drive west for another 0.4 mile and then turn right, staying on FR 10.

Follow this good paved road generally north, avoiding several signed and unsigned, well-graded spur roads. At major junctions, signs point to Caribou Wilderness. After driving 9.9 miles from CA 36, turn left onto FR 30N25 to reach Hay Meadow Trailhead, where a sign reads CARIBOU WILDERNESS TRAIL-HEAD-2. Proceed northwest on this narrow, rough, steadily ascending dirt road for 1.4 miles to a junction on a ridge. Bear right there and descend for another 0.2 mile to the road's end at the trailhead. There you will find room enough to park 15 or more vehicles, and a stock loading ramp.

To reach Cone Lake, continue generally north on FR 10 for 14.9 miles from its junction with FR 30N25, then turn left (west) onto FR 32N09, signed for Cone Lake. After 2 miles, continue straight ahead on the narrow gravel road at the junction with northbound Pole Springs Road (FR 32N09). The Cone Lake Trailhead is located at the road's end 0.8 mile from that junction.

If you are approaching from the north or east via CA 44, you will find FR 10 branching west from the highway 0.2 mile south of the Bogard Work Center, and 23.6 miles southeast of the CA 44/89 junction at Old Station. Follow FR 10 west from the highway for 5.9 miles to the junction with FR 32N09, then continue straight ahead for 2.8 miles to Cone Lake.

This trail traverses the wilderness north to south, making a grand tour of the lake-dotted, forest-covered volcanic landscape of the Caribou. Typical of Caribou trails, this is a pleasant, nearly level route through the forest, passing more than a dozen lakes.

The trail ascends gradually southwest from the Cone Lake Trailhead, winding beneath a canopy of ponderosa, lodgepole pine, and red fir. In less than a mile, you reach the wilderness boundary and trail register, then skirt a blocky lava flow and enter a moderately dense lodgepole forest, typical of low-lying, poorly drained areas in the Caribou. Triangle Lake, about 2 miles from the trailhead, is one of the largest lakes in the Caribou—and the deepest, at 55 feet—and receives heavy use on summer weekends. An abandoned trail that heads west from Triangle Lake leads toward Widow Lake in the Lassen Volcanic Wilderness and affords excellent opportunities for solitude.

The main trail continues a southbound course beyond Triangle Lake, gently rising and falling past Twin Lakes to Turnaround Lake, one of the gems of the Caribou, bounded by broken volcanic cliffs. A good route following a southwest course to Red Cinder can be taken from the top of the moraine north of Turnaround Lake.

Between Turnaround and Black Lakes, a 3-mile trail branches east toward the Caribou Lake Trailhead. At 4.6 miles you meet the next eastbound trail to Caribou Lake at the north shore of North Divide Lake. Follow the southbound trail that continues past South Divide Lake, then descend gradually through pine and fir forest into the Bailey Creek drainage, reaching large Long Lake at 6.9 miles.

At the southern shore of Long Lake, you can take the eastbound trail leading past the Hidden Lakes for 3.5 miles to Hay Meadow, or take the longer trail to the southwest. That trail visits Posey, Beauty, and Evelyn Lakes, leading 4.3 miles to the Hay Meadow Trailhead.

Thousand Lakes Wilderness

28

Location: 40 miles east-northeast of Redding.
Size: 16,335 acres.
Administration: USDAFS–Lassen National Forest.
Management status: National Forest wilderness.
Ecosystems: Sierran Forest–Alpine Meadows province, Southern Cascades section, characterized by a glaciated shield volcano; Pliocene and Pleistocene volcanic rocks; potential natural vegetation is northern yellow pine forest, yellow pine-shrub forest, Sierran montane forest, upper montane-subalpine forests, and chaparral; numerous lakes and tarns.
Elevation range: 5,520 feet to 8,677 feet.
System trails: 21.1 miles.
Maximum core-to-perimeter distance: 3 miles.
Activities: Day hiking, backpacking, cross-country skiing and snowshoeing, horseback riding, fishing.
Maps: Lassen National Forest visitor map; Thousand Lakes Wilderness visitor map; see Appendix D for a list of USGS 1:24,000 quads.

OVERVIEW: The southern extension of the Cascade Range in California contains few prominent landscape features other than Lassen Peak and Mount Shasta. There are large areas of lava flows, and cinder cones are scattered across the landscape, but overall the area is a gently rolling, forest-covered plateau. Several miles north of Lassen Volcanic National Park, two high, prominent volcanoes punctuate this rolling landscape: the Magee Peak/Crater Peak massif and Burney Mountain. Burney Mountain hosts a fire lookout tower accessed by a forest road, but the lands surrounding Crater and Magee peaks remain wild.

For hikers on the summit of Lassen Peak, views of Magee Peak and its satellite summits appear unimpressive—simply another sloping, steep-sided feature so typical of the southern Cascade Range. Yet when viewed from the north, the area displays considerable glacial modification.

Magee, Crater, and Fredonyer Peaks and Red Cliff are the primary features rising above the cirque at the head of Thousand Lakes Valley. These summits rise just above timberline, with mats of krummholz whitebark pines on their flanks. Much of the wilderness is composed of steep to moderate slopes covered with mountain hemlock, red fir, white fir, and Jeffrey, western white, and

28 THOUSAND LAKES WILDERNESS

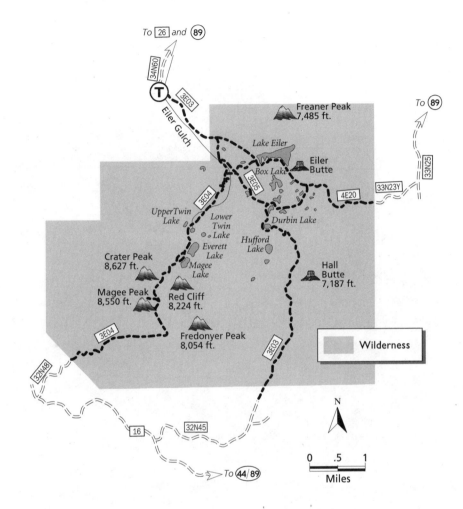

lodgepole pine. Montane chaparral covers many slopes with a south- and west-facing aspect. Numerous cinder cones and lava flows rise above fields of brush and the forests, including Freaner Peak, Hall Butte, and Tumble Buttes.

Two glaciers carved the northern flanks of the Magee Peak highland, one carving the Everett Lake/Magee Lake basin, the other hollowing out the eastern slopes and creating Durbin and Hufford Lakes. The glaciers coalesced two

Red Cliff rises above Magee Lake, the highest lake in the Thousand Lakes Wilderness.

miles below the volcanic crest of the mountain, excavating a broad, gentle basin—Thousand Lakes Valley—dotted with more than 20 lakes and tarns, and now mantled in cool, conifer forests. Although there are not a "thousand lakes" in the wilderness, there is a high concentration of lakes and tarns covering three square miles of the valley.

RECREATIONAL USES: Four trailheads, two in the north and two in the south, provide access to the trail network here. Tamarack Trailhead in the northeast receives the heaviest use, as it allows one-hour access via Trail 4E20 to Thousand Lakes Valley. The easiest trailhead to reach by car is Cypress, where Trail 3E03 ascends 1,000 feet in 2 miles into the valley. Trail 3E04 from the Magee Trailhead receives the least use, since it ascends very steeply to the crest of Magee Peak, and is used mostly by peak-baggers en route to Magee, Fredonyer, or Crater Peaks. The longest, and most interesting, approach to Thousand Lakes Valley begins at the Bunchgrass Trailhead. From there, Trail 3E05 ascends among cinder cones and fields of chaparral to the valley, affording contrasting perspectives of the sloping south side, and glacier-carved north side, of the volcano.

Fishing in the lakes is one of the primary attractions of this wilderness. Brook and rainbow trout are stocked in Eiler, Box, Barrett, Durbin, Lower Twin, Everett, Magee, and Hufford Lakes. The ease of access from Cypress and Tamarack Trailheads makes the area well suited for an easy hike and a day of fishing. Since the trail network in Thousand Lakes Valley traverses rolling terrain, the area is popular for short backpack trips, and is particularly well suited for families with children.

Campsites are abundant in Thousand Lakes Valley, and few show signs of overuse. In general, campsites are located around the many lakes, and are shaded by mixed conifers. The upper reaches of the basin at Everett and Magee lakes display typical timberline scenery, with subalpine forests fringing the lakes and ice-carved volcanic cliffs rising above. That part of the basin is one of the more attractive high-elevation destinations in California's Cascades, making it susceptible to overuse, though most backpackers seem to prefer camping in the more forested areas of Thousand Lakes Valley.

Use is concentrated around the lakes in Thousand Lakes Valley, though, except on holiday weekends, it is seldom heavy. There are ample opportunities for solitude, particularly if you visit during weekdays or camp well away from the trails. The area is well suited for winter ski and snowshoe tours, but lack of plowed roads requires a long trip over snow-covered forest roads to reach any of the trailheads.

Day Trip or Backpack

Thousand Lakes Valley

Distance: 10 to 14 miles, round trip or semi-loop.
Low/high elevations: 5,358 feet/7,215 feet.
Difficulty: Moderate.
Best season: July through early October.
Topo map: Thousand Lakes Valley-CA.
Permits: Wilderness permits not required. A California Campfire Permit is required for open fires and backpack stoves.

HOW TO GET THERE: Follow California Highway 89 to westbound Forest Road 26 in the Hat Creek Valley, and turn west. Find the turnoff 10.5 miles south of the CA 89/299 junction, 0.4 mile north of the Hat Creek Work Center, and 11 miles north of the CA 89/44 junction.

FR 26 is signed for BURNEY SPRINGS, 1000 LAKES WILDERNESS, and BURNEY MOUNTAIN LOOKOUT immediately west of the junction with CA 89. Follow this good gravel road west for 7.9 miles, then turn left (south) onto FR 34N60, signed for CYPRESS CAMP. Continue south, staying left at two junctions, for 2.6 miles to the spacious parking area at Cypress Trailhead.

This interesting hike leads through hushed forests, passes four major wilderness lakes, and ends in an impressive cirque surrounded by precipitous cliffs and alpine peaks. Except during the early summer snowmelt period, the only water usually available in the area comes directly from the lakes. Mosquitoes are thick in Thousand Lakes Valley, and most hikers either pack a headnet or wait until late summer to visit.

Trail 3E03 begins on the east side of the Cypress Trailhead parking area, drops down to boulder-clogged Eiler Gulch, then begins a lengthy, sustained steep ascent. Jeffrey pine and white fir are scattered across nearby slopes, joined by the juniper-like Modoc (or Baker) cypress, a rare tree found in only a few isolated locations in extreme northern California.

The steady ascent provides occasional views, ahead, of pyramidal Crater Peak, the highest point in the wilderness, and behind, of Mount Shasta. Trail 3E03 is a remarkably straight corridor which leads 1.5 miles to the wilderness boundary through manzanita, ceanothus, and chinquapin chaparral, and the mixed conifer forest. At the junction at 1.7 miles, you can follow either fork and make a 4.6-mile loop around Lake Eiler and Box and Barrett Lakes and return to this junction.

Take the right fork to reach the high lakes and to scale Magee Peak. That trail continues to ascend through mixed conifer forest alongside Eiler Gulch for 0.4 mile to a junction with southeast-branching Trail 3E05 leading to Barrett and Durbin Lakes. Follow that trail if you are taking the loop through

Thousand Lakes Valley. Otherwise, turn right onto Trail 3E04 and begin a series of switchbacks ascending a shady, north-facing slope. As you gain elevation, brush-clad Freaner Peak comes into view, the northern sentinel of the wilderness. The massive andesite volcano of Burney Mountain meets your gaze in the northwest, and beyond rises the bold, snowy cone of Mount Shasta.

After the trail levels off in a sparse pine and fir forest 1.5 miles from the previous junction, you cross usually dry Eiler Gulch. Mountain hemlock now joins the subalpine forest as you climb briefly past small, shallow Upper Twin Lake, spectacular with its backdrop of precipitous Red Cliff crags. These cliffs are largely gray, but they're streaked with the red volcanic rock (rich in iron) that gave the mountain its name.

Presently in a subalpine forest of western white and lodgepole pine, red fir, and mountain hemlock, you wind your way up to beautiful Everett Lake. Behind the lake rises majestic Red Cliff and the impressive glacial cirque at the head of Thousand Lakes Valley.

A short jaunt beyond Everett Lake brings you to a junction with the right-branching trail leading to Magee Peak. The left fork proceeds around the shores of Magee Lake, the highest lake in the wilderness, 5 miles from Cypress Trailhead.

South Warner Wilderness

29

Location: 12 miles east of Alturas.
Size: 70,385 acres.
Administration: USDAFS–Modoc National Forest.
Management status: National Forest wilderness.
Ecosystems: Sierran Forest–Alpine Meadows province, Modoc Plateau section, characterized by a north- to south-aligned mountain block, very steep on the east side and moderately steep to steep on the west side; Miocene and Tertiary volcanic rocks, and glacial deposits; potential natural vegetation is yellow pine-shrub forest, Sierran montane forest, upper montane-subalpine forests, juniper-shrub savanna, sagebrush steppe, and smaller areas of alpine communities; many perennial springs and streams, numerous wet meadows, and few moderately high lakes.
Elevation range: 4,800 feet to 9,892 feet.
System trails: 79.4 miles.
Maximum core-to-perimeter distance: 9.25 miles.
Activities: Backpacking, day hiking, horseback riding, fishing, cross-country skiing, and snowshoeing.
Maps: Modoc National Forest visitor map; South Warner Wilderness map (topographic; 1 inch/mile); see Appendix D for a list of USGS 1:24,000 quads.

OVERVIEW: The Warner Mountains is the second longest mountain range in California, stretching some 100 miles north from near the town of Susanville to the Oregon state line. The Warners extend an additional 40 miles north into Oregon. These little-known and lightly visited mountains are among the most unique and beautiful in California. The highest reaches of the Warners, in the central part of the range, were set aside as a primitive area in 1931; the South Warner Wilderness was created in 1964, and its boundaries were expanded in 1984.

The landscapes and ecosystems of the South Warner Wilderness are similar in appearance to parts of the Rocky Mountains and the Cascades, making them quite different from most other mountains in California. The Warner Mountains are part of the Modoc Plateau, and they are the most profoundly block-faulted highland in this volcanic region. The Warner crest divides waters that flow west into the Pit/Sacramento River drainage and east into the Alkali Lakes of Surprise Valley, an enclosed Great Basin valley.

The eastern face of the Warners in the wilderness is an abrupt escarpment rising as much as 5,500 vertical feet in a lateral distance of 5 miles. Typical of

29 SOUTH WARNER WILDERNESS

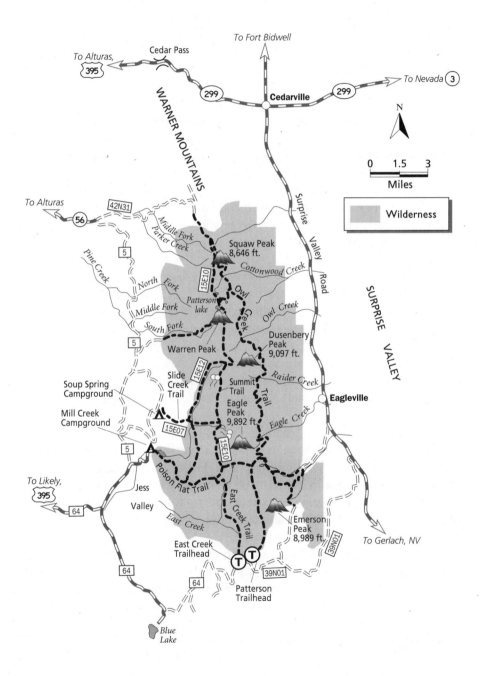

volcanic terrain, the escarpment stair-steps up from Surprise Valley in a series of cliff bands and terraces. Numerous narrow, precipitous gorges cleave the eastern face of the South Warner Wilderness below glacier-carved cirques. Woodlands of western juniper stud the lower slopes, and a narrow, yet dense band of Jeffrey pine and white fir occupies the middle slopes. Grasses, forbs, and shrubs mantle the cirques above timberline.

The western side of the wilderness is a steadily rising slope incised by numerous shallow drainages east of the valleys near Alturas. The western slopes are heavily forested, with conifers extending nearly to the 9,000-foot crest. Jeffrey and ponderosa pine, white fir, and red fir dominate the forest in the low to middle elevations on the west slopes. The highest elevations support lodgepole and whitebark pines, often stunted or in ground-hugging mats of krummholz. Many openings exist in the westside forests, and these clearings are rich with grasses, fields of sagebrush and bitterbrush, and groves of aspen. The deep volcanic soils nurture richer vegetation than in most other parts of California, and innumerable springs and perennial streams issue from the porous volcanic rock.

Much of the Warner Mountains crest in the wilderness is a narrow ridgeline with few prominent peaks. Warren Peak (9,710 feet) in the north and Eagle Peak (9,892 feet) in the south are the highest. Other significant peaks in the wilderness include Squaw Peak (8,646 feet), Dusenbery Peak (9,097 feet), Cole Peak (8,971 feet), and Emerson Peak (8,989 feet). Vistas from these peaks and from the Warner crest are outstanding, stretching west and southwest across the Modoc Plateau to Mount Shasta and Lassen Peak, north past Goose Lake into southern Oregon, and east across the volcanic landscape of the Black Rock Desert in Nevada.

Glacial cirques define the head of nearly all the drainages east of the crest, and since the Warners are composed of volcanics, there are few lakes. Pine Creek Basin, a 3-square-mile cirque, is one of the most outstanding features of the western slope. Of the five cirque lakes in the wilderness, Patterson Lake is the largest, highest, and most beautiful, and so attracts a disproportionate amount of use. Clear Lake is a landslide-dammed lake only 0.5 miles from Mill Creek Campground on the western slopes.

Extending into the wilderness from the west is part of a 6,016-acre state game refuge. In addition to the refuge, the South Warner Wilderness also includes important spring, summer, and early autumn range, fawning areas, and winter range for Rocky Mountain mule deer. A wide variety of other mammals and rodents dwells here, including marten, coyote, badger, bobcat, mountain lion, beaver, and western gray squirrel. Lying in the path of the Pacific Flyway, the Warners attract a variety of waterfowl, and opportunities for bird watching are exceptional.

With an abundance of forage, the South Warner Wilderness supports six cattle and three sheep grazing allotments. Some of these allotments extend outside the wilderness. Roughly 1,650 cattle and 3,000 sheep use these allotments during the general grazing season from about July 1 through September 30.

RECREATIONAL USES: Lying far from population centers, the South Warner Wilderness is very lightly used. The area is just too far out of reach for most wilderness travelers in California, making it one of the best getaway spots in the state. The South Warners contain a network of nearly 80 miles of trails, plus an additional 23 miles of unmaintained pathways not considered system trails. Possibilities for loop trips abound, stretching as long as 45 miles, and cross-country travel further extends recreational opportunities.

Hikers comprise the majority of summer users, with visitors on horseback generally accounting for less than 20 percent of the traffic. Eight trailheads located along well-maintained forest roads provide access to the trail network. Day use and overnight trips are the most popular activities, though use is so light that solitude is almost guaranteed at all but the most popular locations, such as at Clear Lake and Patterson Lake. The Mill Creek Trailhead is most frequently used, primarily by day-hikers en route to Clear Lake. The small number of backpackers who come to the South Warners tend to concentrate at Patterson Lake, and its timberline campsites bear scars from years of use. The least-used trailheads are located at the southern end of the wilderness, and include Emerson, Patterson, and East Creek.

The trail system surveys the spectrum of wilderness landscapes, including open hillsides, forested canyons, timberline forests, and alpine slopes. The Summit Trail extends 22.4 miles between Pepperdine Trailhead in the north and Patterson Trailhead in the south. This trail is one of the premier high-elevation routes in California, and, as its name suggests, it follows the crest of the Warners for much of the way. The Owl Creek Trail branches off from the Summit Trail and follows a lower contour on the east side of the mountains for 18.3 miles. That trail climbs and descends a series of east side canyons, making the way much more rigorous than the Summit Trail. Combine the two trails, beginning at either Patterson or Pepperdine Trailheads, and you have a loop trip extending from 38 to 45 miles.

Hunting districts within and outside the South Warner Wilderness are very popular, as it is one of the few areas in California to hunt Rocky Mountain mule deer. During the autumn hunting season, the normally quiet forest roads and the six campgrounds surrounding the wilderness are bustling with activity, as are some of the backcountry trails.

Many of the streams in the wilderness offer good fishing for rainbow, brown, and brook trout. Patterson, North Emerson, and South Emerson Lakes are stocked with trout, while Clear Lake on Mill Creek supports a self-sustaining population. Deep and cold Patterson Lake provides the most productive lake fishing in the wilderness.

Cross-country skiing and snowshoeing are possible, but like so many wild-lands in California, the lack of plowed roads is a limiting factor. Some of the lower west side trailheads can be reached during winter and early spring. Clear Lake is a popular ice fishing spot. Probably the easiest winter access is via the Mill Creek Campground/Trailhead, which affords access to Clear Lake and the Mill Creek Trail. To reach other trailheads, long approaches on skis are required over snow-covered forest roads.

Backpack

North Emerson Lake

Distance: 12.8 miles, round trip; or 16.2 miles, loop trip (2 to 4 days).
Low/high elevations: 7,100 feet (round trip); 6,300 feet (loop trip)/8,400 feet.
Difficulty: Moderate.
Best season: Early July through September.
Topo maps: Emerson Peak-CA, Eagle Peak-CA.
Permits: Wilderness permits not required. A California Campfire Permit is required for open fires and backpack stoves.

HOW TO GET THERE: Follow U.S. Highway 395 to the small town of Likely, 88 miles north of Susanville and 18.9 miles south of Alturas. Turn east onto Modoc County Road 64, which eventually becomes designated Forest Road 64 ahead. After driving east along the South Fork Pit River for 9.4 miles, turn south onto FR 64 (labeled FR 39N01 on the South Warner Wilderness map) at the junction in the west end of Jess Valley.

FR 64 leads 6.7 miles up to a junction with the southbound road to Blue Lake, where the pavement ends. Continue straight ahead at that junction, and again at the junction with the red-surfaced road to Madeline 1.9 miles ahead. Avoid the northbound road to Mahogany Ridge after another 0.7 miles (18.7 miles from Likely) and continue east, following signs pointing to Patterson Campground at the junctions ahead.

Turn left to reach Patterson Campground 23.8 miles from Likely. Almost immediately, avoid the entrance to Patterson Guard Station, and instead bear right and circle around through the campground to the trailhead at the road's end just above the guard station, 24.2 miles from Likely and US 395.

Beginning at the second most lightly used trailhead in the wilderness, this memorable trip follows the Summit Trail to North Emerson Lake, which rests in an eastside cirque below the apex of the South Warner Wilderness, 9,892-foot Eagle Peak. An option is to loop back to FR 64 at Patterson Meadow via

Eagle Peak (9,892 feet) is the highest point in the South Warner Wilderness.

the seldom-traveled Poison Flat and East Creek Trails, which allows you to survey the spectrum of wilderness landscapes on the west slopes of the range.

The Summit Trail begins a northbound course a few yards west of the trailhead register and information signboard at Patterson Campground. Initially it follows a fenceline, then gradually ascends through white fir and ponderosa pine forest. Soon the trail opens up into a sagebrush-clad opening fringed with aspen and conifer forest. Beyond the clearing, the trail reenters forest, passes the wilderness boundary, and begins ascending in earnest.

After rising 680 feet in 1 mile, the grade moderates as you curve around the shoulder of Point 7,942. There, among volcanic boulders and gnarled clumps of curl-leaf mountain mahogany, panoramic vistas open up, vistas that you will enjoy for much of the remainder of the trip.

Ahead the trail rises into a forest of whitebark and lodgepole pine, then dips into a long saddle studded with wind-flagged ponderosa pines. With the towering alpine dome of Eagle Peak to guide you, the Summit Trail begins a steady northbound ascent. The trail ahead stays just below, or runs along the fringe of, the narrow band of stunted whitebark pines that tops off the upper slopes of the range. After 2.6 miles, the trail crosses a wet, sloping meadow covered with corn lilies, then rises into the timberline forest, where you reach more gentle terrain.

Vistas of North Emerson Lake and Surprise Valley spread out east of the crest of the Warner Mountains.

At 3.5 miles you cross a lovely meadow drained by an early-season stream. The trail ahead begins to break out of the forest onto more open slopes, where the whitebarks are stunted and wind-flagged. The pyramid of Eagle Peak commands the view ahead to the north.

After 5.1 miles the Summit Trail turns west and the North Emerson Trail branches right (northeast). Turn right to reach North Emerson Lake, and rise gradually to the flat-topped 8,400-foot crest of the Warner Mountains, fringed with whitebark pines. From that crest, expansive vistas stretch down the steep eastern face of the range to Lower Alkali Lake and the vast dune fields on its eastern shore in Surprise Valley. Beyond, flat-topped volcanic ranges march eastward into northwest Nevada.

After 0.6 mile the trail drops to an 8,388-foot saddle, where the Owl Creek Trail begins and descends north into Eagle Basin. Stay right at that junction and descend open slopes, studded with mountain mahogany, down to the outlet of 7,700-foot North Emerson Lake, 6.4 miles from the trailhead. There are good campsites in groves of white fir, lodgepole, and whitebark pine near the lake's outlet, and above the north and east shores. Although this lake is stocked with trout, fishing is only fair, yet the lake basin is scenic and very remote.

To loop back to the trailhead via East Creek after passing your first night at North Emerson Lake, return to the Summit Trail and follow it west. (Taking the loop in this direction, rather than starting at East Creek Trailhead, involves less, and more gradual, elevation gain.)

The Summit Trail descends gradually while traversing the open headwaters bowl of the North Fork East Creek, on the south slopes of Eagle Peak, slopes clothed in sagebrush and grass, and studded with aspen. After 1 mile you pass a pair of perennial springs at the source of the North Fork. At 1.5 miles you meet the Poison Flat Trail, heading southwest at 8,080 feet. It may be hard to pass up the temptation of scaling Eagle Peak from that junction, for its southwest ridge, rising above, affords the easiest walk-up route. Although the off-trail ascent climbs nearly 2,000 feet in 1.5 miles, it crosses open slopes among krummholz whitebarks and features expansive vistas.

Follow the Poison Flat Trail, descending steeply southwest into pine and fir forest for 1 mile to a junction at 7,320 feet. The Poison Flat Trail continues west down the slopes of Bald Mountain, but you turn left (southeast) onto the East Creek Trail, and quickly rise to a saddle. Descending the opposite side, you soon pass a good spring with camping areas nearby, then drop via switchbacks through stands of aspen and white fir, and verdant openings for 1 mile to the North Fork East Creek at 6,800 feet.

A steady descent follows, leading down the course of the North Fork, shaded by a canopy of predominantly white fir forest. At 6,280 feet, 2.1 miles from the previous junction, you begin to follow the contour southeast and away from the North Fork. After 0.8 mile the trail crosses a draw watered by an upslope spring, then rises 0.6 mile to a forested saddle southeast of Point 6,841. A short, moderate descent leads another 0.3 mile to a crossing of Little North Fork East Creek, a reliable stream with ample opportunities for camping on the gentle, fir-forested terrain.

The trail rises gradually south away from the Little North Fork, then begins a moderately steep ascent to the wilderness boundary on a pine- and fir-clad saddle at 7,150 feet. From there you quickly descend down to East Creek Trailhead (the most lightly used in the wilderness), then follow the dirt road for 0.3 mile down to FR 64 above Patterson Meadow; turn left (east) and walk another 0.7 mile back to Patterson Trailhead.

Lava Beds Wilderness

30

Location: 7 miles south of Tulelake, 45 miles northeast of Mt. Shasta City, and 35 miles northwest of Canby.
Size: 28,460 acres (in two separate units).
Administration: USDI–National Park Service, Lava Beds National Monument.
Management status: National Monument wilderness.
Ecosystems: Sierran Forest–Alpine Meadows province, Southern Cascades section, characterized by an undulating basalt plain interrupted by many moderately steep to steep volcanic domes and cinder cones; Pliocene, Pleistocene, recent basalt flows, and small areas of alluvial deposits; potential natural vegetation is sagebrush steppe, yellow pine-shrub, and Sierran montane forest; no surface streams or drainages, many lava tube caves.
Elevation range: 4,050 feet to 5,650 feet.
System trails: 17 miles.
Maximum core-to-perimeter distance: 4 miles.
Activities: Spelunking, day hiking, backpacking.
Maps: Lava Beds National Monument visitor map; Modoc National Forest visitor map; see Appendix D for a list of USGS 1:24,000 quads.

OVERVIEW: Lava Beds National Monument spreads out immediately north of the Medicine Lake Highlands, a high collapsed shield volcano that is part of the southern Cascade Range. The monument lies at the interface between the Cascade Range to the west and the Modoc Plateau to the east. Lava Beds Wilderness protects over half the national monument in an east unit and a west unit, and it is a landscape of vast basalt lava flows, some ancient, others so young that vegetation has not yet gained a toehold. Among the recent flows is the Callahan Flow in the southwest corner of the wilderness, a vast stretch of black basalt that issued from vents in the Medicine Lake Highlands. The Devils Homestead Flow spreads out in the northeast corner of the west unit; and the vast Schonchin Flow mantles the landscape northeast of Schonchin Butte in the east unit of the wilderness.

The landscape of Lava Beds is characterized by a gently northward-sloping volcanic plain. Cinder cones, spatter cones, shield volcanoes, chimneys, and stratovolcanoes punctuate the plain, and the volcanic rock ranges from "aa" lava (rough and clinker-like) to "pahoehoe" lava (smooth and ropy).

30   LAVA BEDS WILDERNESS

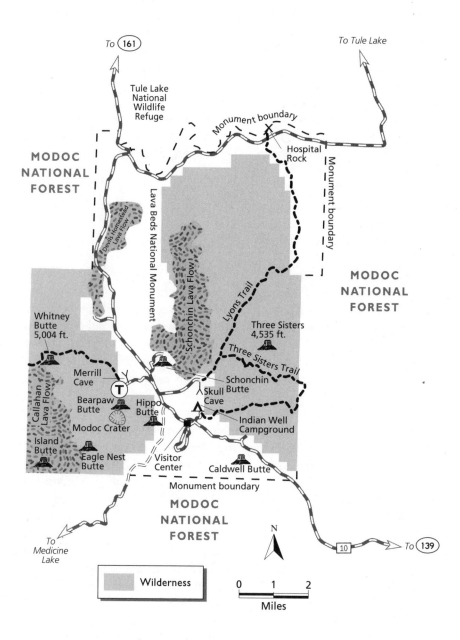

To (161)

To Tule Lake

Tule Lake
National
Wildlife
Refuge

Monument boundary

Hospital
Rock

Monument boundary

MODOC
NATIONAL
FOREST

Devils Homestead Lava Flow

Lava Beds National Monument

Schonchin Lava Flow

MODOC
NATIONAL
FOREST

Whitney
Butte
5,004 ft.

Lyons Trail

Three Sisters
4,535 ft.

Three Sisters Trail

Merrill
Cave

T

Schonchin
Butte

Callahan Lava Flow

Bearpaw
Butte

Hippo
Butte

Skull
Cave

Indian Well
Campground

Modoc Crater

Island
Butte

Eagle Nest
Butte

Visitor
Center

Caldwell Butte

Monument boundary

MODOC
NATIONAL
FOREST

To
Medicine
Lake

N

10

To (139)

Wilderness

0   1   2

Miles

The west unit of the wilderness contains the highest elevations and greatest variety of landforms, and represents a transition from a montane environment to a high desert-type environment. Numerous cones punctuate the southern reaches of this unit, and the Callahan Flow dominates the southwest corner. Ponderosa pine grows in park-like stands in the highest elevations near the southern boundary, with woodlands of western juniper occupying most of the land above 5,000 feet. Fields of sagebrush, bitterbrush, curl-leaf mountain mahogany, and grasslands mantle much of the landscape of both the east and west units. Because of the semi-arid climate, no surface drainage, and relative youth of the volcanic features, little erosion has taken place here, yet the volcanics have broken down to form enough soil to support a well-developed vegetative cover.

The volcanic rocks and abundant vegetation create habitat for a variety of rodents such as yellow-bellied marmot, kangaroo rat, and jackrabbit, and birds such as California quail, sage grouse, and meadowlark. Mule deer winter in Lava Beds, where there is abundant feed and light snow cover. Feeding on the rodent population are abundant coyotes, and a large concentration of raptors, including falcons, owls, and 24 species of hawk. Bald eagles winter in the northern portion of the wilderness adjacent to Tule Lake, in larger numbers than anywhere outside of Alaska. Since Lava Beds is located along the Pacific Flyway, and is adjacent to Tule Lake and other wetlands surrounding Lower Klamath Lake and Clear Lake, the area sees the semi-annual migration of waterfowl that number in the millions. Waterfowl nest on the region's lakes in spring and pass through in even greater numbers each autumn. Migrants include more than 20 species of duck, several varieties of geese, pelicans, herons, cormorants, grebes, terns, coots, and avocets.

Beneath the surface of Lava Beds are more than 300 lava tube caves, many of them well known by Paleo-Indians and Modocs for centuries before settlers arrived. Some caves were used as campsites, providing the only readily available water in the lava fields. The primary camp of the Lava Beds Modocs was located at Indian Well Cave, near where the visitor center stands today. During the Modoc War of 1872 to 1873, the Modocs sought refuge from the U.S. Army in numerous Lava Beds caves.

RECREATIONAL USES: Most visitors come to Lava Beds not so much to experience its terrestrial landscapes but to explore the subterranean world of its lava tubes. Lava Beds' caves range in length from 6,900 feet of surveyed passages in Catacombs Cave to only a few yards. Some caves are surface tubes, lying above the land surface, while others extend to depths of 150 feet. Several contain ice, and some are decorated with dripstone formations. Visitors are advised to register at the visitor center before entering wilderness caves. Hard hats and lights

The Callahan Lava Flow dominates the southwestern corner of Lava Beds Wilderness.

are available for rent at the visitor center. Be sure not to enter any cave without at least one flashlight per person, and beware of low ceilings, slippery footing, sudden drop-offs, and unstable areas.

Above ground, there are only three maintained trails in the Lava Beds Wilderness, yet they are all worth hiking. Far-ranging vistas, first-hand examples of the variable nature of lava flows, plant colonization of the lava, the chance to explore wilderness caves, and brilliant displays of spring wildflowers are among the rewards of hiking in Lava Beds. Yarrow, buckwheat, collomia, penstemon, and fiddleneck are among more common blooms that decorate the slopes. Several other trails shown on topo maps are overgrown, abandoned, and virtually impossible to find on the ground. The three trails receive only light to moderate use, primarily by day-hikers.

Few hikers take backpack trips in Lava Beds. Two factors limiting overnights here are the need to carry all your water and the general lack of suitable campsites in the rocky, brush-covered terrain. There are a few open spots for a tent but you'll have to search for them. Since Lava Beds is small and the trails are gentle and relatively short, one could establish a backcountry base camp and spend time exploring wilderness caves, most of which are not marked on maps. Backpackers should remember that wood fires are not allowed and campsites must be located more than 0.25 mile from roads, trails, parking areas, and overlooks. Camping is not allowed in caves or cave entrances.

The western unit of the wilderness has only the Whitney Butte Trail, and it is perhaps the most scenic of all. Off-trail travel is possible throughout the wilderness, and is made challenging by the lava flows, shrublands, and abundant rattlesnakes.

The eastern unit of the wilderness has two trails but less landscape diversity. Traversing the volcanic plain are the Lyons Trail, an 8.2-mile trail connecting the Skull Cave Trailhead in the south with the Hospital Rock parking area near Tule Lake in the north. Only the southern 5.2 miles of the Lyons Trail lie inside wilderness boundaries. The more popular Three Sisters Trail is an 8.7-mile semi-loop trail that begins on the Lyons Trail 1.2 miles from the Skull Cave Trailhead. This interesting trail skirts the Three Sisters Buttes to the eastern wilderness boundary, then swings west through juniper woodlands and passes several caves along the way to Indian Wells Campground near the visitor center. All three wilderness trails provide excellent day hikes, and solitude is almost guaranteed if you stay overnight on the trails.

Day Hike

Whitney Butte Trail

Distance: 7 miles, round trip.
Low/high elevations: 4,693 feet/4,900 feet.
Difficulty: Moderate.
Best seasons: Late April through June; mid-September through October.
Topo map: Schonchin Butte-CA.
Permits: Not required.

HOW TO GET THERE: From California Highway 299 at the west end of the small town of Canby, turn north onto CA 139. After 27.3 miles, turn left (west) onto the two-lane pavement of County Road 97, signed for Lava Beds National Monument. After another 2.6 miles, turn right (northwest) onto Forest Road 10, still paved but full of potholes.

This rough road leads 9.9 miles to Lava Beds National Monument, and then another 3.6 miles to the monument visitor center, where you pay the entrance fee. Continue straight ahead (north) past the visitor center for another 2.1 miles where, opposite lookout-capped Schonchin Butte, you turn left (west) onto a two-lane paved road signed for Merrill Cave. That road leads 0.9 mile to the trailhead parking area on the edge of the west unit of Lava Beds Wilderness.

The Whitney Butte Trail provides one of the finest hikes in Lava Beds Wilderness. It surveys lava flows both old and recent and offers long-range vistas that extend far into the Oregon Cascades. Shade is a precious commodity along this trail, and it does get hot during summer. Take this hike from spring through early summer, and later in autumn. Winters are cold here, often with light snow cover, yet a winter trip can be memorable, with the white snow contrasting with the dark volcanic landscape.

The Whitney Butte Trail begins at the north side of the road's end, alongside the short trail into Merrill Ice Cave. You quickly enter Lava Beds Wilderness, then pass a trail register. Since most visitors to the monument prefer exploring caves, you likely won't have much company along the trail.

The trail is quite easy, with only minor ups and downs. It passes over lava flows nearly hidden by a dense mantle of sagebrush, bitterbrush, and curl-leaf mountain mahogany. Only a scattering of western junipers stud the gently sloping landscape. Fine vistas along the way extend north down the sloping lava flows to distant Tule Lake. Far to the northwest rises the pointed cone of Oregon's Mount McLaughlin, and on clear days, even more distant Mount Thielson can be seen. On the eastern horizon are the Warner Mountains, defining the eastern reaches of the Modoc Plateau. Many cinder cones dot the Lava Beds landscape, but as its name suggests, the wilderness is dominated by lava flows.

More broken, dark brown lava flows appear after 1 mile as the trail passes south of the small red cone of Bat Butte. At 1.7 miles, as you rise over a 4,800-foot shoulder, the low wooded cone of Whitney Butte appears a short distance ahead to the west, and ice-clad Mount Shasta towers on the southwest skyline. The trail soon curves northwest, then swings back toward Whitney Butte. Below the butte's north slopes, the trail skirts a lava-rimmed depression and becomes a narrow corridor through the brush. The trail then bends south along the western base of the butte; you can leave the trail and scramble up to the summit of the butte, weaving your way up the grassy, shrub-studded slopes.

The highlight of the hike is the Callahan Flow, which comes into view as the trail winds south through the shrub-dotted landscape. This vast field of jagged, black basalt covers several thousand acres and extends northward into Lava Beds from the densely forested Glass Mountain highlands. The trail approaches the foot of the flow, then curves west and becomes a faint path as it skirts the edge of the basalt for several yards to a cable blocking a very old road at the wilderness boundary. Just beyond the boundary there's an exceptional view of Mount Shasta.

Mount Shasta Wilderness

Location: 5 miles east of Mt. Shasta City, and 30 miles southeast of Yreka.
Size: 41,158 acres.
Administration: USDAFS—Shasta-Trinity National Forest.
Management status: National Forest wilderness (38,200 acres); roadless nonwilderness (2,958 acres) allocated to unroaded nonmotorized recreation in the Forest Plan.
Ecosystems: Sierran Forest–Alpine Meadows province, Southern Cascades section, characterized by an extensive, steep to moderately steep stratovolcano, with secondary cinder cones and plug domes, and seven major glaciers, moraines, and cirques; Pliocene and Pleistocene basalt and andesite flows, Recent basalt flows and thick pyroclastic deposits, volcanic ash, and glacial till, outwash, and debris flow deposits; potential natural vegetation is sagebrush steppe, Sierra montane forest, upper montane-subalpine forests, alpine communities, and cold alpine desert; many perennial glacier-fed streams with a concentric drainage pattern, and many perennial springs.
Elevation range: 4,300 feet to 14,162 feet.
System trails: 20 miles.
Maximum core-to-perimeter distance: 5 miles.
Activities: Mountaineering, day hiking, backpacking, cross-country skiing, snowshoeing, ski mountaineering.
Maps: Shasta-Trinity National Forest visitor map; Mount Shasta Wilderness and Castle Crags Wilderness map (topographic, 2 inches/mile); see Appendix D for a list of USGS 1:24,000 quads.

OVERVIEW: Mount Shasta is the single largest mountain in the lower 48 states, and it is California's most outstanding peak. Dominating the landscape of north-central California, Mount Shasta is in view from such distant points as the Warner Mountains in the northeast corner of the state and the Siskiyou Mountains near the north coast. This huge volcano spreads out to a diameter of 17 miles at its base, and rises more than 10,000 feet from surrounding lowlands to a height of 14,162 feet. Mount Shasta is one of only two peaks in California, outside of the Sierra Nevada, that rise above 14,000 feet. The other peak is White Mountain Peak, in the Great Basin of east-central California. Geologists consider Shasta to be a youthful volcano, with the potential for renewed eruptions.

Decades of intensive logging and road construction on Federal and private land surrounding the base of Mount Shasta, combined with "checkerboard" ownership (alternating sections of public and private land), have left a patch-

31   MOUNT SHASTA WILDERNESS

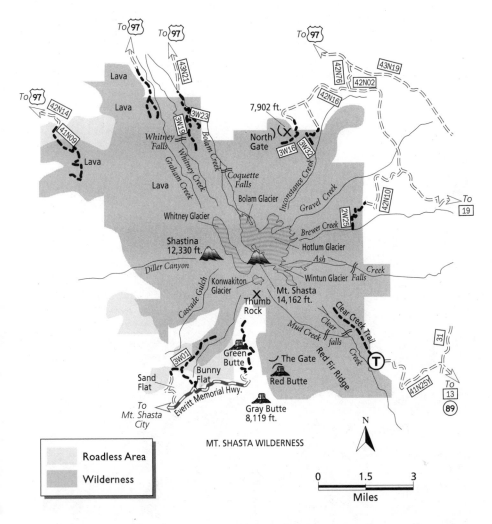

To 97
To 97
To 97

43N21

To 97
42N14
41N09
Lava

Lava

Lava

Lava

Lava

42N76 43N19
42N02
42N16

7,902 ft.
X
North
Gate
3W16 3W32

3W23
3W19
Bolam Creek

Whitney
Falls
Whitney Creek
Graham Creek

Coquette
Falls
Bolam Glacier

Inconstance Creek

Gravel Creek
42N10

To
19

Whitney Glacier

Brewer Creek
2W25

Shastina
12,330 ft.

Hotlum Glacier

Diller Canyon
Ash   Creek
Wintun Glacier Falls

Konwakiton
Glacier
Thumb
Rock
Mt. Shasta
14,162 ft.

Cascade Gulch

Clear Creek Trail

Mud Creek
Clear
falls
Creek
Red Fir Ridge

31

3W01
Green
Butte
The Gate

T

Bunny
Flat
Sand
Flat

Red Butte

41N25
To
13
89

To
Mt. Shasta
City
Everitt Memorial Hwy.

Gray Butte
8,119 ft.

N

MT. SHASTA WILDERNESS

Roadless Area

Wilderness

0   1.5   3
Miles

work of clearcuts and a veritable maze of logging roads. Less than half of the mountain remains roadless. Much of the land that was designated wilderness either contains little timber of commercial value or is dominated by brushy lava flows, barren land, and ice. The Mount Shasta Wilderness is a classic example of the "rock and ice" wild areas that dominate the western U.S., areas that contain few exploitable resources and are deemed suitable only for wilderness designation. Yet Mt. Shasta has long been recognized for the value of its scenic, geologic, and recreational attributes, and scaling its slopes and glaciers to the summit is one of the classic nontechnical climbs in California.

Mud Creek canyon on the southeast slopes of Mount Shasta.

Pristine forests still remain within wilderness boundaries. White fir, sugar pine, Douglas-fir, and incense-cedar mantle the lower elevations, and just below timberline are extensive forests of Shasta red fir. Fingers of the subalpine conifers whitebark pine and mountain hemlock, most often in the ground hugging, krummholz form, extend up the mountain's slopes to timberline, lying between 8,800 and 9,600 feet.

Dominating the Mount Shasta Wilderness is, of course, Mount Shasta itself, but there is much more to this wilderness than simply a towering volcano. One mile west of the Mount Shasta summit is a satellite cone called Shastina, lying at an elevation of 12,330 feet. While glaciers have modified the landscape of Shasta, the cone of Shastina formed after the melting of ice-age glaciers and displays no effects of glacial erosion. On the northern flank of the mountain are several long, sloping lava flows. Composed of andesite and basalt, some of these flows erupted little more than 200 years ago. Volcanic plug domes pimple both the north and south slopes of the mountain. But most of the wilderness consists of barren rock and ice, covering some 25 square miles. Four major glaciers and three smaller ones mantle the upper slopes of Shasta, with the Wintun Glacier extending from just below the summit down to an elevation of 9,100 feet—the lowest-elevation glacier in the state. Three small lakes, frozen for much of the year, dot the upper elevations of the mountain. The Red Banks, located about one-half mile south of Shasta's summit, are composed of volcanic rocks that have been altered by hot spring activity, and very near the summit is an active hot sulfur spring.

With the summit as a hub, the glaciers and their meltwater creeks, along with many springs and other streams, radiate outward in all directions. Long, fir-clad ridges separate drainages on the south slopes. The streams, augmented by melting snow and ice, fall off the mountain in foaming, silt-laden torrents. Consequently, the only potable water is obtained from springs issuing from the mountain's slopes, or by melting snow with a backpack stove. Four of these streams tumble over a named waterfall, yet there are falls on nearly every stream draining the slopes of Shasta, cascading over resistant volcanic ledges. Most streams have eroded only shallow creases on the mountain's flanks, but two streams, Mud and Clear Creeks, flow through gorges that are 800 feet deep in places.

RECREATIONAL USES: The beauty and dominance of this tremendous mountain act like a magnet to attract moderate to heavy use by wilderness recreationists who pursue a variety of activities. Ten trailheads surrounding the wilderness afford access to the slopes of Mount Shasta by way of a series of short trails. Unlike other famous Cascade Range volcanoes, there is no extensive trail system on Mount Shasta. Most of Shasta's short trails lead up the side of the mountain to trailless alpine climbing routes leading to the summit. Yet there are still prime attractions for day-hikers and overnight backpackers who tread these short trails. Close-up views of the mountain, timberline forests and alpine slopes, and a host of beautiful waterfalls can be accessed on wilderness trails. Cross-country routes leading above timberline and beyond the trails are possible, yet the higher one ascends, the greater the danger of unstable slopes and rockfall.

Being a very high, solitary mountain, Mount Shasta frequently creates its own climate and wind flow, and it intensifies existing weather conditions. The formation of a cloud cap, or a cumulus cloud buildup by late morning or early afternoon in summer, often signals impending stormy weather or thunderstorms by afternoon; thus hikers and climbers must keep an eye on developing weather, particularly when exposed above timberline.

Being hit by falling rocks is one of the biggest dangers here, and when traveling above timberline it's a good idea to keep a safe distance between members of your party and not ascend in a vertical line. Altitude sickness is also a threat, since any route to the summit involves 6,000 to 7,000 feet of elevation gain.

Although there are numerous routes leading to Shasta's summit, the so-called Shasta Summit Trail is the most frequently used, and "easiest" of routes to the summit. It's not as much of a trail as it is a route. Starting at either the Sand Flat (6,800 feet) or Bunny Flat (7,000 feet) Trailheads, this route ascends Avalanche Gulch on the southwest flank of the mountain, goes past Red Banks, over Misery Hill, and on to the summit. Though it requires considerable effort and the use of ice axe and crampons, this route is passable to almost any experienced hiker. Other routes are more technical and require experience in mountaineering and glacier travel.

June and July are considered the best months for climbing Shasta, when routes are still snow-covered and travel is smoother over snow and ice. Even during that time, an early, pre-dawn start is essential, so that you are on your way down from the summit before afternoon thunderstorms develop, and before the snow becomes too soft and afternoon rockfall danger increases. In late summer rockfall danger is highest, and the snow-free volcanic slopes are soft and difficult to ascend. Late summer and early fall are the safest times to climb glacier routes, when crevasses are more visible.

A parking permit is required to park at Mount Shasta Wilderness trailheads. These permits are available for $5 per day per vehicle at the McCloud Ranger District office in McCloud, on CA 89, or at the Mount Shasta Ranger District office in Mt. Shasta City, off Interstate 5, and from dispensers at trailheads. Free wilderness permits are required for parties ascending to the summit, plus a *Summit Pass* is required for each climber. The pass is $15 and good for three days. Climbers are **required** to pack out human waste.

Mount Shasta towers above the Clear Creek Trail.

Day Hike

Clear Creek Trail

Distance: 5 miles, round trip.
Low/high elevations: 6,500 feet/8,200 feet.
Difficulty: Moderate.
Best season: Mid-July through early October.
Topo maps: Ash Creek Butte-CA, Elk Spring-CA, Mount Shasta-CA.
Permits: Not required for day hiking.

HOW TO GET THERE: From CA 89 about 3 miles east of McCloud, turn north onto the signed Pilgrim Creek Road (Forest Road 13). Signs read MOUNT SHASTA WILDERNESS TRAILHEADS at the turnoff point. Follow the two-lane pavement of FR 13 north, then northeast, for 5.3 miles, then turn left onto FR 41N15, which is signed CLEAR CREEK TRAILHEAD-8. Follow this steadily ascending graded and graveled road, avoiding numerous unsigned spur roads, and always continuing toward the big white mountain. After 5.1 miles, FR 31 branches left and right. Continue straight ahead across FR 31, ascending steadily past a network of logging roads branching right and left. Signs at most junctions beyond FR 31 point to Clear Creek Trailhead. The road becomes narrow as you proceed, is rough and rutted in places, receives minimal maintenance, and is not recommended for low-clearance vehicles.

The trailhead is located at 6,500 feet, 3 miles from FR 31 and 13.4 miles from CA 89. A fee of $5 per day per vehicle is required. You may self-issue your parking permit from the dispenser at the trailhead by filling out a fee envelope.

This excellent day hike follows a good trail through timberline forests along the rim of Mud and Clear creeks, and offers unforgettable close-up views of Mount Shasta, the Konwakiton Glacier, and a pair of thundering waterfalls.

The Clear Creek Trail (2W01) leads northwest across a corrugated landscape mantled in shady, red fir forest to the rim of Mud Creek canyon, where it turns northwest, ascending along the rim at a moderate grade. As you ascend, the fir forest gradually thins out, affording tremendous views of Mount Shasta, towering 7,000 feet above and 3 miles away. After 1.5 miles, at 7,200 feet, you reach a point on the rim opposite the mouth of Mud Creek, which plunges down a precipitous gorge beneath the small Konwakiton Glacier. About one mile inside Mud Creek's canyon, you see a high, wide waterfall pouring over a volcanic ledge. Walk a little farther up the trail and you will see another, slightly smaller but no less beautiful waterfall in Clear Creek canyon, just above its confluence with Mud Creek.

Some hikers turn around at this point, but you can continue up the trail along the rim to 8,200 feet, where the trail essentially ends. Just above is a steep scree slope covered in a mat of ground-hugging whitebark pine. One can scramble 700 feet up this slope to a timberline bench at 8,900 feet. The summit of Shasta, looming high above, is visible as an ice-encrusted crag.

Phillip Burton Wilderness

32

Location: I mile west of Olema and 20 miles northwest of San Francisco.
Size: 32,730 acres.
Administration: USDI–National Park Service, Point Reyes National Seashore.
Management status: National Seashore wilderness (24,200 acres), with the remainder (8,530 acres) roadless areas designated as "potential wilderness" and managed as wilderness.
Ecosystems: California Coastal Steppe–Mixed Forest-Redwood Forest province, Northern California Coast section, characterized by steep hills and mountains adjacent to the San Andreas Rift Zone, and an elevated coastal plain; Mesozoic granitic rocks, middle Miocene marine sedimentary rocks, lower Pliocene marine sedimentary rocks, extensive areas of beach and dune deposits; potential natural vegetation is coastal saltmarsh, northern seashore communities, coastal prairie-scrub mosiac, coastal cypress and pine forests, and mixed hardwood forest; numerous short, mostly seasonal drainages, large areas of saltmarsh, estuaries, sandy beaches, and rocky headlands.
Elevation range: Sea level to 1,407 feet.
System trails: 71.1 miles.
Maximum core-to-perimeter distance: 4 miles.
Activities: Day hiking, backpacking.
Maps: Point Reyes National Seashore visitor map; USGS 1:48,000 Point Reyes National Seashore and Vicinity-CA ; see Appendix D for a list of USGS 1:24,000 quads.

OVERVIEW: Point Reyes National Seashore embraces one of the most diverse landscapes along the California coast. Nearly half of this unique area is preserved as wilderness or legislatively designated "potential wilderness." The Phillip Burton Wilderness is three separate units in the park, stretching from Tomales Point in the northwest to the southeastern tip of Inverness Ridge near Bolinas Bay. The designated "potential wilderness" includes 30 miles of coastline and the quarter-mile offshore strip and wetlands, primarily along the west coast between Point Reyes and Tomales Point. The Phillip Burton is the only designated wilderness along the California coast, and it maintains a high degree of natural integrity despite its proximity to the San Francisco metropolitan area.

Point Reyes sits immediately west of the famous San Andreas Fault (or Rift) Zone, lying along the eastern edge of the Pacific Plate. Movement along the fault zone has, over time, moved Point Reyes more than 300 miles northwest of corresponding rocks in the Tehachapi Mountains. With its rich grasslands,

32A   PHILLIP BURTON WILDERNESS

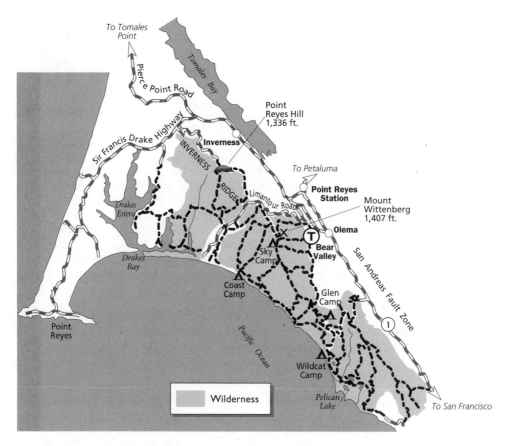

Point Reyes was an important dairy farming region, and grazing of beef and dairy cattle continues today.

The two most dominant features of the Phillip Burton Wilderness are its long coastline and the high crest of Inverness Ridge. Both of these features combine with hills, coastal terraces, coves, beaches, and several small inland lakes in the largest, southeastern segment of the wilderness. Bear Valley, lying along a branch of the San Andreas Fault, is the only break in the barrier of Inverness Ridge between Olema Valley and the sea, and this valley supports a dense canopy of riparian vegetation, with California buckeye being the dominant species. Rich forests of Douglas-fir mantle Inverness Ridge, while coastal chaparral and grasslands dominate in the lower elevations on terraces and coastal foothills.

The central unit of the Phillip Burton, which is separated from the southeast portion by the corridor of Limantour Road, includes the crest area of Inverness Ridge, coastal hills and terraces, the east shores of Estero de Limantour, and Limantour Spit. Open grasslands and forests of Bishop pine, a rare coastal tree endemic to California, dominate the flora of Inverness Ridge here, while chaparral and grasslands clothe lower-elevation seaward slopes. Next to the coast are two interconnected estuaries, Drakes and Limantour, and their mud flats, salt marshes, shallow waters, and sandy bottoms provide habitat for a variety of plants and animals.

Inverness Ridge stretches northwest to Tomales Point, the northwesternmost extension of land on the Point Reyes peninsula. The wilderness includes Tomales Point, an open peninsula covered in grasslands that is the location of a reserve for reintroduced Tule elk. Surrounded by rocky headlands, Tomales Point separates the Pacific Ocean on the west, and Tomales Bay, a submerged valley along the San Andreas Fault Zone, on the east. The rugged shoreline below Tomales Point features unique intertidal areas where plants and animals are adapted to both terrestrial and marine environments. The rocky headlands support populations of Steller and California sea lion, and a recovering population of elephant seals.

Biological diversity compliments the dramatic landscapes of Point Reyes. This diversity and its importance were recognized in 1988 when Point Reyes was declared an International Biosphere Reserve by the United Nations. The more than 850 plant species in the park include 42 rare and endangered plants. Point Reyes has the greatest avian diversity of any national park, with 468 bird species. Black-tailed deer, mountain lion, bobcat, and mountain beaver are among the 37 species of land mammals, and marine mammals add another dozen species. The largest population of mainland harbor seals in California dwells on Point Reyes. The beaches and headlands are some of the best places on the West Coast to observe migrating gray whales.

RECREATIONAL USES: As a whole, both within the wilderness and beyond its boundaries, Point Reyes National Seashore consistently ranks among the top twenty most heavily visited parks in the national park system, with visitation exceeding 2.5 million each year. With that in mind, you may believe that finding solitude in the Phillip Burton Wilderness would be difficult, if not impossible, and in many areas, that's true. With 11 trailheads serving the wilderness trail network, combined with their easy access via mostly paved roads, at least half the trails in the backcountry are very heavily used. Proximity to major population centers and the diversity of unique coastal landscapes makes the Phillip Burton a premier recreation getaway.

32B   PHILLIP BURTON WILDERNESS (TOMALES POINT)

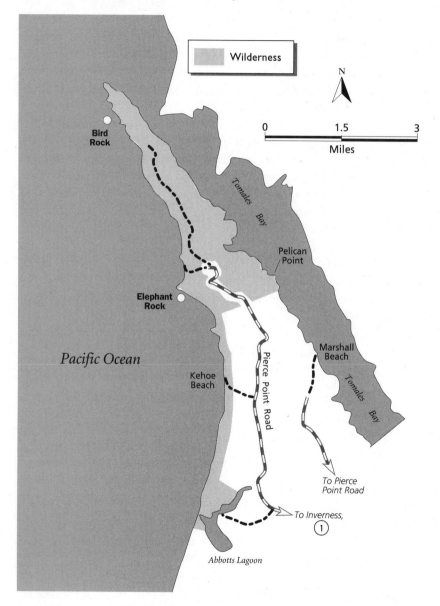

Day hikers make up the majority of users. They visit to pursue a variety of activities, from simply hiking, to bird watching, beachcombing, wildlife watching that includes sea mammals along the coast and deer and elk inland, and whale watching in winter. Or they're satisfied simply by panoramic ocean vistas. There are several miles of trails open to mountain bikes, and they're well used. In the wilderness legislation four trails or trail segments were left open for the use of mechanical equipment including: 1) the Ridge Trail from the Palomarin Road to Pablo Point; 2) the Coast Trail in the slide areas from Palomarin westward; 3) the Coast Trail between the Stewart Trail and the Bear Valley Trail; 4) the closed Lake Ranch Road from the Ridge Trail to the Coast Trail.

Backpackers are limited to overnight stays in one of four backcountry trail camps, and a permit is required. You can get one at the Bear Valley visitor center off California Highway 1 near Olema. Camping is allowed only in one of four campgrounds specified on your permit. All the campsites are located in the southeastern unit; Wildcat and Coast camps are located near the beach, while Sky and Glen camps are located farther inland below Inverness Ridge.

Backpackers should request a copy of *Backpack Camping Information* from the visitor center (see Appendix B). That publication will give you all the information you need to plan a backpack in the Phillip Burton. Reservations are strongly suggested for backcountry trail camps, and fees are required. Permits must be picked up at the Bear Valley Visitor Center. Trail camps can be reserved up to two months in advance. (See Appendix B for more information.)

The trail network surveys the spectrum of Point Reyes landscapes, from the Douglas-fir forests and meadows of Inverness Ridge, to coastal canyons, open ridges and terraces, to broad sandy beaches and rocky headlands. Cross-country travel is possible but requires precautions around crumbling cliffs and steep slopes, and a watchful eye for stinging nettles and poison oak in many places.

Despite the heavy use of the Phillip Burton, several trails are comparatively lightly used. If you're looking for a modicum of solitude, follow one of the trails listed below.

IN THE CENTRAL UNIT:
—Estero Trail
—Glenbrook Trail
—Bucklin Trail
IN THE SOUTHEASTERN UNIT:
—Fire Lane Trail
—Woodward Valley Trail
—Old Pine Trail
—Baldy Trail
—Greenpicker Trail
—Lake Ranch Trail between the Bolema Trail junction and the Coast Trail
—Ridge Trail between Palomarin Road and the Bolema Trail junction
—Teixeira Trail between CA 1 and the Ridge Trail.

Day Hike

Mount Wittenberg

Distance: 4.7 miles, loop trip.
Low/high elevations: 105 feet/1,470 feet.
Difficulty: Moderate.
Best season: April through November.
Topo map: Inverness-CA.
Permits: Not required for day hiking.

HOW TO GET THERE: From CA 1 in the small hamlet of Olema, about 36 miles north of San Francisco and 20 miles west of San Rafael, turn west where a large sign indicates the Point Reyes National Seashore Headquarters. After driving 0.5 mile from CA 1, turn left where a sign points to the Bear Valley visitor center. You reach the trailhead after another 0.3 mile. Park in the large parking lot opposite the visitor center.

This hike leads through forests of Douglas-fir and across lush, green meadows. Views from the top of Mount Wittenberg, the high point of the Phillip Burton Wilderness, are panoramic of the varied landscapes that characterize the Point Reyes region. Portions of the trail are heavily used, but the natural attractions of the area help compensate for the lack of solitude. The weather in the area is highly variable. During winter the area is swept by strong Pacific storms, and during the summer a cold fog often enshrouds the coastal slopes.

From the large Bear Valley trailhead parking area, walk south past the locked gate, avoiding the signed Earthquake Trail that immediately branches left. Stroll 0.2 mile south on the closed road, then turn right onto the signed Mount Wittenberg Trail. A moderate ascent brings you into a shady forest of tanbark-oak and towering Douglas-fir. The lush understory is dominated by ferns.

After a few switchbacks, your trail breaks into the open in a beautiful green meadow surrounded by dense Douglas-fir forest. From this point, Inverness Ridge can be seen rising on the western skyline, crowned by the grassy summit of your goal, Mount Wittenberg.

The trail continues climbing through a series of lovely meadows, and with the help of switchbacks, you soon reach a junction with a northwest-bound path leading to the summit of Mount Wittenberg. Turn right there, and ascend grassy slopes dotted with occasional Douglas-fir, and soon surmount the grassy, wildflower-carpeted summit region of 1,470-foot Mount Wittenberg, crowned by stunted Douglas-fir.

After absorbing the panoramic vistas, avoid a faint, northwest-bound path and descend southward, soon picking up a steep trail that descends to a wide, grassy saddle where you rejoin the Mount Wittenberg Trail. Just before reach-

The Sky Trail traverses the rich grasslands of Inverness Ridge.

ing the destination and mileage sign at the saddle, avoid another northwest-bound trail, and proceed west on the Sky Trail. A sign indicates that the Meadow Trail, the return leg of your loop, is 0.4 mile ahead.

Begin descending the wide trail west, then south, around a grassy hill, passing a few stunted Douglas-firs en route. You reach a signed, four-way junction 0.4 mile from the last; turn left (east) onto the Meadow Trail, and reenter Douglas-fir forest. After hiking another 0.5 mile east on the Meadow Trail, you break into the open and proceed through a quarter-mile-long ridgetop meadow, then duck back into the forest of Douglas-fir, California bay, and tanbark-oak. The descent soon becomes moderate as you approach Bear Valley.

At length you cross a small creek on a wooden bridge, then turn left and stroll down the closed road for 0.8 mile to complete the hike at the trailhead.

Snow Mountain Wilderness Complex   `33`

Location: 65 miles north of Santa Rosa, 30 miles northeast of Ukiah, and 65 miles southwest of Red Bluff.
Size: 40,482 acres.
Administration: USDAFS–Mendocino National Forest.
Management status: National Forest wilderness (37,679 acres); roadless nonwilderness (2,803 acres), allocated for backcountry management (no development) in the Forest Plan.
Ecosystems: Sierran Forest–Alpine Meadows province, Northern California Coast Ranges section, characterized by mountains with rounded ridges, steep sides, and narrow, deep canyons; Jurassic and Cretaceous metamorphic rocks, intensely folded and faulted, and alluvial deposits; potential natural vegetation is chaparral, and Coast Range montane forest; dendritic drainage pattern with many perennial streams and springs, and wet and dry meadows.
Elevation range: 1,800 feet to 7,056 feet.
System trails: 37 miles.
Maximum core-to-perimeter distance: 5.75 miles.
Activities: Day hiking, backpacking, horseback riding, fishing, cross-country skiing, and snowshoeing.
Maps: Mendocino National Forest visitor map; Snow Mountain Wilderness map (topographic; 1 inch/mile); see Appendix D for a list of USGS 1:24,000 quads.

OVERVIEW: The North Coast Ranges head north for 180 miles from the San Francisco Bay Area into northwestern California, where they merge with the Klamath Mountains. These mountains are made up of numerous mountain ranges aligned in a northwest-southeast pattern. Remote Snow Mountain lies near the southern end of one such mountain crest that some geologists refer to as the Mendocino Range, one of the longest crests in the interior North Coast Ranges complex. Snow Mountain's 7,000-foot summit stands at timberline, bears the brunt of Pacific storms, and captures an average of 60 inches of moisture annually, mostly in the form of snow.

The wilderness embraces a 13-mile stretch of the crest of this North Coast Range mountain divide. The west slopes of the divide form the headwaters of tributaries to the main stem and Rice Fork Eel River, and on the east slopes are the headwaters of the Middle and South Forks of Stony Creek. The Middle Fork Stony Creek flows through a precipitous canyon that in places is more than 2,000 feet deep. It is an important wild rainbow trout fishery and the

33 SNOW MOUNTAIN WILDERNESS COMPLEX

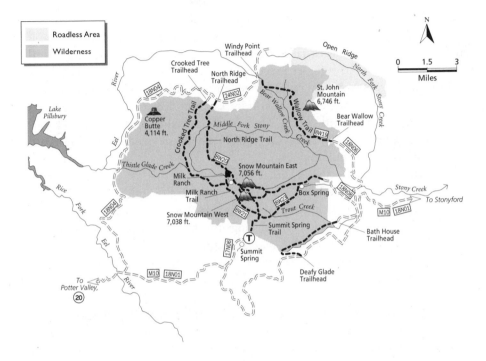

principal trout stream here. Many other streams also support healthy, self-sustaining populations of rainbow trout. Much of the Middle Fork, however, is rugged and inaccessible, with trail access at only two points via unmaintained trails, and special wild trout fishing regulations apply to anglers fishing this stream (refer to California state fishing regulations).

Forests of mixed conifers, primarily red fir, white fir, incense-cedar, and Jeffrey pine, dominate the higher elevations. Early-season wet meadows interrupt the forests and barren slopes in the high country, but these grasslands quickly dry up as summer weather sets in. On the crest of Snow Mountain and its high spur ridges, barren rocky slopes are studded with stunted red firs, representing the only subalpine-like environment in the wilderness. Middle elevations host mixed conifers and black oak, fields of chaparral, and oak woodlands. Oak woodlands, chaparral, and rocky cliffs and bluffs dominate the lowest elevations on the eastern side of the wilderness. Stands of very old, gnarled curl-leaf mountain mahogany, a fragrant shrub that is one of the preferred browse plants for the black-tailed deer population, occurs on higher exposed ridges with shallow soils. More than 500 species of plants have been identified in the Snow Mountain Wilderness, and more than one-quarter of these species are growing here at the extreme margin of their geographical range.

The diverse ecosystems contain important habitat for northern spotted owl, goshawk, fisher, and marten, only four of the 122 species of wildlife that dwell here. Black bear and black-tailed deer are common, and Snow Mountain contains key winter and summer range for the deer population. Mountain lions thrive in the Snow Mountain area, feeding primarily on the abundant deer. Hunters also visit the area in autumn in search of deer, most taking day trips into the wilderness with stock. There is also an abundance of upland bird species, including California valley quail, mountain quail, mourning dove, sooty grouse, and bandtail pigeon.

Adjacent to the northeast corner of the wilderness is the 2,803-acre Snow Mountain Backcountry Area, an area that was part of the original Snow Mountain roadless area not included when the area was designated wilderness in 1984. This area contains key winter range for deer; it lies between the wilderness boundary and Open Ridge, and is bounded on the south by Forest Road 18N45, embracing the headwaters of North Fork Stony Creek. Elevations range from 2,000 feet to 3,900 feet.

RECREATIONAL USES: The Snow Mountain area is remote, reached only after long drives on winding forest roads. Although the area lies within four hours' driving distance of the population centers of the Bay Area, Santa Rosa, and Sacramento, backcountry use is generally light, except during hunting season, when peripheral roads, trailheads, and trails are kept busy by hunters.

The Snow Mountain Wilderness is growing increasingly popular with day-hikers, particularly during the spring months. When the Sierra Nevada and other backcountry destinations in northern California are buried by deep snowpack, Snow Mountain attracts more visitors. Snow Mountain is well suited for day hiking and short backpack trips, particularly in early season when abundant water is still available. Water sources, especially those in high elevations, tend to dry up during summer.

The trail network is serviced by eight trailheads and provides opportunities for a variety of short hikes, both round trips and loop trips. In addition to the 37 miles of maintained trails, there are another 18.5 miles of unmaintained pathways. The summit area of Snow Mountain, featuring an east and west peak, is the destination of the majority of visitors, and for good reason. This 7,000-foot crest is one of few subalpine-like areas in the North Coast Ranges, and vistas are panoramic and far-ranging. The highest trailheads—Summit Springs, Crooked Tree, North Ridge, and Windy Point—all lie above 5,000 feet, but even so, they are often accessible in winter by cross-country skiers and snowshoers. The North Ridge and Crooked Tree Trailheads lie close together, and by following the unmaintained, 7-mile Crooked Creek Trail and the 9.5-mile North Ridge Trail, which converge in the meadows of Milk Ranch, you can make a two-day loop.

The lower-elevation trailheads on the east side lead to lower elevations of the wilderness that are attractive from late autumn through early spring. The Bear Wallow Trailhead takes you to the Bear Wallow Trail (8W19) that traverses the southern and western slopes of 6,746-foot Saint John Mountain. This fine trail heads for the Middle Fork Stony Creek, with excellent views into that creek's gorge and of Snow Mountain. The Trout Creek Trailhead will take you to the unmaintained Trout Creek Trail, which is a steep route that ascends a ridgeline past Rattlesnake Glade to the Box Springs Loop Trail east of High Rock. The Bath House Trailhead leads to the Bath House Trail (7W15), which follows the south wilderness boundary along the course of the South Fork Stony Creek. This trail currently ends at the Deafy Glade Trailhead on the south wilderness boundary. A proposed trail may eventually be constructed from Deafy Glade up the steep slopes to the Summit Springs Trail (8W21).

Day Hike or Overnighter

Snow Mountain

Distance: 7.8 miles, round trip.
Low/high elevations: 5,240 feet/7,056 feet.
Difficulty: Moderate.
Best season: Mid-May through October.
Topo maps: Crockett Peak-CA, Potato Hill-CA, Fouts Springs-CA, St. John Mountain-CA.
Permits: Wilderness permits are not required. A California Campfire Permit is required for open fires and backpack stoves.

HOW TO GET THERE: From Interstate 5 in the Sacramento Valley, 70 miles south of Red Bluff and 63 miles north of Sacramento, turn west onto California Highway 20. After 8.6 miles, turn right onto Leesville Road at a hard-to-spot junction where a sign reads STONYFORD–30. After 30 miles, you pass the Stonyford Ranger Station on your right. One-half mile beyond, turn left onto Market Street in downtown Stonyford.

After driving 0.2 mile from Stonyford, turn left again onto Fouts Springs Road (Forest Road M10/18N01). A sign here points to Fouts Springs and Letts Lake. Follow this road, paved at first, with a graded dirt surface farther on, into the mountains via the Stony Creek drainage, avoiding several signed spur roads. After 19.1 miles, turn right onto FR 24N02, leaving FR

Red firs stud the slopes of Snow Mountain.

M10/18N01 where a sign points to Summit Springs. Very soon, bear right again where a sign indicates Blue Slide Ridge. After 1.7 miles from FR M10/18N01, you reach a four-way junction at the Lake/Colusa County line. Take the northbound road where the sign points to Summit Springs and the Summit Springs Trail. Climb steeply on this good, dirt, ridgetop road for another 0.1 mile to the trailhead at the end of the road, avoiding two right-branching roads along the way.

The trailhead can also be reached from the town of Upper Lake, which lies above the north end of Clear Lake. From CA 20 in Upper Lake, turn north where a sign indicates the ranger station is 1 mile ahead and Lake Pillsbury is 31 miles ahead. After reaching the ranger station, follow paved northbound County Road 301 for 15.5 miles, then turn right onto dirt FR M10/18N01. The sign here indicates Bear Creek and Snow Mountain. Following this road into the mountains, you pass occasional signs pointing to Bear Creek Station. At one point the road fords wide and shallow Bear Creek. When FR M10/18N01 branches south, stay left, soon passing Bear Creek Station, and very soon thereafter turn right onto FR 17N16, 7.3 miles from CR 301. Follow this road for 5.5 miles to the above-mentioned four-way junction at the Lake/Colusa County line, and drive 1.8 miles to the trailhead. The trailhead is 31 miles from Upper Lake.

This memorable hike features far-ranging vistas and visits timberline environments en route to the subalpine summits of Snow Mountain. The trail rises nearly 2,000 feet from the trailhead, though grades are moderate, and the vistas and scenery are so absorbing that most hikers probably won't notice the significant elevation gain.

From the trailhead at 5,240 feet, shaded by ponderosa and sugar pine, white fir, and black oak, the wide, steep trail ascends northeastward. The trail very soon leaves the forest and climbs to an open hillside sparsely vegetated with grasses and lupine. After 1.8 miles you level off on the flat crest and enter a cool red fir stand, then reach a junction with the eastbound Box Springs Loop Trail. Bear left here and proceed north on the faint trail. Watch for blazes if you lose the route.

After a minor descent, you soon reach another junction. The left-branching trail leads northwest to Milk Ranch and could be used to loop back via the basin just west of Snow Mountain. But for now, turn right; the sign indicates that Snow Mountain is 2 miles ahead. Another sign at the meadow's edge calls the area Cedar Camp, although there are no cedars here. Your trail crosses a meadow and heads north. Soon it crosses over the crest of the range and traverses northeast facing slopes above the head of the Trout Creek drainage.

You then top out on a 6,600-foot saddle and pass into the Dark Hollow Creek drainage, a tributary of the Middle Fork Stony Creek. In an open, forested bowl, accompanied by a ground-hugging understory of manzanita and ceanothus, your route passes a right-branching (northbound) trail leading to the East Snow Mountain and Box Springs Loop Trails. Bear left here and proceed on the level through a northeast-facing bowl, passing a few grassy-banked, seasonal streams en route.

You soon reach a small creek and climb to a tiny meadow at its source. The red fir forest becomes sparse as you ascend the increasingly rocky basin. The trail soon bends southwest while ascending a few small grassy benches to the crest of the range, where there is a four-way junction.

The trail straight ahead (northwest) descends into a north-facing bowl, crosses the ridge just south of 6,684-foot Signal Peak, and then descends to Milk Ranch. The left-branching (southbound) trail climbs 190 feet in 0.5 mile to the open summit of Snow Mountain West, rising to 7,038 feet. Turn right and ascend the faint trail for 0.5 mile to the 7,056-foot summit of Snow Mountain East. The view from the summit, an all-encompassing 360-degree panorama, is superb. From your vantage point high atop this North Coast Range divide you can gaze northwestward to the Yolla Bolly Mountains near the northern tip of the range, to Mount Shasta, Lassen Peak, and the Sacramento Valley.

King Range   **34**

Location: North Coast, 40 miles south of Eureka, and 15 miles west of Garberville.
Size: 33,635 acres.
Administration: USDIBLM–Ukiah District, Arcata Resource Area.
Management status: BLM Wilderness Study Area (WSA).
Ecosystems: California Coastal Steppe–Mixed Forest–Redwood Forest province, Northern California Coast section, characterized by rocky shoreline and very steep mountains and precipitous canyons; Cretaceous, Jurassic, and Tertiary marine sedimentary rocks, and Tertiary marine sediments; potential natural vegetation is coastal prairie-scrub mosaic, and mixed evergreen forest with rhododendron; many perennial springs and streams with small drainage areas and a dendritic drainage pattern.
Elevation range: Sea level to 4,087 feet.
System trails: 15.5 miles.
Maximum core-to-perimeter distance: 3 miles.
Activities: Day hiking, backpacking, surf and stream fishing.
Maps: BLM King Range National Conservation Area recreation map; see Appendix D for a list of USGS 1:24,000 quads.

OVERVIEW: The Coast Ranges of California typically jut abruptly skyward from the shores of the Pacific Ocean, making them seem much higher than their modest elevations would suggest. One such mountain chain, the King Range, located along northern California's "Lost Coast," boasts the greatest relief in the shortest distance of all the state's Coast Ranges. Its chaparral-clad slopes soar from the ocean's edge to more than 4,000 feet in a lateral distance of only 3 miles.

Despite the dry appearance of the brush-clad seaward slopes of the range, this region is one of the wettest in the continental U.S. The small hamlet of Honeydew in the Mattole River valley northwest of Kings Peak averages 100 inches of moisture annually. November through March bring heavy rains to the region, while in summer, fog often blankets the coastline.

The shoreline beneath the King Range is known as the Lost Coast, the wildest and most remote coastal strip remaining in California. The Lost Coast Trail is a superb hiking route along this coastline, stretching 24 miles from the mouth of the Mattole River in the north to Shelter Cove in the south.

34A KING RANGE WILDERNESS STUDY AREA (NORTH)

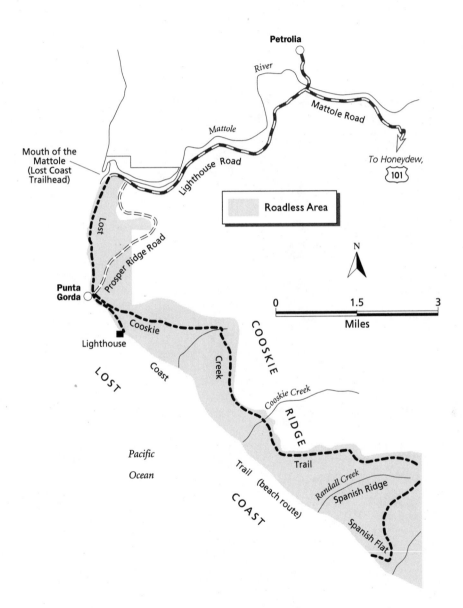

34B   KING RANGE WILDERNESS STUDY AREA (SOUTH)

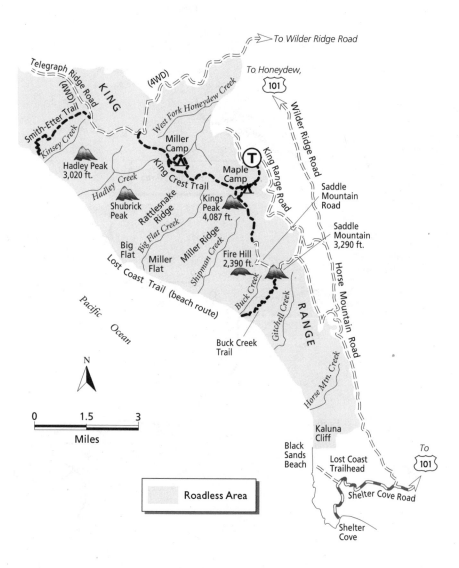

To Wilder Ridge Road

Telegraph Ridge Road (4WD)

KING

(4WD)

West Fork Honeydew Creek

To Honeydew, 101

Smith-Etter Trail

Kinsey Creek

Miller Camp

Maple Camp

T

Wilder Ridge Road

Hadley Peak 3,020 ft.

Hadley Creek

King Crest Trail

King Range Road

Saddle Mountain Road

Shubrick Peak

Rattlesnake Ridge

Kings Peak 4,087 ft.

Saddle Mountain 3,290 ft.

Big Flat Creek

Miller Ridge

Shipman Creek

Fire Hill 2,390 ft.

Big Flat

Miller Flat

Lost Coast Trail (beach route)

Buck Creek

Gitchell Creek

Horse Mountain Road

RANGE

Pacific Ocean

N

Buck Creek Trail

Horse Mtn. Creek

0   1.5   3

Miles

Kaluna Cliff

Black Sands Beach

Lost Coast Trailhead

To 101

Roadless Area

Shelter Cove Road

Shelter Cove

Much of this area, including the coastline and the King Range, lies within the boundaries of the King Range National Conservation Area, and 33,635 acres therein are currently roadless. Since this area is still under study for inclusion into the Wilderness Preservation System, several alternatives proposed in the Wilderness Study Area EIS are under consideration, ranging from designating all roadless lands as wilderness to maintaining current management with no wilderness designation.

Commercial forest land, dominated by Douglas-fir, occupies 6,500 acres of the WSA. The potential for developing mineral and energy resources in the WSA is considered low to moderate. The most contentious issue regarding wilderness designation of the King Range involves off-highway vehicle use. Users of OHVs account for about one-quarter of all visitors to the WSA, primarily along peripheral roads in the northern and eastern portions and primarily during hunting season. Black Sands Beach, a 3-mile strip stretching from Kaluna Cliff to Gitchell Creek, is one of only two beach areas open to OHV use in California, and OHV interests are fighting tooth-and-nail to keep the beach open to motorized recreation. This beach is also important to hikers, since it is the final 3 miles of the Lost Coast Trail.

There are many environmental, scenic, and recreational attributes to the King Range WSA to recommend it for wilderness designation. The Lost Coast is the last wild stretch of California's vast coastline, stretching some 25 miles from the mouth of the Mattole River in the north to Shelter Cove in the south. The King Range, rising abruptly from the sea, provides an extremely rugged barrier between the coast and inland areas. The four significant botanical resources in the WSA include 1,500 acres of old-growth Douglas-fir forest in the Honeydew Creek drainage on the east slopes of the King Range; the Mattole dune system; undisturbed coastal prairie; and stands of leafy reedgrass along the coastal strand, a candidate for listing as being threatened with extinction.

Wildlife here is as diverse as the landscapes. Offshore areas, kelp beds, and tidal areas are inhabited by harbor seals, Steller and California sea lions, and various marine birds, including cormorants. Terrestrial wildlife inhabiting forests, chaparral, and grasslands include black-tailed deer, mountain lion, black bear, and transplanted Roosevelt elk. Upland game species include mountain quail, blue grouse, bandtailed pigeon, mourning dove, gray squirrel, brush rabbit, and black-tailed jackrabbit. A variety of raptors use the WSA for wintering, including sharp-shinned and Cooper's hawks. Turkey vultures summer here and a small population of osprey occupies the areas surrounding larger streams and the Mattole River. Bald eagles forage on winter-spawning anadromous fish. The Honeydew Creek Wildlife Preserve, located north of Kings Peak, covers 2,980 acres in the WSA, and in its old-growth and hardwood forests you'll find wintering areas for bald eagles and important habitat for spotted owls, black bear, mink, and anadromous fish.

Nine tributaries to the Mattole River arise on the inland side of the WSA, and there are 12 drainages on the coastal side of the King Range. All of these streams support spawning salmon and steelhead, but the inland streams provide the better rearing habitat. Resident fish include sculpin in all drainages and rainbow trout in many streams.

Despite the biological diversity of the WSA, it is the landscape, and the sense of remoteness it provides, that makes it a premier wilderness destination. In the north, the King Range begins to rise southeast of the estuary of the Mattole River. There the broad river plain blends into a large sandy beach that extends south to historic Punta Gorda Lighthouse. This stretch of coast is bounded by cliffs and slopes that rise abruptly into the stream-dissected King Range. Above the beach, the slopes of the King Range are mantled in grasslands, with coastal chaparral and Douglas-fir in sheltered stream drainages. Several terraces interrupt the rugged shoreline farther south, and broad, grassy flats extend to the beach in places such as Miller Flat, Big Flat, and Spanish Flat. The southern end of the Lost Coast is covered in black sand and is one of the most beautiful beaches on the North Coast.

RECREATIONAL USES: The Lost Coast/King Range area provides outstanding opportunities for primitive recreation, not only because it is one of the most rugged and scenic parts of the California coast, but also because its isolation and topography largely protect it from human intrusion. The topography of the King Range WSA concentrates use on the beaches and along the developed trail network, and the majority of use is confined to late spring through early autumn. Yet opportunities for solitude are still excellent.

The Lost Coast Trail is the area's primary attraction, and backpacking use by both round-trip and through-hikers increased markedly during the 1990s. More than 60% of hikers stay on the beach. The Lost Coast Trail really is a 24-mile beach route, rather than a trail. Some points along the route may be impassable during very high tides, so it is advisable to use a tide table when hiking here. Not only does the Lost Coast Trail provide one of the best coastal backpack trips on the West Coast, it also provides opportunities for both surf and stream fishing.

Seven trailheads provide access to backcountry. In the north, the Mouth of the Mattole recreation site is the usual jump-off point for a hike along the Lost Coast Trail. The Smith-Etter Road and Telegraph Ridge Road, both suitable for four-wheel-drive vehicles only, will take you to the Spanish Ridge Trail. The north King Crest Trailhead is also located along Smith-Etter Road atop North Slide Peak. The Lightning Trailhead is the only route to the King Crest from the north slopes of the range. The Saddle Mountain Road leads to the Buck Creek Trail and the south King Crest Trailhead. And finally, on the south at Black Sands Beach, just northwest of Shelter Cove, is where most through-hikers on the Lost Coast Trail end their journey.

The 7.5-mile King Crest Trail traverses the crest of the range between the Smith-Etter four-wheel-drive road on the northwest and the Saddle Mountain Road on the southeast. Only one foot trail goes down to the beach from the King Crest—the 3-mile Buck Creek Trail, a rigorous trail that descends more than 3,000 feet from the Saddle Mountain Road southeast of Kings Peak. The only other trail descending to the beach is the Spanish Ridge Trail and four-wheel-drive road; it is currently closed to motorized use, except for emergencies and livestock operators.

While backpackers can camp wherever they wish (above the high tide line) along the beach, three trail camps provide overnight accommodations in the King Range. Miller Camp, Maple Camp, and Big Rock Camp are all located in shady, mixed hardwood–Douglas-fir forests on the north slopes of the range adjacent to small streams. These lightly used campsites are ideal for short loop or round trips via the King Crest Trail, but few hikers stay overnight in the King Range. Most of the mountain trails are used by day-hikers, and not heavily. Autumn hunters account for half the annual use.

Day Hike or Overnighter

Kings Peak

Distance: 6.1 miles, semi-loop trip.
Low/high elevations: 2,184 feet/4,087 feet.
Difficulty: Moderate.
Best seasons: April through June; mid-September through mid-November.
Topo maps: Honeydew-CA, Shubrick Peak-CA.
Permits: A California Campfire Permit is required for open fires and backpack stoves.

HOW TO GET THERE: Follow U.S. Highway 101 either 63 miles south from Eureka or 91 miles north from Ukiah to the Redway exit. Proceed west into the small town of Redway and then turn west onto the Briceland Road, heading toward Briceland and Shelter Cove. After a long mile from Redway you bridge the Eel River and proceed through the Whittemore Grove of redwoods.

Pass through the small town of Briceland 5.7 miles from Redway, and after another 4.2 miles, avoid a right turn signed for Honeydew and Petrolia. Ignore a signed left turn to Whitethorn 12 miles from Redway, and continue along the steep and winding paved road, avoiding the signed left-branching road leading to Nadelos and Wailaki campgrounds 17.1 miles from Redway.

Presently the road climbs to another ridge, and just before attaining the summit, avoid a left-forking paved road. At the summit, another paved road continues ahead for 4 miles to Shelter Cove, but you should turn right onto a dirt road, indicated by a large BLM sign. Almost at once avoid a paved road that forks right, and instead follow the steep, narrow, and winding dirt road northwest, passing the entrances to Tolkan Campground after 3.7 miles, and Horse Mountain Campground after 6.4 miles. Be sure to avoid the left-branching Saddle Mountain Road 0.1 mile before reaching Horse Mountain Camp (that road leads to the south King Crest Trailhead).

After driving 9.3 miles from the pavement, or 26.8 miles from Redway, you will reach a prominently signed junction. Turn left here onto King Range Road. This wide and smooth dirt road is a noticeable improvement over the past 9.3 miles. Stay to the right where a signed spur forks off to the Saddle Mountain Road after 2 miles, then curve into and out of several drainages to the signed Lightning Trailhead after 6.4 miles. Parking space is available for several cars just north of the trailhead.

This hike follows the Lightning Trail, a steadily climbing spur to the 7.5-mile-long King Crest Trail, which you follow to the apex of the King Range. En route, you pass through coastal forests of Douglas-fir, madrone, tanbark-oak, and coastal chaparral. Two trail camps along the way invite hikers to stay overnight.

From the trailhead, the smooth tread of the Lightning Trail climbs quickly past a trailhead register, then switchbacks at a moderate grade to a ridgeline. As you climb steadily southward, salal soon joins the understory, and after 0.8 mile you meet a signed spur trail branching right to Big Rock Camp. There is only one campsite here, just a few feet off the main trail, next to a small stream.

Beyond the trail camp, you switchback steadily for 1.0 mile among stately Douglas-fir to a signed junction. Here trails fork right and left, both leading to Kings Peak and forming a pleasant loop. Maple Camp lies along the left-branching trail, which descends for 150 feet from the junction. Once the trail begins to rise again you enter Douglas-fir forest and soon reach signed Maple Camp, 2 miles from the trailhead. Backpackers will find seven campsites carved into the steep trailside slopes. A spring issues from the draw just below the camp.

Beyond Maple Camp, the trail climbs up the draw before leaving it to ascend brush-clad slopes, winding upward to the crest of the King Range and a junction with its namesake trail after 0.6 mile.

A 0.1-mile traverse across slopes thick with manzanita and scrub oak brings you to another junction. The crest trail continues the traverse, but to reach the peak you must take the left fork, which climbs steeply and is noticeably rougher. Just below the peak another trail branches right, leading back down to the King Crest Trail. You will use that trail for your return trip. First climb the final few feet to the summit, passing a crude shelter just below the high point, 0.4 mile from the King Crest Trail. The far-reaching vistas from Kings Peak are breathtaking, encompassing mountains, forest, valleys, and the ocean.

Eventually hikers must abandon the memorable vistas and begin the trek back to the trailhead. First descend to the aforementioned trail and turn left, following switchbacks through the brush for 0.2 mile to the junction with the King Crest Trail, where you bear left once again, and soon follow switchbacks steadily downhill to another junction 0.6 mile from the peak. You should bear right here to the end of the loop at the junction with the trail to Maple Camp after 0.4 mile. From here turn left and retrace your steps 1.75 miles to the trailhead.

Yolla Bolly–Middle Eel Wilderness Complex

35

Location: 30 miles west of Red Bluff.
Size: 173,289 acres.
Administration: USDAFS–Mendocino, Shasta-Trinity, and Six Rivers National Forests; USDIBLM–Arcata Resource Area.
Management status: National Forest wilderness (156,000 acres); roadless nonwilderness (15,289 acres) released for multiple-use management; BLM Wilderness Study Area (2,000 acres).
Ecosystems: Sierran Forest–Alpine Meadows province, Northern California Coast Range section, characterized by mountains with rounded ridges, steep sides, and narrow canyons; Jurassic and Cretaceous metamorphic rocks, intensely folded and faulted; potential natural vegetation is chaparral, Coast Range montane forest, mixed evergreen forest with chinquapin, Klamath montane forest with Douglas-fir; Klamath montane forest with yellow pine, and mixed evergreen forest with rhododendron; many perennial springs, and streams with a dendritic drainage pattern, numerous wet meadows, and few moderately high cirque lakes.
Elevation range: 2,700 feet to 8,092 feet.
System trails: 274 miles.
Maximum core-to-perimeter distance: 11.75 miles.
Activities: Backpacking, day hiking, horseback riding, fishing.
Maps: Mendocino, Shasta-Trinity, and Six Rivers National Forests visitor maps; Yolla Bolly–Middle Eel Wilderness map (topographic, 1 inch/mile); see Appendix D for a list of USGS 1:24,000 quads.

OVERVIEW: The Yolla Bolly–Middle Eel Wilderness, or the "Yolla Bollys," as the area is called by locals, lies near the northern terminus of one of the North Coast Ranges' most prominent divides. Its western and northern flanks drain the Middle Fork Eel River, the North Fork Eel River, the Mad River, and the South Fork Trinity River. Eastside streams eventually empty their waters into the Sacramento, California's mightiest river. The unusual name Yolla Bolly is derived from the language of Wintun Indians, and means "snow-covered high peak."

Only the highest peaks in the area ever hosted glaciers, and some of the finest examples of this minor glaciation can be seen in the vicinity of the North Yolla Bolly Mountains. In total, there are eight small, glacier-excavated lakes in the wilderness, all of them located at high elevations on north- and northeast-facing slopes.

The highest peaks in the wilderness stand at or just above timberline, clustered at the north and south ends of a high divide that separates the drainages of the Middle Fork Eel River to the west, and Cottonwood Creek and Buck Creek that drain eastward to the Sacramento. The North Yolla Bolly Mountains are an array of rocky peaks rising above 7,700 feet at the north end of the wilderness, and their northern flanks represent the most obvious effects of glaciation. The south end of the principal north-south divide is crowned by the 7,500-foot summits of Solomon Peak and Hammerhorn Mountain. At Sugarloaf Peak, 1.5 miles north of Solomon Peak, a spur ridge extends east from the main divide for 6 miles to the eastern wilderness boundary. Crowning this ridge are the South Yolla Bolly Mountains, including Mount Linn, the apex of the wilderness at 8,092 feet, and the only peak above 8,000 feet in the Yolla Bollys.

In the northwestern reaches of the wilderness, another prominent divide winds westward. A spur ridge trending northwest from this divide separates the northwest-flowing South Fork Trinity River from the Mad River. The bulk of the wilderness embraces the headwaters of the Middle Fork Eel River and is characterized by long, rounded ridges extending west and southwest from the high divides. Principal drainages include Rattlesnake Creek, Balm of Gilead Creek, Middle Fork Eel River, and the North Fork of Middle Fork Eel River. The canyons and lower ridges are covered with thick conifer forests, grassy glades, and mixed conifer/oak woodlands. On higher elevation ridges and in high basins, Brewer oak and red fir dominate.

The most unusual conifer in the Yolla Bollys is the foxtail pine, a tree endemic to California. It is found in two general areas separated by more than 300 miles. The southernmost population in the North Coast Ranges is found in the Mount Linn area of the South Yolla Bolly Mountains.

The wilderness and adjacent roadless areas contain critical habitat for a number of aquatic and terrestrial wildlife species. The area contains a significant population of black-tailed deer, and this herd produces the largest trophy-size bucks in the state. Key winter and summer ranges for black-tailed deer are present in the wilderness. With environments ranging from oak woodlands to subalpine conifer forests, the Yolla Bollys also contain important habitat for black bear. There's critical habitat for northern spotted owl, too, along with nesting areas for goshawk, and denning areas for fisher and marten. The Middle Fork Eel River, North Fork of Middle Fork Eel River, and Balm of Gilead Creek provide summer holding habitat for summer-run steelhead. A 24-mile stretch of the Middle Fork Eel River, from the Mendocino National Forest boundary upstream to Fern Point in the wilderness, is designated as a Wild and Scenic River. Under consideration for Wild and Scenic River designation is the remainder of the Middle Fork in the wilderness, and Balm of Gilead Creek. This drainage provides habitat not only for summer-run steelhead, but also for winter-run steelhead, spring-run Chinook salmon, and resident rainbow trout.

35A YOLLA BOLLY–MIDDLE EEL WILDERNESS COMPLEX (WEST)

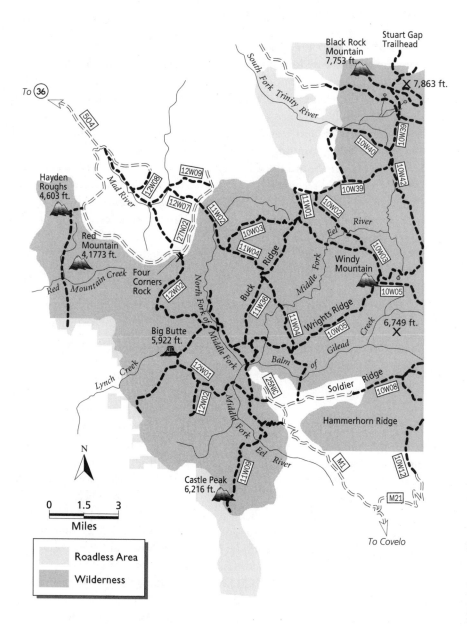

Black Rock Mountain 7,753 ft.

Stuart Gap Trailhead

South Fork Trinity River

× 7,863 ft.

To 36

504

10W39

10W40

10W42

10W39

Hayden Roughs 4,603 ft.

12W09

12W08

Mad River

12W07

27N02

11W02

10W41

10W02

Eel River

10W03

Red Mountain 4,1773 ft.

Red Mountain Creek

Four Corners Rock

12W02

North Fork of Middle Fork

10W03

11W04

Buck Ridge

11W36

Middle Fork

Windy Mountain

10W05

6,749 ft. ×

11W04

Wrights Ridge

10W05

Big Butte 5,922 ft.

12W01

Creek of Gilead

Balm

Lynch Creek

12W02

Middle Fork

25N1C

Soldier Ridge

10W08

Hammerhorn Ridge

N

Eel River

M1

10W12

Castle Peak 6,216 ft.

11W06

M21

To Covelo

| 0 | 1.5 | 3 |
Miles

Roadless Area

Wilderness

35B YOLLA BOLLY–MIDDLE EEL WILDERNESS COMPLEX (EAST)

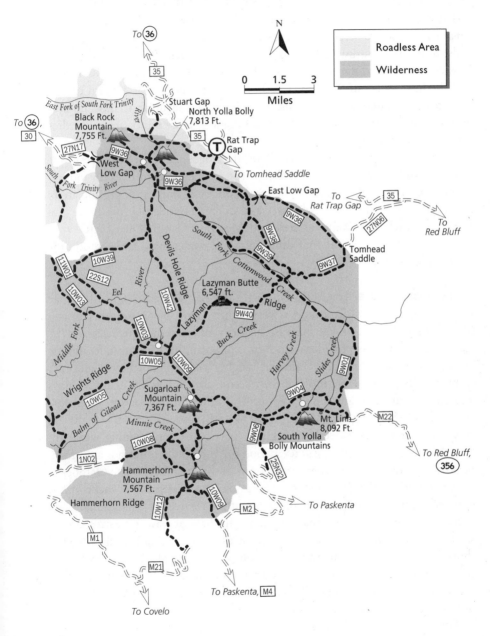

Roadless Area

Wilderness

0 1.5 3
Miles

N

To 36

35

East Fork of South Fork Trinity River

Stuart Gap

North Yolla Bolly
7,813 Ft.

Black Rock
Mountain
7,755 Ft.

To 36,
30

27N17

9W36

West
Low Gap

35

Rat Trap
Gap

T

To Tomhead Saddle

9W36

South Fork Trinity River

South Fork

East Low Gap

To
Rat Trap Gap

35

To
Red Bluff

27N06

9W36

9W38

9W39

Tomhead
Saddle

9W37

11W01

10W39

22S12

Eel River

Devils Hole Ridge

Lazyman Butte
6,547 ft.

Cottonwood Creek

Ridge

10W03

10W42

Lazyman

9W40

10W03

Buck Creek

Harvey Creek

Slides Creek

9W01

10W05

10W05

Wrights Ridge

Middle Fork

Balm of Gilead Creek

Sugarloaf
Mountain
7,367 Ft.

Minnie Creek

9W04

Mt. Linn
8,092 Ft.

M22

10W08

9W06

South Yolla
Bolly Mountains

To Red Bluff,
356

1N02

Hammerhorn
Mountain
7,567 Ft.

25N32

Hammerhorn Ridge

10W42

10W09

M2

To Paskenta

M1

M21

To Paskenta, M4

To Covelo

Significant roadless areas are adjacent to the wilderness on the north and west boundaries. Three roadless units in the Shasta-Trinity National Forest include Penney Ridge (4,844 acres), Murphy Glade (1,018 acres), and East Fork (5,195 acres). The western boundary is adjacent to a BLM Wilderness Study Area covering 2,000 acres at the headwaters of Antone and Casoose Creeks. Finally, along the southwest boundary is the 4,242-acre Big Butte–Shinbone roadless area, including the 6,000-foot summits of Castle Peak and Red Rock and the headwaters of Williams Creek. All the roadless areas contain critical wildlife habitat, undisturbed forests, woodlands, and shrublands, most notably on the 3,380 acres in the Maple Creek and Smokehouse Creek areas, but they offer minimal recreational opportunities.

From the late 1800s to the early 1900s, the ridgelines of the wilderness were heavily grazed by both cattle and sheep. Today, grazing continues on four allotments covering 28,700 acres. The most noticeable impacts of grazing are in the west-central part of the wilderness, in an area bounded by Big Butte and Ant Point, including Willow Creek and Morrison Camp. There, cattle routinely trample springs and foul campsites, and sometimes, cattle invade the Johnson Headquarters area.

RECREATIONAL USES: The Yolla Bolly–Middle Eel Wilderness is California's largest "forgotten" wildland and is very lightly used, being overlooked as a backcountry destination by the vast majority of wilderness travelers in the state. This wilderness provides tremendous opportunities for solitude, unique environments and landscapes, and far-ranging vistas of northern California from its lofty ridges. Here in this highly scenic area, hikers can roam for days and see few hikers, if any. The exception is during hunting season, when forest roads surrounding the wilderness, trailheads, and backcountry trails are very busy with black-tailed deer hunters, particularly on opening weekend. Deer hunting season is the peak use period for Yolla Bolly trailheads and many backcountry trails, and runs generally from mid-September to late October.

Many trails in the Yolla Bollys are faint, owing to light use by backcountry enthusiasts and the minimal maintenance they receive on a rotational basis every 5 to 6 years. Nearly all backcountry trails have at least some exceedingly steep sections, dating back to their origin as "cowboy" trails, following the shortest and fastest way between two points on a straight line. Blowdowns, slumping of unstable slopes, and overgrown brush, combined with the steep grades, make travel on many wilderness trails challenging, and help to keep the numbers of backcountry visitors low.

During the 1990s, the Yolla Bollys have seen an increase in visitation, primarily by autumn deer hunters. In fact, deer hunters using pack and saddle stock make up the majority of backcountry users, and some of them have the most significant impacts on wilderness campsites, including ringed trees, large campfire rings, meat poles, and other "improvements." The greatest increase in foot travel is by day hikers who walk to easily accessible wilderness highlights. These include the North Yolla Bolly Mountains, the Summit Trail to Hammerhorn Mountain and Solomon Peak, and one of the most popular trails, the Ides Cove Loop National Recreation Trail, a 7.5-mile route through the South Yolla Bolly Mountains. The wilderness occasionally sees an increase in visitation during years when heavy snowpack renders other well-known destinations in the Sierra Nevada and Klamath Mountains inaccessible well into the summer. Early spring and late autumn are the preferred seasons for most visitors to the Yolla Bollys. Winter backcountry use is almost nonexistent, due to very long distances from open roads. Generally the wilderness is inaccessible from late November through mid-May.

Fifteen trailheads provide access to the extensive trail network on all sides of the wilderness, and most trailheads are located either on or very near wilderness boundaries. A wide variety of backcountry trips can be devised using this trail network, ranging from round-trip day hikes and overnighters to long-distance, multi-day backpacks. Water is relatively abundant in streams and from numerous hillside springs, and rarely are water sources separated by more than a few miles. The driest trail in the Yolla Bollys is the Wrights Ridge Trail in the south-central portion. Along that often steep trail, 6 miles separate the water sources at Upper Glade Camp and Frying Pan Meadow. Water flows can subside markedly in the wilderness, particularly following dry winters. There are dozens of camps labeled on the wilderness map, and these are traditional sites that most often provide the only suitable terrain for camping near water, and so they are the focal point for most overnight use in the wilderness.

Wilderness travelers searching for solitude (and safety) are advised to steer clear of the Yolla Bollys during hunting season. At other times, solitude is generally the rule, but to ensure solitude, you might consider avoiding the following campsites and trails:

—Frying Pan Meadow (used heavily by stock parties)
—French Cove (popular with stock parties)
—Minnie Lake (popular with stock parties and hikers)
—Summit Trail from Green Springs Trailhead to Frying Pan Meadow (popular with stock parties)
—Georges Valley Trail to Haynes Delight, Balm of Gilead Creek crossing camp, Lower Glade Camp, and Upper Glade Camp (popular with stock parties and hikers)

—Watertrough Camp and Yellowjacket Creek crossing camp (popular with stock parties)

—Sulphur Glade (popular with stock parties)

Day Hike or Overnighter

North Yolla Bolly Mountains

Distance: 11.2 miles, loop trip.
Low/high elevations: 6,000 feet/7,700 feet.
Difficulty: Moderately strenuous.
Best season: Late June through mid-October.
Topo map: North Yolla Bolly-CA 1:25,000 (7.5 x 15-minute) quad.
Permits: Wilderness permits are not required. A California Campfire Permit is required for open fires and backpack stoves.

HOW TO GET THERE: From Red Bluff, follow California Highway 36 west for 38 miles, then turn left (southwest) onto signed Tedoc Road, Forest Road 45. Or from Eureka, drive south on U.S. Highway 101 for 22 miles, then proceed east on CA 36 for 96 miles to the Tedoc Road. This turnoff is about 9.6 miles east of the Harrison Gulch Ranger Station.

Follow this road, mostly dirt with remnant sections of oiled surface, for 12.2 miles to a multi-signed junction at Tedoc Gap. Turn right here; a sign indicates that Stuart Gap is 7 miles ahead. Bear left in less than 0.25 mile where the signed right-branching road heads toward Stuart Gap.

Continuing on FR 45, avoid several signed spur roads as you proceed. After driving 5.3 miles from Tedoc Gap, you reach a multi-branched road junction and the signed trailhead at Rat Trap Gap.

This rewarding hike, involving some moderate cross-country travel, tours the high country of the North Yolla Bolly Mountains and features far-ranging vistas of a wide variety of Yolla Bolly landscapes. The first 1.6 miles of the trip ascend through the pristine Murphy Glade roadless area, an area that deserves the protection of wilderness designation.

From Rat Trap Gap at 6,000 feet, follow the Cold Fork Trail south, very soon passing the homebound segment of your loop, the North Yolla Bolly Lake Trail, on the right. The route then climbs moderately to steeply under a shady canopy of Douglas-fir, red fir, and white fir. You soon negotiate a few elevation-gaining switchbacks and pass just above a reliable spring. Another moderately steep ascent follows, bringing you to a small creek draining the area labeled Barker Camp on the quad. Campsites can be located here and this is the last reliable water source until reaching Pettijohn Basin, more than 4.5 miles ahead.

North Yolla Bolly Lake lies along the northern boundry of the Yolla Bolly–Middle Eel Wilderness.

Beyond Barker Camp, you enter the Yolla Bolly–Middle Eel Wilderness, and just beyond, an opening in the forest allows hikers to view the Sacramento Valley and Lassen Peak in the east. Soon thereafter, you reach a junction on a major east-west ridge at 7,027 feet.

There you turn right onto the faint North Yolla Bolly Mountain Trail. This route heads west through a corridor in the red fir forest and soon breaks into the open on grassy, south-facing slopes interrupted by scattered stands of stunted red fir. On these open slopes, you are treated to unobstructed southward views into the heavily forested interior of the Yolla Bolly–Middle Eel Wilderness. The trail is often faint on these slopes.

Your trail briefly reenters a red fir stand, and just ahead, you may notice some rare foxtail pines joining the sparse forest just southwest of Peak 7531. Your ridgecrest route then passes above the glacier-carved valley of Beegum Basin, lying on the north slopes of the North Yolla Bolly Mountains. Soon the trail disappears altogether, and you continue your grassy, ridgeline jaunt where occasional ducks (cairns) help guide you.

Your trail briefly reappears long enough to get you into a stand of foxtail pines just east of the south summit of the North Yolla Bolly Mountains before disappearing for good. From the foxtail pine stand, scramble a short distance west to the rocky high point of the south summit of the North Yolla Bolly Mountains, Peak 7,700. The north summit, Peak 7,863, lies due north, separated from the south peak by a low gap, and is an easy 0.3-mile cross-country jaunt. The wilderness map shows a trail leading to that peak, but some "trails" in the Yolla Bollys are difficult to locate on the ground.

Vistas from the south peak are excellent, and the Trinity Alps are especially striking. To the northwest rises the summit of 7,755-foot Black Rock Mountain, separated from the south peak by a low saddle. You presently head for that saddle, first scrambling down steep and often loose rock west of the south peak. Once that obstacle is behind you the going is easier, although you are still forced to go over or around some rocky sections on the ridge.

Upon reaching the saddle after less than a mile, you can continue west up the ridge on a faint trail to Black Rock Mountain for more boundless views, or you can turn right on the Pettijohn Trail to loop back to the trailhead. To do so, descend a series of switchbacks into Pettijohn Basin. You soon pass several springs forming the headwaters of the East Fork of South Fork Trinity River, then jog northwest and begin traversing high above meadow-floored Pettijohn Basin, where secluded campsites can be located. You then splash through the runoff of several cold, reliable, but cattle-trampled springs, and within 0.25 mile you begin watching for an unmarked right-branching trail, the North Yolla Bolly Lake Trail. When you locate this trail, turn right and proceed east through fir forest while steadily ascending to the ridge above the deep, cliff-bound cirque containing North Yolla Bolly Lake. You then negotiate numerous switchbacks before leveling off and reaching the lake. It's a small, fishable lake with a backdrop of precipitous 700-foot cliffs, and it makes an excellent rest spot or campsite.

The trail traverses to the west side of the lake, crosses its seasonal outlet, and descends into another small basin lying below a group of striking black pinnacles. Your route soon curves south to reach a hop-across fork of South Fork Beegum Creek. Beyond that crossing, Douglas-fir joins the red fir and white fir forest as you contour along north-facing slopes toward another small creek. You then pass a spring issuing from beneath a large boulder, cross another small creek, and soon reach the initial leg of your loop, where you turn left and stroll back to the trailhead.

Castle Crags Wilderness

36

Location: 40 miles north of Redding and 35 miles south-southeast of Yreka.
Size: 12,232 acres.
Administration: USDAFS—Shasta-Trinity National Forest (10,020 acres); Castle Crags State Park (480 acres).
Management status: National forest and state park wilderness; Castle Crags roadless area (1,732 acres), part of which may be allocated to timber production.
Ecosystems: Sierran Forest–Alpine Meadows province, Klamath Mountains section, characterized by steep-sided mountains, narrow, precipitous drainages, with a subrange of granitic towers, glaciated cirques in the highest elevations; Cambrian, Ordovician, Silurian, and Devonian ultramafic (dark, iron-rich igneous) rocks, intruded by Mesozoic granitic rocks; potential natural vegetation is northern yellow pine forest, Sierran montane forest, and Klamath montane forest with yellow pine; few lakes, several perennial streams.
Elevation range: 2,500 feet to 7,200 feet.
System trails: 27.8 miles.
Maximum core-to-perimeter distance: 2.5 miles.
Activities: Day hiking, backpacking, rock climbing.
Maps: Shasta-Trinity National Forest visitor map; Mount Shasta Wilderness and Castle Crags Wilderness visitor map (topographic; 2 inches/mile); see Appendix D for a list of USGS .1:24,000 quads.

OVERVIEW: Castle Crags Wilderness is located on the easternmost slopes of the Trinity Mountains, one of many interconnected mountain ranges that make up the Klamath Mountains province of northwestern California. Proximity to the coast, abundant precipitation, the northerly latitude, and unusual rock types combine to give the region great biological diversity and an abundance of subalpine landscapes at relatively low elevations.

Located on an east-trending spur ridge off the Trinity Mountains, Castle Crags features two distinctly different landscapes. The southeast half of the wilderness is dominated by the Castle Crags, a prominent array of spires and sheer cliffs that, along with Mount Shasta, are major regional landmarks. The crags are composed of granitic rocks, similar in both age and composition to those of the Sierra Nevada, and the landscape of the crags is reminiscent of parts of Yosemite or the Dome Land Wilderness in the Sierra.

The northern portion of the wilderness is more typical of the Klamath Mountains. Here there is a high, east-trending divide strongly modified by gla-

36 CASTLE CRAGS WILDERNESS

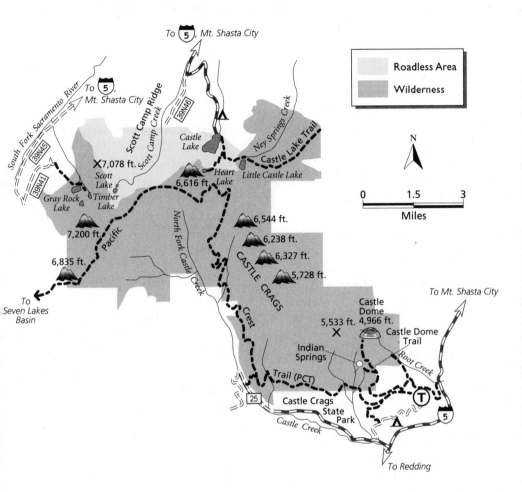

cial activity and crowned by 6,000- and 7,000-foot peaks. Small cirques have been gouged out of the north and east slopes of this divide, and three of these cirques in the Castle Crags complex contain lakes. On the north flank of Peak 7,200, three lakes occupy depressions in a small cirque, including Lower Gray Rock, Timber, and Upper Gray Rock Lakes. Scott Lake lies at the head of Scott Camp Creek, and large Cliff Lake rests in a deep cirque in the headwaters of Castle Lake Creek, both tributaries to the South Fork Sacramento River.

The wilderness is bounded on the east by the Sacramento River, on the north and northwest by the river's South Fork, and on the south by the canyon of Castle Creek. The North Fork Castle Creek is the principal drainage in the wilderness, gathering its waters from the high divide and flowing down the steep south slopes of the wilderness. The northern boundary generally follows the high divide, and the few streams that originate on the north slopes of the divide all empty into the South Fork Sacramento River.

There are a few wet meadows in the drainage headwaters and riparian vegetation hugs the banks of many stream courses, including trees such as big-leaf maple, vine maple, and Pacific dogwood. Much of the wilderness that is not dominated by bare rock is covered in an evergreen mantle of montane chaparral. Dominated by greenleaf and pinemat manzanita, huckleberry oak, mountain whitethorn, and wedge-leaf ceanothus, these brush fields, combined with the steep slopes that predominate in the wilderness, make off-trail travel very difficult if not impossible. Conifers cover the most sheltered slopes, and on south-facing slopes where deeper soils are found. Open woodlands in low to middle elevations contain black oak, tanbark-oak, and live oak. Castle Crags contains more than 300 species of wildflowers, including the endemic Castle Crags harebell. Moist sites host tiger lily, Indian rhubarb, pitcher plant, and yellow monkey flower, while drier sites feature various species of buckwheat, and yarrow, aster, and cycladenia. Poison oak is common in lower elevations, fringing many trails and dictating caution when hikers and climbers travel off-trail.

The habitats in Castle Crags, ranging from brush fields to forests and from rocky outcrops to riparian areas, support a variety of wildlife species. One of the more common animals visitors are likely to encounter is the western rattlesnake. Particularly in brush fields and rocky areas, hikers may unexpectedly meet one of these reptiles, some of which can exceed four feet in length. During the spring months, hikers in grassy and brushy areas may become host to the abundant ticks found in the area. Bobcats feed on an abundant rodent population, while mountain lions stalk deer throughout the crags. Black bears are common, as are coyotes; marten and fisher are seldom observed, though they do dwell here.

Only one roadless area lies adjacent to the wilderness, and since there is little commercial timber standing there, this 1,732-acre area will likely remain undeveloped. The Castle Crags roadless area contains two prominent cirques at the head of Scott Camp and Castle Lake Creeks, on the north slopes of the divide that forms the wilderness boundary. The three high lakes in the area include large Castle Lake, which is where the 1855 Battle of Castle Crags initiated 18 years of conflict between white settlers, the U.S. Army, and the Modoc people of northeastern California and southern Oregon.

RECREATIONAL USES: Castle Crags State Park, which lies on the southeast boundary of the wilderness and extends 480 acres of its land inside the wilderness, is the focal point of recreational activity in the Castle Crags area. Five trails beginning at three trailheads lead into the wilderness from here. The Pa-

The Castle Dome Trail leads into the heart of the Castle Crags.

cific Crest Trail (PCT) enters on the east boundary of the state park adjacent to Interstate 5 at the Soda Creek Trailhead, and its traverse through the wilderness for 19 miles, passes beneath the Castle Crags and follows the high divide in the northern reaches. The Bobs Hat Trail follows a closed road and foot trail from the park entrance station for 1.2 miles to the PCT. The Vista Point Trailhead at the end of the road in the state park provides access to three trails: the dead-end Root Creek Trail, the PCT, and the Castle Dome Trail—the only trail leading into the Castle Crags.

You can also get to the PCT by three short spur trails. One begins at the Dog Trailhead to the south along the North Fork Castle Creek, off the Whalan Road (Forest Road 25). Another trail takes you there from the South Soapstone Trailhead, located along a logging road north of FR 25. The third route is from the North Soapstone Trailhead, located at the end of a primitive logging road in Soapstone Gulch, off FR 26 in the South Fork Sacramento River canyon. Although the PCT is the longest trail in the wilderness, most of the use it receives is by through-hikers northbound toward Oregon, usually in late summer. The trail traverses at low elevations around the south and west sides of the Castle Crags; it provides dramatic vistas but offers few campsites. It passes several creeks draining into the North Fork Castle Creek, the falls on Burstarse Creek, and several springs, but it is dry, open, and hot as it traverses the high divide in the northern reaches of the wilderness.

FR 26 affords access into the northern slopes of the wilderness from Siskiyou Lake near Mt. Shasta City. The popular Castle Lake area, on the boundary of the Castle Crags roadless area, can be reached via FR 26 and the paved Castle Lake Road. Two trails begin at the road's end; one follows the shore of the 5,500-foot lake, and the other—the Castle Lake Trail— ascends the slopes of the Castle Lake cirque, crosses over the divide and into the wilderness, and leads to Little Castle Lake in less than one mile. That trail follows the divide east from Little Castle Lake, ultimately leaving the wilderness en route to lookout-capped Mount Bradley. An unmaintained trail leaves the Castle Lake Trail one-half mile from the trailhead and climbs to Heart Lake, a 6,000-foot tarn just inside the wilderness.

The Castle Lake Road is plowed in winter to a cross-country ski area trailhead, 0.5 mile north of Castle Lake. There are numerous opportunities for snowshoeing and cross-country ski touring and ski mountaineering. One can ski over the divide into the wilderness in the Heart Lake and Little Castle Lake areas on day trips or overnights, or one can tour into the trailless drainage of Scott Camp Creek on FR 39N46, which stops at the roadless area boundary. Advanced skiers can loop over the divide between Scott Camp Creek and Castle Lake.

The only sizable lakes located inside the wilderness can be reached on a long, unmaintained network of forest roads that follows the southeast side of

Grand views of Mount Shasta unfold from the Castle Dome Trail.

the South Fork Sacramento River canyon to the Gray Rock Lake Trailhead. From there the Gray Rock Lake Trail leads into a beautiful cirque that contains Gray Rock, Timber, and Upper Gray Rock Lakes. The trail ends after one mile at Timber Lake, but Upper Gray Rock Lake and the upper reaches of the cirque beneath Peak 7,200 can easily be traversed cross-country.

Because of moderately long approaches, the Castle Crags receive fairly light use by rock climbers. Climbers who do make the trek are rewarded by a variety of climbing opportunities, ranging in difficulty from Class 5 to Class 5.13a. The granitic rocks of the crags are massive, but due to exfoliation, there are areas of unstable slabs.

Day Hike

Castle Dome

Distance: 5.5 miles, round trip.
Low/high elevations: 2,600 feet/4,750 feet.
Difficulty: Strenuous.
Best season: Mid-May through mid-October.
Topo map: Dunsmuir-CA.
Permits: Not required.

HOW TO GET THERE: From I-5, 12.5 miles south of Mt. Shasta City and 46 miles north of Redding, take the Castella Exit, signed for Castle Crags State Park. Proceed west from I-5 for 0.5 mile, then turn right (northwest) to the

Castle Dome anchors the east end of the Castle Crags divide.

state park entrance station and pay a day-use fee. The paved road beyond the entrance station winds through the shady campground to the Vista Point Road, 0.8 mile from the park entrance. Turn left onto that steep, winding one-lane road, and drive another 1.3 miles to the parking area at the Vista Point Trailhead.

The granite spires of the Castle Crags are the highlight of the Castle Crags Wilderness, and there is no better way to experience them than by hiking the Castle Crags Trail, which happens to be called the Castle Dome Trail on the wilderness map. The trail to Castle Dome is strenuous, but nevertheless it receives moderate use. Many hikers go no farther than Indian Springs, where they can enjoy inspiring views of the crags from the shady hillside springs.

The signed Castle Crags Trail begins in Castle Crags State Park, 100 yards north of the Vista Point parking area, at 2,600 feet. The trail begins as a wide, level singletrack traversing the steep slopes of Kettlebelly Ridge beneath a shady canopy of white fir, ponderosa pine, incense-cedar, and big-leaf maple. After 0.25 mile, the Root Creek Trail branches right, and the Castle Crags Trail quickly leads you up to the crest of the ridge on three steep switchbacks. On the ridgetop, the PCT crosses your trail beneath the intrusion of overhead power lines, while the increasingly loud rumble of I-5 traffic reverberates from the Sacramento River canyon.

Even at 3,000 feet on these south-facing slopes, the forest cover is moderate; nevertheless, Douglas-fir, incense-cedar, and ponderosa pine form a shady canopy overhead. Poison oak grows at the trailside and there are rattlesnakes, so remain alert. At length the Bobs Hat Trail joins from the south, and beyond that junction your trail rises steadily higher through the mixed conifer forest, reaching the wilderness boundary at 3,200 feet, shortly after the trail turns north. Ascend steadily beyond the boundary to the curve of a switchback, from where you enjoy the first glimpse of the towering spires of Castle Crags.

The trail levels out on a 3,500-foot ridge in a parklike forest of mixed conifers, and soon traverses west-facing slopes high above Winton Canyon, where fine vistas unfold that reach into Castle Creek canyon and to the high rocky peaks of the Trinity Mountains. At 3,600 feet you meet the spur trail to Indian Springs, a worthwhile destination for a side-trip. That trail, nearly level along its 0.25-mile course, leads to a series of cold, vigorous springs issuing from cracks in the granite. Pine, fir, and big-leaf maple shade the springs beneath the 2,000-foot face of the crags.

North of the Indian Springs junction, tremendous views unfold, revealing gargantuan Mount Shasta and towering Castle Dome just ahead. A series of steep switchbacks rising among conifers and black and live oaks leads to a prolonged ascent into the realm of the crags, where the trail is often carved into solid granite. Up and up it climbs, offering excellent views. The final several hundred yards pass over granite slopes mantled with clumps of manzanita and huckleberry oak and studded with sugar and ponderosa pine. Keep an eye out for the few rare weeping spruce trees in the draw just below Castle Dome.

Finally, at the end of a long 2.7 miles, at 4,750 feet, you reach the trail's end in a rocky notch immediately west of Castle Dome, its cliffs framing an unobstructed view of Mount Shasta. One can explore the ridge a short distance to the west among boulders and low domes, above which the crags rise defiantly to 5,500 feet in an array of spires, needles, buttresses, couloirs, and sheer, smooth cliffs.

Trinity Alps Wilderness Complex   37

Location: 40 miles northeast of Eureka, and 35 miles northwest of Redding.
Size: 636,218 acres.
Administration: USDAFS–Klamath, Six Rivers, and Shasta-Trinity national forests; USDIBLM.
Management status: National Forest wilderness (512,005 acres, including 4,433 acres administered by the BLM); with the remainder roadless nonwilderness (124,213) located in 14 separate units, some of which may be allocated to future development.
Ecosystems: Sierran Forest–Alpine Meadows province, Klamath Mountains section, characterized by mountains with rounded ridges, steep sides, and narrow canyons, with the higher elevations dominated by glacier-modified mountains, with horns, aretes, cirques, and U-shaped valleys; Cambrian, Ordovician, Silurian, and Devonian ocean crust intruded by Mesozoic granitic rocks, Mesozoic granitics, Paleozoic to Jurassic gabbro, metavolcanic, and metasedimentary rocks, and alluvial, earthflow, and glacial deposits; potential natural vegetation is Oregon oak forest, mixed evergreen forest with chinquapin, Klamath montane forest with Douglas-fir, Klamath montane forest with yellow pine, and alpine communtities; abundant perennial streams with a dendritic drainage pattern, wet meadows, and many high-elevation lakes.
Elevation range: 400 feet to 9,002 feet.
System trails: 738.5 miles.
Maximum core-to-perimeter distance: 18.5 miles.
Activities: Backpacking, day hiking, horseback riding, fishing, cross-country skiing, and snowshoeing.
Maps: Klamath, Six Rivers, and Shasta-Trinity National Forests visitor maps; Trinity Alps Wilderness map (topographic; 1 inch/mile); see Appendix D for a list of USGS 1:24,000 quads.

OVERVIEW: The vast Trinity Alps Wilderness, drained by the Salmon River on the north, the Trinity River on the south and east, and the Scott River on the northeast, is the southernmost wildland in the Klamath Mountains province. The complex geologic make-up of the Klamath Mountain region, its great vertical relief, and its proximity to the moist North Coast Ranges to the west and south and the drier Cascade Range to the east, results in a unique combination of climate, soil types, and topography, and the landscape supports a diverse assemblage of plants and animals, including several endemic species. Two noteworthy species are Brewer (weeping) spruce and foxtail pine, both of which occur in the higher elevations. These relict species, which are now widely scat-

37 TRINITY ALPS WILDERNESS COMPLEX

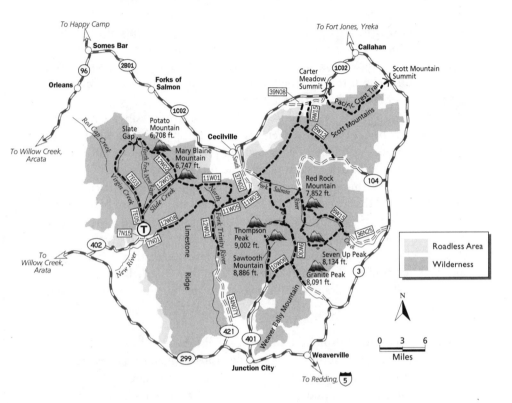

tered and grow in small numbers, are the remains of more extensive past stands that populated unglaciated areas of mostly ultramafic soil types (serpentinite and peridotite).

The principal range that forms the backbone of this rugged, mountainous wilderness is the Salmon Mountains, the same range that winds through the Russian and Marble Mountain wildernesses to the north. This range generally trends from east to west, and in the east-central portion of the wilderness, the Salmons rise to their highest elevations, reaching an apex atop 9,002-foot Thompson Peak, the highest point in the Klamath Mountains region. The high part of the Salmons and several high divides are collectively called the Trinity Alps because this is truly a landscape of alpine peaks. Some harbor permanent snowfields and all exceed 8,000 feet, rising a full mile above a series of deep canyons. Along the northern boundary, the Scott Mountains branch northeast from the Salmons with a crest of 7,000-foot peaks. On the north slopes of the Scotts, glaciers carved a series of cirques that hold nearly two dozen high lakes.

The wilderness as a whole contains 84 named lakes that are stocked with rainbow, eastern brook, brown, and golden trout, and range in size from less than an acre to 200 acres. Two major tributaries to the Trinity River—New River and North Fork Trinity River—support summer-run steelhead. The lower reaches of those streams, and Canyon Creek, also support spring-run Chinook salmon. Fall-run Chinook and winter-run steelhead are widespread in Trinity River tributaries in the wilderness.

Once home to grizzly bear and Roosevelt elk, the Trinity Alps are now populated by black bear, black-tailed deer, and northern spotted owl. A number of important species dwell here; some are either proposed for or are already listed as threatened or endangered, and they are indicative of the wild character of the wilderness. Among these species are bald eagle, peregrine falcon, marbled murrelet, northern goshawk, Pacific fisher, and northwestern pond turtle.

Although the Trinity Alps is one of California's largest wilderness areas, there are significant areas of roadless lands bordering it. Though some of it extends to moderately high divides, much of it is low in elevation. Some of this land contains timber of commercial value, but there's real, lasting value in keeping it wild to maintain wildlife habitat, water quality, and scenic and recreational uses.

RECREATIONAL USES: Despite the size of this wilderness and its excellent network of trails, only a handful of it is heavily visited. Much of the rest receives light to very light use. At present, the Forest Service has identified 234,160 acres, or 46 percent of the wilderness, as "pristine," with no trails or other signs of human modification, while another 37 percent is considered "primitive," with minimal trails or campsites.

The Trinity Alps provides a superb range of hiking opportunities, from day hikes to multi-day backpacks beginning at 76 trailheads. Loop trips of a week or more are possible, yet except for a handful of well-known lake basins, much of the backcountry is only lightly used. Only 5 to 10 percent of wilderness users travel with pack stock, and steep terrain limits some routes to foot travel only (these are marked on the wilderness map). Most stock use is in the autumn hunting season.

Despite difficult access, cross-country skiing can be excellent in the high basins. One of the best places for a ski or snowshoe trip is the Carter Meadow Summit area at 6,200 feet, near the northern wilderness boundary. Here the road between Callahan and Forks of Salmon is plowed in winter and allows access to both the Russian Wilderness to the north and the Trinity Alps to the south. Follow the Pacific Crest Trail south into the Trinity Alps, or any one of

The granite core of the high Trinity Alps.

the north-side drainages, and you'll reach open terrain and broad bowls within a few miles.

Wilderness permits are required for entry into the Trinity Alps Wilderness year-round, by day-hikers and backpackers alike. Currently there are no trailhead quotas. Wilderness permits are available from Shasta-Trinity, Klamath, and Six Rivers ranger district offices surrounding the Trinity Alps.

Solitude seekers can get away from the crowds, with a little effort, by hiking to areas not accessed by trails. Other lightly visited areas include Eagle Creek, Limestone Ridge, North Fork Swift Creek (Poison Canyon), New River, Rush Creek Lakes, Billys Peak, and Packers Peak. The most heavily used trails are listed by ranger district below.

Lower Trinity District
Mill Creek Lakes Trail (6E73)
Tish Tang A Tang Trail (6E18)
Red Cap Hole Trail (6E14)

Salmon River District
China Springs Trail (11W33.2)
Caribou Lake Trail (09W18)

Big Bar District
North Fork Trail (12W01) to Grizzly Meadows
Canyon Creek Trail (10W08)
Boulder Creek Lakes Trail (10W02)

Weaverville District
Stuart Fork Trail (9W20)
Four Lakes Trail (9W13)
Stoddard Lake Trail (7W06)
Bear Lake Trail (7W03)

Backpack

New River/Virgin Creek Loop

Distance: 36.7 miles, loop trip (4 to 6 days).
Low/high elevations: 2,300 feet/6,600 feet.
Difficulty: Moderately strenuous.
Best season: Late June through September.
Topo maps: Dees Peak-CA, Jim Jam Ridge-CA, Salmon Mountain-CA, Trinity Mountain-CA, Youngs Peak-CA.
Permits: Wilderness permit required. California Campfire Permit required for use of open fires and backpack stoves.

HOW TO GET THERE: From Interstate 5 at Redding, follow California Highway 299 west for 98 miles to Hawkins Bar, where a sign indicating DENNY marks the turnoff to paved, northeastbound County Road 402 leading to the New River Trailhead. The Denny turnoff can also be approached from the west by driving about 10 miles southeast of the CA 299/96 junction at Willow Creek.

Proceed northeast on the paved county road; after about 11 miles you pass Denny Campground and the Forest Service station. Continue ahead for 2 miles, then turn left onto dirt Forest Road 7N15. The New River Trailhead is 4 miles ahead at the end of the road.

The New River canyon has always been one of the most isolated areas in California, though the area did support gold mining activity and hosted several "boom" towns in the 1800s; this trip surveys many of these historic sites. From the 1970s to the mid-1980s, the New River area was a focal point for marijuana cultivation, which put a virtual halt to all recreational activity here. Between 1984 and 1987, a law enforcement project eliminated illicit agriculture in this area. However, recreational use of the area is still low. One can expect considerable solitude on this trip, while still enjoying the diversity of deep, shady canyons and high granite basins.

The trailhead lies at 2,300 feet, and Trail 7E05 leads north above the New River beneath a multi-canopied forest that offers several places for camping. After 2.9 miles you reach the confluence of Virgin and Slide Creeks, where the New River and our loop begin.

Turn right onto trail 12W03 and begin ascending into the Slide Creek drainage. The gradually ascending trail follows the stream banks beneath old-growth forests of Douglas-fir, sugar pine, incense-cedar, madrone, and oak. After 2.2 miles, at the confluence with Eagle Creek Trail (8E11), bear right again. Stay on the Slide Creek Trail for the remaining distance past the historic Marysville mining site, up to the Cinnabar Mine, and on to Mary Blaine Mountain on the Salmon Mountains crest, 10.1 miles from the New River trail junction. Vistas are excellent, stretching south past the magnificent Pony Buttes to the Thurston Peaks and Limestone Ridge and northwest along the crest. From Mary Blaine Mountain begin heading northwest along the Salmon Summit Trail (12W02); follow the crest past Dees Peak, Potato Mountain, and Youngs Peak for 9 miles to Slate Gap. The crest trail is landscaped with occasional wet meadows, and fields of chaparral dotted with small groves of sugar and ponderosa pine, Brewer spruce, and occasional red and white fir. Several small creeks cross the trail, often with campsites nearby.

At Slate Gap, short side-trips lead to Knownothing and Rock Lakes, which are the only lakes found along the loop. To continue the loop, begin the descent down Virgin Creek via Trail 7E03. Virgin Creek is a tumultuous stream, with abundant waterfalls in the upper canyon. A lovely mixed conifer and mixed evergreen forest shades the trail in the depths of this canyon. Remains of mining sites can be found as you descend 13.2 miles down to the confluence of Virgin and Slide Creeks at the origin of the New River. From the confluence backtrack for 2.2 miles to the New River Trailhead.

Russian Wilderness Complex   38

Location: 27 miles southwest of Yreka and 65 miles northeast of Eureka.
Size: 29,500 acres.
Administration: National Forest wilderness (12,700 acres); the remainder roadless
nonwilderness (16,800 acres) in three separate units, allocated to possible future
development in the Forest Plan.
Management status: USDAFS–Klamath National Forest.
Ecosystems: Sierran Forest–Alpine Meadows province, Klamath Mountains section,
characterized by steep mountains, deep and narrow-to-wide stream valleys, high-elevation
glacier-modified valleys, and cirques; Mesozoic granitics, and Paleozoic to Jurassic metavolcanic
and metasedimentary rocks, and glacial deposits; potential natural vegetation is Oregon oak
forest, Klamath montane forest with yellow pine, and Klamath montane forest with
Douglas-fir; many perennial streams, wet meadows, and high-elevation lakes.
Elevation range: 2,500 feet to 8,196 feet.
System trails: 34 miles.
Maximum core-to-perimeter distance: 6.25 miles.
Activities: Backpacking, day hiking, horseback riding, and fishing.
Maps: Klamath National Forest visitor map; Russian Wilderness and Marble Mountain
Wilderness map (topographic, 2 inches/mile); see Appendix D for a list of USGS 1:24,000
quads.

OVERVIEW: Often overlooked in favor of larger and better-known wildlands to
the north and south, the small Russian Wilderness offers some of the most spectacular and most easily accessible high country in the Klamath Mountains region. The Russian Wilderness, embracing only 12,700 acres, is a compact
preserve located along the high crest of the Salmon Mountains. Small in size but
long on dramatic scenery, the Russian is dominated by glacier-sculpted granite
crags. Mountains of dark metamorphic rocks are common around the wilderness perimeter. Cirques have been gouged by Pleistocene glaciers into the north,
northeast, and eastern flanks of the mountains and, combined with the cirque
lakes in the roadless lands within and surrounding the Russian Wilderness,
there are 29 subalpine lakes. Only two lightly traveled, light-duty paved roads
separate the Russian from the Trinity Alps Wilderness to the south, and the
Marble Mountain Wilderness to the north, making this part of the Klamath
Mountains region the largest nearly roadless complex in northwest California.

The Russian Wilderness is quite similar in appearance to a well-watered ver-

38   RUSSIAN WILDERNESS COMPLEX

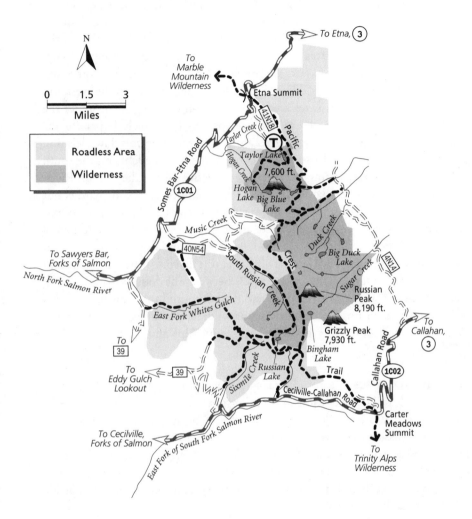

sion of the Sierra Nevada, but of course there are differences that make the Russian area distinctive. The granite of the Russian Wilderness is much more massive, or solid and less fractured, than in the Sierra Nevada. Compared to granitic areas in the nearby Marble Mountain and Trinity Alps wildernesses, there are fewer areas dominated by fields of chaparral in the Russian. Forest trees, where they do grow among areas of solid rock, are dense, and in most cirques there are verdant thickets of mountain alder. As in the Sierra, lake-filled cirques, U-shaped valleys, and bold granite crags dominate the landscape.

The west slopes of the wilderness lie entirely within the North Fork Salmon River drainage. The distant thunder of rushing water is frequently heard from trails, and the source of that sound can be traced to the large streams draining the west slopes: South Russian, Music, Hogan, and Taylor Creeks. East of the Salmon Mountains crest, streams including Sugar, Duck, Horse Range, Paynes Lake, and Meeks Meadow Creeks are among the headwaters of the Scott River.

The Russian roadless area, located in disconnected parcels to the west and north of the wilderness, was released for multiple-use management under the California Wilderness Act of 1984. These roadless lands include part of the Salmon Mountains crest immediately southeast of Etna Summit; low-elevation canyons, including South Russian and East Fork Whites Gulch; and the south slopes of the divide separating the South and North Forks of the Salmon River.

Within these roadless lands are old-growth forests, stands of hardwoods such as oak and madrone, glacial valleys, subalpine lakes, and timberline peaks. Just as in the Russian Wilderness, there are stands of Brewer spruce and foxtail pine and habitat for summer steelhead and resident rainbow trout, northern spotted owl, great gray owl, goshawk, peregrine falcon, fisher, marten, and wolverine. With much of the land roadless between the county roads crossing Carter Meadow Summit in the south and Etna Summit in the north, the Russian Complex is an important corridor for wildlife, including black bear and black-tailed deer, migrating between the Trinity Alps and Marble Mountain Wildernesses.

RECREATIONAL USES: Nearly all trails leading into the Russian Wilderness begin at mid- to high-elevations. Exceptions include the South Russian Creek and East Fork Whites Gulch Trails, which begin at low elevations on the west side of the Russian roadless area. Both trails ascend deep canyons through old-growth, mixed-conifer forests. In contrast to other areas of the Klamath Mountains region, the Russian features up-close alpine grandeur beginning at most trailheads. Nearly half of the trail miles in the complex (16 miles) lie outside the wilderness boundaries.

The Pacific Crest Trail (PCT) traverses the high Salmon Mountains crest for 18.5 miles between Etna Summit and Carter Meadows Summit. This superb high trail affords easy access to nearly all of the high lakes in the Russian Wilderness, and unobstructed vistas into the wild interior of the eastern Klamath Mountains region. Yet the Russian is still relatively undiscovered, being a destination wilderness mainly for hunters and only a small number of backcountry recreationists. In the Marble Mountain, Trinity Alps, and Siskiyou wilderness areas, high country is generally at least one long day's hike from most trailheads. But in the Russian Wilderness, hikers can reach subalpine lakes and windswept timberline ridges in less than two hours.

Taylor Lake, one of the gems of the Russian Wilderness.

Access into the wilderness from the east is limited by private land, and forest roads lead to only two trailheads, where the Duck Lakes and Paynes Lake trails begin. Both lake basins can then be reached in miles, four and three respectively. Access from the west is gained via the South Russian Creek Trail, beginning on Forest Road 40N54 three miles off the Somes Bar–Etna Road southeast of Idlewild Campground, and from the East Fork Whites Gulch Trail, beginning on FR 39 about three miles east of Sawyers Bar. Most hikers, however, enter the wilderness from the north or south via the PCT. There are no loop trails in the Russian Wilderness, so most backcountry trips are round trips.

During winter, the paved roads over Carter Meadow Summit and Etna Summit offer a high-elevation start for a cross-country ski or snowshoe trip into the Russian Wilderness. From the south, following the route of the PCT leads 5 miles to the Salmon Mountains crest at the head of South Russian Creek, where four cirque basins offer excellent telemark skiing and sheltered camping. From Etna Summit in the north, ski and snowshoe trips can be taken along the route of the PCT along the Salmon Mountain crest, which features a series of east-facing cirques, or follow FR 41N18 to the Taylor Lake Trailhead and continue on into the Taylor Lake cirque.

Rich meadows, subalpine forests, and bold granite peaks typify the Russian Wilderness.

Day Hike or Overnighter

Taylor and Hogan Lakes

Distance: 1 mile, round trip to Taylor Lake; 6.5 miles round trip to Hogan Lake.
Low/high elevations: 5,960 feet/6,900 feet.
Difficulty: Easy to Taylor Lake; strenuous to Hogan Lake.
Best season: July through mid-October.
Topo maps: Eaton Peak-CA, Tanners Peak-CA.
Permits: Wilderness permit not required. California Campfire Permit required for open fires and backpack stoves.

HOW TO GET THERE: Hikers approaching from the east will follow California Highway 3 to Etna, 11 miles south of Fort Jones, then turn southwest and follow the main street through downtown Etna. Beyond the town the road becomes County Road 1C01, the Somes Bar–Etna Road. Follow this steep, narrow, and winding paved road up to Etna Summit, 11.6 miles from CA 3, then descend southwest for 0.4 mile to the junction with FR 41N18, signed for Taylor Lake. Turn left (southeast) onto FR 41N18, and follow its narrow, rough, and rocky course for 2.3 miles to the small trailhead parking area. There are some very steep stretches as you approach the trailhead, and though a high-clearance vehicle is recommended, carefully driven passenger cars can reach the trailhead.

Hikers approaching from the south and west will follow CA 96 north for 48 miles from its junction with CA 299 (which is 40 miles east of Arcata and 109 miles west of Redding), to the hamlet of Somes Bar, where it is advisable to top off your gas tank. Drive 0.1 mile south from Somes Bar to the junction with eastbound CR 2B01, signed for Forks of Salmon, Cecilville, and Etna. This junction is located immediately north of the Salmon River bridge on CA 96.

Turn east there and follow the two-lane pavement along the sinuous course of the Salmon River. The road eventually narrows to one lane, with occasional turnouts, and the drive ahead is slow and arduous; drivers must proceed with caution. After driving 17.4 miles from CA 96, you reach a junction in the small town of Forks of Salmon, and bear left onto the Sawyers Bar Road (CR 1C01), signed for Etna and Yreka.

Follow this narrow, winding road for another slow 29.1 miles to the junction with FR 41N18 and turn right, following the directions above to reach the trailhead.

This scenic trip visits two high lakes set beneath ice-gouged granite peaks. For most hikers, Taylor Lake is but a 10-minute stroll down an improved, rock-lined trail. Since it is the easiest-to-reach subalpine lake in the Klamath Mountains region, it is frequently visited. Yet just over the ridge, nearby Hogan Lake is seldom visited. A strenuous, up-and-down trail, which grows more obscure the farther you go, leads to this hidden, fish-filled lake. For solitude, avoid Taylor Lake on holidays and weekends. If you are just passing Taylor en route to Hogan, it doesn't matter when you go, since few hikers tackle the strenuous trail beyond Taylor Lake.

The Taylor Lake Trail begins rising on a gentle uphill grade, leading through red and white fir forest. Within minutes you enter the Russian Wilderness and follow close to the banks of musical Taylor Creek, where lodgepole pine joins the fir forest. After about 10 minutes and 0.3 mile you reach Taylor Lake at 6,500 feet. This fish-filled gem lies beneath an 800-foot headwall of broken granite, with the splintered crest of the Salmon Mountains rising above the east shore. Campsites near the outlet are some of the most severely impacted sites in the wilderness.

The newly-constructed trail ahead follows the west shore of the long, alder- and fir-fringed lake. The trail rises above the boggy meadow beyond the southwest shore. From the slopes southwest of Taylor Lake, the trail leads first west, then southwest. Upslope springs nurture rich flower gardens and alder thickets on these slopes, and sometimes turn the hike into a wet slog in early summer. Soon you regain a firm, rocky tread and ascend a very steep grade into the forest of mountain hemlock and red fir, topping out on a broad ridge at 6,900 feet.

As the trail begins its descent west off the ridge, it briefly crosses an outcrop of black metamorphic rock, where you may notice sagebrush, very unusual in the Klamath Mountains region, sharing space with manzanita and a variety of wildflowers. Views soon open up into the broad Hogan Creek basin, backed up by a towering granite headwall, tumbling waterfalls, and 7,900-foot peaks. The trail continues descending, steeply at times, leading down into mixed conifer forest. The trail grows indistinct as it winds over boulder-littered slopes to the bottom of the descent. Then you begin ascending alongside the noisy stream draining the Twin Lakes basin.

When you reach a small meadow, the tread disappears. Midway through the meadow, turn right (south) and make your way through the tall corn lilies to the Twin Lakes creek, which you ford, then follow the faint tread over a low moraine and down into another meadow. By now you can hear the cascading inlet stream of Hogan Lake. Cross the meadow on a southwest course, traverse another low moraine, and finally you drop to a campsite at the lake's north shore. This is a dusty site impacted by stock parties, who visit during hunting season, but there are many, more attractive, possible places to camp in the basin. Fishing in the lake can be productive for brook, golden, and rainbow trout. Grazing cattle sometimes will be encountered in the Hogan Lake basin.

The lake lies in a dramatic setting, with an ice-polished headwall rising 1,500 feet from the lakeshore to a pair of lofty granite peaks. The inlet stream tumbles and falls 800 feet over a precipitous wall of granite, draining remote and difficult-to-reach Big Blue Lake far above.

Marble Mountain Wilderness Complex 39

Location: 60 miles northeast of Eureka and 25 miles southwest of Yreka.
Size: 298,500 acres.
Administration: USDAFS—Klamath National Forest.
Management status: National Forest wilderness (223,500 acres), the remainder roadless nonwilderness (75,000 acres) allocated for potential future development in the Forest Plan.
Ecosystems: Sierran Forest–Alpine Meadows province, Klamath Mountains section, characterized by complex, moderately high mountains, deep and narrow stream valleys, and cirques; Mesozoic granitics, and Paleozoic and Jurassic metavolcanic and metasedimentary rocks, alluvial and glacial deposits, and slump and earthflow deposits; potential natural vegetation is Oregon oak forest, mixed evergreen forest with chinquapin, Klamath montane forest with Douglas-fir, and Klamath montane forest with yellow pine; complex drainage pattern with many perennial streams, many lakes and tarns in cirque and paternoster basins, and numerous wet meadows.
Elevation range: 400 feet to 8,299 feet.
System trails: 390.4 miles.
Maximum core-to-perimeter distance: 12 miles.
Activities: Backpacking, horseback riding, day hiking, fishing, cross-country skiing, and snowshoeing.
Maps: Klamath National Forest visitor map; Marble Mountain Wilderness and Russian Wilderness map (1 inch/mile); see Appendix D for a list of USGS 1:24,000 quads.

OVERVIEW: Although part of the Klamath Mountains region, many features make the Marble Mountain complex one of the most distinctive wildlands in the United States. With more than 7,000 feet of vertical relief, and soils derived from five very different rock types, the diversity of vegetation and ecosystems is unequaled anywhere else in the country. The ultramafic rocks (serpentinite) common to this region support numerous plant species found nowhere else. Proximity to the Pacific Ocean in northwestern California gives rise to abundant precipitation from autumn through spring, with a typically dry summer season.

Nearly encircled by the Scott, Klamath, and Salmon Rivers, the Marbles are a mosaic of lofty divides and deep canyons, and distinctive, often colorful, rocks. The Klamath Mountains region is not made up of a single mountain range, but rather is an aggregate of mountain ranges and river valleys. One such mountain range, the Salmon Mountains, forms the core of the Marble Mountain Wilderness. Forming a great horseshoe-shaped arc, with the arms opening to the south, the Salmon Mountains also have several prominent spur

39A   MARBLE MOUNTAIN WILDERNESS COMPLEX (NORTH)

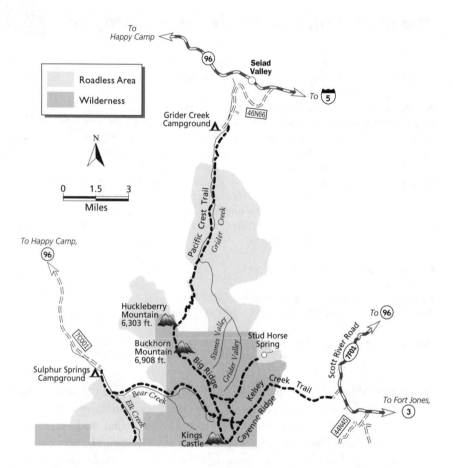

ridges that rise as high, or higher, than the principal crest. Marble Mountain is one of these spur ridges, extending north from the Salmon crest, and its white marble (metamorphosed limestone) peaks, some capped by black metamorphic rocks, are the namesake of the wilderness.

Other prominent spur ridges include the Boulder Peak ridge, which stretches past the apex of the wilderness into the area's northeast corner, and the 22-mile-long English Peak ridge. The granitic and metamorphic crest of that 7,000-foot ridge separates the two principal drainages in the southern half of the wilderness—Wooley Creek and the North Fork Salmon River. Both drainages are extensive. Vegetation ranges from chaparral and mixed hardwoods in their lower reaches to mixed evergreen, mixed conifer, red fir, and mixed subalpine forests as the canyons reach deeper and higher into the wilderness and gather their waters from tributaries draining the Salmon Mountain crest. Wooley Creek and the North Fork have been designated as Wild and Scenic Rivers, and Wooley Creek is one of few streams in the Marbles to support summer steelhead, as well as a spring run of king salmon. Numerous other streams in the Marbles support steelhead and resident rainbow trout, and several of these have been recommended for Wild and Scenic River status, including portions of Ukonom, Grider, Kelsey, Elk, Granite, Burney Valley, Toms Valley, and Rainy Valley Creeks.

The diversity of habitats in the Marbles is not only reflected in its vegetation, but in its animal populations as well. Numerous important species reside in the Marbles and other Klamath Mountains region wildlands, including several that are both classified as threatened and endangered or are candidates for such classification, and Forest Service-recognized species. Bald eagle and peregrine falcon are listed as endangered in California, while the northern spotted owl is listed as a threatened species. Sensitive species present in the Marbles include American marten, Pacific fisher, northern goshawk, great gray owl, and willow flycatcher. The Marbles have a healthy population of black-tailed deer, and black bears are abundant, so caution must be used with food storage. Badger and wolverine are present in limited numbers.

Following the additions made to the Marble Mountain Wilderness under the California Wilderness Act of 1984, 12 roadless areas around the perimeter were released for further evaluation of their suitability to remain roadless. On some of the lands in these roadless areas, salvage logging, road construction, and timber sales have been implemented, while much of the land still remains roadless and, with enough public support, may eventually be added to the wilderness. However, because the Klamath National Forest has determined that the regional supply of wilderness exceeds the current and projected demand, not one acre of these lands is recommended for wilderness designation in any alternative in the Forest Plan.

RECREATIONAL USES: With a number of prominent destination features, including 87 high lakes, the Marbles receive moderate to heavy use, despite its remote location far from population centers. Yet the size of the area, combined with its highly variable terrain, gives the Marbles the ability to absorb large numbers of visitors, so few areas are consistently crowded. The most heavily used trails in the Marbles are those that involve the least amount of elevation gain and the shortest distance to wilderness highlights. Trails beginning at

39B   MARBLE MOUNTAIN WILDERNESS COMPLEX (SOUTHWEST)

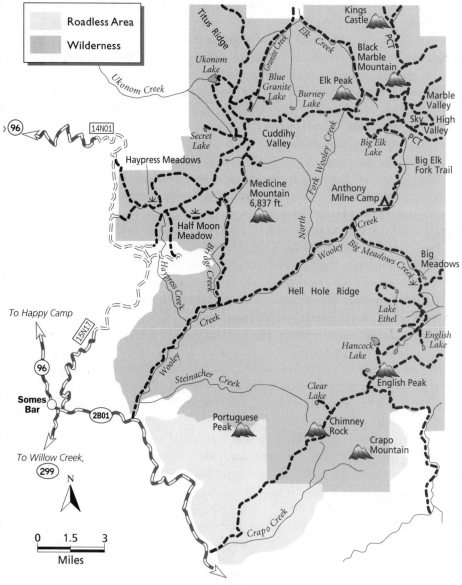

Roadless Area

Wilderness

Titus Ridge

Kings Castle

Elk Creek

Granite Creek

PCT

Ukonom Lake

Black Marble Mountain

Blue Granite Lake

Elk Peak

Burney Lake

Marble Valley

Ukonom Creek

Sky

High Valley

PCT

96

14N01

Secret Lake

Cuddihy Valley

North Fork Wooley Creek

Big Elk Lake

Big Elk Fork Trail

Haypress Meadows

Medicine Mountain 6,837 ft.

Anthony Milne Camp

Half Moon Meadow

North

Creek

Wooley

Big Meadows Creek

Big Meadows

Bridge Creek

To Happy Camp

Haypress Creek

Hell Hole Ridge

Lake Ethel

15N17

Creek

English Lake

Wooley

Hancock Lake

English Peak

96

Somes Bar

Steinacher Creek

Clear Lake

2B01

Portuguese Peak

Chimney Rock

Crapo Mountain

To Willow Creek,

299

N

Crapo Creek

To Forks of Salmon

0   1.5   3
Miles

39C MARBLE MOUNTAIN WILDERNESS COMPLEX (SOUTHEAST)

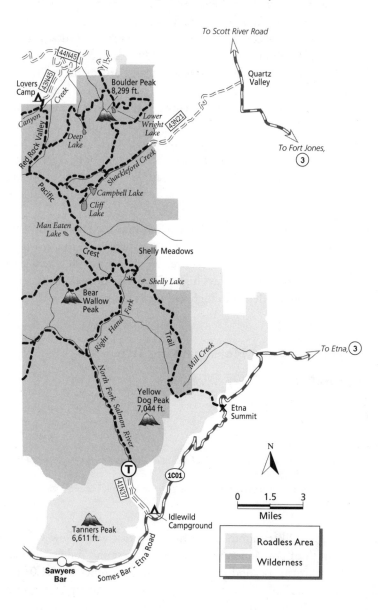

Lovers Camp, Shackleford Creek, and Haypress offer the weekend visitor a chance to visit some of the most attractive landscapes in the Marbles, and these trails are used by a steady stream of hikers and stock parties throughout summer. Places such as Cliff and Campbell Lakes, Paradise Lake, Marble Valley, Sky High Lakes valley, Cuddihy Lakes, and Ukonom Lake, are favorite destinations.

Much of the remainder of the wilderness, including deep canyons and high divides, particularly those in the south and southeast parts of the wilderness, requires considerable time and effort to explore. Yet along these high divides, in the lonely lake basins, and in the dark depths of the low-elevation canyons travelers can enjoy utter solitude far off the beaten tracks of this wilderness.

The Marbles can be accessed on trails and forest roads beginning from County Road 1C01 on the south (Somes Bar–Etna Road), CR 7F01 on the east (Scott River Road), and California Highway 96 on the north and west (Klamath River Road). The most popular is the Scott River Road, which leads to Lovers Camp, Shackleford, and Kidder Creek trailheads.

The plowed Somes Bar–Etna Road (CR 1C01) offers the only good winter access to the wilderness at its southeastern corner, where the Salmon Mountains crest is traversed by the Pacific Crest Trail. A ski or snowshoe trip starting at Etna Summit starts high and stays high. If you ski north along the crest, a number of chutes pose moderate to high avalanche danger.

Multi-day Backpack and Horsepacking Trip

North Fork Salmon River–Wooley Creek Loop

Distance: 59.5 miles, loop trip (5 to 7 days).
Low/high elevations: 2,800 feet/6,900 feet.
Difficulty: Strenuous.
Best season: Late June through September.
Topo maps: Boulder Peak-CA, English Peak-CA, Medicine Mountain-CA, Marble Mountain-CA, Tanners Peak-CA, Yellow Dog Peak-CA.
Permits: Wilderness permit not required. California Campfire Permit required for open fires and backpack stoves.

HOW TO GET THERE: Hikers approaching from the east will follow CA 3 to Etna, 11 miles south of Fort Jones, then turn southwest and follow the main street through downtown. Beyond the town the road becomes CR 1C01, the Somes Bar–Etna Road. Follow this steep, narrow, and winding paved road up to Etna Summit, 11.6 miles from CA 3, then descend a very steep and narrow grade into the canyon below. About 20 miles from Etna is the signed northbound turnoff to Idlewild Campground and the North Fork Trail. Follow Forest Road 41N37 for 2 miles past the campground to the trailhead.

SUSAN MENANNO PHOTO

The moss-draped canyon of Wooley Creek.

Hikers approaching from the south and west will follow CA 96 north for 48 miles from its junction with CA 299, which is 40 miles east of Arcata and 109 miles west of Redding. At the hamlet of Somes Bar, it is advisable to top off your gas tank at the Somes Bar General Store. Drive 0.1 mile south from Somes Bar to the junction with eastbound CR 2B01, signed for FORKS OF SALMON, CECILVILLE, AND ETNA. This junction is located immediately north of the Salmon River bridge on CA 96.

Turn east there and follow the two-lane pavement along the sinuous course of the Salmon River. The road eventually narrows to one lane, with occasional turnouts, and as the drive ahead is slow and arduous, drivers must proceed with caution. After driving 17.4 miles from CA 96, you reach a junction in the small town of Forks of Salmon, and bear left onto the Sawyers Bar Road (CR 1C01): the sign points to Etna and Yreka.

Follow this narrow, winding road for another slow 20 miles to the Idlewild Campground turnoff and the North Fork Trailhead.

This ambitious loop into the heart of the wilderness surveys the spectrum of landscapes in the Marbles, from very low canyons to forested ridges, including a timberline traverse on the PCT and back down to the canyons of the North Fork. A variety of shorter loops, round-trip, and side-trip options makes the North Fork Trailhead one of the best entry points to the wilderness, though trails here receive only light to moderate use.

Marble Mountain and the Salmon Mountains crest rise in the eastern reaches of the wilderness.

From the trailhead at 2,550 feet, the trail follows the North Fork Salmon River closely, passing its many beautiful granite pools, and leads 2.5 miles to the wilderness boundary. Hikers starting late in the day will find numerous campsites in the lower reaches of the river canyon. The leaf-lined trail gently climbs through a diverse mixture of oaks, madrone, Douglas-fir, and ponderosa and sugar pine. At 4.5 miles is The Cedars area, a shady flat beneath a canopy of incense-cedar and an old homestead site.

Farther up-canyon, you reach the confluence of the North and Right Hand Forks of the Salmon at 8.5 miles. The trail that follows the Right Hand Fork, to the north, forms the return leg of the loop. Bear left at the junction and continue up the North Fork for 5.5 miles to the Big Meadows Creek Trail, at Abbotts Upper Cabin site at 4,850 feet, and turn right (northwest). That trail begins ascending toward the English Peak ridge, a spectacular granite crest, via Pierces Draw and Cold Springs Creek. Spur trails en route lead southwest to Horse Range Lake (good fishing for eastern brook trout), and to lakes Ethel and Katherine (with eastern brook and rainbows), lying in granite cirques on the north slope of Hell Hole Ridge.

The trail crests the divide at 6,400 feet, 2.6 miles from the North Fork, then descends 3,600 feet down Big Meadows Creek in 5 miles to the Wooley Creek

Trail. Camping is available at Big Meadows and Wild Lake at the head of the canyon, and at the junction in Wooley Creek canyon. Poison oak abounds along the trail, so caution is advised. Voluminous Wooley Creek is a major tributary to the Salmon River and features clear, deep pools that support salmon, steelhead, and resident rainbow trout. Turn right (north) at the junction and head up the shady canyon of Wooley Creek. Anthony Milne Camp, 2.25 miles up-canyon, offers good camping and even better swimming, at the confluence of the South Fork and main stem of Wooley Creek.

Above Anthony Milne Camp, the lower-elevation mixed evergreen forest changes to mixed conifer forest and areas of montane chaparral and granite outcrops, as the trail ascends the canyon of Big Elk Creek toward Marble Mountain and the Salmon Mountain crest. The trail ascends to a junction just below Big Elk Lake, at 5,500 feet, 6 miles above Anthony Milne Camp. Shallow Big Elk Lake offers good camping and fair fishing for brookies and rainbows, but it can be a popular spot.

To continue the loop, turn right at the junction below Big Elk Lake and ascend 750 feet in one mile to the Pacific Crest Trail (PCT). To visit Marble Valley, follow the PCT for 1 mile north into the unique marble landscape. The loop continues along the crest of the Salmon Mountains, following the PCT southeast for 12.4 miles, with far-ranging vistas into the wild interior of the Marbles in all directions. This is a high, spectacular crest route, but for camping you may need to descend off the crest into Sky High Lakes basin, Rainy Valley, Shackleford Creek, or Kidder Lake. Man Eaten Lake, lying beneath an 800-foot granite headwall, is perhaps the most dramatic high lake in the Marbles, lying a short but challenging distance off the PCT. This 112-foot deep lake is a good producer of large rainbows. Camping is limited.

After following the PCT for 12.4 miles, you reach a junction on Shelly Meadows saddle; turn right (west), and follow the Right Hand Fork down to its confluence with the North Fork of the Salmon, and close the loop after another 16.4 miles.

Siskiyou Wilderness Complex `40`

Location: 25 miles east of Crescent City, 50 miles northeast of Eureka, and 8 miles west of Happy Camp.
Size: 250,200 acres.
Administration: USDAFS–Klamath, Six Rivers, and Siskiyou National Forests.
Management status: National Forest wilderness (153,000 acres); roadless nonwilderness (97,200 acres), some of which has been allocated for future development in the Forest Plan.
Ecosystems: Sierran Forest–Alpine Meadows province, Klamath Mountains section, characterized by moderately high mountains with rounded ridges with steep sides, narrow, deep canyons, and cirques; serpentinite, peridotite, gabbro, and diabase, Paleozoic to Jurassic metavolcanic and metasedimentary rocks, Jurassic marine sedimentary rocks and greenstone, and Mesozoic gabbro and granitic rocks, moderately to intensely folded and faulted, and glacial and landslide deposits; potential natural vegetation is Klamath montane forest with Douglas-fir, and mixed evergreen forest with chinquapin; many perennial streams with a dendritic drainage pattern, numerous wet meadows, and moderately high-elevation lakes.
Elevation range: 770 feet to 7,309 feet.
System trails: 136.3 miles.
Maximum core-to-perimeter distance: 13 miles.
Activities: Backpacking, day hiking, horseback riding, fishing, hunting.
Maps: Klamath and Six Rivers National Forests visitor maps; Siskiyou Wilderness map (topographic, 1 inch/mile); see Appendix D for a list of USGS 1:24,000 quads.

OVERVIEW: The Siskiyou Mountains rise north and west of the Klamath River canyon in the northwest corner of California and form one of the longest continuous crests in the Klamath Mountains region. Trending south to north for 40 miles from near the town of Weitchpec to the Oregon state line and lying an average of 20 miles inland from the Pacific coast, the Siskiyous are crowned by a series of rocky peaks that rise as much as 6,000 feet above surrounding lowlands. Although most peaks reach into the 5,000- to 6,000-foot range, one summit—Preston Peak—rises to 7,309 feet, and its landmark pyramid is visible from many distant viewpoints in the Klamath Mountains region. From its summit you can see redwood forests and the Pacific Ocean.

Glaciers modified the landscape of the Siskiyou crest, carving cirques out of the red peridotite and green serpentinite peaks. More than one dozen cirques contain small lakes, many of them accessible by faint, infrequently maintained trails.

40A SISKIYOU WILDERNESS COMPLEX (NORTH)

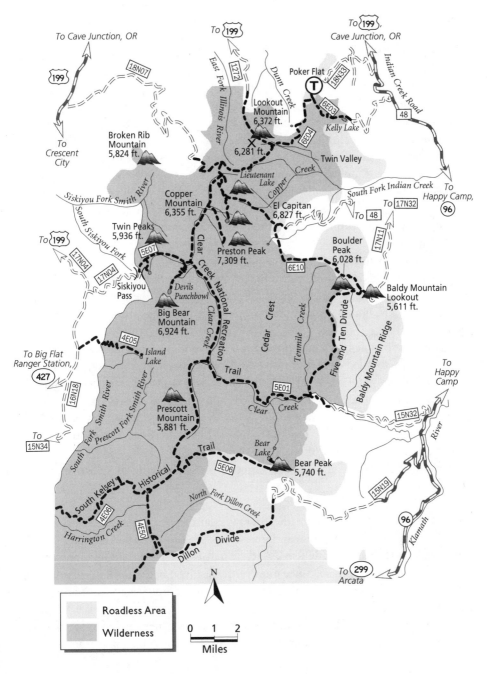

To Cave Junction, OR

To 199

To 199, Cave Junction, OR

18N07

199

Indian Creek Road

East Fork Illinois River

1272

Dunn Creek

Poker Flat

18N33

To Crescent City

T

6E03

Lookout Mountain 6,372 ft.

6E04

Kelly Lake

48

Broken Rib Mountain 5,824 ft.

6,281 ft.

Twin Valley

Lieutenant Lake

Copper Creek

South Fork Indian Creek

To Happy Camp, 96

Siskiyou Fork Smith River

Copper Mountain 6,355 ft.

El Capitan 6,827 ft.

To 17N32

To 48

South Siskiyou Fork

Twin Peaks 5,936 ft.

5E07

Preston Peak 7,309 ft.

6E10

Boulder Peak 6,028 ft.

17N11

To 199

17N04

17N04

Siskiyou Pass

Devils Punchbowl

Clear Creek National Recreation

Baldy Mountain Lookout 5,611 ft.

Big Bear Mountain 6,924 ft.

Clear Creek

Cedar Crest

Tenmile Creek

Five and Ten Divide

Baldy Mountain Ridge

4E05

To Big Flat Ranger Station,

Island Lake

Trail

To Happy Camp

427

16N18

5E01

15N32

River

South Fork Smith River

Prescott Fork Smith River

Prescott Mountain 5,881 ft.

Clear Creek

To 15N34

Trail

Bear Lake

15N19

South Kelsey

Historical

5E06

Bear Peak 5,740 ft.

96

4E06

North Fork Dillon Creek

Klamath

Harrington Creek

4E50

Divide

Dillon

To 299, Arcata

N

Roadless Area

Wilderness

0   1   2

Miles

Aside from its dramatic crest of colorful, rocky crags, the Siskiyou Wilderness is most notable for its vast old-growth forests. Nineteen species of conifer occur in the wilderness, more than in any other wildland in the United States. The Siskiyous also contain a large number of endemic species, including trees, shrubs, and wildflowers, and one of the world's largest concentrations of lily species.

Headwaters of the South Fork Smith River drain the west slopes of the range in the Six Rivers National Forest, as does Blue Creek, a tributary to the lower Klamath River. In its extreme northern reaches, the wilderness boundaries extend into the Siskiyou National Forest 5 miles south of the Oregon state line, thus protecting the last remaining roadless lands at the headwaters of the East Fork Illinois River. The bulk of the wilderness lies east of the Siskiyou crest in the Klamath National Forest. These slopes have been logged, mined, and carved with roads, and only the higher elevations lie within wilderness boundaries. The exception is the 15-mile canyon of Clear Creek, the only low-elevation canyon on the east slopes of the Siskiyous protected behind the veil of wilderness.

Unprotected roadless lands remain, primarily on the eastern slopes of the range. These lands are significant to the integrity of the Siskiyou region, as they contain old-growth forests, fields of montane chaparral, the productive steelhead stream of Dillon Creek, numerous sensitive plant species, and important wildlife habitat.

There's a sizeable black bear population here, and both summer and winter range for black-tailed deer. Indicative of its wild character, the Siskiyous also contain habitat for several rare species, including wolverine, marten, fisher, Roosevelt elk that have migrated into the mountains from coastal areas, northern spotted owl, pileated woodpecker, white-headed woodpecker, barred owl, and peregrine falcon. Both resident rainbow trout and anadromous fish depend on the clear waters of the wilderness. Summer-, fall-, and winter-run steelhead, and spring- and fall-run chinook and coho salmon spawn in the streams of the Siskiyous.

RECREATIONAL USES: Despite the dramatic landscape of the Siskiyou, and good access on well-maintained forest roads leading to 16 trailheads, the wilderness is still very lightly used. And since it is so far from population centers, it will likely remain so. Since most of the Siskiyou backcountry is pristine, with very few signs of human impact, visitors must employ zero-impact practices to the fullest.

One look at the Siskiyou Wilderness map shows a network of more than 130 miles of trails that follow canyon bottoms, traverse ridges, and reach into

40B   SISKIYOU WILDERNESS COMPLEX (SOUTH)

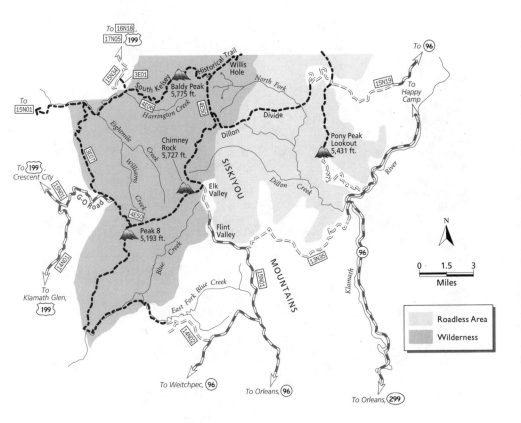

remote cirque basins. Only one of these trails, the 20.5-mile Clear Creek National Recreation Trail (5E01), is regularly maintained. Many other trails receive infrequent maintenance, and are often faint, overgrown, hard to follow, and in some cases blocked by blowdowns for miles as they traverse through heavy forest. The Clear Creek Trail and the South Kelsey Trail (4E06) are the most frequently used. Trail 5E07 from the Doe Flat Trailhead is another popular route leading to Devil's Punchbowl, one of the largest and most spectacular lakes in the Siskiyous.

Remote Twin Valley in the Siskiyou Wilderness.

Day Hike or Overnighter

Poker Flat to Twin Valley

Distance: 7 miles, round trip.
Low/high elevations: 4,800 feet/5,600 feet.
Difficulty: Moderate.
Best season: Late June through mid-October.
Topo map: Polar Bear Mountain-CA.
Permits: A California Campfire Permit is required for open fires and backpack stoves.

HOW TO GET THERE: Follow California Highway 96 along the Klamath River to the small town of Happy Camp, 89 miles north of the CA 299/96 junction at Willow Creek, and 65 miles west of Interstate 5. At the north end of Happy Camp, turn west onto Davis Road at the closed gas station, drive past the post office and grocery store, then follow a right-hand curve that turns onto Indian Creek Road (Forest Road 48). Follow this good, two-lane paved road up through the valley of Indian Creek.

After driving 14.5 miles from CA 96, and 2.6 miles past the turnoff to West Branch Campground, turn left (west) onto FR 18N33. This graded dirt road, locally known as the Powerline Road, leaves the pavement immediately north of where the powerlines cross FR 48. Follow this steadily ascending road along the powerline corridor for 2.5 miles to the junction with FR 18N30, the main north-to-south forest road on the east slopes of the Siskiyous. Turn left onto FR 18N30 at that junction, then after about 50 yards, bear right, uphill, at the unsigned junction, continuing along FR 18N33.

After following this road for another 1.4 miles (3.9 miles from the pavement), bear left (south) toward Poker Flat at the signed junction with north-bound FR 18N36. Your road ascends for another 2.5 miles to an unsigned ridgetop junction. Follow the middle road (avoiding left and right turns) west, soon descending into the lovely, grass-floored bowl of Poker Flat. The inconspicuous trailhead is located at the beginning of a long-closed road, next to an information signboard at the southwest margin of the meadow, 0.7 mile from the ridge, 7.1 miles from FR 48, and 21.6 miles from Happy Camp. There's room enough to park about two vehicles.

(Note: A proposed timber sale in the near future may alter trailhead conditions at Poker Flat.)

This fine trip through old-growth forests is a wonderful introduction to the wild Siskiyous, featuring vistas of the highest summits in the range, open ridges littered with serpentinite, and a remote, lonely meadow with a perennial stream and good campsites. Side-trip options include scaling the nearby summits of Lookout and Polar Bear Mountains, or continuing up the trail to remote Lieutenant Lake, Youngs Valley, or Raspberry Lake. By the time you

Preston Peak, highest in the Siskiyous.

visit, though, the Klamath National Forest may already have logged the magnificent old-growth forests surrounding Poker Flat. But since the wilderness boundary lies less than 0.5 mile from the trailhead, you will quickly leave most signs of civilization behind.

The trail beginning at Poker Flat is actually a long-closed mining road, and it's one of the least visited of the Siskiyou's trailheads. It is also one of the highest, perched near the northern Siskiyou crest in a wildflower-rich meadow. The road begins behind an information signboard, rising into a forest of Douglas-fir, noble fir, and weeping spruce. Expect the possibility of downed trees along much of the infrequently maintained route ahead, and you may expend considerable time and effort climbing over, under, and around blowdowns.

The road winds upward to the wilderness boundary, and to a fork in the road just beyond. The left fork leads to Kelly Lake, so be sure to bear right at the junction. The road ahead leads to the top of a minor ridge, descends a shallow draw, then begins a traverse along the Siskiyou crest. En route you will pass several of the 19 species of conifers present in the wilderness, including Douglas-fir, noble fir, western white pine, ponderosa pine, Jeffrey pine, and incense-cedar.

After curving around the shoulder of Peak 5,463, the trail/road begins a steady descent and dramatic views open up of the craggy northern peaks of the Siskiyous, including the towering pyramid of Preston Peak. The descent ends as you approach the floor of Twin Valley creek. You then rise again along the course of the creek to the rich meadow of Twin Valley at 4,800 feet, 3.5 miles from Poker Flat. Shooting star, cinquefoil, groundsel, and corn lily decorate the grassland. Polar Bear and Lookout Mountains bound the valley to the west, and a clear, cold stream filled with small trout courses through the valley. Campsites can be located among the huge old Douglas-fir and incense-cedar that fringe the meadow.

The trail continues invisibly southwest through the meadow, then continues as a singletrack as it rises past Lieutenant Lake to the crest of the range and beyond into Youngs Valley. The trail is seldom used and is faint in places.

Red Buttes Wilderness Complex   41

Location: 50 miles northeast of Crescent City, 35 miles northwest of Yreka, and 30 miles southwest of Ashland, Oregon.
Size: 60,823 acres.
Administration: USDAFS–Rogue River, Siskiyou, and Klamath National Forests.
Management status: National Forest wilderness (20,323 acres), with the remainder roadless nonwilderness (Kangaroo Roadless Area, 40,500 acres) of which 26,300 acres are managed for semi-primitive nonmotorized recreation, with the remainder released for multiple-use management in the Forest Plan.
Ecosystems: Sierran Forest–Alpine Meadows province, Klamath Mountains section, characterized by an east-to-west drainage divide and mountains with rounded ridges, steep sides, and deep, narrow canyons, small cirques, and narrow terraces and floodplains along tributaries to the Applegate River; a variety of Paleozoic to Triassic metavolcanic and metasedimentary rocks, intruded by Mesozoic granitic rocks; potential natural vegetation is mixed evergreen forest with chinquapin, Klamath montane forest with Douglas-fir, and Klamath montane forest with yellow pine; many perennial streams with a dendritic drainage pattern, numerous moderately high to high-elevation lakes.
Elevation range: 1,400 feet to 6,739 feet.
System trails: 65.3 miles.
Maximum core-to-perimeter distance: 5 miles.
Activities: Backpacking, day hiking, horseback riding, fishing.
Maps: Rogue River National Forest (Oregon) visitor map; Applegate Ranger District visitor map; Red Buttes Wilderness map (topographic, 2 inches/mile); see Appendix D for a list of USGS 1:24,000 quads.

OVERVIEW: The Siskiyou Mountains form one of the longest continuous crests in the Klamath Mountains region of northwest California. The range generally trends north to south, but at the head of Indian Creek, near the isolated hamlet of Happy Camp, the Siskiyous turn northeast and project slightly into Oregon before turning east and reentering California. For 30 miles the Siskiyous stay inside California before exiting the state for good. Along about 12 miles of the east-trending Siskiyous in California and extending 4 miles northwest into Oregon is the small but unique Red Buttes Wilderness, California's northernmost wildland.

The Red Buttes Wilderness stretches along the 6,000-foot Siskiyou Mountains crest and extends north into the drainages of the Middle Fork, Steve Fork, and Butte Fork of the Applegate River, a tributary to Oregon's Rogue River. The northwest portion of the wilderness, in Oregon, drains Sucker

41 RED BUTTES WILDERNESS COMPLEX

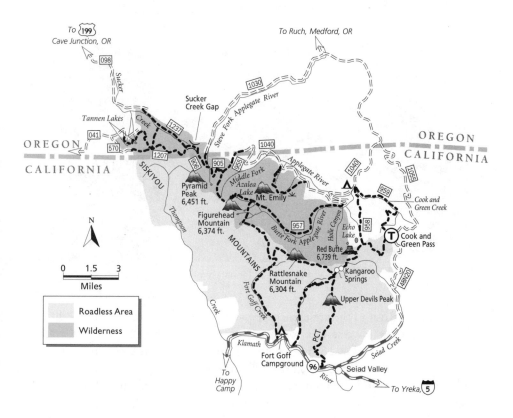

Creek, a tributary to the Illinois River. Separating the Middle and Butte Forks is an isolated high divide of 5,000- and 6,000-foot peaks, rising as much as 3,000 feet above the surrounding canyons in a lateral distance of just one to two miles. Between Cook and Green Pass and Kangaroo Mountain, the crest is composed of ultramafic rocks (dunite, peridotite, serpentinite, and pyroxenite) that weather to a reddish orange color that gives the Red Buttes its name. Red Butte itself is the most outstanding landmark in the area, and the highest at 6,739 feet.

The wilderness was created in 1984 from the Kangaroo roadless area. Except for about 5 to 10 acres surrounding the summit of Red Butte, only the north slopes of the Siskiyou crest were designated wilderness. The south slopes of the crest still contain 40,500 acres of roadless lands in the Klamath River drainage, extending from just above the California Highway 96 corridor along

Red Butte, Kangaroo Mountain, and Figurehead Mountain from the trail above Azalea Lake.

the Klamath River to the crest, encompassing some 5,000 feet of vertical relief. Numerous trails traverse this roadless area, including the Pacific Crest Trail (PCT), which stretches 15 miles between Seiad Valley and Cook and Green Pass. Other trails include the Fort Goff and Portuguese Trails, which traverse their respective canyons. Thompson Creek, in the western reaches of the roadless area, is trailless. Much of the Kangaroo roadless area was burned in two 1987 forest fires. A single low-standard road, constructed by the Federal government in 1940, enters the roadless area from Cook and Green Pass. The road was built to access chromite deposits at the Kubli Mine in upper Hello Canyon for the war effort, and is still used today by motorized recreationists to reach Lily Pad Lake. That portion of the road that crosses over the crest into Hello Canyon lies within wilderness boundaries and is closed to motor vehicles.

The combination of variable terrain, considerable relief, varied climate, several distinct rock types (metamorphic, ultramafic, granitic, and limestone/marble), and overlapping geographic ranges of numerous plant species, results in incredible biodiversity. Species endemic to the Klamath Mountains region include Brewer (weeping) spruce, various ferns, Siskiyou lewisia, and Sadler and Brewer oak, among many others. Other species from different geographic ranges include Baker (Modoc) cypress, which occurs in several stands near the PCT in the West Fork Seiad Creek drainage in the Kangaroo roadless area, and mountain hemlock, Alaska yellow-cedar, noble and silver fir, and knobcone pine. Montane chaparral and at least 12 different species of conifers form a vegetational mosaic across the Red Buttes landscape. The lower Butte Fork canyon is notable for its extensive stands of old growth pine and fir.

The highest elevations of the wilderness, primarily on north-facing slopes, were carved by small mountain glaciers. Numerous cirques were hollowed out below the rocky crest of the Siskiyous, and some are occupied by 15 small lakes and tarns.

Butte Fork and its lower tributaries are the only self-sustaining fisheries in the wilderness. Fish stocking takes place in the Tannen Lakes in Oregon, and in Azalea and Lonesome Lakes on the California side. Wildlife species are typical of those found throughout the Klamath Mountains region. Black-tailed deer use the higher elevations of Red Buttes as summer range, and black bear are very common. Both deer and bear are hunted, and Siskiyou County in California has historically accounted for the highest take of black bear by hunters in the state.

RECREATIONAL USES: Due to its location at the headwaters of Oregon's Applegate River, most access points to the Red Buttes are approached from the Oregon side, and consequently most visitors to the wilderness come from Oregon. Much of the backcountry use in Red Buttes is concentrated in the two major lake basins in the wilderness—Tannen Lakes, and Azalea/Lonesome Lakes. The remainder of the wilderness is lightly used. In fact, the Forest Service has classified more than three-quarters of the wilderness as either primitive or pristine. Opportunities for solitude are great in much of the wilderness and the surrounding roadless lands.

Upper Hello Canyon is a popular destination for day-hikers approaching from Cook and Green Pass and the PCT. Most users of the PCT, however, are through-hikers en route to Oregon and points north, and these hikers usually pass through the area in late summer. The Boundary National Recreation Trail along the Siskiyou crest, the Butte Fork Trail, Steve Fork Trail, and Fir Glade Trail are the most frequently used routes in the wilderness.

Although some areas of the wilderness are considered to be heavily used, use in the Red Buttes is measured in the hundreds, rather than in the thousands and tens of thousands like many California wilderness destinations. Use is concentrated on weekends and holidays from late June through October, although the lower Butte Fork area and the lower canyons in the Kangaroo roadless area are accessible year-round. Outfitter/guide activities are minimal in the Red Buttes, though private stock parties account for a small percentage of wilderness users. Most stock use is limited to day rides and/or overnight trips to Azalea Lake in summer, with the remainder of stock traffic occurring during hunting season. Day hiking and backpacking are the most popular activities.

About 43 miles of trails are maintained within the wilderness, with more than 20 miles of additional trails traversing the Kangaroo roadless area. These trails traverse the spectrum of Red Buttes landscapes, from the lush lower canyons with their mixed conifer forests and groves of oak and madrone, to the open, chaparral-clad ridges and subalpine stands of mountain hemlock and western white pine. High trails afford memorable vistas into the Red Buttes interior, and to distant features including the Marble Mountains, Mount Shasta, and Mount McLoughlin in Oregon. Hikers visiting in May will find the rhododendron, calypso orchid, iris, and various lilies in bloom. Azaleas begin blooming in the higher terrain around the end of June, and earlier in the lower canyons.

Except for trails beginning along CA 96 in the Klamath River canyon, and Forest Road 48N20 at Cook and Green Pass, most access is from forest roads in the Applegate District of the Rogue River National Forest in Oregon. FR 1040 follows the northern wilderness boundary and offers access to seven major trailheads. The Tannen Lakes/Sucker Creek Gap area on the northwest is the only part of the wilderness in Oregon, and trailheads there can be reached via the Indian Creek Road (FR 48) northwest of Happy Camp, California, and FR 4812 and 041.

Day Hike or Overnighter

Cook and Green Pass to Kangaroo Springs

Distance: 10.6 miles, round trip.
Low/high elevations: 4,750 feet/5,900 feet.
Difficulty: Strenuous.
Best season: Late June through September.
Topo map: Kangaroo Mountain-CA.
Permits: California Campfire Permit required for open fires and backpack stoves.

HOW TO GET THERE: Follow CA 96 through the Klamath River canyon to the hamlet of Seiad Valley, 46 miles west of Interstate 5 and 108 miles from the CA 299/96 junction at Willow Creek. Look for your turnoff, the Seiad Creek Road, at the west end of town, immediately west of the Seiad Creek bridge and north of the Old Seiad Valley Store. Once you find the road, turn northeast and follow the pavement up Seiad Valley. After 3.4 miles, FR 46N50 branches right (south) and bridges Seiad Creek. Bear left and drive another 0.6 mile to the end of the pavement, where FR 48N20 begins.

Follow that steep, narrow, and winding gravel road for another 8.1 miles to Cook and Green Pass on the crest of the Siskiyou Mountains, 12.1 miles from CA 96. The southbound Pacific Crest Trail begins at the small trailhead parking area on the west side of the pass.

Red Butte, the highest point in Red Buttes Wilderness.

This memorable hike along the Pacific Crest Trail tours the eastern reaches of the Kangaroo Roadless Area. Traversing the high crest of the Siskiyous and passing beneath the red rock tower of Red Butte, this trip features far-ranging vistas that contrast vast clearcuts with remnant stands of old-growth forests, and leads to a fine base camp at Kangaroo Springs. From there, day hikes along the Boundary Trail or scrambles to the nearby summits of Red Butte, Kangaroo Mountain, and Rattlesnake Mountain can keep hikers busy for several days.

At the trailhead, avoid the descending Cook and Green Trail (959) and bear left onto the ascending course of the Pacific Crest Trail (PCT). The trail contours south, rising moderately on a course above the old mining road leading to Hello Canyon. At first the trail traverses through old-growth Douglas-fir and white fir, but soon opens up onto rubbly, red rock slopes dominated by huckleberry oak and silktassel. Vistas expand as the rising traverse leads out to the shoulder of a south-trending ridge, from which you can see Mount Shasta, the Trinity Mountains, and the Marble Mountains, all forming a vast landscape of high ridges and deep river valleys.

As the trail curves around the shoulder of the ridge, Jeffrey and western white pine shade the trail, and views reach into the headwaters of the West Fork Seiad Creek, bounded by Red Butte and Kangaroo Mountain. Panoramic vistas continue as you gradually rise among wind-flagged conifers to a 5,900-foot saddle at 2.5 miles. The Horse Camp Trail (958) descends from the saddle to Echo Lake and eventually leads to a trailhead on FR 1040 along the Butte Fork Applegate River. From immediately north of the saddle you can see shallow Echo Lake in the cirque below and gaze far beyond into the canyon of the Applegate River.

A steady descent from the saddle on the PCT ensues, leading into a cool forest of incense-cedar and white fir. After dropping 250 feet in 0.3 mile, the PCT crosses the old mining road, traverses a shallow, rocky basin beneath the tower of Red Butte, then bridges a small, cold, spring-fed stream. After curving around a minor ridge, the trail leads into a larger ice-gouged basin, thick with fir and cedar and flanked on its south side with ice-polished bedrock.

The trail becomes increasingly narrow and overgrown as you traverse above shallow, aptly named Lily Pad Lake. Above the lake is a signed junction with a faint, rarely used trail descending the West Fork Seiad Creek. The PCT curves around the bowl above Lily Pad Lake, then crests a ridge atop gray marble—the same rock present on Marble Mountain far to the south. Another 0.5 mile of walking through montane chaparral and scattered conifers leads to another small cirque basin, this one lying beneath the tree-fringed crest of 6,694-foot Kangaroo Mountain. Here at 5,700 feet, the trail reenters a cool fir forest where you will find reliable Kangaroo Springs and several good campsites, 5.3 miles from Cook and Green Pass.

APPENDIX A

Recommended Equipment for Wilderness Travel

Hiking, backpacking, and winter travel beyond the roads require ample planning, and one of the first steps to being well prepared is packing the right equipment. Don't overburden your pack with too much equipment and unnecessary items; bring only what you really need. Scan the checklist below before your trip into wild country to ensure you haven't forgotten an essential item.

—Backpack
—Day pack
—Extra pack straps
—Water bottles (1- to 2-quart Nalgene bottles are best)
—Collapsible bucket (for settling silty water)
—Water filter (with brush to clean in the field)
—Pocket knife
—Hiking poles (1 or 2)
—Foam or self-inflating sleeping pad
—Sleeping bag (or sheet, or sleeping bag liner for summer)
—Tent, stakes, ground sheet and/or tarp
—Hat with brim
—Sunglasses (with UV protection)
—Sunscreen (with an SPF of 15 or greater)
—Backpack stove, fuel bottle (full)
—Signal mirror
—First-aid kit
—Medication: prescriptions, anti-inflammatory and/or pain medication
—Knee and/or ankle wraps (neoprene is best)
—First-aid tape
—Moleskin, Second Skin
—Bandaids, bandages
—Aspirin (or other pain medication)
—Lip balm
—Toothbrush, toothpaste
—Toilet paper
—Lightweight trowel
—Boots (well broken-in)
—Camp shoes or sandals
—Extra shirt

—Extra underwear
—Extra socks
—Hiking socks; wool outer, polypropylene or nylon liner
—Parka (synthetic pile works best)
—Sweater
—Pants
—Hiking shorts
—Swimsuit
—Rain gear (Gore-tex or similar fabric that is both waterproof and windproof)
—Biodegradable soap, small towel
—Cookware, cup, pot handle, pot scrubber
—Spoon and fork
—Matches in waterproof container
—Insect repellent
—Nylon tape or duct tape
—Pack cover
—Bear-resistant food canister
—Topo maps
—Flashlight, with spare bulb and fresh batteries
—Zipper-lock bags (for packing out trash and used toilet paper)
—Enough food, plus a little extra
—Watch
—Compass
—Binoculars
—Thermometer
—Camera, film, lenses, filters, lens brush and paper
—Small sewing kit
—Notebook, pencils
—Field guidebooks
—Water
—Wilderness Permit (where required)
—California Campfire Permit

Add the following for winter travel:
—Gaiters
—Instep crampons
—Wool or polypro cap or balaclava
—Space blanket
—Layers of warm clothing
—Sleeping bag with a rating of at least -10 degrees F.
—Waterproof/windproof clothing

—Mittens or gloves
—Thermal underwear (wool or polypropylene)
—Cross-country skis, poles, climbing skins, extra tips, wax, cork, scraper
—Snowshoes
—Avalanche probes (threaded ski poles)
—Avalanche tranceivers
—Four-season tent
—Internal frame backpack
—Closed-cell foam pad
—Foam pad for stove
—Snow shovel

APPENDIX B

Federal Agencies

Bureau of Land Management

California Desert District
6221 Box Springs Blvd.
Riverside, CA 92507
(909) 697-5200

Caliente Resource Area
3801 Pegasus Dr.
Bakersfield, CA 93308
(805) 391–6120

Ridgecrest Resource Area
300 South Richmond Rd.
Ridgecrest, CA 93555
(760) 384–5400

Arcata Resource Area
1695 Heindon Rd.
Arcata, CA 95521
(707) 825–2300

National Park Service

Sequoia–Kings Canyon National Parks
Three Rivers, CA 93271
(209) 565–3341

Wilderness Permit Reservations
Sequoia–Kings Canyon National Parks
HCR 89 Box 60
Three Rivers, CA 93271
FAX (209) 565–4239

(**For wilderness permit reservations:** request a copy of *Backcountry Basics*, a wilderness trip-planning guide, from the phone number above, or consult the Web site at www.nps.gov/seki. Permit reservations require a fee.)

Yosemite National Park
P.O. Box 577
Yosemite, CA 95389
(209) 372–0200

Wilderness Permits
P.O. Box 545
Yosemite, CA 95389
(209) 372–0740

Lassen Volcanic National Park
P.O. Box 100
Mineral, CA 96063
(530) 595–4444

Lava Beds National Monument
Box 867
Tulelake, CA 96134
(530) 667–2282

Point Reyes National Seashore
Point Reyes Station, CA 94956
(415) 663–8522
(For permit reservations, accepted between 9:00 AM and 2:00 PM, Monday through Friday, call (415) 663–8054. Reservations are also accepted in person at the Bear Valley visitor center. A recorded message, indicating trail camps availability, can be heard by phoning (415) 663–1092, ext. 400.)

California State Parks
Castle Crags State Park
Castella, CA 96001
(530) 235–2684

Forest Service
Pacific Southwest Region Headquarters (Region 5)
630 Sansome St.
San Francisco, CA 94111
(415) 705–2874

Sequoia National Forest
Forest Supervisor
900 W. Grand Ave.
Porterville, CA 93257
(209) 784–1500
www.r5.fs.fed.us/sequoia

Hume Lake Ranger District
36273 E. Kings Canyon Rd.
Dunlap, CA 93621
(209) 338–2251

Tule River Ranger District
32588 Highway 190
Springville, CA 93265
(209) 539–2607

Hot Springs Ranger District
Rt. 4, Box 548
California Hot Springs, CA 93207
(805) 548–6503

Greenhorn Ranger District
15701 Hwy. 178
P.O. Box 6129
Bakersfield, CA 93386-6129
(805) 871–2223

Cannell Meadow Ranger District
P.O. Box 6
Kernville, CA 93238
(760) 376–3781

Inyo National Forest
Forest Supervisor
873 N. Main
Bishop, CA 93514
(760) 873–2400
www.r5.fs.fed.us/inyo

Mono Lake Scenic Area Visitor Center
Mono Lake Ranger District
P.O. Box 130
Lee Vining, CA 93541
(760) 647–3044

Mammoth Ranger District
P.O. Box 148
Mammoth Lakes, CA 93546
(760) 934–2505

White Mountain Ranger District
798 Main St.
Bishop, CA 93514
(760) 873–2500

Mt. Whitney Ranger Station
P.O. Box 8
Lone Pine, CA 93545
(760) 876–6200

(For wilderness permit reservations in the Inyo National Forest, contact by mail or fax: Inyo National Forest Wilderness Reservation Office, 873 North Main Street, Bishop, CA 93514, or fax applications to (760) 873–2484. A fee is required for reservations.)

Sierra National Forest
Forest Supervisor
1600 Tollhouse Rd.
Clovis, CA 93611-0532
www.r5.fs.fed.us/sierra

Minarets and Mariposa Ranger Districts
P.O. Box 10
North Fork, CA 93643
(559) 877-2218

Kings River Ranger District
34849 Maxon Rd.
Sanger, CA 93657
(559) 855-8321

Pineridge Ranger District
29688 Auberry Rd.
Prather, CA 93651
(559) 855-5360

Stanislaus National Forest
Forest Supervisor
19777 Greenley Rd.
Sonora, CA 95370
(209) 532-3671

Summit Ranger District
#1 Pinecrest Rd.
Pinecrest, CA 95364
(209) 965-3434

Miwok Ranger District
P.O. Box 100
Hwy. 108 E.
Mi-Wuk Village, CA 95346
(209) 586-3234

Groveland Ranger District
Star Rt., Box 75G
Groveland, CA 95321
(209) 962-7825

Calaveras Ranger District
P.O. Box 500
Hathaway Pines, CA 95233
(209) 795-1381

Toiyabe National Forest
Forest Supervisor
1200 Franklin Way
Sparks, NV 89431
(775) 331-6444

Carson Ranger District
1536 South Carson St.
Carson City, NV 89701
(775) 882-2766

Bridgeport Ranger District
P.O. Box 595
Bridgeport, CA 93517
(760) 932-7070

Eldorado National Forest
Forest Supervisor
100 Forni Rd.
Placerville, CA 95667
(530) 622-5061

Amador Ranger District
26820 Silver Dr.
Pioneer, CA 95666
(209) 295-4251

Tahoe National Forest
Forest Supervisor
Nevada City Ranger District
631 Coyote St.

P.O. Box 6003
Nevada City, CA 95959-6003
(530) 265–4531

Downieville Ranger District
15924 Hwy. 49
Camptonville, CA 95922-9707
(530) 288–3231

Foresthill Ranger District
22830 Foresthill Rd.
Foresthill, CA 95631
(530) 367–2224

Sierraville Ranger District
P.O. Box 95
Sierraville, CA 96126
(530) 994–3401

Truckee Ranger District
10342 Hwy. 89 N.
Truckee, CA 96161
(530) 587–3558

**Lake Tahoe Basin
Management Unit**
870 Emerald Bay Rd., Suite 1
South Lake Tahoe, CA 96150
(530) 573–2669

Plumas National Forest
Forest Supervisor
159 Lawrence St.
P.O. Box 11500
Quincy, CA 95971
(530) 283–2050

Quincy Ranger District
39696 Hwy. 70
Quincy, CA 95971
(530) 283–0555

Oroville Ranger District
875 Mitchell Ave.
Oroville, CA 95965–4699
(530) 534–6500

Lassen National Forest
Forest Supervisor
55 S. Sacramento St.
Susanville, CA 95971
(530) 257–2151

Almanor Ranger District
P.O. Box 767
Chester, CA 96020
(530) 258–2141

Hat Creek Ranger District
P.O. Box 220
Fall River Mills, CA 96028
(530) 336–5521

Shasta-Trinity National Forests
Forest Supervisor
2400 Washington Ave.
Redding, CA 96001
(530) 244–2978

Weaverville Ranger District
P.O. Box 1190
Weaverville, CA 96093-1190
(530) 623–2131

Hayfork Ranger District
P.O. Box 159
Hayfork, CA 96041
(530) 628–5227

Big Bar Ranger District
Star Rt. 1, Box 10
Big Bar, CA 96010
(530) 623–6106

Shasta Lake Ranger District
6543 Holiday Dr.
Redding, CA 96003
(530) 275–1587

Mt. Shasta Ranger District
204 West Alma St.
Mt. Shasta City, CA 96067
(530) 926–4511

McCloud Ranger District
Drawer 1
McCloud, CA 96057
(530) 964–2184

Modoc National Forest
Forest Supervisor
441 N. Main St.
Alturas, CA 96101
(530) 233–5811

Warner Mountain District
P.O. Box 220
Cedarville, CA 96104
(530) 279–6116

Mendocino National Forest
Forest Supervisor
825 N. Humboldt Ave.
Willows, CA 95988
(530) 934–3316

Stonyford Ranger District
Stites-Lodoga Rd.
Stonyford, CA 95979
(530) 963–3128

Covelo Ranger District
78150 Covelo Rd.
Covelo, CA 95428
(707) 983–6118

Corning Ranger District
P.O. Box 1019
Corning, CA 96021
(530) 824–5196

Yolla Bolly Ranger District
Platina, CA 96076
(530) 352–4211

Klamath National Forest
Forest Supervisor
1312 Fairlane Rd.
Yreka, CA 96097
(530) 842–6131

Scott River and Salmon River Ranger
Districts
11263 S. Hwy. 3
Fort Jones, CA 96032
(530) 468–5351

Happy Camp Ranger District
P.O. Box 377
Happy Camp, CA 96039
(530) 493–2243

Ukonom Ranger District
P.O. Drawer 410
Orleans, CA 95556
(530) 627–3291

Goosenest Ranger District
37805 Hwy. 97
Macdoel, CA 96058
(530) 398–4391

Oak Knoll Ranger District
22541 Hwy. 96
Klamath River, CA 96050
(530) 465–2241

Six Rivers National Forest
Forest Supervisor
1330 Bayshore Way
Eureka, CA 95501-3834
(707) 442–1721

Mad River Ranger District
Star Rt., Box 300
Bridgeville, CA 95428
(707) 574–6233

Lower Trinity Ranger District
P.O. Box 68
Willow Creek, CA 95573
(530) 629–2118

Smith River National Recreation Area
P.O. Box 228
Gasquet, CA 95543
(707) 457–3131

Siskiyou National Forest
Forest Supervisor
P.O. Box 440
200 Northeast Greenfield Rd.
Grants Pass, OR 97526
(541) 479–5301

Illinois Valley Ranger District
26568 Redwood Highway
Cave Junction, OR 97523
(541) 592–2166

Rogue River National Forest
Forest Supervisor
P.O. Box 520
333 W. 8th St.
Medford, OR 97501
(541) 776–3600

Applegate Ranger District
6941 Upper Applegate Rd.
Jacksonville, OR 97530
(541) 899–1812

Regional Map Sales
4260 Eight Mile Road
Camino, CA 95709
(530) 647–5390
(for wilderness and national forest maps)

APPENDIX C

Public Lands Conservation Groups in California

California Wilderness Coalition
2655 Portage Bay E., Suite 5
Davis, CA 95616
(530) 758–0380

The Wilderness Society
Presidio Building 1016
P.O. Box 29241
San Francisco, CA 94129-0241
(415) 561–6641

Sierra Club
85 Second St.
San Francisco, CA 94105
(415) 977–5500

Wilderness Watch
P.O. Box 9175
Missoula, MT 59807
(406) 542–2048

(Note: There are numerous other conservation groups in California. Contact any one of the above organizations, and they can inform you of the conservation group that is involved with the area you are interested in.)

APPENDIX D

Topographic Map Lists

(Note: All maps listed are 1:24,000-scale (2.5 inches/mile) USGS quadrangles for California, unless otherwise indicated. Lists are arranged in alphabetical order.)

1. **KIAVAH:** Cane Canyon-CA, Freeman Junction-CA, Horse Canyon-CA, Onyx-CA, Owens Peak-CA, Walker Pass-CA.

2. **OWENS PEAK:** Freeman Junction-CA, Lamont Peak-CA, Ninemile Canyon-CA, Owens Peak-CA, Walker Pass-CA.

3. **DOME LAND:** Cannell Peak-CA, Crag Peak-CA, Lamont Peak-CA, Onyx-CA, Rockhouse Basin-CA, Sacatar Canyon-CA, Sirretta Peak-CA, Weldon-CA, White Dome-CA.

4. **SACATAR TRAIL:** Coso Junction-CA, Lamont Peak-CA, Little Lake-CA, Long Canyon-CA, Ninemile Canyon-CA, Sacatar Canyon-CA.

5. **SOUTH SIERRA:** Crag Peak-CA, Haiwee Pass-CA, Long Canyon-CA, Monache Mountain-CA, Olancha-CA, Templeton Mountain-CA.

6. **GOLDEN TROUT:** Bartlett-CA, Camp Nelson-CA, Camp Wishon-CA, Casa Vieja Meadows-CA, Cirque Peak-CA, Hockett Peak-CA, Johnson Peak-CA, Kern Lake-CA, Kern Peak-CA, Mineral King-CA, Monache Mountain-CA, Moses Mountain-CA, Olancha-CA, Quinn Peak-CA, Templeton Mountain-CA.

7. **SEQUOIA–KINGS CANYON:** Aberdeen-CA, Blackcap Mountain-CA, Case Mountain-CA, Cedar Grove-CA, Chagoopa Falls-CA, Giant Forest-CA, Johnson Peak-CA, Kearsarge Peak-CA, Kern Lake-CA, Lodgepole-CA, Marion Peak-CA, Mineral King-CA, Moses Mountain-CA, Mount Brewer-CA, Mount Clarence King-CA, Mount Darwin-CA, Mount Goddard-CA, Mount Henry-CA, Mount Kaweah-CA, Mount Langley-CA, Mount Pinchot-CA, Mount Silliman-CA, Mount Thompson-CA, Mount Whitney-CA, Mount Williamson-CA, Muir Grove-CA, North Palisade-CA, Quinn Peak-CA, Rough Spur-CA, Shadequarter Mountain-CA, Silver City-CA, Slide Bluffs-CA, Sphinx Lakes-CA, Split Mountain-CA, Tehipite Dome-CA, The Sphinx-CA, Triple Divide Peak-CA, Wren Peak-CA.

8. JENNIE LAKES: Mount Silliman-CA, Muir Grove-CA.

9. MONARCH: Cedar Grove-CA, Hume-CA, Luckett Mountain-CA, Patterson Mountain-CA, Rough Spur-CA, Sacate Ridge-CA, Slide Bluffs-CA, Tehipite Dome-CA, Verplank Ridge-CA, Wren Peak-CA.

10. JOHN MUIR: Aberdeen-CA, Balloon Dome-CA, Blackcap Mountain-CA, Bloody Mountain-CA, Cirque Peak-CA, Convict Lake-CA, Coyote Flat-CA, Courtright Reservoir-CA, Crystal Crag-CA, Fish Springs-CA, Florence Lake-CA, Graveyard Peak-CA, Kearsarge Peak-CA, Manzanar-CA, Mount Abbot-CA, Mount Clarence King-CA, Mount Darwin-CA, Mount Goddard-CA, Mount Henry-CA, Mount Hilgard-CA, Mount Langley-CA, Mount Morgan-CA, Mount Pinchot-CA, Mount Thompson-CA, Mount Tom-CA, Mount Whitney-CA, Mount Williamson-CA, North Palisade-CA, Sharktooth Peak-CA, Split Mountain-CA, Toms Place-CA, Ward Mountain-CA.

11. DINKEY LAKES: Courtright Reservoir-CA, Dogtooth Peak-CA, Mount Givens-CA, Nelson Mountain-CA, Ward Mountain-CA.

12. KAISER: Huntington Lake-CA, Kaiser Peak-CA, Mammoth Pool Dam-CA, Mount Givens-CA, Musick Mountain-CA.

13. ANSEL ADAMS: Balloon Dome-CA, Cattle Mountain-CA, Crystal Crag-CA, Graveyard Peak-CA, Mammoth Mountain-CA, Mount Lyell-CA, Mount Ritter-CA, Sharktooth Peak-CA, Sing Peak-CA, Squaw Dome-CA, Timber Knob-CA.

14. PIPER MOUNTAIN: Chocolate Mountain-CA, Cowhorn Valley-CA, Deep Springs Lake-CA, Horse Thief Canyon-CA, Joshua Flats-CA, Soldier Pass-CA, Sylvania Canyon-CA/NV.

15. SYLVANIA MOUNTAINS: Horse Thief Canyon-CA, Last Chance Mountain-CA/NV, Sylvania Canyon-CA/NV, Sylvania Mountains-NV/CA.

16. YOSEMITE: Ackerson Mountain-CA, Buckeye Ridge-CA, Cherry Lake North-CA, Cherry Lake South-CA, Dunderberg Peak-CA, El Capitan-CA, El Portal-CA, Emigrant Lake-CA, Falls Ridge-CA, Fish Camp-CA, Half Dome-CA, Hetch Hetchy Reservoir-CA, Kibbie Lake-CA, Koip Peak-CA, Lake Eleanor-CA, Mariposa Grove-CA, Matterhorn Peak-CA, Merced Peak-CA, Mount Dana-CA, Mount Lyell-CA, Piute Mountain-CA, Sing Peak-CA,

Tamarack Flat-CA, Tenaya Lake-CA, Ten Lakes-CA, Tiltill Mountain-CA, Tioga Pass-CA, Tower Peak-CA, Vogelsang Peak-CA, Wawona-CA, White Chief Mountain-CA, Yosemite Falls-CA.

17. HOOVER: Buckeye Ridge-CA, Dunderberg Peak-CA, Emigrant Lake-CA, Fales Hot Springs-CA, Lundy-CA, Matterhorn Peak-CA, Mount Dana-CA, Pickel Meadow-CA, Sonora Pass-CA, Tioga Pass-CA, Tower Peak-CA, Twin Lakes-CA.

18. EMIGRANT: Cherry Lake North-CA, Cooper Peak-CA, Dardanelle-CA, Emigrant Lake-CA, Kibbie Lake-CA, Pickel Meadow-CA, Pinecrest-CA, Sonora Pass-CA, Tiltill Mountain-CA, Tower Peak-CA.

19. CARSON-ICEBERG: Coleville-CA, Dardanelle-CA, Dardanelles Cone-CA, Disaster Peak-CA, Donnell Lake-CA, Ebbetts Pass-CA, Lost Cannon Peak-CA, Pacific Valley-CA, Pickel Meadow-CA, Sonora Pass-CA, Spicer Meadow Res.-CA, Tamarack-CA, and Wolf Creek-CA.

20. MOKELUMNE: Bear River Reservoir-CA, Calaveras Dome-CA, Caples Lake-CA, Carson Pass-CA, Mokelumne Peak-CA, Pacific Valley-CA, Tamarack-CA.

21. DARDANELLES: Caples Lake-CA, Echo Lake-CA, Freel Peak-CA.

22. FREEL: Freel Peak-CA, South Lake Tahoe-CA.

23. GRANITE CHIEF: Granite Chief-CA, Homewood-CA, Tahoe City-CA, Wentworth Springs-CA.

24. BUCKS LAKE: Bucks Lake-CA, Caribou-CA, Meadow Valley-CA, Storrie-CA.

25. ISHI: Barkley Mountain-CA, Devils Parade Ground-CA, Ishi Caves-CA, Panther Springs-CA.

26. LASSEN VOLCANIC: Lassen Peak-CA, Manzanita Lake-CA, Mount Harkness-CA, Prospect Peak-CA, Reading Peak-CA, West Prospect Peak-CA.

27. CARIBOU: Bogard Buttes-CA, Red Cinder-CA.

28. THOUSAND LAKES: Jacks Backbone-CA, Thousand Lakes Valley-CA.

29. SOUTH WARNER: Eagle Peak-CA, Eagleville-CA, Emerson Peak-CA, Jess Valley-CA, Shields Creek-CA, Snake Lake-CA, Soup Creek-CA, Warren Peak-CA.

30. LAVA BEDS: Caldwell Butte-CA, Captain Jacks Stronghold-CA, The Panhandle-CA, Lava Beds National Monument-CA, Schonchin Butte-CA.

31. MOUNT SHASTA: Ash Creek Butte-CA, City of Mount Shasta-CA, Elk Spring-CA, Hotlum-CA, McCloud-CA, Mount Shasta-CA, The Whaleback-CA.

32. PHILLIP BURTON: Bolinas-CA, Double Point-CA, Drakes Bay-CA, Inverness-CA, Tomales-CA.

33. SNOW MOUNTAIN: Crockett Peak-CA, Fouts Spring-CA, Potato Hill-CA, Saint John Mountain-CA.

34. KING RANGE: Cooskie Creek-CA, Honeydew-CA, Petrolia-CA, Shelter Cove-CA, Shubrick Peak-CA.

35. YOLLA BOLLY: USGS 1:25,000 Black Rock Mtn.-CA, Buck Rock-CA; Four Corners Rock-CA, North Yolla Bolly-CA, South Yolla Bolly-CA.

36. CASTLE CRAGS: Dunsmuir-CA, Seven Lakes Basin-CA.

37. TRINITY ALPS: Billys Peak-CA, Callahan-CA, Caribou Lake-CA, Carrville-CA, Cecil Lake-CA, Cecilville-CA, Covington Mill-CA, Deadman Peak-CA, Dees Peak-CA, Dedrick-CA, Del Loma-CA, Denny-CA, Grasshopper Ridge-CA, Hayfork Bally-CA, Helena-CA, Hopkins Butte-CA, Jim Jam Ridge-CA, Mount Hilton-CA, Rush Creek Lakes-CA, Salmon Mountain-CA, Scott Mountain-CA, Siligo Peak-CA, Tangle Blue Lake-CA, Thompson Peak-CA, Thurston Peaks-CA, Tish Tang Point-CA, Trinity Mountain-CA, Ycatapom Peak-CA, Youngs Peak-CA.

38. RUSSIAN: Deadmans Peak-CA, Eaton Peak-CA, Etna-CA, Grasshopper Ridge-CA, Tanners Peak-CA.

39. MARBLE MOUNTAIN: Boulder Peak-CA, English Peak-CA, Forks of Salmon-CA, Grider Valley-CA, Huckleberry Mountain-CA, Marble Mountain-CA, Sawyers Bar-CA, Somes Bar-CA, Ukonom Lake-CA, Ukonom Mountain-CA, Yellow Dog Peak-CA.

40. SISKIYOU: Bear Peak-CA, Broken Rib Mountain-CA/OR, Chimney Rock-CA, Devils Punchbowl-CA, Dillon Mountain-CA, Hurdygurdy Butte-CA, Lonesome Ridge-CA, Polar Bear Mountain-CA, Prescott Mountain-CA, Preston Peak-CA, Ship Mountain-CA, Summit Valley-CA.

41. RED BUTTES: Deadman Point-CA, Figurehead Mountain-CA, Kangaroo Mountain-CA, and Seiad Valley-CA; Carberry Creek-OR/CA, Grayback Mountain-OR, Oregon Caves-OR.

FINDING THE RIGHT MAPS: There are several different useful kinds of maps for exploring the areas covered in *Wild Northern California*. First, there are the U.S. Geological Survey (USGS) 1:24,000-scale topographic maps listed above, and these detailed maps are useful for on-the-ground navigation. Many wilderness areas in California have been created since some of these maps were published, so some maps will not show wilderness boundaries. The USGS also produces maps that cover the national parks and monuments in the state, and statewide maps on a scale of 1:1,000,000 (5/8-inch/mile). The best place to start when choosing USGS maps is the California index of topographic maps, available free of charge from the USGS.

Order maps and state indexes from the USGS at: USGS Information Services, Box 25286, Denver, CO 80225, or by calling 1-800-USA-MAPS or 1-800-HELP-MAP. USGS maps are $6 each, with a handling charge of $3.50 added to all orders. Over-the-counter sales of USGS maps are available at USGS, Building 3, Room 3128, 345 Middlefield Road, Menlo Park, CA 94025. USGS maps are also widely available at various outdoor and sporting goods stores.

Other maps that are listed under "Maps" in the trip-planning chart for each California wildland are national forest maps and wilderness maps. National forest maps are useful for an overview and for finding trailheads. Wilderness maps are available for most wilderness areas in California. All of these maps are topographic, and show a usually accurate representation of trails and access roads. These maps are available from most national forest district offices, forest supervisor's offices, from the Pacific Southwest Region headquarters, and from the Regional Map Sales Office, all listed in Appendix B.

Finally, for wilderness areas within the BLM's California Desert District, which includes the extreme southern Sierra Nevada, the Mojave Desert, and the Great Basin, there are 1:2,500,000-scale maps available that show land ownership, roads, and wilderness areas. You can request a map index and order maps from the BLM offices listed in Appendix B.

APPENDIX E

Trips at a Glance

SOUTHERN SIERRA

Trip Name	Area and (Chapter #)	Type	Distance	Difficulty
Skinner Peak	Kiavah (1)	Day hike	8.2	Moderately strenuous
Lamont Peak	Owens Peak (2)	Day hike	4	Strenuous
Rockhouse Basin	Dome Land (3)	Backpack	14	Moderate
Sacatar Trail	Sacatar Trail (4)	Day hike/ overnighter	9	Moderately strenuous
Lost Mdws.	South Sierra (5)	Backpack	15	Moderate
Kern Peak	Golden Trout (6)	Backpack	26.6	Moderate
Sky Blue Lake	Sequoia–Kings Canyon (7)	Backpack	25.6	Moderately strenuous
Mitchell Peak	Jennie Lakes (8)	Day hike/ overnighter	10.6	Moderate
Agnew Grove	Monarch (9)	Day hike/ overnighter	8.4	Strenuous
North Lake to Pine Creek	John Muir (10)	Backpack	22	Moderate
Dogtooth Peak	Dinkey Lakes (11)	Day hike/ overnighter	11.6	Moderate
George Lake/ Kaiser Peak	Kaiser (12)	Day hike/ backpack	6-9	Moderate to strenuous
North Fork San Joaquin River	Ansel Adams (13)	Backpack	28	Strenuous

NORTHERN GREAT BASIN

Trip Name	Area and (Chapter #)	Type	Distance	Difficulty
Soldier Pass Canyon	Piper Mountain (14)	Day hike	6.4	Moderate
Sylvania Mountains	Sylvania Mountains (15)	Day hike	9	Moderate

NORTHERN SIERRA

Trip Name	Area and (Chapter #)	Type	Distance	Difficulty
Virginia Canyon	Yosemite (16)	Backpack	19	Moderately strenuous
Leavitt Lake Loop	Hoover (17)	Backpack/ horsepacking trip	20.8	Moderately strenuous
Upper Relief Valley	Emigrant (18)	Backpack/ horsepacking trip	16.4	Moderate
Fish Valley Loop	Carson-Iceberg (19)	Backpack	14	Moderate
Wheeler Lake/ Underwood Valley	Mokelumne (20)	Backpack	15	Moderate
Showers Lake	Dardanelles (21)	Day hike/ backpack	8.2	Moderate
Freel Mdws.	Freel (22)	Day hike/ overnighter	7.6	Moderate
Twin Peaks	Granite Chief (23)	Day hike/ overnighter or ski/snow-shoe tour	9.2	Moderately strenuous
Spanish Peak	Bucks Lake (24)	Day hike	7.5	Moderate

CASCADE RANGE/MODOC PLATEAU

Trip Name	Area and (Chapter #)	Type	Distance	Difficulty
Mill Creek	Ishi (25)	Day hike/ overnighter	9	Easy
Butte Lake/ Snag Lake Loop	Lassen Volcanic (26)	Backpack	11.9	Moderate
Cone Lake to Hay Mdw.	Caribou (27)	Day hike/ backpack	10.75	Moderate
Thousand Lakes Valley	Thousand Lakes (28)	Day hike/ backpack	10-14	Moderate
North Emerson Lake	South Warner (29)	Backpack	12.8-16.2	Moderate
Whitney Butte Trail	Lava Beds (30)	Day hike	7	Moderate
Clear Creek Trail	Mount Shasta (31)	Day hike	5	Moderate

NORTH COAST RANGES/KLAMATH MOUNTAINS

Trip Name	Area and (Chapter #)	Type	Distance	Difficulty
Mount Wittenberg	Phillip Burton (32)	Day hike	4.7	Moderate
Snow Mountain	Snow Mountain (33)	Day hike/ overnighter	7.8	Moderate
Kings Peak	King Range (34)	Day hike/ overnighter	6.1	Moderate
North Yolla Bolly Mtns.	Yolla Bolly– Middle Eel (35)	Day hike/ overnighter	11.2	Moderately strenuous
Castle Dome	Castle Crags (36)	Day hike	5.5	Strenuous
New River/ Virgin Creek Loop	Trinity Alps (37)	Backpack	36.7	Moderately strenuous
Taylor and Hogan Lakes	Russian (38)	Day hike/ overnighter	1-6.5	Easy to strenuous
North Fork Salmon River/ Wooley Creek Loop	Marble Mountain (39)	Backpack/ horsepacking trip	59.5	Strenuous
Twin Valley	Siskiyou (40)	Day hike/ overnighter	7	Moderate
Kangaroo Springs	Red Buttes (41)	Day hike/ overnighter	10.6	Strenuous

APPENDIX F

Wilderness Designation in Northern and Central California

1931—establishment of South Warner Primitive Area, Marble Mountain Primitive Area, and Emigrant Basin Primitive Area.

1932—establishment of Salmon–Trinity Alps Primitive Area.

1933—Salmon–Trinity Alps Primitive Area expanded.

1936—establishment of High Sierra Primitive Area (including what is now Kings Canyon National Park, John Muir and Monarch Wildernesses).

1940—southern part of High Sierra Primitive Area transferred to National Park Service to create Kings Canyon National Park.

1964—Wilderness Act leads to creation of the following wilderness areas: Caribou, Dome Land, Hoover, John Muir, Marble Mountain, Minarets, Mokelumne, South Warner, Thousand Lakes, and Yolla Bolly–Middle Eel.

1972—Lassen Volcanic and Lava Beds wilderness areas established by two separate Acts of Congress.

1975—Emigrant Wilderness established.

1976—Kaiser Wilderness and Phillip Burton Wilderness established.

1978—Golden Trout Wilderness established under the Endangered American Wilderness Act.

1984—California Wilderness Act creates Yosemite, Snow Mountain, Dinkey Lakes, Monarch, Jennie Lakes, Carson-Iceberg, Sequoia–Kings Canyon, Bucks Lake, Castle Crags, Mount Shasta, Russian, Siskiyou, and South Sierra Wilderness areas. The Act also expanded the South Warner, Mokelumne, Marble Mountain, John Muir, Emigrant, Dome Land, and Yolla Bolly–Middle Eel

Wildernesses. The Salmon–Trinity Alps Primitive Area is designated the Trinity Alps Wilderness. Minarets Wilderness is also expanded, and renamed Ansel Adams Wilderness. Red Buttes Wilderness is created by both the California Wilderness Act and the Oregon Wilderness Act.

1994—California Desert Protection Act creates 69 wilderness areas in the Great Basin, the Colorado and Mojave deserts, and southern Sierra Nevada. Wilderness areas covered in this book that were established in 1994 include: Sylvania Mountains, Piper Mountain, Kiavah, Owens Peak, and Sacatar Trail. The Dome Land Wilderness was also expanded in 1994.

Index

ABOUT THE AUTHOR

Ron Adkison, an avid hiker and backpacker, began his outdoor explorations at age six. In more than 30 years of hiking he has logged nearly 9,000 trail miles in ten western states. He has walked, or snowshoed, every trail and route in this guide, and has an extensive background exploring wild country in California since 1965. When he's not on the trail, Ron lives on his mountain ranch in southwest Montana where he raises sheep.

Ron shares his love and enthusiasm for wild places in this, his twelfth guidebook.

Other FalconGuides by Ron Adkison include: *Hiking California, Hiking Grand Canyon National Park, Hiking Washington, Hiking Wyoming's Wind River Range, Hiking Grand Staircase–Escalante and the Glen Canyon Region, Best Easy Day Hikes Grand Canyon, Best Easy Day Hikes Grand Staircase–Escalante and the Glen Canyon Region, Hiking Northern California,* and *Best Easy Day Hikes Northern Sierra.*